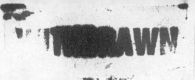

THE
PRAIRIE STATE

THE PRAIRIE STATE

A DOCUMENTARY HISTORY OF ILLINOIS
Colonial Years to 1860

Edited by

Robert P. Sutton
Director of Local and Regional Collections,
Western Illinois University Libraries

William B. Eerdmans Publishing Company

Copyright © 1976 by Wm. B. Eerdmans Publ. Co.
255 Jefferson Ave., SE; Grand Rapids, Mich. 49502

Printed in the United States of America

Library of Congress Cataloging in Publication Data
Main entry under title:

The Prairie state.

  Contents: v. 1. Colonial years to 1860.
  1. Illinois—History—Sources. 2. Illinois—
History—Addresses, essays, lectures. I. Sutton,
Robert P.
F536.P7   977.3   76-21805
ISBN 0-8028-1651-7

To Christopher, Rebecca, and Abigail—my children.

"There is little that is more important for an American to know than the history and traditions of his country. Without such knowledge, he stands uncertain and defenseless before the world."

—John F. Kennedy

Acknowledgments

A documentary of the chronological scope of these volumes is the product of many individuals' assistance in the identification and collection of material. I am particularly indebted to Donna A. Goehner, Periodicals Librarian, Lois P. Mills, Documents and Legal Reference Librarian, and the entire staff of Memorial Library, Western Illinois University. Indispensable to the completion of *The Prairie State* was the assistance given to me by William K. Alderfer, State Historian, and Ellen M. Whitney, editor of the *Journal of the Illinois State Historical Society*. John J. Hartnett, a graduate assistant in the History Department of Western Illinois University, toiled diligently with me almost daily during the past year and thereby relieved me of hours of work. A special thanks goes to my wife, Alice, for her encouragement and for her careful reading of the manuscript. Finally, had it not been for the support of Reinder Van Til, Editor of the American History Series at Eerdmans, this documentary history might never have appeared in print.

Contents

List of Illustrations

Preface

It would seem that nature had intended Illinois to be the keystone state of the Republic, though that name was first claimed by one of the original eastern commonwealths. Illinois's lush prairie soil and varied growing seasons were to yield the most productive grain farms on the North American continent, and under the surface lay the nation's largest deposits of bituminous coal. Bounded on the west by the Mississippi River, on the south by the Ohio, on the east by the Wabash, and on the northeast by Lake Michigan—with the addition of excellent interstate waterways—the state's geographical location has helped make it the transportation heart of the country; all the major commercial arteries enter and leave it. Illinois's population has been formed from the widely varying peoples who claimed America as their home: the Illiniwek Indians and French *coureurs de bois,* the English land settlers, the Southern frontiersmen and Yankee farmers, the nineteenth-century European emigrants, and the black freedmen. Illinois's contributions to American arts and culture have surpassed those of every state but New York; and, of course, it has produced many giants of American politics.

Until the publication of Robert Howard's *Illinois: A History of the Prairie State,* much of the focus of Illinois history had been on politics and wars, particularly Lincoln and the Civil War. But history—especially that of the Prairie State—goes far beyond the so-called drum-and-trumpet story. The processes that shaped Illinois find their sources not in the regimental chronicles and political speeches but in contemporaneous perceptions and original accounts of events that moved the territory and state, within a span of four generations, from a sparsely inhabited prairie to the "third state and second city" of the land.

Volume One of this documentary history is organized into two chronological units: "The Formative Period, 8,000 B.C. to A.D. 1818," and "The Prairie State, 1818-1860." Each unit is divided into topical chapters. "The Formative Period" deals with Illinois before the arrival of the Europeans, during the French explorations, the English period of control, and, finally, the Illinois Territory. "The Prairie State" covers the first years of statehood, pioneer life, and mid-century expansion. Each chapter has a section of special accounts (interpretive essays and selections from scholarly historical works intended to highlight important events of that era) followed by a section of original narratives, which include letters, diaries, speeches, travelogues, eyewitness reports, and reminiscences.

Part I

THE FORMATIVE PERIOD, 8,000 B.C. to A.D. 1818

Introduction

About 10,000 years ago, the ice mass known as the Wisconsin Glacial Drift retreated northward from what is now the state of Illinois. In the wake of this last of four distinct glacial drifts, which in the Pleistocene age covered nine-tenths of the future state, lay the pulverized soil and table-flat terrain on which would flower the prairie grass tall enough to hide a man on horseback. Beneath the surface was a layer of rich loam unsurpassed in fertility, and below the soil itself were deep deposits of soft coal. As the glacier vanished, the ancient Indians (or Paleo-Indians) appeared in the Illinois River valley, and over the next five millennia these stone-age hunters evolved through a spear-throwing and basket-weaving culture to agriculture, pottery, and village life. Burying their dead in elaborate ritual mounds, these Hopewell Indians, as they have been labeled by archaeologists, spread their civilization up the Ohio River as far eastward as the Appalachian Mountains. The Hopewellians disappeared mysteriously about A.D. 500 and were replaced by other Mound Builders. These successors constructed more impressive temple mounds and mastered the bow and arrow, but their aesthetic achievements were inferior. By the time of the arrival of the Europeans, the Mound Builders had vanished. The simple hunters and fishermen who met the first *coureurs de bois* referred to their predecessors only as the "ancient ones." And instead of the traditions of a burial-mound culture, the gift of the Illiniwek Indians to the French was the canoe.

The first European explorers to reach Illinois, the traders and missionaries, were as much impressed with the land as with its inhabitants. The earliest arrivals, Marquette and Jolliet, marveled at the high blue grass and the sprawling waterways which in legend opened to the Pacific. They were warned by the Indians of the giant man-eating dragon bird called the Piasa, who supposedly haunted a tributary of the Mississippi River. Next came the epic voyages of Robert Cavelier, sieur de La Salle and his loyal Italian companion, Henri de Tonti. La Salle claimed all of the Mississippi Valley for his king, constructed a fort at Starved Rock in honor of Louis, and laid

3

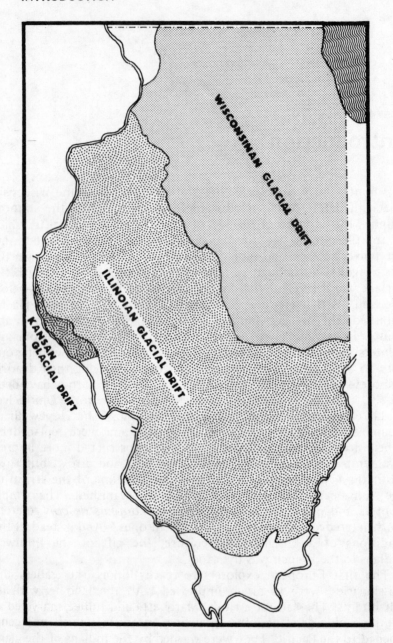

The extent of glaciation in Illinois

the economic foundations of New France by starting the fur trade with the Indians. Over the next half century the French established a precarious claim to La Salle's empire in a string of small white-stained villages along a hundred-mile stretch from Genieve to St. Louis. However, the French had not come to stay; they preferred the romantic life of the riverboat trader to permanent settlements and farming. In 1763, less than a century after the arrival of Jolliet and Marquette, France surrendered all claims east of the Mississippi River to the English.

Where the French had failed, the English succeeded; or, more precisely, the English colonial—the American—conquered, surveyed, and settled the Illinois territory. During the American Revolution, George Rogers Clark, a Virginia-born surveyor, captured Kaskaskia and Vincennes for the American cause in a brilliant military campaign. The Virginia General Assembly then created the gargantuan County of Illinois, which extended westward from Pennsylvania to the Mississippi River and southward from Canada to Kentucky. The county was simply too vast to be governed, and the endless squabbles between the French *habitants* and the incoming American settlers, along with the failure of the British to evacuate troops from the western fortifications, combined to make the years under Governor John Todd chaotic indeed. A major step toward restoring order in the far-flung county came with the enactment of the Northwest Ordinances of 1785 and 1787. In these ordinances the Confederation Congress reorganized the area into governable units, provided for orderly land survey, and established the steps to be taken for full statehood.

However, the settlement of the Northwest proceeded slowly. By 1800 there were only about 2500 inhabitants along the navigable streams between St. Louis and the Ohio River. Predominantly from the upper South, these backwoodsmen built crude cabins, eked out a subsistence life from small vegetable farming, and hunted game in the rolling woodlands of what was called the American Bottom. Settlement picked up slightly after the completion of the grid-like land surveys required in the Ordinance of 1785, only to be set back by Indian troubles during the War of 1812. With the coming of peace, a spurt of land speculation brought more pioneers into the Illinois territory. This development, along with adroit political maneuvering in Washington by Daniel Pope Cook, brought "instant statehood" to the frontier civilization in 1818.

1: Prairies and Indians

Clarence W. Alvord's *The Illinois Country, 1673-1818,* a contribution to the historical series published in commemoration of the centennial of Illinois statehood in 1918, opens this section with a detailed appraisal of Indian life. Professor of history at the Universities of Illinois and Minnesota, Alvord was from 1914 until 1923 the editor of the *Mississippi Valley Historical Review.* In addition to numerous contributions to scholarly journals, he wrote the prize-winning two-volume book *Mississippi Valley in British Politics* (New York, 1917), and *The First Explorations of the Trans-Alleghany Region by the Virginians, 1650-1674* (Cleveland, 1912). Useful monographs on Illinois before the coming of the Europeans are Elaine A. Bluhm, *Illinois Archeology* (Urbana, 1959) and Wayne C. Temple, *Indian Villages of the Illinois Country: Historic Tribes* (Springfield, 1958). See also Ellen M. Whitney, "Indian History and the Indians of Illinois," *Journal of the Illinois State Historical Society,* LXIX (May 1976), 139-146.

Special Account

The First Illinoisans

CLARENCE W. ALVORD

Most baffling of all are the Indian mounds in the central part of the state.[1] Their wide variety, the uncertainty of their chronology, the lack of distinguishing characteristics, make it particularly dif-

---

From Clarence W. Alvord, *The Illinois Country, 1673-1818* (Springfield, 1920), pp. 23-35, 38-48.

[1] It must be borne in mind that in practically no region of the state is there one and only one type of mound. On the contrary, mounds representing quite different cultures are often found in the same locality; this, of course, argues a succession of tribes, but may also in many cases mean a modification of a particular tribe's customs through imitation of another tribe. The only practicable method of classification, therefore, is to mark out roughly the boundaries of areas in which a particular type of mound occurs more frequently than any other one type.

ficult to decipher by what tribe or succession of tribes they may have been built. . . .

In the lower valley of the Illinois river and along the alluvial flats of the Mississippi river—the American Bottom—the Indian monuments grant greater satisfaction to the curiosity of the investigator. Here a distinctive type predominates—the pyramidal mound, built up from either a square or a circular base, and truncated. The mounds vary in size from insignificant knolls to the Cahokia mound, a "mountain made by man," rising to a height of a hundred feet and covering an area of about seventeen acres, the greatest ancient earthwork in the United States. . . .

Who made these great works? . . . Probably it will never be known; no one will ever be able to identify with any of the Indians known to the white men the tribe or group of tribes who labored here. Yet the white men saw in the southern Mississippi valley just such mounds as these being used as temples and dwelling places by Muskhogean peoples who had developed a surprisingly complex organization and had reached an advanced state of civilization.[2] The customs of the Natchez in particular may reflect dimly those of the men who in very early days hunted on the prairies of the Illinois country and left in the mounds monuments of their passage.

The articles found in these mounds offer further evidence of the relation between their builders and the southern tribes. The hoes and other farming implements skillfully chipped out of flint or other hard stone and fashioned to fit wooden handles could have been the product only of a people to whom agriculture was of long-standing importance. Still more striking is the similarity between the pottery which has been unearthed from these mounds and that described by early travelers among the Natchez. According to Le Page du Pratz, an early French traveler in the Mississippi valley, "The Natchez Indians make pots of extraordinary size, cruses with a medium sized opening, jars, bottles with long necks holding two pints, and pots or cruses for holding bear's oil." He says further that these vessels were colored by painting with ocher, which became red after firing. Among the vessels discovered in the mounds of southern Illinois, southeastern Missouri, and Arkansas

---

[2] The Indians may be conveniently classified according to geographical location, physical characteristics, general culture, or language. The linguistic criterion is generally the most satisfactory as being the most readily attained; it applies to fundamental differences in syntax and vocabulary, not merely to dialectic variations. Broadly speaking, this classification is generally borne out by division on the lines of the other criteria; there are, of course, numerous exceptions. For the distribution of Indian stocks in North America see the map at the back of *Handbook of American Indians*, volume I. The principal tribes of the Muskhogean group were: Creeks, Seminole, Muskogee, of the eastern gulf states, the Chickasaw and Alibamu of Alabama and northern Mississippi, and the Choctaw and the Natchez along the Mississippi.

are specimens of all the types mentioned by Du Pratz, and many of
the pieces have not only the characteristic red coloring, but even
designs worked out in red, white, and yellow figures.[3] The specimens belong to a high order of craftsmanship; the clay has been
tempered with pounded shell, producing pottery far more thin and
fragile than the ordinary sand-tempered kind in use among the tribes
of the upper Mississippi valley. In shapes and sizes these pots
exhibit great variety; and many, fashioned as effigies of animals,
reveal striking originality and play of imagination in the primitive
artists. These animal effigy types are almost certainly of southern
origin, for they are found in greatest abundance in a district which
seems to radiate from Pecan Point, Arkansas.

Many bits of evidence pointing in the same direction make it
appear highly probable that the southern Muskhogean stock,
originating somewhere on the upper reaches of the Red and the
Arkansas rivers, migrated gradually southeastward; . . . it would
have been easy for some of the tribes, possibly exterminated in
time, to diverge to a course north of these river valleys and to
establish themselves finally in the fertile lands of Missouri and
southern Illinois. Their stay must have extended over many generations; their numbers must have been large, judging from the mounds
they left. Eventually these builders of mounds were forced to
retreat before more barbarous tribes. What became of them is
unknown; perhaps they were annihilated or absorbed by their
conquerors; perhaps they saved themselves by fleeing southward,
there to survive to historic times as the Natchez or kindred tribes.

Other mounds within the state give evidence of the occupation
by a third Indian stock, the Siouan. . . . Students have located its
place of origin with some degree of certainty in the eastern part of
the present United States, possibly in the Carolinas and Virginia.
Thence the main part of the family moved westward, one group—
the Dakota, Winnebago, and cognate tribes—following a northerly
course along the Great Lakes; another group—the Dhegiha—moving
down the Ohio. This latter division, some time after reaching the
Mississippi, divided into two parts; one going south to the mouth of
the Arkansas became designated Quapaw, or "downstream people;"
the other moving northward and up the Missouri river became
known as the Omaha, or "upstream people." Subsequently the
Omaha group was differentiated into four tribes, the Omaha proper,
Osage, Kansa, and Ponca.

This migration must have occurred some time prior to 1541.

. . . .

[3] A cache containing many pieces of pottery was discovered near the base of the great
Cahokia mound, and there are fragments on the surface at many of the sites in this
district.

The northern Sioux had two chief groups, the Dakota—often called the Sioux proper—and the Chiwere group, made up of four tribes closely allied linguistically, the Iowa, Missouri, Oto, and Winnebago. Tradition says that at one time these four dwelt together as one in the region of the lakes, whence they migrated south and west in pursuit of game.[4]

. . . .

The passing of the Siouan tribes from an eastern to a western habitat must have formed one of the most important events in the prehistoric period of Mississippi valley history. The movement must have unsettled the equilibrium among the tribes, many of which were permanently driven from their homes and their places taken by members of alien stocks. Possibly the wide extension of the Algonquian tribes discovered by the first white men to visit the valley may have been made possible by the movement, or possibly the migration of the Siouans may have been occasioned by the invasion of these powerful northern neighbors.

The Algonquian, one of the largest and most important of Indian families, probably originated in the north Atlantic region, but its tribes were distributed over so extensive a territory that it is almost impossible to designate a common home.

. . . .

It may without great hazard be inferred that the Shawnee formed the vanguard of the Algonquian advance into the Mississippi valley from some point north of the Great Lakes. In moving southward they came in contact with more civilized tribes, possibly the builders of the Cahokia mound. These the Shawnee drove out or assimilated, but by this contact with a superior culture the customs of the Shawnee themselves were modified. They adopted the custom of building mounds, learned to make pottery similar to that of the Cahokia people, and took on the characteristic customs of sedentary agricultural life. In the course of time the tide of migration carried some of them to the valley of the Cumberland and some into northern Georgia, but not even after the coming of the whites and the subsequent revolution in all Indian development was the link broken between the Shawnee and the kindred Illinois, Foxes, Sauk, and other tribes of the central Algonquian group who followed them into the great valley.[5]

[4] An interesting piece of evidence corroborating the traditions of these tribes is the Chippewa tradition that their tribe found the Sioux in possession of the land somewhere east of Detroit, and after waging many wars finally succeeded in driving them west of the Mississippi.
[5] The Shawnee and Kickapoo called the Foxes and Sauk their younger brothers.

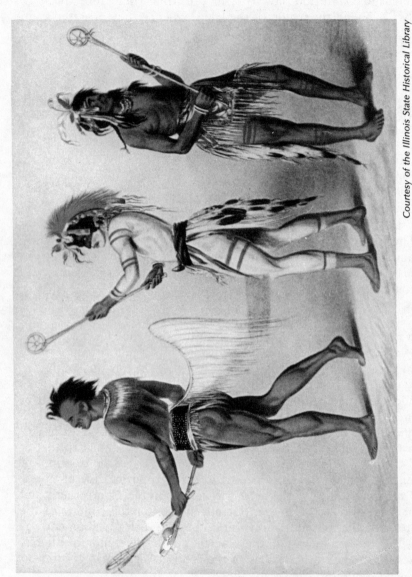

George Catlin's painting of the Illiniwek Indians

Of these tribes the Illinois, or, to give them their proper name, the Iliniwek, were easily first in importance and probably also in point of time.[6]

. . . .

The bands of the Illinois continued to act together against their common enemies, but their bond of union, throughout historic times, remained kinship rather than a deliberate and formal political alliance comparable to the league of the Iroquois. When understood as a family alliance, the term "Illinois confederacy" is in a general sense an accurate enough designation.

In the heyday of their prosperity, the Illinois probably ranged over almost the entire area of the present state as well as into southern Wisconsin and Iowa. Farthest south were the Michigamea, who may have lived for some time in the region of the American Bottom—where they doubtless came in contact with the Shawnee or other southern agricultural peoples—and then pushed on over into what is now the territory of southeastern Missouri and northern Arkansas, in the region of Big Lake, where Marquette found them in 1673.

. . . .

The main body of the Illinois in historic times centered in the valley of the river of their name, and it is highly probable that this had been their seat for a considerable period prior to the seventeenth century.

The nearest kin of the Illinois were the Miami, the two being so similar in language and customs that the first impression of the French was that they formed one tribe. The tribes had probably been long separated, however, when first known to the Europeans. Tradition relates that the Illinois and the Miami were associated in their migration from the west, and it may be assumed that the latter took possession of the valley of the Wabash at a very early date. They were split into bands, known in later years as Piankashaw, Eel River, Wea, and others, some of which in time acquired the attributes of separate tribes. Like their kinsmen, the Miami were continually at war with the tribes lying south of the Ohio river, the Cherokee and Chickasaw.

. . . .

The tribes of the Illinois country, using this term to designate a more extensive territory than that indicated by the early writers,

[6] "*Iliniwek*, from *ilini* 'man,' *iw* 'is,' *ek* plural termination, changed by the French to *ois*."

belonged to the Algonquian stock, with the exception of the Winnebago, whose hunting grounds in later years extended south of the Wisconsin boundary. A description, therefore, of the principal group of tribes, the one that has given its name to the state, will answer in a general way for all. . . .

A writer who knew the Illinois well has written the following description: "There never were people better made than they; they are neither large nor small—generally there are some of them whom you can circle with your two hands. They have tapering legs which carry their bodies well, with a very haughty step, and as graceful as the best dancer. The visage is fairer than white milk so far as savages of this country can have such. The teeth are the best arranged and the whitest in the world. They are vivacious, but withal indolent."

The country and the climate disposed them to indolence, for it was not difficult to secure a living; the wealth of wild fruits, berries, and edible roots went far to sustain life even without effort, and game was abundant. Nevertheless, the real staff of life, the year-round food of the Illinois Indians, was maize; and maize was by no means a gratuitous gift of nature, nor were beans, squashes, and other vegetables; hence the cultivation of the soil loomed large in their economy—far larger than has popularly been supposed. Even with the fertile treeless prairies ready at hand, the work of breaking and preparing the ground with implements rudely wrought from stone was highly laborious, and a cornfield once brought under cultivation was not lightly abandoned. Village sites, therefore, took on a degree of permanency which has not always been recognized.[7]

In the summer, after the crops were planted, and again in the winter after they had been gathered and stored in pits in the village, the whole group would move to some spot in a wilder part of the country, often a hundred or more miles away, and set up a hunting camp; here they would spend from six to twelve weeks hunting all kinds of animals which could be made to furnish meat for the kettle, furs for clothing, ornaments for personal decoration, or which, in short, could serve any purpose whatever. The spoils of the hunt would for the most part be prepared for human use on the spot, the meat being cut into thin strips and slowly dried on a wooden rack four or five feet above an open fire; the pelts of the buffalo, deer, bear, and the smaller fur bearing animals were dressed with the hair on if they were to be used as robes, or with the hair

---

[7] An excellent illustration of this is seen in the failure of the whites at the time of the Black Hawk War to comprehend what it meant to the Sauk and Foxes to give up their ancient domain in the Rock river valley.

removed if they were to be made into any of the dozens of articles the Indian knew how to fashion out of dressed skins. The animals' bones were often utilized in the making of weapons or domestic utensils; the horns and teeth of the elk and deer and various parts of the smaller animals and of birds went to adorn the warriors or to serve some ceremonial purpose; there was scarcely a portion of any animal for which the Indian could not find some use—although if his need for a particular article was not immediate, he felt no necessity of conserving against possible future wants.

If at any time there was a scarcity of meat, the deficiency could be supplied by fish from the rivers or lakes, but as game was usually plentiful the Indians of the Illinois country never developed such prowess as fishermen as was achieved by the northern tribes of the lakes region. "They take little trouble to make nets suitable for catching fish in the rivers," writes a missionary. "However, when they take a fancy to have some, they enter a canoe with their bows and arrows; they stand up that they may better discover the fish, and as soon as they see one they pierce it with an arrow."

Their weapon for all purposes was the bow and arrow. The bows were simple affairs, and the arrows consisted of long shafts to which were attached the triangular stone heads that are still to be found on the site of many an old Indian village or battlefield. The bow was most important in the world of the Indian; upon his skill in using it depended his livelihood and his reputation as a hunter, and his accuracy was a matter of life or death in war. For the chase as well as for war he supplemented it with clubs and knives; the clubs were of wood, "shaped like a cutlass," with a ball at the end, or of a deer's horn trimmed of all save one or two tines; the knives were of chipped flint, much like the arrowheads but larger. Daggers also were sometimes made from some long bone such as the shank of a deer.

The manufacture as well as the use of these weapons was the peculiar province of the men; the warriors were expected to provide their families with meat and furs and to protect them from all attack; and since hunting was both arduous and dangerous and war a constantly threatening emergency, life was no sinecure. To the women, with the assistance of the old men and children, fell the tasks of preparing food and clothing, tilling the fields, attending to the construction as well as the care of the dwellings, and carrying all the baggage when on the march to and from the seasonal hunting camps. The line between the work of the two sexes was sharply drawn, but it can hardly be said to have been unfair, being based very directly on the necessities of their mode of life.

Courtesy of the Illinois State Historical Library

P. Rendisbacher's painting of a war dance of the Sauks and Foxes

The waging of war among the Illinois, as among most American Indians, was largely a matter of individual choice, over which the tribe as a whole had little control; hence the difficulty of making a permanent treaty with any particular group of Indians. . . . The opportunity was always present, for practically continuous war existed between the Illinois and their southern neighbors, the Chickasaw and the Cherokee, and their neighbors on the north, the Sioux. . . .

Large campaigns were always an exception in Indian warfare, and except for a few instances such as the Winnebago war, the fighting of the Illinois consisted chiefly of desultory raids, a primary aim of which was the taking of captives to be kept in the tribe or sold as slaves to other groups. . . . [An early Jesuit observer says,] "Their method is to follow on the trail of their enemy, and to kill some one of them while he is asleep,—or, rather, to lie in ambush in the vicinity of the villages, and to split the head of the first one who comes forth,—and, taking off his scalp, to display it as a trophy among their countrymen. . . . For several days this scalp is hung from the top of his cabin, and then all the people of the village come to congratulate him upon his valor, and bring presents to show him the interest that they take in his victory. Sometimes they are satisfied with making the enemy prisoners; but they immediately tie their hands and compel them to run on before at full speed, fearing that they may be pursued, as sometimes happens, by the companions of those whom they are taking away. The fate of these prisoners is very sad; for often they are burned by a slow fire, and at other times they are put into the kettle, in order to make a feast for all the fighting men."

The cannibalism suggested was probably very rare; the Illinois seem most frequently to have kept prisoners alive, for they were notorious slave traders. . . .

In spite of a reputation for humane treatment of captives, the Illinois, like other Indians, found pleasure in torturing their prisoners, a custom commonly found among all people in the low stages of development. The slow fire, the pulling of finger nails, and the cutting with knives were spectacles, prolonged for days, in which men, women, and children participated. Cruelty to enemies and stoical patience under suffering were basic principles in the education of Indian children.

. . . .

As the women are said to have outnumbered the men four to one, it is not surprising to find that polygamy was common among the Illinois; the only limit set upon the number of wives a man might have was his ability to provide food and clothing for them. A custom very usual among the Algonquians was for a man to espouse the younger sisters of his first wife, a practice no doubt followed to some extent by the tribes of the Illinois. The men were very jealous of their wives and commonly punished them for any infidelity by cutting off the nose; divorce apparently could take place whenever either of the couple desired, but public opinion was rather against such procedure. The chief element in holding any pair together, since the element of affection was in most instances negligible, was the offspring; as the strength and wealth of a clan was measured chiefly by the number of its members, children were an important factor; moreover, since Indian women were not especially prolific and infant mortality was high, a woman with children was not likely to be put away by her husband nor to go unavenged by her relatives if in any way wronged.

. . . .

The world known to the Illinois was circumscribed; they knew only the territory watered by the Mississippi and its principal tributaries, and the Great Lakes region. . . . Over this world of theirs they saw the sun, the moon, and the stars; they felt the wind, the rain, and the snow, and heard the thunder. Their explanation of nature reproduced this limitation of knowledge. The earth was humanized; it was a person with emotions and passions; it bestowed life on all who fed on it. Objects of the world also were similarly humanized; some had the freedom of motion—such were the bears and deer; but others like the reeds of the swamp, the oaks, and the persimmon trees, had been attached firmly to the earth by some mighty wizard. In like manner the rivers and creeks were men-beings who at times were bound by the spell of the winter magician and ceased their continuous running. All inanimate objects—stones, streams, trees, hills, the wind, and the sun—possessed a magic power that might be used to aid or harm man and must therefore be propitiated. Indian tribes called this magic power by different names, but by the Algonquians it was named "manitou" or "manito."

The Indians lived in a world of terror, surrounded as they imagined themselves by these manitous, and their lives were struggles to appease the manitou beings and to bribe or compel them to give aid and not to harm. . . . In every project of his life the Indian believed himself watched and warned by special protectors, who communicated with him by means of dreams and omens the disregard of which was sure to be attended with the most disastrous consequences. . . . A dream, the cry of a bird, the unexpected appearance of some animal, would seem to the Indian a direct revelation and order from a supernatural power.

In the midst of this world filled with animate objects possessing magic power man was helpless without the support and aid of some personal manitou. Hence the principal spiritual experience of the Indian occurred when he won the control of some power as a personal guide.

. . . .

Original Narratives

The first of the original narratives records the impressions of the first white men to see the Illinois country, the Jesuit missionary Father Marquette and his Canadian-born companion Louis Jolliet. They entered from Lake Michigan in the spring of 1673, and Jolliet, in a dispatch dated August 1, 1674, related their first perceptions of "these treeless lands." This selection is taken from that treasure of historical material on early Illinois, the seventy-three-volume *The Jesuit Relations and Allied Documents, 1610-1791* (Cleveland, 1896-1903), edited by the prolific Reuben G. Thwaites, who was secretary and superintendent of the State Historical Society of Wisconsin. The most recent treatment of Jolliet and the French is by Virginia S. Eifert in *Louis Jolliet, Explorer of Rivers* (New York, 1961) and *Of Men and Rivers: Adventures and Discoveries Along American Waterways* (New York, 1966).

The Prairie

LOUIS JOLLIET

"At first, when we were told of these treeless lands, I imagined that it was a country ravaged by fire, where the soil was so poor that it could produce nothing. But we have certainly observed the contrary; and no better soil can be found, either for corn, for vines, or for any other fruit whatever.

From Reuben G. Thwaites, ed., *The Jesuit Relations*, LVIII (Cleveland, 1900), pp. 105-109.

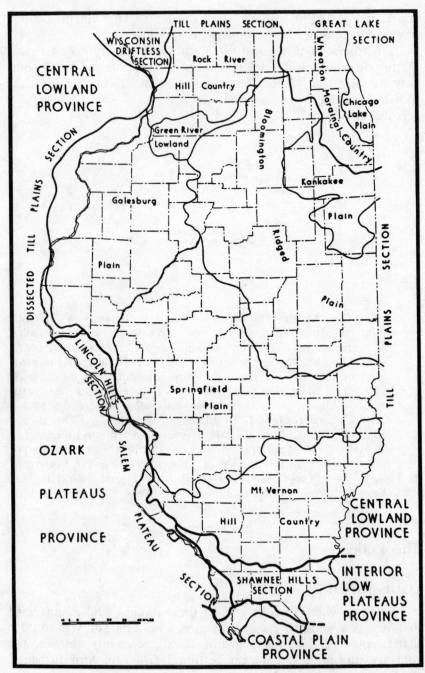

The Physiographic Division of Illinois

"The river which we named for Saint Louis, which rises near the lower end of the lake of the Illinois, seemed to me the most beautiful, and most suitable for settlement. The place at which we entered the lake is a harbor, very convenient for receiving vessels and sheltering them from the wind. The river is wide and deep, abounding in catfish and sturgeon. Game is abundant there; oxen, cows, stags, does, and Turkeys were found there in great numbers than elsewhere. For a distance of eighty leagues, I did not pass a quarter of an hour without seeing some.

"There are prairies three, six, ten, and twenty leagues in length, and three in width, surrounded by forests of the same extent; beyond these, the prairies begin again, so that there is as much of one sort of land as of the other. Sometimes we saw the grass very short, and, at other times, five or six feet high; hemp, which grows naturally there, reaches a height of eight feet.

"A settler would not there spend ten years in cutting down and burning the trees; on the very day of his arrival, he could put his plow into the ground. And, if he had no oxen from France, he could use those of this country, or even the animals possessed by the Western Savages, on which they ride, as we do on horses.

"After sowing grain of all kinds, he might devote himself especially to planting the vine, and grafting fruit-trees; to dressing ox-hides wherewith to make shoes; and with the wool of these oxen he could make cloth, much finer than most of that which we bring from France. Thus he would easily find in the country his food and clothing, and nothing would be wanting except salt, but, as he could make provision for it, would not be very difficult to remedy that inconvenience."

The above is a brief abstract of matters which are fully related in the journal that was lost. If we can secure the copy of it, we shall observe therein many things which will please the curious, and satisfy geographers regarding the difficulties that they may encounter in preparing descriptions of that part of North America.

René-Robert Cavelier, sieur de La Salle, gives his opinion of the Illinois country in this letter to Monsieur de Frontenac, then governor of New France. The document, dated November 9, 1680, surveys the economic opportunities for France in the West. This intrepid aristo-crat was the first to grasp the vision of a vast French empire stretched along the interior waterways of North America. Between 1679 and his untimely death in 1685, La Salle, along with the Italian adventurer Henri de Tonti, established the basis of New France. The drama of La Salle's adventures is vividly told by Francis Parkman in *La Salle and the Dis-covery of the Great West* (Boston, 1869). A contemporary treatment is found in Timothy Severin, *Explorers of the Mississippi* (New York, 1967).

The Illinois Country, 1680

LA SALLE

The Niagara River is innavigable [?] for ten leagues from the falls to the entrance into Lake Erie, it being impossible to bring up a vessel, at least without enough men to handle the sail, to haul at the bow, and to warp at the same time, and even with such great caution one cannot hope to be successful always. The entrance into Lake Erie is so obstructed with shallow bars that, in order not to risk losing the vessel every voyage, it is necessary to leave it in a river six leagues away along the lake, which is the nearest harbor or anchorage. There are in Lake Erie three large peninsulas, of which two jut out more than ten leagues. These are sand bars which one may run afoul of before seeing them unless one takes great pre-cautions.

A change of wind is necessary to enter the straits between Lake Erie and Lake Huron, where there is more water and a strong current. Great difficulties confront one at the Straits of Michilli-mackinac in entering from Lake Huron into the lake of the Illinois.[1] The wind there is usually counter to the current, and the channel is narrow on account of the bars which extend out from the two shores. There are very few or no anchorages in Lake Huron, and no more harbors than in the lake of the Illinois along the north, west, and south shores. There are great numbers of islands in both lakes. Those of the Illinois are a hazard on account of the sand bars

From Theodore C. Pease and Ray Werner, eds., "The French Foundations, 1680-1693," *Collections of the Illinois State Historical Library*, XXIII (1934), 1-16. Footnotes in the original identifying persons and places have been retained.
[1] Lake Michigan.

which are off them. This lake is not deep and is subject to terrific winds from which there is no shelter, and the bars border upon the approaches to the islands; but it is possible that with more frequent voyages the dangers will be lessened and the ports and harbors better known as has happened in the case of Lake Frontenac,[2] on which navigation is now safe and easy.

The haven which one enters in order to go from the lake of the Illinois to the Divine River[3] is not at all suitable for navigation as there are no winds in the roadstead, nor any passageway for a vessel, nor even for a canoe, at least in a great calm. The prairies over which communication is maintained are flooded by the great volume of water flowing down from the neighboring hills whenever it rains. It is very difficult to make and maintain a canal that does not immediately fill up with sand and gravel; one need only dig into the ground to find water; and there are some sand dunes between the lake and the prairies. And, although a canal would be possible with a great deal of expense, it would be useless because the Divine River is innavigable for forty leagues, the distance to the great village of the Illinois. Canoes cannot traverse it during the summer, and even then there are long rapids this side of that village.

Mines have not yet been seen although pieces of copper have been found in a number of places where the water is low. There is excellent stone [?] and coal. The Indians relate having sold some yellow metal from the village, but from their description it was too pure to have come from a gold mine.

The buffalo are becoming scarce here since the Illinois are at war with their neighbors; both kill and hunt them continually.

It is possible to go by water from Fort Crèvecoeur to the sea. New Mexico is not over twenty days' journey distant to the west from this fort. The Oto, who have come to see Monsieur de la Salle, have brought with them a piebald belonging to some Spaniards whom they killed in their country only ten days' journey distant from this fort; one could go from the one to the other by the river. These Indians relate that the Spanish who make war against them use lances more than muskets.

There are no Europeans at the mouth of the great river Colbert.[4] The monster a sketch of which the Sieur Jolliet brought back is a grotesque painted by some Indian of the river: no one will avow its origin. It is a day and a half's journey from Crèvecoeur, and if the

[2] Lake Ontario.
[3] Applied to the Illinois River and its various sources. Here it probably refers to the Desplaines, while later in the paragraph to the main branch of the river.
[4] The Mississippi River.

Sieur Jolliet had descended a little farther he would have seen another more frightful still.[5]

He has not reflected that the Mosopelea,[6] whom he notes on his map, were completely wiped out before his voyage. He notes on this same map numerous nations which are only the names of some of the tribes composing the nation of the Illinois—the Peoria, Kaskaskia, Tamaroa, Coiracoentanon, Chinko, Cahokia, Chepoussa, Amonokoa, Cahokia, Quapaw,[7] and many others forming the village of the Illinois made up of about 400 huts covered with reed mats and without any fortification. I have reckoned up almost 1,800 fighting men who are at war only with the Iroquois; with them it would be easy to come to an understanding if there were not cause to fear that, being at peace with the Iroquois and feeling secure from their direction, the Illinois might wish to make war against the Ottawa, whom they hate exceedingly, and thus interrupt our commerce. But so long as it can be contrived to keep them dependent upon us, they may readily be held to their duty, and through them the more distant nations by whom they are feared.

There is some very fine wood for shipbuilding along the seven or eight rivers flowing into the Colbert, the least of which has a course of 300 leagues without falls.

Monsieur de la Salle has seen the Indians of three nations through whom Fernando de Soto passed, namely, Chickasaw, Casqui, and Aminoya.[8] From them these people go into Mexico; they assure us that they have a very good water route from Crèvecoeur to their homes.

It is important that this exploration be carried out because the river on which the Chickasaw live, and which probably is the Sakakoüa,[9] has its source near Carolina, where the English are, 300 leagues to the east of the river Colbert in French Florida near Apalachee; whence the English would be able to come by ship to the Illinois, to the Miami,[10] and close to the Baye des Puans[11] and the country of the Sioux, and secure thereby a great portion of our trade.

[5] These pictographs were on a rock along the river near Alton, Illinois. Evidence of one of them remained at least to 1848.
[6] Marquette's map locates them on the east bank of the Mississippi south of the Ohio.
[7] Peoria, Kaskaskia, Tamaroa, Coiracoentanon, Chinko, Cahokia, Chepoussa, and Amonokoa were tribes and bands of the Illinois. The name Oouka is undoubtedly a corruption of Cahokia. The Akansea were the Quapaw, a southern Siouan tribe who once ranged the southern part of Illinois.
[8] The Chickasaw, a Muskhogean tribe, were at this time in northern Mississippi. Casqui and Aminoya are Indian towns west of the Mississippi, visited either by De Soto or his followers.
[9] Franquelin's map of 1708 would indicate that this is the Yazoo.
[10] The Miami were at this time located about the southern end of Lake Michigan and along the St. Joseph River.
[11] Green Bay, Wisconsin.

Courtesy of the Illinois State Historical Library

A war canoe on the Mississippi River

It was colder this year in the Illinois than at Fort Frontenac.[12] Planting is done here only once a year and that is in the month of May, as there is always a hard freeze in April. It is true that the mildness of the month of January, which is the same at Fort Frontenac, at first caused us to believe that this country would be as mild as Provence, but since then we have learned that the winter is not less severe than that of the Iroquois inasmuch as on March 22, the river was still frozen; and the lake of the Illinois was again as full of ice along the south shore as Lake Frontenac ordinarily is in January, although Lake Erie was so clear eight days later that no ice was apparent at all in the quiet waters or in the open water along the north shore.

The entire country between the lake of the Illinois and Lake Erie for the space of 100 or 120 leagues, has only one chain of mountains, whence a number of rivers flow to the west into the lake of the Illinois, to the north into Lake Huron, to the east into Lake Erie, and to the south into the Ohio River. Their sources are so near

---

[12] The modern Kingston, Ontario.

together on the summits of these mountains that in three days of marching we have passed twenty-two or twenty-three more considerable than the Sorel or the Richelieu. The tops of these mountains are flat and covered with perpetual marshes, which, during periods of thawing weather, have given us considerable trouble. There is also some dry country and very good land overrun with an unbelievable number of bears, deer, roebucks, and wild turkeys, on whom the wolves make relentless war; these last are so bold that we have often been in danger of not being able to defend ourselves with shots from our guns.

There is a river[13] at the end of Lake Erie ten leagues from Detroit by which one should be able to go up far along the road toward the Illinois, as it is navigable for canoes to within two leagues of the river which leads there; but there is yet another route, the Ohio, which is shorter and better, and is navigable for sailing vessels; by it one may avoid the difficulty of the harbor at the end of the lake of the Illinois and that of getting over into the Divine River, and making it navigable to Fort Crèvecoeur.

It should not be supposed that these lands of which we speak in the country of the Illinois are lands to which one has only to put the plow, for the greater part are drowned by ever so little rain. Others are too dry, and the best require considerable labor to clear off the aspens which cover them, as well as to drain the marshes which comprise wide areas.

The possession of a calumet of peace enables one to pass safely through all of these nations. The greater part of them through whom we had to go already knew of our coming and were prepared to receive us well.

The Illinois offered to escort us to the sea from the hope that we have given them that thence will come everything which they need. That other tribes need knives, hatchets, and so forth increases their desire to have us among them

The buffalo calves are easy to tame and can be of great use as well as the slaves in which these people are accustomed to traffic and whom they compel to labor for them. There are as many rogues among them as elsewhere; there are more women among them than men. There is not a man who does not have several wives—some having as many as ten and as far as possible all sisters, that they may agree better among themselves, as indeed they do.

I have seen three healthy children baptized—one was named Pierre, the other Joseph, and the third, Marie—the children of the brother of Chicagou. They are in grave danger of growing up to be

[13] Probably the Maumee.

like their father, who has three sisters as wives. It does not appear that they will have further instruction, since Father d'Allouez,[14] who baptized them, has left the Illinois, unless a staff which he has left wrapped up behind to indicate that this country is to be the field of his labor, has any extraordinary virtue. These are the only Christians I know who cannot but be in the faith of the church.

Father d'Allouez has retired to a village composed partly of Miami and partly of Mascouten and Wea who have abandoned their old village and most of their kinsmen in order to make an alliance with the Iroquois and along with them carry on war against the Illinois. For that reason they sent five men and a woman last summer as an embassy with a letter from Father d'Allouez. The purpose of their embassy was to urge the Iroquois to join them in making war on the Illinois. This matter had been under negotiation for twenty-four days when I arrived at the Sanchioragon village of the Seneca, but as it was known that I was at Kanagaro[15] where Father Raffeix[16] was, a woman who had once upon a time been captured by the Miami came from this village to tell the ambassadors their heads would be broken, and they had better flee, fearing perhaps that by my being there I might learn the object of this embassy.

It is nevertheless true that the Iroquois had no desire to harm them for, although their flight was bound to raise suspicions against them, they were well received after they had been ensnared, but they had no desire to talk so long as I was present.

Having since met in their own country these same ambassadors, one of whom spoke Huron, I became aware of things which I wish to believe were the invention of Indian maliciousness. However, when the news that I had arrived in the Illinois had been carried to the village where Father d'Allouez is, a man called Monceau, one of the chiefs, who carried four large copper kettles, a dozen hatchets, and twenty knives secretly to the Illinois, was sent to say that I was a brother to the Iroquois, that I was breathing his breath, that I ate the serpents of his country, that they had given me a net to hem them in from one side while the Iroquois came from the other, that I was abhorred by all the black-robes, who, regarding me as an Iroquois, had given me up, that I previously had wished to kill the Miami, that I had taken two prisoners, and that I possessed a drug to be used in poisoning them all.

It was easy for me to disprove all these lies, and this poor

[14] Claude Jean Allouez, S. J., 1622-1689.
[15] Kanagaro, a Seneca town, destroyed during Denonville's expedition of 1687.
[16] Pierre Raffeix, S. J., 1633 [?]-1724. He devoted a number of years to the Cayuga and Seneca missions.

Monceau was almost obliged to stay there as a hostage, he having been told that it was he that had the Iroquois serpent under his tongue, that his comrades who had been sent there as ambassadors had brought some and had not been able to smoke the same calumet without inhaling the breath of the Iroquois. If I had not intervened, the Illinois would have killed this Monceau.

Here is another matter wherein I suspect a trap and which is apparently a sequel of the desire which they have that Monseigneur the Comte de Frontenac make war on the Iroquois if it becomes apparent that he has abandoned the Illinois. The vehemence with which the Iroquois wished him to make war is entirely abated although, in fact, there are some who have taken the warpath, a fact which is concealed from the Ottawa in order that they may continue to go to trade, and that the Iroquois, taking them for the Illinois, may kill them in order to embroil them. Moreover, negotiations are being carried on that the greater part of the Miami, who are our allies, will come to live with the Illinois. Thus the Iroquois could not fall upon one without the other; and thus Monseigneur the comte might be compelled either to abandon his allies or make war on the Iroquois in order to prevent them from warring on the Illinois. Perhaps this is rash judgment, but nevertheless the small number of Miami, among whom Father d'Allouez has retired, seeing that the Iroquois did not begin the war soon enough against the Illinois, have killed some of the Iroquois this winter in order to precipitate it, and have cut off the fingers of a Seneca, whom they then sent back to his own country to say that the Miami joined with the Illinois to kill Iroquois. Perhaps the knowledge which Father d'Allouez must have had of the evil intentions of these savages and of their bad faith is what is obliging him to leave them as he was to do this spring.

However, I am certain of stopping this war, especially if Monseigneur the comte will come this year to lament for the deaths of the Onondaga, as I have prevented the Illinois from going in search of the Iroquois and obtained of them the return of some slaves that they have; the Iroquois learning this of me appeared perfectly satisfied.

It is not to be wondered at that the Iroquois speak of waging war against our allies inasmuch as they receive affronts from them every year. I have seen, among the Potawatomi and Miami at Michilli-mackinac, the spoils and scalps of numerous Iroquois whom the Indians from this region had treacherously killed while hunting last spring and earlier; which is not unknown to the Iroquois, our allies having the imprudence of celebrating this feat in their presence while they were trading among them, as I have seen Potawatomi at

Michillimackinac who, dancing with the calumet, boasted of this treachery, holding up the scalps at arm's length in the sight of three Mohawk who were there to trade.

I cannot omit a conversation that I had with an Indian of the Mahican[17] tribe as to the causes of his difficulty in choosing between our religion and that of the English on account of the two differences which he found between the apostles, some of the missionaries of this country and the English ministers. He perceived that the latter did not imitate the celibacy of the apostles and the former were far removed from their disinterestedness, judging by their pursuit of riches. Finally, he found consolation in seeing the Recollect fathers' love for poverty which determined him to come to seek baptism in our religion.

Following the murder of La Salle in 1687, Tonti shifted the center of French operations to a new fort constructed at the future site of Peoria. Tonti's nephew, the sieur de Liette, under the pen name De Gannes, wrote a valuable description of that Central Illinois locale and its inhabitants. It was published by the Illinois Historical Library in 1934 as *Degannes Memoir*. The standard biography of Tonti is Edmund R. Murphy, *Henry de Tonty: Fur Trader of the Mississippi* (Baltimore, 1941).

Memoirs of the Illinois Country

DE GANNES

The Illinois country is undeniably the most beautiful that is known anywhere between the mouth of the St. Lawrence River and that of the Mississippi, which are a thousand leagues apart. You begin to see its fertility at Chicago which is 140 leagues from Michillimackinac, at the end of Lake Michigan. The Chicago is a little stream only two leagues long bordered by prairies of equal dimension in width. This is a route usually taken to go to this

From "De Gannes Memoir" in Pease and Werner, *Collections of the Illinois State Historical Library*, XXIII (1934), 302-310, 320-324. Footnotes identifying place names have been retained.

[17] The Mahican, called Loups by the French, at one time lived along the upper Hudson River, but pressure of the Iroquois, along with other causes, pushed them westward.

country. At this river a portage is made, of a quarter of a league in low water and of an arpent in high water. One finds a streamlet for half a league which comes from two little lakes that extend a league and a half, at the end of which, on the rising ground at this point, is made a short portage simply of one's baggage. When the water is favorable one reëmbarks at once, but when it is low it is necessary to go a league. This is called the Portage of the Oaks; and it costs considerable effort to get the boat into this streamlet, which empties into the river which the French call the Illinois. However, this is not the Illinois, as we only come to that stream twenty leagues farther on. The passage is very difficult on account of the low waters which virtually render this river impracticable, because one ordinarily reaches this region only in summer or autumn. There are ten places where for half a league it is necessary to take out half of the baggage, and very often to remove it entirely, until the deep water is reached. It is necessary also sometimes to carry the canoe. There is a place even, called Mount Joliet, where there are four leagues of rapids, and where this must nearly always be done.

This place is called Illes, because a *voyageur* who bore that name was detained here a long time. The Illinois and Miami call it Missouratenouy, which signifies an earthen vessel. . . .

Here you ordinarily begin to see the buffalo. As for turkeys, there are quantities of them. There is a game bird that is abundant, which is a good deal like the French pheasant, and which is very good. . . . Here you begin to see the beauty of this country, both for the soil, which yields bountifully, and for the abundance of animals. You see places on the one side that are unwooded prairies requiring only to be turned up by the plow, and on the other side valleys spreading half a league before reaching the hills, which have no trees but walnuts and oaks; and behind these, prairies like those I have just spoken of. Sometimes you travel a league, seeing all this from your boat. Afterwards you find virgin forest on both sides, consisting of tender walnuts, ash, whitewood, Norway maple, cottonwood, a few maples, and grass, taller in places than a man. More than an arpent in the woods you find marshes which in autumn and spring are full of bustards, swans, ducks, cranes, and teals. Ten steps farther on are the hills covered with wood extending about an eighth of a league, from the edge of which are seen prairies of extraordinary extent. Three leagues from the fork is the river Mazon,* which signifies the tow, in which neighborhood are found parrakeets that live in bands of fifty to sixty. They make a very strange noise. They are a little bigger than turtledoves.

*Mazon Creek in Grundy County, Illinois.

Seven leagues from here is a rapid where, in low waters, you have to portage for an eighth of a league. Three leagues farther are some places that are very flat because of several islands that are located here, and a river flowing from the north, which the Illinois call Pestequouy,† near the outlet of which there is a rich quarry of coal. This river comes from the northeast. It has nothing but prairies on either side, except for a little strip of wood consisting of oaks and walnuts, and running the whole length of its banks. From here it is two leagues to the old fort. This is a steep rock, very favorably situated, which induced the late Monsieur de la Salle to build a fort here in 1682 or 1683. . . .

There were also a hundred families of Shawnee. But, aside from the fact that I never saw them except for two years, I had so little inclination for their language, and so great a desire to know that of the Illinois, that I learned very little of it. What spurred my desires still more was that I was told that the languages of the Illinois and of the Miami were the same, and this is true, there being no difference except that the accent of the Illinois is very short and that of the Miami very long. One pronounces the *h* and the other the *f*. This was my reason, in 1688, for begging Monsieur de Tonti to allow me to accompany a village of Illinois who were going off on a buffalo hunt for five weeks. This request he readily granted, being pleased to have me learn this language, for which task he saw I had some talent, that he might safely absent himself when his affairs demanded it, and leave me in his place. He recommended me to the chief of this village, and with my servant I was placed in a cabin of savage men, if one may say that there be any among barbarians.

We went into camp two leagues away. As I saw only old men, women, and girls, and five or six men, I asked them, partly with the few words that I knew and partly by signs, how it happened that there were so few young men. They gave me to understand that they were out on a hunting expedition. The women had thrown down their packs and had run, each with an axe, into the woods to cut poles and to peel bark for their summer hunting cabin. . . .

The few young men who were with us while the women and girls were making the cabins went an arpent into the woods to cut three poles of which they made a large tripod from which they hung a big kettle, which they filled with water and then seated themselves around the fire which they had made underneath. My man and I settled down near them. A short time after, two men arrived each with a buck on his back. Two of our cooks went to meet them. The

---

†Fox River, Illinois.

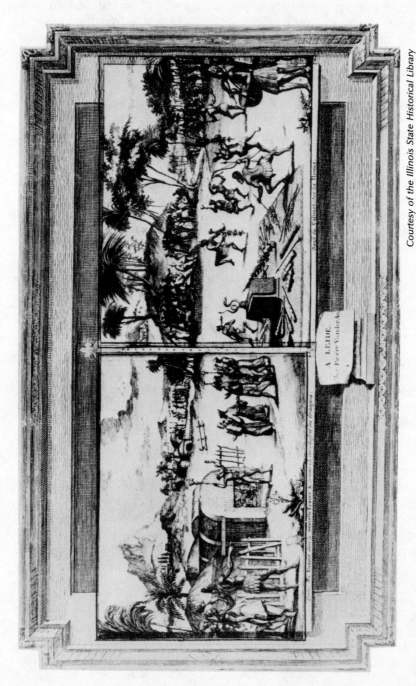

VanderAa's paintings of Illinois Indians introducing strangers and performing the dance of the calumet

hunters, on seeing them approach, threw down their load and advanced proudly toward them, highly elated at being the first to bring meat to the camp. Our servitors soon had the bucks cut up and put into the kettle. When they were cooked the old men were called and came to eat. We were the first served and got the best there was. I noticed that this happened every day, and that some young men always came by turns with the old men. They are called guards, and prevent anyone from separating from the band and going off alone, because this frightens away the game. A man and woman once tried to escape from the band while the guards were busy gathering strawberries; one of the guards saw them and ran after them, took away the man's load, cut the collar and the bear skins which they used as a mattress, smashed the kettles which the woman was carrying, and came near killing a child, which she had upon her load, by pulling it from her head; and all this happened without the man or woman saying a single word.

. . . .

We found in these woods a vast number of trees laden with medlars, and others with nuts which have a wonderfully delicate taste. They are ordinarily olive-shaped but twice as big. The shells are very thin. There is a testa inside dividing in two the kernel, which is very bitter. There were other trees as thick as one's leg, which bend under a yellowish fruit of the shape and size of a medium-sized cucumber, which the savages call *assemina*. The French have given it an impertinent name. There are people who would not like it, but I find it very good. They have five or six nuclei inside which are as big as marsh beans, and of about the same shape. I ate, one day, sixty of them, big and little. This fruit does not ripen till October, like the medlars. Grapes grow here in such abundance that one cannot travel four arpents without finding trees full of trellises of charming beauty, with clusters sometimes as large as those in France; but most of them have the berries far apart. I cannot say as much of their quality, for out of all those that I have tasted, I have found none that are edible. I tried to cook some and used more than a quarter of a pound of sugar to a pint of this juice, yet it was impossible for me or my serving man to swallow it.

There are wood rats here as big as a French cat, which have white fur inclining to reddish, as long as that of a marten. It is very fine and the women make garters of it. They have tails a foot long and as thick as a finger, just like that of the muskrat. The female has two skins under her belly which gives the effect of a justaucorps closed at the top and the bottom and open in the middle. They have as many as eight young, which they carry inside when they walk. Some savages brought me a couple of them once during the winter. I hoped to send them to France, but I was surprised some days after to find their tails missing. The cold had frozen them, and they had broken off like glass. Sometime later their ears also dropped off, so that I was obliged to kill them. Some savages to whom I told this informed me that the mothers always kept them in their holes until they were as big as themselves, and that, moreover, they did not go out when it was very cold. They are very good to eat. They are very heavy, and there is no need of running after them for when they see anyone they do not flee; they only open their mouths and you smash their heads with a stick.

There is also a great abundance of stinking animals, who produce an infectious stink with the smell of their urine. This is their defense; when one tries to approach them to kill them, they immediately turn tail and urinate if they can. The dogs, after having strangled them, are often like mad for a very long time. They do all they can by rolling on the ground to get rid of this bad smell, which sticks to them for a long time. This does not keep the savages from making dresses of their skin, the fur being white and black and very warm. The meat is very tender, but despite all precautions taken in washing it, it develops an unpleasant odor when eaten.

Plums are also very abundant here, and not inferior in beauty to those of France. I found some at one time which, as regards appearance, were nowise different from our *Imperiale*, but they had a very different flavor indeed. They are never freestone, and have a very thick skin.

There are also in the prairies many orchards whose trees are laden with apples as big as the Api, but very bad. I was never able to eat them except after boiling them, and after they had been frozen.

We got back from our hunt toward the middle of July. From that time up to the end of September there arrived continually bands of ten and fifteen and twenty Illinois, to the number of 800, whom the late Monsieur de Tonti had sent out at the beginning of March against the Iroquois, by order of Monsieur the Marquis Denonville. They brought in this summer, captive or killed, sixty men, women, and children.

In the autumn Monsieur de la Forest arrived, who told us that the Iroquois had killed many French and that everybody was in great dismay. He and Monsieur de Tonti used all their address to induce as many Illinois as possible to set out against them. In this they were fairly successful, for the following summer we burned six Iroquois, and they brought in more than twenty scalps.

In 1691 Monsieur de Tonti left for some business which he had at Michillimackinac, leaving me to take command in his place.

Before his departure, he assembled all the principal Illinois and told them that he was leaving me in his place, and that in case any matters turned up regarding the service of the king or the well-being of their village, they had only to apply to me—he would approve whatever I might do. I learned afterward that this speech had had not a little effect on their minds, for I can truthfully say to their praise that never had Indians been so submissive as they were during this time.

2: French Explorations

Reuben G. Thwaites, in a selection from *France in America, 1497-1763* (New York, 1905), summarizes the pattern of French exploration and settlement and of the growing—but unappreciated—rivalry with the English. Then the great literary historian Francis Parkman describes the attempts of France to take possession of the West. Writing in the grand style of the nineteenth-century historian, he canvasses the last days of Jesuit activity on the lakes, portraying the ceremony in which Daumont de Saint-Lusson, a French officer on orders of the Intendant Jean Talon, proclaimed an empire in the name of Louis XIV. Although justly criticized for his personal biases for the heroic explorers and against the Indians, particularly the Iroquois, Parkman's works still stand among the most readable narratives of the French failure in the New World. The description in this selection is from *La Salle and the Discovery of the Great West* (Boston, 1869).

Special Accounts

France in America

REUBEN G. THWAITES

French Jesuits had operated in the Illinois country as early as Marquette, but their ministrations were in Indian villages along the Illinois River. In 1699 the Sulpicians opened a mission at Cahokia, on the Mississippi, and the year following the Jesuits removed their establishment to the neighboring Kaskaskia. Fort Chartres (1720)— a stout fortress, designed to check growing English encroachments

From Reuben G. Thwaites, *France in America, 1497-1763* (New York, 1905), pp. 84-95.
Footnotes in the original have been omitted.

on the Ohio and the Mississippi—St. Philippe (1723), and Prairie du
Rocher (1733) followed in due course.

By the time of the founding of New Orleans, the little group of
Illinois settlements had from their productive soil, facilities of
transportation, and location at the centre of profitable Indian trade,
already grown into a neighborhood of great importance in the
agricultural and commercial development of New France. In 1719,
Louisiana and the Illinois entered upon the brief period of "boom"
which was inaugurated by Law's somewhat fantastic speculative
scheme. Cahokia and Kaskaskia greatly increased in size and importance, eight hundred new settlers being imported, chiefly from
Canada and New Orleans, and placed on large land grants; several
stone-mills and storehouses were constructed, the *habitants* were
encouraged to grow tobacco, and negro slaves were introduced.

Throughout the first half of the eighteenth century the Illinois
became noted for agricultural products, which were shipped in large
quantities to Detroit on the north, Ohio River ports on the east,
and southward to New Orleans and Mobile, whence they found
their way to the West Indies and Europe. At Kaskaskia the Jesuits
maintained an academy; at Cahokia, the Sulpicians had a considerable school for Indian youth; and Fort Chartres was known as "the
centre of life and fashion in the West." It is recorded that "about
the year 1746 there was a scarcity of provisions at New Orleans,"
and the Illinois French "sent thither in one winter, upward of eight
hundred thousand weight of flour." In exchange for their products,
the thrifty Illinois *habitants* received many luxuries and refinements
directly from Europe and other French colonies—sugar, rice, indigo,
cotton, manufactured tobacco, and goods of like character—and
these interior settlements were long regarded as the garden of New
France.

At first the Illinois settlements were governed from Canada,
although their trade relations were naturally more intimate with
Louisiana than with the lower St. Lawrence. Indeed, despite the
protests of the Quebec officials, who were alarmed over this diversion of the Mississippi trade, there was now but slight connection
with Canada. The old portage routes connecting the divergent
drainage systems of the St. Lawrence and the Mississippi had fallen
into comparative disuse. Several causes contributed to this result:
the reduction of trading-posts on the Great Lakes, under the economical policy of Governor Callières's administration; the continued hostility of the Fox Indians in Wisconsin; the physical
hardships of these routes; but in large measure the careful fostering
of the more convenient southern trade and the growing bulk of

exports. The people of the Illinois henceforth looked upon the Mississippi as their natural highway to the markets of the world.

Law's financial project collapsed in 1720, but its Louisiana branch had become merged in the Company of the Indies, which continued to operate here for several years upon a dwindling career. The enormous expense of a long but successful war with the Natchez Indians was in the end the determining factor, and at its close the corporation gladly surrendered its charter (January 23, 1731), Louisiana becoming once more a royal province.

In the mean while both Louisiana and the Illinois had materially prospered, chiefly as the result of improved navigation facilities, and stimulation of business and manufacturing enterprise, increased immigration, and the efforts made to broaden not only the area of tillage but the variety of crops. From Louisiana rice, indigo, and tobacco were exported; fig trees from Provence and orange trees from Santo Domingo had become acclimated; there was also a small acreage of cotton; the population along the lower Mississippi had increased from some six hundred whites and a score of negroes to five thousand whites and two thousand blacks. As a province, Louisiana, in the leisurely fashion of the subtropics, had continued to thrive. But in Illinois the easy-going *habitants*—farmers, hunters, traders by turn, with a strong admixture of unprogressive Indian blood—soon forgot the feverish and unwonted energy of artificial stimulus. The villages of the mid-country resumed their natural status of sleepy little fur-trade and mission stations, and thus remained until the downfall of New France.

The War of the Spanish Succession, in America called Queen Anne's War (1702-1713), had greatly impoverished France. Louis XIV died in 1715, overwhelmed with disappointment, for the wide-spreading empire which he had reared was now shorn on every hand, and numerous domestic calamities faced the throne. Immediately following his death the country came under the practical control of the benign Cardinal Fleury, preceptor to the young king, and in 1726 he was made actual minister. Early in his career commercial restrictions were largely removed, to the immediate benefit of French commerce. We have already seen that earnest, although economically unsound, measures had been taken for the development of Louisiana; Guadeloupe, Martinique, and the French half of Hayti also felt new life. In Canada, ice-bound half the year and with a roving population that lived largely on the fur-trade, feudalism seemed an ill-nurtured exotic; but Louisiana and these West Indian possessions were, with their subtropical climate, particularly adapted to the profitable use of slave labor and to the paternal form of government which France employed alike at home and in the colonies. Coffee and sugar from the French colonies began to drive from the European markets the production of rival English islands of Jamaica, Barbadoes, and their smaller neighbors; England was also, for a time, losing ground along the Mediterranean, in the Levant, and in far-off India. French merchant shipping grew from three hundred vessels, at the time of Louis's death, to eighteen hundred in 1735.

While Fleury was dominating France, the English prime-minister was Sir Robert Walpole. Both statesmen strongly desired peace in western Europe, and in the face of many difficulties long maintained it. But there were irresistible forces at work, largely originating in differences of temperament between the two peoples, which tended to neutralize their efforts at a good understanding. France and England were engaged in a long-standing rivalry for the possession of lands over-seas, which might be colonized and thereby made to assist in the development of national commerce. Naval strength is the predominant factor in colonizing and the pushing of colonial trade. The mistress of the seas controls the ocean lanes, can keep open against all comers the necessary lines of communication between the colonies and the mother-land, and in need can defend colonial coasts.

England, more clearly than France, recognized this principle, and in a measure acted upon it. Her perception had not at the time of our narrative attained to a thorough understanding; her efforts were lacking in continuity and cohesion, and much stupidity was sometimes displayed by her naval and military boards; but, impelled in great measure by the necessities of her insular position, she did much better than France, whose statesmen were so steeped in the back-door turmoil of continental dynastic bickerings that they often quite lost sight of their colonies and the sea. The result was that soon her neglected navy had shrunk to half the strength of that of Great Britain, ill-manned and ill-equipped as the latter generally was; and complications arose for which France was unprepared and the reasons for which were not always at once comprehended by her leaders.

English trade rivalry among the tribes of both the Ohio and the upper Great Lakes early became a serious matter with the officials and merchants of New France, and we find frequent references to it in the French documents of the period. Not only did wandering French and English traders visit and tamper with each other's Indians; but . . . there was much smuggling across the lines—French merchants obtaining low-priced goods from New York and Albany; Englishmen purchasing peltries from

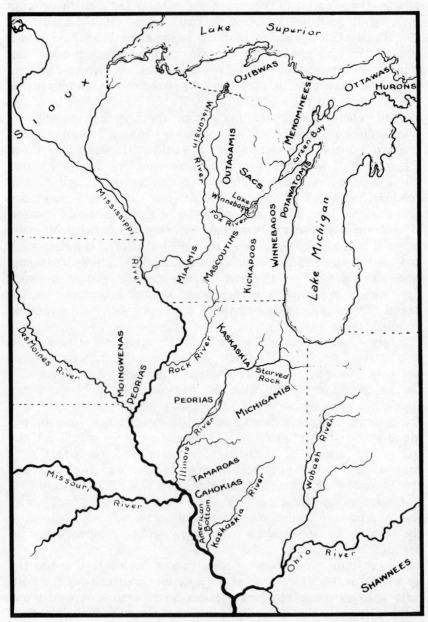

The location of historic Indian tribes of the Northwest in 1763

French dealers, and even directly from *coureurs de bois* who operated in the region of Mackinac and Sault Ste. Marie and surreptitiously sought the English market. In 1724 it was affirmed by a careful observer that, contrary to law, Albany merchants, instead of exclusively patronizing tribes allied to the English, were obtaining four-fifths of their skins "from the French of Mont Royall and Canada"; and several English traders were prosecuted and punished for this serious offence.

The issue relative to the proprietorship of the trans-Alleghany region was soon raised by English colonial officials. In 1686 Denonville reported to Versailles that letters written to him by Governor Dongan of New York "will notify you sufficiently of his pretensions which extend no less than from the lakes, inclusive, to the South Sea. Missilimakinac is theirs. They have taken its latitude; have been to trade there with our Outawas and Huron Indians, who received them cordially on account of the bargains they gave." Denonville pleads for definite information from the court, relative to the French claims, based on "a great many discoveries that have been made in this country, with which our registers ought to be loaded." As usual, however, nothing was then done to check the fast-opening bud of English aspirations. Versailles waited until it had grown into a stout tree.

. . . .

La Salle

FRANCIS PARKMAN

What were the Jesuits doing? Since the ruin of their great mission of the Hurons, a perceptible change had taken place in them. They had put forth exertions almost superhuman, set at naught famine, disease, and death, lived with the self-abnegation of saints and died with the devotion of martyrs; and the result of all had been a disastrous failure. From no short-coming on their part,

From Francis Parkman, *La Salle and the Discovery of the Great West* (Boston, 1869), pp. 36-45, 48-53. Footnotes in the original have been omitted.

but from the force of events beyond the sphere of their influence, a very demon of havoc had crushed their incipient churches, slaughtered their converts, uprooted the populous communities on which their hopes had rested, and scattered them in bands of wretched fugitives far and wide through the wilderness. They had devoted themselves in the fulness of faith to the building up of a Christian and Jesuit empire on the conversion of the great stationary tribes of the lakes; and of these none remained but the Iroquois, the destroyers of the rest,—among whom, indeed, was a field which might stimulate their zeal by an abundant promise of sufferings and martyrdoms, but which, from its geographical position, was too much exposed to Dutch and English influence to promise great and decisive results. Their best hopes were now in the North and the West; and thither, in great part, they had turned their energies.

We find them on Lake Huron, Lake Superior, and Lake Michigan, laboring vigorously as of old, but in a spirit not quite the same. Now, as before, two objects inspired their zeal,—the "greater glory of God," and the influence and credit of the Order of Jesus. If the one motive had somewhat lost in power, the other had gained. The epoch of the saints and martyrs was passing away; and henceforth we find the Canadian Jesuit less and less an apostle, more and more an explorer, a man of science, and a politician. The yearly reports of the missions are still, for the edification of the pious reader, filled with intolerably tedious stories of baptisms, conversions, and the exemplary deportment of neophytes,—for these have become a part of the formula; but they are relieved abundantly by more mundane topics. One finds observations on the winds, currents, and tides of the Great Lakes; speculations on a subterranean outlet of Lake Superior; accounts of its copper-mines, and how we, the Jesuit fathers, are laboring to explore them for the profit of the colony; surmises touching the North Sea, the South Sea, the Sea of China, which we hope ere long to discover; and reports of that great mysterious river of which the Indians tell us,—flowing southward, perhaps to the Gulf of Mexico, perhaps to the Vermilion Sea,—and the secrets whereof, with the help of the Virgin, we will soon reveal to the world.

. . . .

Prefixed to the *Relation* of 1671 is that monument of Jesuit hardihood and enterprise, the map of Lake Superior,—a work of which, however, the exactness has been exaggerated, as compared with other Canadian maps of the day. While making surveys, the priests were diligently looking for copper. Father Dablon reports that they had found it in greatest abundance on Isle Minong, now

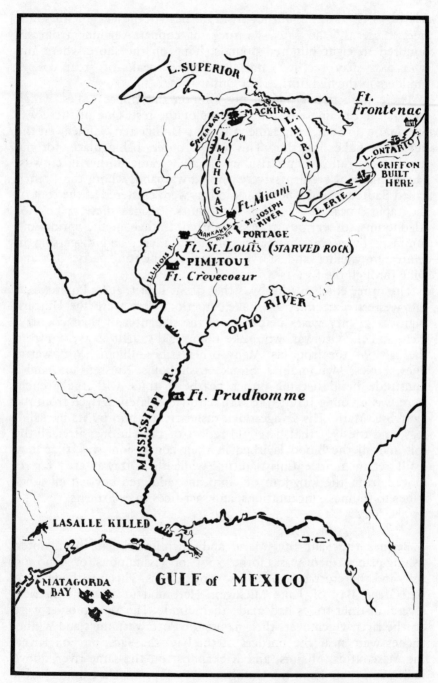

LaSalle's explorations in North America

Isle Royale. "A day's journey from the head of the lake, on the south side, there is," he says, "a rock of copper weighing from six hundred to eight hundred pounds, lying on the shore where any who pass may see it;" and he further speaks of great copper boulders in the bed of the river Ontonagan.

There were two principal missions on the Upper Lakes, which were, in a certain sense, the parents of the rest. One of these was Ste. Marie du Saut,—the same visited by Dollier and Galinée,—at the outlet of Lake Superior. This was a noted fishingplace; for the rapids were full of white-fish, and Indians came thither in crowds. The permanent residents were an Ojibwa band, whom the French called Sauteurs, and whose bark lodges were clustered at the foot of the rapids, near the fort of the Jesuits. Besides these, a host of Algonquins, of various tribes, resorted thither in the spring and summer,—living in abundance on the fishery, and dispersing in winter to wander and starve in scattered hunting-parties far and wide through the forests.

The other chief mission was that of St. Esprit, at La Pointe, near the western extremity of Lake Superior. Here were the Hurons, fugitives twenty years before from the slaughter of their country-men; and the Ottawas, who, like them, had sought an asylum from the rage of the Iroquois. Many other tribes—Illinois, Pottawatta-mies, Foxes, Menomonies, Sioux, Assiniboins, Knisteneaux, and a multitude besides—came hither yearly to trade with the French. Here was a young Jesuit, Jacques Marquette, lately arrived from the Saut Ste. Marie. His savage flock disheartened him by its backslid-ings; and the best that he could report of the Hurons, after all the toil and all the blood lavished in their conversion, was, that they "still retain a little Christianity;" while the Ottawas are "far re-moved from the kingdom of God, and addicted beyond all other tribes to foulness, incantations, and sacrifices to evil spirits."

. . . .

Besides the Saut Ste. Marie and Michilimackinac, both noted fishing-places, there was another spot, no less famous for game and fish, and therefore a favorite resort of Indians. This was the head of the Green Bay of Lake Michigan. Here and in adjacent districts several distinct tribes had made their abode. The Menomonies were on the river which bears their name; the Pottawattamies and Winne-bagoes were near the borders of the bay; the Sacs, on Fox River; the Mascoutins, Miamis, and Kickapoos, on the same river, above Lake Winnebago; and the Outagamies, or Foxes, on a tributary of it flowing from the north. Green Bay was manifestly suited for a mission; and, as early as the autumn of 1669, Father Claude

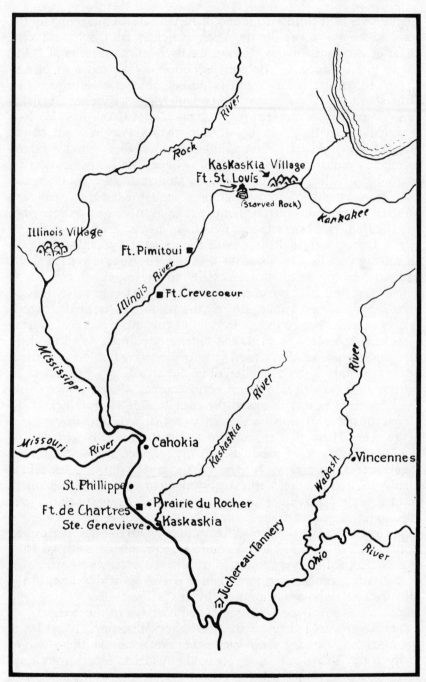

Rock River

Kaskaskia Village
Ft. St. Louis
(Starved Rock)

Kankakee

Illinois Village

Ft. Pimitoui

Illinois River

Ft. Crevecoeur

Mississippi

Missouri River

Cahokia

Kaskaskia River

Wabash River

Vincennes

St. Phillippe

Ft. de Chartres
Ste. Genevieve

Prairie du Rocher
Kaskaskia

Juchereau Tannery

Ohio River

Courtesy of the Illinois State Historical Library

The Illinois country in the days of the French

Allouez was sent thither to found one. After nearly perishing by the way, he set out to explore the destined field of his labors, and went as far as the town of the Mascoutins. Early in the autumn of 1670, having been joined by Dablon, Superior of the missions on the Upper Lakes, he made another journey, but not until the two fathers had held a council with the congregated tribes at St. François Xavier; for so they named their mission of Green Bay. Here, as they harangued their naked audience, their gravity was put to the proof; for a band of warriors, anxious to do them honor, walked incessantly up and down, aping the movements of the soldiers on guard before the governor's tent at Montreal. "We could hardly keep from laughing," writes Dablon, "though we were discoursing on very important subjects; namely, the mysteries of our religion, and the things necessary to escaping from eternal fire."

The fathers were delighted with the country, which Dablon calls an earthly paradise; but he adds that the way to it is as hard as the path to heaven. He alludes especially to the rapids of Fox River, which gave the two travellers great trouble. Having safely passed them, they saw an Indian idol on the bank, similar to that which Dollier and Galinée found at Detroit,—being merely a rock, bearing some resemblance to a man, and hideously painted. With the help of their attendants, they threw it into the river. Dablon expatiates on the buffalo, which he describes apparently on the report of others, as his description is not very accurate. Crossing Winnebago Lake, the two priests followed the river leading to the town of the Mascoutins and Miamis, which they reached on the fifteenth of September. These two tribes lived together within the compass of the same enclosure of palisades,—to the number, it is said, of more than three thousand souls. The missionaries, who had brought a highly colored picture of the Last Judgment, called the Indians to council and displayed it before them; while Allouez, who spoke Algonquin, harangued them on hell, demons, and eternal flames. They listened with open ears, beset him night and day with questions, and invited him and his companion to unceasing feasts. They were welcomed in every lodge, and followed everywhere with eyes of curiosity, wonder, and awe. Dablon overflows with praises of the Miami chief, who was honored by his subjects like a king, and whose demeanor towards his guests had no savor of the savage.

Their hosts told them of the great river Mississippi, rising far in the north and flowing southward,—they knew not whither,—and of many tribes that dwelt along its banks. When at length they took their departure, they left behind them a reputation as medicine-men of transcendent power.

. . . .

Jean Talon, intendant of Canada, was full of projects for the good of the colony. On the one hand, he set himself to the development of its industries, and, on the other, to the extension of its domain. He meant to occupy the interior of the continent, control the rivers, which were its only highways, and hold it for France against every other nation. On the east, England was to be hemmed within a narrow strip of seaboard; while, on the south, Talon aimed at securing a port on the Gulf of Mexico, to keep the Spaniards in check, and dispute with them the possession of the vast regions which they claimed as their own. But the interior of the continent was still an unknown world. It behooved him to explore it; and to that end he availed himself of Jesuits, officers, fur-traders, and enterprising schemers like La Salle. His efforts at discovery seem to have been conducted with a singular economy of the King's purse. La Salle paid all the expenses of his first expedition made under Talon's auspices; and apparently of the second also, though the intendant announces it in his despatches as an expedition sent out by himself. When, in 1670, he ordered Daumont de Saint-Lusson to search for copper mines on Lake Superior, and at the same time to take formal possession of the whole interior for the King, it was arranged that he should pay the costs of the journey by trading with the Indians.

Saint-Lusson set out with a small party of men, and Nicolas Perrot as his interpreter. Among Canadian *voyageurs*, few names are so conspicuous as that of Perrot; not because there were not others who matched him in achievement, but because he could write, and left behind him a tolerable account of what he had seen. He was at this time twenty-six years old, and had formerly been an *engagé* of the Jesuits. He was a man of enterprise, courage, and address,—the last being especially shown in his dealings with Indians, over whom he had great influence. He spoke Algonquin fluently, and was favorably known to many tribes of that family.

Saint-Lusson wintered at the Manitoulin Islands; while Perrot, having first sent messages to the tribes of the north, inviting them to meet the deputy of the governor at the Saut Ste. Marie in the following spring, proceeded to Green Bay, to urge the same invitation upon the tribes of that quarter. They knew him well, and greeted him with clamors of welcome. The Miamis, it is said, received him with a sham battle, which was designed to do him honor, but by which nerves more susceptible would have been severely shaken. They entertained him also with a grand game of *la crosse*, the Indian ball-play. Perrot gives a marvellous account of the authority and state of the Miami chief, who, he says, was attended day and night by a guard of warriors,—an assertion which would be incredible, were it not sustained by the account of the same chief given by the Jesuit Dablon. Of the tribes of the Bay, the greater part promised to send delegates to the Saut; but the Pottawattamies dissuaded the Miami potentate from attempting so long a journey, lest the fatigue incident to it might injure his health; and he therefore deputed them to represent him and his tribesmen at the great meeting. Their principal chiefs, with those of the Sacs, Winnebagoes, and Menomonies, embarked, and paddled for the place of rendezvous, where they and Perrot arrived on the fifth of May.

Saint-Lusson was here with his men, fifteen in number, among whom was Louis Joliet; and Indians were fast thronging in from their wintering grounds, attracted, as usual, by the fishery of the rapids or moved by the messages sent by Perrot,—Crees, Monsonis, Amikoués, Nipissings, and many more. When fourteen tribes, or their representatives, had arrived, Saint-Lusson prepared to execute the commission with which he was charged.

At the foot of the rapids was the village of the Sauteurs, above the village was a hill, and hard by stood the fort of the Jesuits. On the morning of the fourteenth of June, Saint-Lusson led his followers to the top of the hill, all fully equipped and under arms. Here, too, in the vestments of their priestly office, were four Jesuits,— Claude Dablon, Superior of the Missions of the lakes, Gabriel Druilletes, Claude Allouez, and Louis André. All around the great throng of Indians stood, or crouched, or reclined at length, with eyes and ears intent. A large cross of wood had been made ready. Dablon, in solemn form, pronounced his blessing on it; and then it was reared and planted in the ground, while the Frenchmen, uncovered, sang the *Vexilla Regis*. Then a post of cedar was planted beside it, with a metal plate attached, engraven with the royal arms; while Saint-Lusson's followers sang the *Exaudiat*, and one of the Jesuits uttered a prayer for the King. Saint-Lusson now advanced, and, holding his sword in one hand, and raising with the other a sod of earth, proclaimed in a loud voice,—

"In the name of the Most High, Mighty, and Redoubted Monarch, Louis, Fourteenth of that name, Most Christian King of France and of Navarre, I take possession of this place, Sainte Marie du Saut, as also of Lakes Huron and Superior, the Island of Manitoulin, and all countries, rivers, lakes, and streams contiguous and adjacent thereunto,—both those which have been discovered and those which may be discovered hereafter, in all their length and breadth, bounded on the one side by the seas of the North and of the West, and on the other by the South Sea: declaring to the nations thereof that from this time forth they are vassals of his Majesty, bound to obey his laws and follow his customs; promising them on his part all succor and protection against the incursions and invasions of their enemies: declaring to all other potentates, princes, sovereigns, states, and republics,—to them and to their subjects,—that they cannot and are not to seize or settle upon any parts of the aforesaid countries, save only under the good pleasure of His Most Christian Majesty, and of him who will govern in his behalf; and this on pain of incurring his resentment and the efforts of his arms. *Vive le Roi.*"

The Frenchmen fired their guns and shouted "Vive le Roi," and the yelps of the astonished Indians mingled with the din.

What now remains of the sovereignty thus pompously proclaimed? Now and then the accents of France on the lips of some straggling boatman or vagabond half-breed,—this, and nothing more.

. . . .

Original Narratives

The first two original narratives are Marquette's own accounts of his contacts with the Indians, the second being specifically about his three-day visit in an Indian town at the headwaters of the Fox River. (Spelling, capitalization, and punctuation have been reproduced exactly from the original documents.) His travels on the river to the Jesuit mission at De Pere near Green Bay mark the extent of his explorations. After becoming critically ill in the autumn of 1674, he spent the winter of 1675 in a small hut on the Chicago River; that spring, after traveling to the eastern shore of Lake Michigan, he died. A somewhat unseemly controversy developed over the exact site of Marquette's burial. For more on the fight over the priest's bones, see Joseph P. Donnelly, *Jacques Marquette, S.J., 1637-1675* (Chicago, 1968). For a reliable sketch of his life, consult Raphael N. Hamilton, *Father Marquette* (Grand Rapids, 1970), in the *Great Men of Michigan* series published by Eerdmans.

The 'Unknown Countries'

FATHER JACQUES MARQUETTE

Accordingly, on The 17th day of may, 1673, we started from the Mission of st. Ignace at Michilimakinac, where I Then was. The Joy that we felt at being selected for This Expedition animated our

From Reuben G. Thwaites, ed., *The Jesuit Relations*, LIX (Cleveland, 1900), pp. 91-93, 99-107.

Courage, and rendered the labor of paddling from morning to night agreeable to us. And because We were going to seek Unknown countries, We took every precaution in our power, so that if our Undertaking were hazardous, it should not be foolhardy. To that end, we obtained all the Information that we could from the savages who had frequented those regions; and we even traced out from their reports a Map of the whole of that New country; on it we indicated the rivers which we were to navigate, the names of the peoples and of the places through which we were to pass, the Course of the great River, and the direction we were to follow when we reached it.

Above all, I placed our voyage under the protection of the Blessed Virgin Immaculate, promising her that, if she granted us the favor of discovering the great River, I would give it The Name of the Conception, and that I would also make the first Mission that I should establish among Those New peoples, bear the same name. This I have actually done, among the Illinois.

Section 2nd. The Father Visits, in Passing, the
Tribes of the Folle Avoine. What That
Folle Avoine is. He Enters the Bay Des
Puants; Some Particulars About That Bay.
He Arrives Among the Fire Nation.

With all these precautions, we Joyfully Plied our paddles on a portion of Lake huron, on That of the Illinois and on the bay des Puants.

The first Nation that we came to was That of the folle avoine. I entered Their river, to go and visit these peoples to whom we have preached The Gospel for several years,—in consequence of which, there are several good christians among Them.

The wild oat, whose name they bear because it is found in their country, is a sort of grass, which grows naturally in the small Rivers with muddy bottoms, and in Swampy Places. It greatly resembles the wild oats that Grow amid our wheat. The ears grow upon hollow stems jointed at Intervals; they emerge from the Water about the month of June, and continue growing until they rise About two feet above it. The grain is not larger than That of our oats, but it is twice as long, and The meal therefrom is much more abundant. The Savages Gather and prepare it for food as Follows. In The month of September, which is the suitable time for The harvest, they go in Canoes through These fields of wild oats; they shake its Ears into the Canoe, on both sides, as they pass through. The grain falls out easily, if it be ripe, and they obtain their supply In a short time. But, in order to clean it from the straw, and to

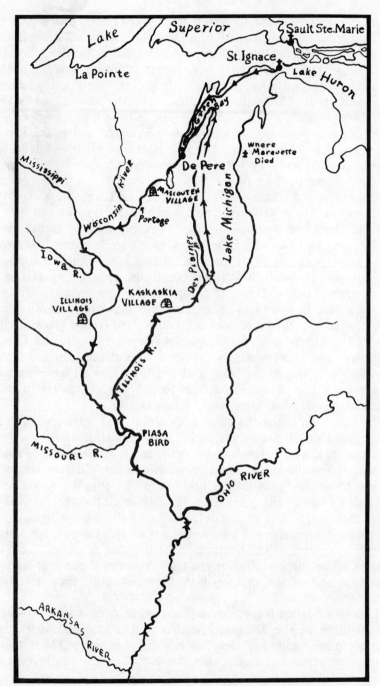

Courtesy of the Illinois State Historical Library

The exploration route of Marquette and Jolliet

remove it from a husk in which it is Enclosed, they dry it in the smoke, upon a wooden grating, under which they maintain a slow fire for some Days. When The oats are thoroughly dry, they put them in a Skin made into a bag, thrust It into a hole dug in the ground for This purpose, and tread it with their feet—so long and so vigorously that The grain separates from the straw, and is very easily winnowed. After this, they pound it to reduce it to flour,—or even, without pounding it, they Boil it in water, and season it with fat. Cooked in This fashion, The wild oats have almost as delicate a taste as rice has when no better seasoning is added.

I told these peoples of the folle avoine of My design to go and discover Those Remote nations, in order to Teach them the Mysteries of Our Holy Religion. They were Greatly surprised to hear it, and did their best to dissuade me. They represented to me that I would meet Nations who never show mercy to Strangers, but Break Their heads without any cause; and that war was kindled Between Various peoples who dwelt upon our Route, which Exposed us to the further manifest danger of being killed by the bands of Warriors who are ever in the Field. They also said that the great River was very dangerous, when one does not know the difficult Places; that it was full of horrible monsters, which devoured men and Canoes Together; that there was even a demon, who was heard from a great distance, who barred the way, and swallowed up all who ventured to approach him; Finally that the Heat was so excessive In those countries that it would Inevitably Cause Our death.

I thanked them for the good advice that they gave me, but told them that I could not follow it, because the salvation of souls was at stake, for which I would be delighted to give my life; that I scoffed at the alleged demon; that we would easily defend ourselves against those marine monsters; and, moreover, that We would be on our guard to avoid the other dangers with which they threatened us. After making them pray to God, and giving them some Instruction, I separated from them. Embarking then in our Canoes, We arrived shortly afterward at the bottom of the Bay des puantz,* where our Fathers labor successfully for the Conversion of these peoples, over two thousand of whom they have baptized while they have been there.

This bay bears a Name which has a meaning not so offensive in the language of the savages; For they call it *la baye sallée* ["salt bay"] rather than Bay des Puans,—although with Them this is almost the same and this is also The name which they give to the

---

*Green Bay.

Sea. This led us to make very careful researches to ascertain whether there were not some salt-Water springs in This quarter, As there are among the hiroquois, but we found none. We conclude, therefore, that This name has been given to it on account of the quantity of mire and Mud which is seen there, whence noisome vapors Constantly arise, Causing the loudest and most Continual Thunder that I have ever heard.

The Bay is about thirty leagues in depth and eight in width at its Mouth; it narrows gradually to the bottom, where it is easy to observe a tide which has its regular ebb and flow, almost Like That of the Sea. This is not the place to inquire whether these are real tides; whether they are Due to the wind, or to some other cause; whether there are winds, The precursors of the Moon and attached to her suite, which consequently agitate the lake and give it an apparent ebb and flow whenever the Moon ascends above the horizon. What I can Positively state is, that, when the water is very Calm, it is easy to observe it rising and falling according to the Course of the moon. although I do not deny that This movement may be Caused by very Remote Winds, which, pressing on the middle of the lake, cause the edges to Rise and fall in the manner which is visible to our eyes.

We left This bay to enter the river that discharges into it; it is very beautiful at its Mouth, and flows gently; it is full Of bustards, Ducks, Teal, and other birds attracted thither by the wild oats of which they are very fond. But, after ascending the river a short distance, it becomes very difficult of passage, on account of both the Currents and the sharp Rocks, which Cut the Canoes and the feet of Those who are obliged to drag them, especially when the Waters are low. Nevertheless, we successfully passed Those rapids; and on approaching Machkoutens, the fire Nation, I had the Curiosity to drink the mineral Waters of the River that is not Far from That village. I also took time to look for a medicinal plant which a savage, who knows its secret, showed to Father Alloues with many Ceremonies. Its root is employed to Counteract snake-bites, God having been pleased to give this antidote Against a poison which is very common in these countries. It is very pungent, and tastes like powder when crushed with the teeth; it must be masticated and placed upon the bite inflicted by the snake. The reptile has so great a horror of it that it even flees from a Person who has rubbed himself with it. The plant bears several stalks, a foot high, with rather long leaves; and a white flower, which greatly resembles The wallflower. I put some in my Canoe, in order to examine it at leisure while we continued to advance toward Maskoutens, where we arrived on The 7th of June.

Section 3rd. Description of the Village of Mas-
koutens; What Passed There Between the
Father and the Savages. The French
Begin to Enter a New and Unknown
Country, and Arrive at Missisipi.

Here we are at Maskoutens. This Word may, in Algonquin, mean
"the fire Nation,"—which, indeed, is the name given to this tribe.
Here is the limit of the discoveries which the french have made, For
they have not yet gone any farther.

This Village Consists of three Nations who have gathered there—
Miamis, Maskoutens, and Kikabous. The former are the most civil,
the most liberal, and the most shapely. They wear two long locks
over their ears, which give them a pleasing appearance. They are
regarded as warriors, and rarely undertake expeditions without
being successful. They are very docile, and listen quietly to What is
said to Them; and they appeared so eager to Hear Father Alloues
when he Instructed them that they gave Him but little rest, even
during the night. The Maskoutens and Kikabous are ruder, and seem
peasants in Comparison with the others. As Bark for making Cabins
is scarce in this country, They use Rushes; these serve Them for
making walls and Roofs, but do not afford them much protection
against the winds, and still less against the rains when they fall
abundantly. The Advantage of Cabins of this kind is, that they
make packages of Them, and easily transport them wherever they
wish, while they are hunting.

When I visited them, I was greatly Consoled at seeing a handsome
Cross erected in the middle of the village, and adorned with many
white skins, red Belts, and bows and arrows, which these good
people had offered to the great Manitou (This is the name which
they give to God). They did this to thank him for having had pity
On Them during The winter, by giving Them an abundance of game
When they Most dreaded famine.

I took pleasure in observing the situation of this village. It is
beautiful and very pleasing; For, from an Eminence upon which it is
placed, one beholds on every side prairies, extending farther than
the eye can see, interspersed with groves or with lofty trees. The
soil is very fertile, and yields much indian corn. The savages gather
quantities of plums and grapes, wherewith much wine could be
made, if desired.

No sooner had we arrived than we, Monsieur Jollyet and I,
assembled the elders together; and he told them that he was sent by
Monsieur Our Governor to discover New countries, while I was sent
by God to Illumine them with the light of the holy Gospel. He told

them that, moreover, The sovereign Master of our lives wished to be known by all the Nations; and that in obeying his will I feared not the death to which I exposed myself in voyages so perilous. He informed them that we needed two guides to show us the way; and We gave them a present, by it asking them to grant us the guides. To this they very Civilly consented; and they also spoke to us by means of a present, consisting of a Mat to serve us as a bed during the whole of our voyage.

On the following day, the tenth of June, two Miamis who were given us as guides embarked with us, in the sight of a great crowd, who could not sufficiently express their astonishment at the sight of seven frenchmen, alone and in two Canoes, daring to undertake so extraordinary and so hazardous an Expedition.

We knew that, at three leagues from Maskoutens, was a River which discharged into Missisipi. We knew also that the direction we were to follow in order to reach it was west-southwesterly. But the road is broken by so many swamps and small lakes that it is easy to lose one's way, especially as the River leading thither is so full of wild oats that it is difficult to find the Channel. For this reason we greatly needed our two guides, who safely Conducted us to a portage of 2,700 paces, and helped us to transport our Canoes to enter That river; after which they returned home, leaving us alone in this Unknown country, in the hands of providence.

Thus we left the Waters flowing to Quebeq, 4 or 500 Leagues from here, to float on Those that would thenceforward Take us through strange lands. Before embarking thereon, we Began all together a new devotion to the blessed Virgin Immaculate, which we practiced daily, addressing to her special prayers to place under her protection both our persons and the success of our voyage; and, after mutually encouraging one another, we entered our Canoes.

The River on which we embarked is called Meskousing. It is very wide; it has a sandy bottom, which forms various shoals that render its navigation very difficult. It is full of Islands Covered with Vines. On the banks one sees fertile land, diversified with woods, prairies, and Hills. There are oak, Walnut and basswood trees; and another kind, whose branches are armed with long thorns. We saw there neither feathered game nor fish, but many deer, and a large number of cattle. Our Route lay to the southwest, and, after navigating about 30 leagues, we saw a spot presenting all the appearances of an iron mine; and, in fact, one of our party who had formerly seen such mines, assures us that The One which We found is very good and very rich. It is Covered with three feet of good soil, and is quite near a chain of rocks, the base of which is covered by very fine trees. After proceeding 40 leagues on This same route, we arrived at the mouth of our River; and, at 42 and a half degrees Of latitude, We safely entered Missisipi on The 17th of June, with a Joy that I cannot Express.

First Contact with the Indians

FATHER JACQUES MARQUETTE

We advanced constantly, but as we did not know where we were going, having already made more than a hundred leagues without having discovered anything but beasts and birds, we kept well on our guard. Accordingly we make only a little fire on the shore at night to prepare our meal, and after supper keep as far from it as possible, passing the night in our canoes, which we anchor in the river pretty far from the bank. Even this did not prevent one of us being always as a sentinel, for fear of a surprise.

. . . .

At last, on the 25th of June, we perceived footprints of men by the water-side, and a beaten path entering a beautiful prairie. We stopped to examine it, and concluding that it was a path leading to some Indian village, we resolved to go and reconnoitre; we accordingly left our two canoes in charge of our people, cautioning them strictly to beware of a surprise; then M. Jollyet and I undertook this rather hazardous discovery for two single men, who thus put themselves at the discretion of an unknown and barbarous people. We followed the little path in silence, and having advanced about two leagues, we discovered a village on the banks of the river, and two others on a hill, half a league from the former.

Then, indeed, we recommended ourselves to God, with all our hearts; and, having implored His help, we passed on undiscovered, and came so near that we even heard the Indians talking. We then deemed it time to announce ourselves, as we did by a cry, which we raised with all our strength, and then halted without advancing any farther. At this cry the Indians rushed out of their cabins, and having probably recognized us as French, especially seeing a black gown, or at least having no reason to distrust us, seeing we were but two, and had made known our coming, they deputed four old men to come and speak with us. Two carried tobacco-pipes well-adorned, and trimmed with many kinds of feathers. They marched slowly, lifting their pipes toward the sun, as if offering them to him to smoke, but yet without uttering a single word. They were a long time coming the little way from the village to us. Having reached us at last, they stopped to consider us attentively. I now took courage, seeing these ceremonies, which are used by them only with friends, and still more on seeing them covered with stuffs, which made me to judge them to be allies. I, therefore, spoke to them first, and asked them who they were; they answered that they were Ilinois, and, in token of peace, they presented their pipes to smoke. They then invited us to their village where all the tribe awaited us with impatience. These pipes for smoking are called in the country, calumets, a word that is so much in use, that I shall be obliged to employ it in order to be understood, as I shall have to speak of it frequently.

At the door of the cabin in which we were to be received, was an old man awaiting us in a very remarkable posture, which is their usual ceremony in receiving strangers. This man was standing perfectly naked with his hands stretched out and raised toward the sun, as if he wished to screen himself from its rays, which nevertheless passed through his fingers to his face. When we came near him, he paid us this compliment: "How beautiful is the sun, O Frenchman, when thou comest to visit us! All our town awaits thee, and thou shalt enter all our cabins in peace." He then took us into his, where there was a crowd of people, who devoured us with their eyes, but kept a profound silence. We heard, however, these words occasionally addressed to us: "Well done, brothers, to visit us!"

As soon as we had taken our places, they showed us the usual civility of the country, which is to present the calumet. You must not refuse it, unless you would pass for an enemy, or at least for being impolite. It is, however, enough to pretend to smoke. While all the old men smoked after us to honor us, some came to invite us on behalf of the great sachem of all the Ilinois to proceed to his town, where he wished to hold a council with us. We went with a good retinue, for all the people who had never seen a Frenchman among them could not tire looking at us; they threw themselves on the grass by the wayside, they ran ahead, then turned and walked back to see us again. All this was done without noise, and with marks of a great respect entertained for us.

Courtesy of the Illinois State Historical Library

Robert Thom's painting of Marquette and Jolliet meeting the Illiniwek

Having arrived at the great sachem's town, we espied him at his cabin-door, between two old men, all three standing naked, with their calumet turned to the sun. He harangued us in a few words, to congratulate us on our arrival, and then presented us his calumet and made us smoke; at the same time we entered his cabin, where we received all their usual greetings. Seeing all assembled and in silence, I spoke to them by four presents which I made; by the first, I said that we marched in peace to visit the nations on the river to the sea; by the second, I declared to them that God their Creator had pity on them, since, after their having been so long ignorant of Him, He wished to become known to all nations; that I was sent on His behalf with this design; that it was for them to acknowledge and obey Him; by the third, that the great chief of the French informed them that he spread peace everywhere, and had overcome the Iroquois. Lastly, by the fourth, we begged them to give us all the information they had of the sea, and of the nations through which we should have to pass to reach it.

When I had finished my speech, the sachem rose, and laying his hand on the head of a little slave, whom he was about to give us, spoke thus: "I thank thee, Blackgown, and thee, Frenchman," addressing M. Jollyet, "for taking so much pains to come and visit us; never has the earth been so beautiful, nor the sun so bright, as today; never has our river been so calm, nor so free from rocks, which your canoes have removed as they passed; never has our tobacco had so fine a flavor, nor our corn appeared so beautiful as we behold it today. Here is my son, that I give thee, that thou mayest know my heart. I pray thee to take pity on me and all my nation. Thou knowest the Great Spirit who has made us all; thou speakest to Him and hearest His word; ask Him to give me life and health, and come and dwell with us, that we may know Him." Saying this, he placed the little slave near us and made us a second present, an all-mysterious calumet, which they value more than a slave; by this present he showed us his esteem for our governor, after the account we had given of him; by the third, he begged us, on behalf of his whole nation, not to proceed further, on account of the great dangers to which we exposed ourselves.

I replied, that I did not fear death, and that I esteemed no happiness greater than that of losing my life for the glory of Him who made all. But this these poor people could not understand.

The council was followed by a great feast which consisted of four courses, which we had to take with all their ways; the first course was a great wooden dish full of sagamity, that is to say, of Indian meal boiled in water and seasoned with grease. The master of ceremonies, with a spoonful of sagamity, presented it three or four

times to my mouth, as we would do with a little child; he did the
same to M. Jollyet. For the second course, he brought in a second
dish containing three fish; he took some pains to remove the bones,
and having blown upon it to cool it, put it in my mouth, as we
would food to a bird; for the third course, they produced a large
dog, which they had just killed, but learning that we did not eat it,
it was withdrawn. Finally, the fourth course was a piece of wild ox,
the fattest portions of which were put into our mouths.

After this feast we had to visit the whole village, which consists
of full three hundred cabins. While we marched through the streets,
an orator was constantly haranguing, to oblige all to see us without
being troublesome; we were everywhere presented with belts, garters, and other articles made of the hair of the bear and wild cattle,
dyed red, yellow, and gray. These are their rarities; but not being of
consequence, we did not burthen ourselves with them.

We slept in the sachem's cabin, and the next day took leave of
him, promising to pass back through his town in four moons. He
escorted us to our canoes with nearly six hundred persons, who saw
us embark, evincing in every possible way the pleasure our visit had
given them. On taking leave, I personally promised that I would
return the next year to stay with them, and instruct them. But
before leaving the Ilinois country, it will be well to relate what I
remarked of their customs and manners.

To say Ilinois is, in their language, to say "the men," as if other
Indians compared to them were mere beasts. And it must be
admitted that they have an air of humanity that we had not
remarked in the other nations that we had seen on the way. The
short stay I made with them did not permit me to acquire all the
information I would have desired. The following is what I remarked
in their manners:

They are divided into several villages, some of which are quite
distant from that of which I speak, and which is called Peouarea.
This produces a diversity in their language which in general has a
great affinity to the Algonquin, so that we easily understood one
another. They are mild and tractable in their disposition, as we
experienced in the reception they gave us. They have many wives,
of whom they are extremely jealous; they watch them carefully,
and cut off their nose or ears when they do not behave well; I saw
several who bore the marks of their infidelity. They are well-
formed, nimble, and very adroit in using the bow and arrow; they
use guns also, which they buy of our Indian allies who trade with
the French; they use them especially to terrify their enemies by the
noise and smoke, the others lying too far to the west, have never

seen them, and do not know their use. They are war-like and formidable to distant nations in the south and west, where they go to carry off slaves, whom they make an article of trade, selling them at a high price to other nations for goods.

The distant nations against whom they go to war, have no knowledge of Europeans; they are acquainted with neither iron or copper, and have nothing but stone knives. When the Ilinois set out on a war party, the whole village is notified by a loud cry made at the door of their huts the morning and evening before they set out. The chiefs are distinguished from the soldiers by their wearing a scarf ingeniously made of the hair of bears and wild oxen. The face is painted with red lead or ochre, which is found in great quantities a few days' journey from their village. They live by game, which is abundant in this country, and on Indian corn, of which they always gather a good crop, so that they have never suffered from famine. They also sow beans and melons, which are excellent, especially those with a red seed. Their squashes are not of the best; they dry them in the sun, to eat in the winter and spring.

Their cabins are very large; they are lined and floored with rush-mats. They make all their dishes of wood, and their spoons of the bones of the buffalo, which they cut so well, that it serves them to eat their sagamity, easily.

They are liberal in their maladies, and believe that the medicines given them operate in proportion to the presents they have made the medicine-man. Their only clothes are skins; their women are always dressed very modestly and decently, while the men do not take any pains to cover themselves. Through what superstitition I know not, some Ilinois, as well as some Nadouessi [Sioux or Dacotas], while yet young, assume the female dress, and keep it all their life. There is some mystery about it, for they never marry, and glory in debasing themselves to do all that is done by women; yet they go to war, though allowed to use only a club, and not the bow and arrow, the peculiar arm of men; they are present at all the juggleries and solemn dances in honor of the calumet; they are permitted to sing, but not to dance; they attend the councils, and nothing can be decided without their advice; finally, by the profession of an extraordinary life, they pass for manitous [that is, for genii], or persons of consequence.

It now only remains for me to speak of the calumet, than which there is nothing among them more mysterious or more esteemed. Men do not pay to the crowns and sceptres of kings the honor they pay to it; it seems to be the god of peace and war, the arbiter of life and death. Carry it about you and show it, and you can march fearlessly amid enemies, who even in the heat of battle lay down their arms when it is shown. Hence the Ilinois gave me one, to serve as my safeguard amid all the nations that I had to pass on my voyage. There is a calumet for peace, and one for war, distinguished only by the color of the feathers with which they are adorned, red being the sign of war. They use them also for settling disputes, strengthening alliances, and speaking to strangers. It is made of a polished red stone, like marble, so pierced that one end serves to hold the tobacco, while the other is fastened on the stem, which is a stick two feet long, as thick as a common cane, and pierced in the middle; it is ornamented with the head and neck of different birds of beautiful plumage; they also add large feathers of red, green, and other colors, with which it is all covered. They esteem it particularly because they regard it as the calumet of the sun; and, in fact, they present it to him to smoke when they wish to obtain calm, or rain, or fair weather. They scruple to bathe at the beginning of summer, or to eat new fruits, till they have danced it. They do it thus:

The calumet dance, which is very famous among these Indians, is performed only for important matters, sometimes to strengthen a peace or to assemble for some great war; at other times for a public rejoicing; sometimes they do this honor to a nation who is invited to be present; sometimes they use it to receive some important personage, as if they wished to give him the entertainment of a ball or comedy. In winter the ceremony is performed in a cabin, in summer in the open fields. They select a place surrounded with trees, so as to be sheltered beneath their foliage against the heat of the sun. In the middle of the space they spread out a large party-colored mat of rushes; this serves as a carpet, on which to place with honor the god of the one who gives the dance; for every one has his own god, or manitou as they call it, which is a snake, a bird, or something of the kind, which they have dreamed in their sleep, and in which they put all their trust for the success of their wars, fishing, and hunts. Near this manitou and at its right, they put the calumet in honor of which the feast is given, making around about it a kind of trophy, spreading there the arms used by the warriors of these tribes, namely, the war-club, bow, hatchet, quiver, and arrows.

Things being thus arranged, and the hour for dancing having arrived, those who are to sing take the most honorable place under the foliage. They are the men and the women who have the finest voices, and who accord perfectly. The spectators then come and take their places around under the branches; but each one on arriving must salute the manitou, which he does by inhaling the smoke and then puffing it from his mouth upon it, as if offering incense. Each one goes first and takes the calumet respectfully, and supporting it with both hands, makes it dance in cadence, suiting himself to the air of the song; he makes it go through various figures, sometimes showing it to the whole assembly by turning it from side to side.

After this, he who is to begin the dance appears in the midst of the assembly, and goes first; sometimes he presents it to the sun, as if he wished it to smoke; sometimes he inclines it to the earth; and at other times he spreads its wings as if for it to fly; at other times, he approaches it to the mouths of the spectators for them to smoke, the whole in cadence. This is the first scene of the ballet.

The second consists in a combat, to the sound of a kind of drum, which succeeds the songs, or rather joins them, harmonizing quite well. The dancer beckons to some brave to come and take the arms on the mat, and challenges him to fight to the sound of the drums; the other approaches, takes his bow and arrow, and begins a duel against the dancer who has no defence but the calumet. This spectacle is very pleasing, especially as it is always done in time, for one attacks, the other defends; one strikes, the other parries; one flies, the other pursues; then he who fled faces and puts his enemy to flight. This is all done so well with measured steps, and the regular sound of voices and drums, that it might pass for a very pretty opening of a ballet in France.

The third scene consists of a speech delivered by the holder of the calumet, for the combat being ended without bloodshed, he relates the battles he was in, the victories he has gained; he names the nations, the places, the captives he has taken, and as a reward, he who presides at the dance presents him with a beautiful beaver robe, or something else, which he receives, and then he presents the calumet to another, who hands it to a third, and so to all the rest, till all having done their duty, the presiding chief presents the calumet itself to the nation invited to this ceremony in token of the eternal peace which shall reign between the two tribes.

*　*　*　*　*

We take leave of our Ilinois about the end of June, at three o'clock in the afternoon, and embark in sight of all the tribe, who admire our little canoes, having never seen the like.

In 1698, Father Jean François Buisson de St. Cosmé and two priests were ordered by the Bishop of Canada to extend French missions to the southwest. Cosmé describes their voyage, beginning with a statement on conditions at the Jesuit Mission of the Guardian Angel, located on the future site of Chicago, then giving a brief account of the journey down the Illinois River. Louise Phelps Kellogg published extensively on the French and British occupancy of the Old Northwest.

The Mission of the Illinois

JEAN FRANÇOIS BUISSON DE ST. COSMÉ

We remained five days at Kipikaoui,* leaving on the 17th and after being windbound on the 18th and 19th we camped on the 20th at a place five leagues from Chikagou. We should have arrived there early on the 21st but the wind which suddenly arose on the lake compelled us to land half a league from Chikagou. We had considerable difficulty in landing and in saving our canoes; we all had to jump into the water. One must be very careful along the lakes, and especially Lake Mixcigan, whose shores are very low, to take to the land as soon as possible when the waves rise on the lake, for the rollers become so high in so short a time that one runs the risk of breaking his canoe and of losing all it contains. Many travellers have already been wrecked there. We, Monsieur de Montigny, Davion, and myself, went by land to the house of the Reverend Jesuit Fathers while our people remained behind. We found there Reverend Father Pinet and Reverend Father Binneteau, who had recently arrived from the Illinois country and was slightly ill.

I cannot describe to you, my lord, with what cordiality and manifestations of friendship these Reverend Fathers received and embraced us while we had the consolation of residing with them. Their house is built on the bank of a small river, with the lake on one side and a fine and vast prairie on the other. The village of the savages contains over a hundred and fifty cabins, and a league up the river is still another village almost as large. They are all Miamis. Reverend Father Pinet usually resides there except in winter, when the savages are all engaged in hunting, and then he goes to the Illinois. We saw no savages there; they had already started for their hunt. If one may judge of the future from the short time the Reverend Father Pinet has passed in this mission, we may believe that if God will bless the labors and the zeal of that holy missionary

From Louise Phelps Kellogg, ed., *Early Narratives of the Northwest, 1634-1649* (New York, 1917), pp. 346-351. Footnotes of identification in the original have been retained.
*The Root River, which empties into Lake Michigan at Racine, Wisconsin.

THE MISSION OF THE ILLINOIS

there will be a great number of good and fervent Christians. It is true that but slight results are obtained with reference to the older persons, who are hardened in profligacy, but all the children are baptized, and the jugglers even, who are the most opposed to Christianity, allow their children to be baptized. They are also very glad to let them be instructed. Several girls of a certain age and also many young boys have already been and are being instructed, so that we may hope that when the old stock dies off, they will be a new and entirely Christian people.

On the 24th of October the wind fell and we sent for our canoes with all our effects, and finding that the water was extraordinarily low, we made a cache in the ground with some of them and took only what was absolutely necessary for our journey, intending to send for the remainder in the spring. We left Brother Alexandre in charge thereof, as he agreed to remain there with Father Pinet's man. We started from Chikagou on the 29th, and slept about two leagues from it on the little river that afterward loses itself in the prairies. On the following day we began the portage, which is about three leagues in length when the waters are low, and is only one-fourth of a league in the spring, for then one can embark on a small lake that discharges into a branch of the river of the Illinois, and when the waters are low a portage has to be made to that branch. On that day we got over half our portage, and would gone still further, when we perceived that a little boy given us by Monsieur de Muis, and who had set out alone although he was told to wait, was lost. We had not noticed it because all our people were busy. We were obliged to stop to look for him; everybody went and several gun-shots were fired, but he could not be found. It was a rather unfortunate accident; we were pressed for time, owing to the lateness of the season, and the waters being very low, we saw quite well, that as we were obliged to carry our baggage and our canoe, it would take a long time to reach the Illinois. This compelled us to separate. Messieurs de Montigny, de Tonty, and Davion continued the portage on the following day, while I with four other men went back to look for the little boy. While retracing my steps I met Fathers Pinet and Binneteau, who were on the way to the Illinois with two Frenchmen and a savage. We looked for the boy during the whole of that day also, without finding him. As it was the day before the feast of All Saints, I was compelled to go to Chikagou for the night with our people. After they had heard mass and performed their devotions early in the morning, they spent the whole of that day also looking for the little boy without getting sight of him. It was very difficult to find him in the long grass, for this country consists of nothing but prairies with a few groves of trees.

"Summer Evening in a French Village" from John Drury's Midwest Heritage

We were afraid to set fire to the long grass lest we might burn the boy. Monsieur de Montigny had told me to remain only one day, because the cold weather pressed us, and this compelled me to proceed, after giving orders to Brother Alexandre to seek him and to take some Frenchmen who were at Chikagou.

I started in the afternoon of the 2nd of November. I crossed the portage and passed the night at the river or branch of the River of the Illinois. We descended the river as far as an island. During the night we were surprised to see a slight fall of snow, and on the following day the river was frozen over in several places. We had therefore to break the ice and haul the canoe, because there was no open water. This compelled us to leave our canoe and go by land to seek Monsieur de Montigny, whom we met on the following day, the 5th of the month, at the Isle aux Cerfs. They had already gone over two leagues of portage. We still had four leagues to do, as far as Mont Joliet. This took us three days, and we arrived on the 8th of the month.

From the Isle à la Cache to the said Mount Jolliet,* a distance of seven leagues, everything has to be portaged, as there is no water in the river except in the spring. The banks of this river are very agreeable; they consist of prairies bounded by small hills and very fine thickets; there are numbers of deer in them and along the river are great quantities of game of all kinds, so that after crossing the portage one of our men, while taking a walk, procured enough to provide us with an abundant supper as well as breakfast on the following day. Mont Jolliet is a very fine mound of earth in the prairie to the right, descending a little. It is about thirty feet high. The savages say that at the time of the great deluge one of their ancestors escaped, and that this small mountain is his canoe which he upset there.

On leaving Mont Jolliet we proceeded about two leagues by water. We remained two whole days at our short portage, about a quarter of a league in length. As one of our men named Charbonneau had killed several turkeys and bustards in the morning, together with a deer, we were very glad to give our people a good meal and to let them rest for a day. On the tenth we made the short portage and found half a league of water, after which two men carried the canoe for about a league, the others walking behind, each carrying his load; and we then embarked for a league and a half. We slept at a short portage, five or six arpents in length. On the eleventh, after making the short portage, we came to the river

*One finds both Joliet and Jolliet in travelers' accounts. The explorer spelled his name "Jolliet," but the official spelling of the Illinois city is "Joliet."

Courtesy of the Illinois State Historical Library

Festivities of the early French of Illinois

Teatiki,† which is the true river of the Illinois, that which we descended being only a distant branch. We put all our baggage in the canoe, which two men paddled, while Monsieur de Tonty and ourselves, with the remainder of our men, proceeded by land, walking all the time through fine prairies. We came to the village of the Peangichias, Miamis who formerly dwelt at the falls of the Miçipi and who have for some years been settled at this place. There was no one in the village, for all had gone hunting. That day we slept near Massane,‡ a small river which falls into the River of the Illinois. On that day we began to see oxen, and on the morrow two of our men killed four; but as these animals are in poor condition at this season we contented ourselves with taking the tongues only. These oxen seem to me to be larger than ours; they have a hump on their backs; their legs are very short; the head is very large and so covered with long hair that it is said a bullet cannot penetrate it. We afterward saw some nearly every day during our journey as far as the Acansças.

†The Kankakee River.
‡Mazon Creek in Grundy County, Illinois.

After experiencing considerable difficulty during three days in carrying and hauling our baggage in the canoe, owing to the river being rapid, low, and full of rocks, we arrived on the 15th of November at the place called the Old Fort. This is a rock on the bank of the river, about a hundred feet high, whereon Monsieur de la Salle had caused a fort to be built, which has been abandoned, because the savages went to reside about twenty-five leagues further down. We slept a league above it, where we found two cabins of savages; we were consoled on finding a woman who was a thoroughly good Christian. The distance between Chicagou and the fort is considered to be about thirty leagues. There we commenced the navigation, that continues to be always good as far as the fort of Permetaoui, where the savages now are and which we reached on the 19th of November. We found there Reverend Father Binetot and Reverend Father Marais who, owing to their not being laden when they left Chigaou, had arrived six or seven days before us. We also saw Reverend Father Pinet there. All the Reverend Jesuit Fathers gave us the best possible reception. Their sole regret was to see us compelled to leave so soon on account of the frost. We took there a Frenchman who had lived three years with the Acansças and who knows a little of their language.

This mission of the Illinois seems to me the finest that the Reverend Jesuit Fathers have up here, for without counting all the children who are baptized, a number of adults have abandoned all their superstitions and live as thoroughly good Christians; they frequently attend the sacraments and are married in church. We had not the consolation of seeing all these good Christians often, for they were all scattered down the bank of the river for the purpose of hunting. We saw only some women savages married to Frenchmen, who edified us by their modesty and their assiduity in going to prayer several times a day in the chapel. We chanted high mass in it, with deacon and subdeacon, on the feast of the Presentation of the most Blessed Virgin, and after commending our voyage to her and having placed ourselves under her protection we left the Illinois on the 22nd of November—we had to break the ice for two or three arpents to get out of Lake Pemsteoui. We had four canoes: that of Monsieur de Tonty, our two, and another belonging to five young voyageurs who were glad to accompany us, partly on account of Monsieur de Tonty, who is universally beloved by all the voyageurs, and partly also to see the country. Reverend Fathers Binneteau and Pinet also came with us a part of the way, as they wished to go and spend the whole winter with their savages.

3: English Colonization

In discussing the transition from French to English control of Illinios after the Treaty of Paris (signed in 1763), Clarence E. Carter traces the murky trail of British colonial policy regarding the newly acquired western territory. His analysis points up the basic reasons why England never made full claim by way of settlement to the Illinois country and why George Rogers Clark, in 1779, met little effective British resistance in his conquest of the West for the patriot cause. Carter, an Illinois native, taught history at Miami University, Ohio State University, the University of Illinois, and the University of Texas before becoming editor of the Territorial Papers of the United States in 1931.

Special Account

The Illinois Country

CLARENCE E. CARTER

The conclusion of the Seven Years' war saw a tremendous change in the relative position of France and England in North America: the former had lost and the latter gained an empire. The final struggle for supremacy was the culmination of a series of continental and colonial wars beginning near the close of the seventeenth century and ending with the definitive treaty of 1763. During the first quarter of the century France occupied a predominant position among the powers. Through the aggressiveness of Louis XIV and his ministers her boundaries had been pushed eastward and northward, thereby seriously threatening the balance of power in Europe.

. . . .

From Clarence E. Carter, *Great Britain and the Illinois Country 1763-1774* (New York, 1910), pp. 1-3, 27-31, 110-117, 123-125, 129-136, 141-144. Footnotes in the original have been omitted.

In North America the pioneers of France had won for her the greater part of the continent, the extensive valleys of the St. Lawrence and the Mississippi with all the land watered by their tributaries. The French claim to this region was based almost entirely upon discovery and exploration, for in all its extent less than one hundred thousand people were permanently settled. Canada at the north and the region about New Orleans on the extreme south contained the bulk of the population, while throughout the old Northwest settlements were few and scattering. Trading posts and small villages existed at Vincennes on the Wabash River, at Detroit, at St. Joseph near Lake Michigan, and at other isolated places. Outside of Detroit the most important and populous settlement was situated along the eastern bank of the Mississippi, in the southwestern part of the present State of Illinois, where about two thousand people were living.

In contrast to this vast area of French territory and the sparseness of its population were the British colonies, with more than a million people confined to the narrow strip between the Alleghany mountains and the Atlantic Ocean. These provinces were becoming comparatively crowded, and many enterprising families of English, Scotch-Irish, and German extraction were pushing towards the mountains. Each year saw the pressure on the western border increased. The great unoccupied valley of the Ohio invited home-seekers and adventurers westward in spite of hostile French and Indians. By 1750 the mountain barriers were being crossed by constantly increasing numbers, and the French found their possession of the West and their monopoly of the fur trade threatened.

. . . .

By the treaty of Paris the title to the Illinois region passed to Great Britain, but Fort de Chartres was not immediately occupied. Detachments of British troops had taken possession of practically every other post in the newly ceded territory as early as 1760. The occupation of the forest posts of Green Bay, Mackinac, St. Joseph, Ouiatanon, Detroit, Fort Miami, Sandusky, Niagara, and others seemed to indicate almost complete British dominion in the West. The transfer of the Illinois posts, however, remained to be effected, and although in the summer of 1763 orders were forwarded from France to the officers commanding in the ceded territory to evacuate as soon as the English forces appeared, almost three years elapsed before the occupation was accomplished; for soon after the announcement of the treaty of cession, the chain of Indian tribes stretching from the fringe of the eastern settlements to the Mississippi River rose in rebellion. This unexpected movement had to be reckoned with before any thought of the occupation of the Illinois country could be seriously entertained.

. . . .

The mass of the Indians rose chiefly from resentment, but Pontiac, the great chief of the Ottawas, acted from a deeper motive. He determined to rehabilitate French power in the West and to reunite all the Indian nations into one great confederacy in order to ward off approaching dangers. During the years 1761-1762 he developed the plot and in 1762 he despatched his emissaries to all the Indian nations. The ramifications of the conspiracy extended to all the Algonquin tribes, to some of the nations on the lower Mississippi, and even to a portion of the Six Nations. The original aim of the plot was the destruction of the garrisons on the frontier, after which the settlements were to be attacked. The assault on the outposts, beginning in May, 1763, was sudden and overwhelming; Detroit, Fort Pitt, and Niagara alone held out, the remainder of the posts falling without an attempt at defense. . . . Peaceful pacification was now, however, out of the question. During the summers of 1763 and 1764 Colonel Bouquet raised the siege of Fort Pitt, penetrated the enemy's country in the upper Ohio Valley, and completely subdued the Shawnee and Delaware tribes upon whom Pontiac had depended. Previous to Bouquet's second campaign, Colonel Bradstreet had advanced with a detachment along the southern shore of Lake Erie, penetrating as far west as Detroit, whence companies were sent to occupy the posts in the upper lake region. In the campaign as a whole the Bouquet expedition was the most effective. After the ratification of a series of treaties, in which the Indians promised allegiance to the English crown, the eastern portion of the rebellion was broken.

. . . .

General Gage, who succeeded Amherst as commander-in-chief of the British army in America in November, 1763, was convinced that the early occupation of the western posts was essential, since it would in a measure cut off communication between the French and the Indian nations dwelling in that vicinity. The Indians, finding themselves thus inclosed, would be more easily pacified.

. . . .

The next definite schemes of which we have knowledge appeared in 1766, although it is probable that there were many others, for during those years half of England was said to have been "New Land mad and every body there has their eye fixt on this Country."

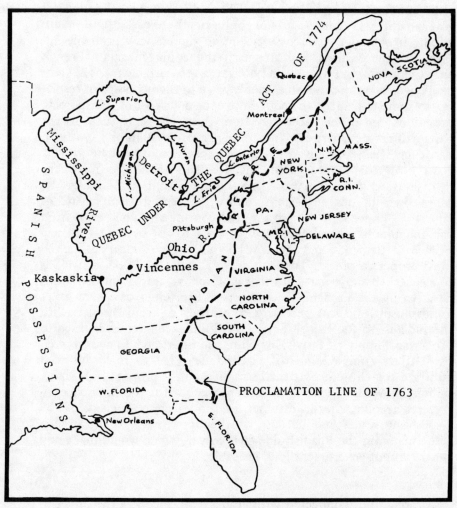

Courtesy of the Illinois State Historical Library

The Illinois country under the English

It is hardly probable, therefore, that the few definite proposals of which we have record were the only plans projected during those years.

. . . .

In 1766, the year of the repeal of the Stamp Act, the imperial government was conscious not only of the necessity of main-taining in America a force sufficient to put down a probable up-rising of the Indians and to guard the country against French encroachments, but also of the obligation to curtail expenses. Gen-eral Gage, therefore, became keenly alive to the necessity of resort-ing to some expedient to reduce the enormous cost of transporting provisions and other necessities from the seacoast to such distant parts as Fort de Chartres. With reference to the Illinois country in particular, he reported to the home government that he was "a good deal disappointed that any Demand should be made for Provisions, as the country used to abound with it, and none can be supplied from our Provisions, but with great difficulty, and at enormous Expense." "This want," he continued, "must arise from the Inhabitants abandoning their Farms to go over to the new French Settlements, and the only method which appears to me the most proper to obviate Difficulties on account of Food, as well as to strengthen those parts at the least Expense, is to grant the Lands deserted by the French, which I presume forfeited, as well as other Lands unsettled, using necessary Precautions to avoid Disputes with the Indians, to the British Settlers. All Endeavours must be used to procure a Supply of Provisions upon the Spot, and I have directed the Officer commanding to get seed, and try to make his men cultivate the Ground near the Fort." Gage next proposed . . . that a military governor be appointed immediately for the Illinois coun-try, on account of the distance of the villages from any of the English provinces and because of their proximity to the French settlements on the Spanish side of the river, which would make any other form of government impracticable.

. . . .

Although not connected with any other projects of the time this proposal of General Gage undoubtedly gave some encouragement to the promoters of a larger colony. . . . About the same time Gover-nor William Franklin of New Jersey, together with the Philadelphia firm of Baynton, Wharton and Morgan, and Joseph Galloway and John Hughes, also of the colony of Pennsylvania, conceived the idea of forming a land company for the definite purpose of purchasing such lands at the Illinois villages as the French might desire to sell, as well as to obtain a grant for other lands in the adjoining country. Accordingly, in March, 1766, they drew up some articles of agreement for the proposed company, which provided among other things that application was to be made to the crown for a grant of 1,200,000 acres of land in the Illinois country or "more if to be procured". Provision was also made for ten equal shareholders, the stipulation to be subject to change in case others desired to enter the company. Apparently Sir William Johnson and his deputy, Croghan, were not directly concerned in the formation of this company, but they were immediately invited to enter, and Croghan, who was then in Philadelphia, signed the contract on behalf of himself and Johnson.

The land company thus organized was intended to be the foundation of a permanent colony in the northwest country. Governor Franklin, in a letter to his father, Dr. Franklin, who was at the time in London as agent for the colony of Pennsylvania, explained the proposition to him as follows: "A few of us, from his [Croghan's] Encouragement, have form'd a Company to Purchase of the French Settled at the Illinois, such Lands as they have a good Title to, and are inclined to dispose of. But as I thought it would be of little Avail to buy Lands in that Country, unless a Colony were established there, I have drawn up some Proposals for that Purpose, which are much approved of by Col. Croghan and the other Gent^m. concerned in Philad^l. and are sent by them to S^r. W. for his Sentiments which when we receive, the whole will be forwarded to you. It is proposed that the Comp^y. shall consist of 12 now in America, and if you like the Proposals, you will be at Liberty to add yourself, and such other gentlemen of Character and Fortune in England as you may think will be likely to promote the Undertaking."

The proposals mentioned in Governor Franklin's letter were outlined by him along with the Articles of Agreement; indeed the substance of the latter was included in the proposals for a colony.

. . . .

In the meantime the Rockingham ministry, which had been in power since July, 1765, had resigned; the Earl of Chatham had been made prime minister in August, 1766, and Lord Shelburne had displaced Conway as secretary of state for the southern department. Johnson's letter to Conway and the proposals for a colony went, therefore, into Shelburne's hands. . . .

Shelburne was pleased with the plan submitted, but openly confessed to Franklin that there were members of the government with whom the scheme did not find approval. . . . The task of

creating a sentiment among the leading members of the government sufficiently strong to bring the whole question to a conclusion was slow and tedious. Although Shelburne and some of
his subordinates were personally favorable to the project, many
months elapsed before they were ready to recommend the proposals to the Board of Trade for its consideration.

. . . .

On October 1, 1767, . . . Shelburne presented a plan providing
for the establishment of three distinct colonies in the Northwest.
The center of one of the proposed governments was to be "at the
Detroit between Lakes Erie and Huron," another "at or near the
Mouth of the Ohio," and the third "in the Illinois Country at or
near the Mouth of the River of that name." In each colony there
were to be one hundred original proprietors, each of whom was to
be allowed "to take up twenty thousand acres of land (without
paying any fine or consideration to the King for them), and to sell
to undertenants; and the proprietors were also to have possessed
their lands fifteen years, without paying any quit-rent or taxes; . . .
at the expiration of the 15 years, they were to have paid a quit-rent
to the King of two shillings per hundred acres; and this quit-rent
was to have been altogether applied to the payment of the contingencies of the government." What form of government Shelburne
had in mind for the new colonies does not appear. It is probable
that that question was left in abeyance until the decision of the
Board of Trade was made known.

. . . .

Soon after this the Board called for the opinion of the merchants, whether the settlement of colonies in the Illinois country
and at Detroit would promote in any way the commerce of Great
Britain. Dr. Franklin, who was present at the meeting, says that
they answered unanimously in the affirmative.

Whatever may have been the prospect in October or November
for a favorable report on the colonial project, the hopes of the
promoters were dashed in the following months. . . .

Throughout 1767 Shelburne was under the necessity of carrying
out the will of the ministry and of Parliament, distasteful though it
was. Friction between himself and the cabinet became so pronounced that for months he failed to attend the meetings. In
September, Townshend, the most influential minister in the cabinet, died and there was an opportunity for Grafton to reconstruct
the policy of the government along the liens advocated by Chatham
and Shelburne. But he chose to continue the policy of Townshend

and admitted into the ministry members of the Bedford party, who were advocates of the adoption of a firm policy toward the colonies. The retirement of Shelburne as colonial minister was made a condition of the support of Bedford. The King was likewise using his influence against the retention of the liberal minister. Shelburne was finally relieved of his unhappy situation; for in January, 1768, the office of secretary of state for the colonies was created, and Lord Hillsborough was appointed to fill the office. The Board of Trade, now deprived of all its executive powers, was under the nominal direction of Lord Clare, Hillsborough having resigned the presidency in December, 1766. . . .

To men like Franklin, therefore, the adverse report made in March, 1768, must have been no surprise. The Board of Trade, under the inspiration of Hillsborough, indorsed the recommendations of the former colonial minister that the management of the Indian trade should be transferred to the colonies and that certain interior posts might then be reduced, but declared a disbelief in the western colonial plan as a further means of reducing imperial expenses.

. . . .

Hillsborough was a bitter opponent of colonial expansion in general, and the objections summarized in this report represent in a large measure his own opinions as well as the point of view held by a large body of conservative Englishmen of that time, who had not yet reached the broader notions held by Shelburne, Franklin, and Adam Smith as to the end for which colonies ought to be created.

. . . .

There was still another important reason for the rejection of interior settlements, which comes to light in contemporary correspondence, but which is not contained in the report of the Board of Trade. During this period Louisiana, with New Orleans commanding the mouth of the Mississippi River, was in the hands of Spain. New Orleans was practically the only outlet for the western country, and it was the settled conviction of many that so long as it remained in the possession of a foreign power, it was useless to expect much from the West. In 1768 Lieutenant George Phyn of the regular army was sent from Fort Pitt down the Ohio and Mississippi rivers to Mobile, and in writing to Sir William Johnson he declared that the country in and about the Illinois region would never be settled "with any advantage to England" unless New Orleans were procured.

In a communication to Secretary Hillsborough in 1770, in which he argued at length against the establishment of settlements or of any additional military posts in the West, General Gage declared that no further time or money should be expended on that country, and particularly the Illinois country, because it would be of no conceivable "advantage to the King's subjects, unless New Orleans was added to His Majesty's Possessions".

In the same year Lord Hillsborough himself mentioned one of the chief objections which he considered to "lie against Colonies in the Illinois with a view to the Peltry Trade, which is the peculiar Commerce of that Country." "This Commerce", he affirmed, "cannot (I apprehend) be useful to Great Britain otherwise than as it furnishes a material for her Manufactures, but it will on the contrary be prejudicial to her in proportion as other Countries obtain that material from us without its coming here first; and whilst New Orleans is the only Port for Exportation of what goes down the Mississippi, no one will believe that that town will not be the market for Peltry or that those Restrictions, which are intended to secure the Exportation of that Commodity directly to G. Britain, can have any effect under such circumstances."

. . . .

In conclusion it may be observed that after 1768 the attention of those most interested in the colonizing of Illinois was turned in another direction. In that year, at the treaty of Fort Stanwix, the boundary line between the Indians and the whites was determined, thus opening for settlement a large tract of land in the region south of the Ohio River. There was formed in the same year a company, called the Walpole or Vandalia Company, for the purpose of establishing a colony there. Although Hillsborough again opposed the scheme, he was overruled, and the grant was made. But the Revolution put an end to further progress in the scheme. In the Illinois country there was another revival of land speculation in 1773, which, however, was simply an attempt of individuals and companies to purchase large tracts of land from the Indians without applying to the crown, a proceeding manifestly contrary to the proclamation of 1763.

Original Narratives

The two original narratives are reports of military missions. Concerned about rumors of deteriorating conditions in the western forts, General Gage, in the spring of 1766, ordered Captain Harry Gordon on an inspection trip to examine installations from Fort Pitt to Pensacola. Gordon left Philadelphia in early May and reached the mouth of the Wabash on the sixth of August. From there he journeyed down the Illinois and Mississippi rivers and arrived at Pensacola in mid-November. On December 6, with his assignment completed, he left New Orleans for Philadelphia by sea. The accounts in this section are selected from Gordon's journal of that mission. The Illinois Historical Library has published three volumes dealing with the British period of Illinois history, under the editorship of Clarence W. Alvord and Clarence E. Carter: *The Critical Period, 1763-1765* (Springfield, 1915), *The New Regime, 1765-1767* (1916), and *Trade and Politics, 1767-1769* (1921).

Gordon's Journal

CAPTAIN HARRY GORDON

The Situation of this Fort is a good one, jetting with a Point a little into the River, the Reach of which up & down it discovers to a considerable Distance. A Garrison here will protect the Traders that come down the Ohio, untill they have Accounts from the Illinois. It will prevent those of the French going up the Ohio or among the Wabash Indians. Hunters from this Post may be sent amongst the Buffaloe, any Quantity of whose Beef they can procure in proper Season, & the Salt may be got from the above mentioned Saline at any easy Ratc to cure it, for the Use of the Troops at the Illinois & in the other Posts on the Mississipi. The Situation is a good one no where commanded from, nor can the Retreat of the Garrison, (a Consideration in the Indian Countries) ever be cut off—The River being, from the Entrance of that called the Cherokee, from 7 to 800 yds. wide. It will in a political Light hold the Ballance between the Cherokee & Wabash Indians, as it favours the Entrance of the former, across the Ohio, into the laters Country, and covers their Retreat from it. There is no proper Spot for a Post nearer the

From "Journal of Capt. H. Gordon," *Collections of the Illinois State Historical Library*, XI (1916), 296-301. Footnotes in the original have been omitted.

Cherokee River above or the Mississipi below but This, as the Grounds on the Banks of the Ohio begin to be very low. The Current of the River towards the Mississipi is very still and may be easily ascended if Affairs are any Way doubtfull at or near the Illinois.

7th We got to the Fork of the Ohio in Lat. 36.43. about 40 Miles below Massiac; we took a Survey of the River in coming down. Our Bearings and Distances from the Method we imagined, and carefully pursued have a considerable Right to be exact, & have been corrected with Observations on the Lat: that are to be depended on. The gentle Ohio is push'd back by the impetuous Stream of the Mississipi, whose muddy white Water is to be seen above 200 yds. up the former. we examined the Ground for several Miles within the Fork. It is an Aggregation of Mud & Dirt interspersed wth Marsh and some Ponds of Water, and is in high Times of the Mississipi overflowed, which is the Case with the other Sides of both Rivers.

9th & 10th repaired the Boats, and fitted them strongly with every-Thing in our Power, to encounter the Stream of the Mississipi, which we thought hardly possible, having been so long used to the much gentler One of the Pleasant Ohio.

11th Augt having been joined by a Party of the 34 Regt from F. Chartres, we began to ascend the Mississipi—whose rapid Stream has broke thro the Country, and divided it every where into a Number of Islands. The low Lands on each Side continue 8 Leagues upwards —when it becomes broken and small Ridges appear for the Rest of the Way to Kaskaskias. There are many Islands in this Distance, some of which entirely of Rock; That called by the French La Tour, which it much resembles, is 11 Leagues below the Kaskaskias River. The Distance of This River from the Forks is 31 Leagues.

The Mississipi's principal Stream is from 5 to 700 yds wide, but it is scarcely ever to be seen together; and some small Parts are above a mile distant from one another—the Principall Stream likewise often shifts & the deep Chanels also, which makes the Pilotage of the River extremely difficult, & boats often get a Ground in ascending, chiefly when endeavouring to avoid the rapid Current.

The 19th we got in the morning to the small River of the Kaskaskias 60 Yds. wide at the Mouth but Deep 5 Feet which it carries up to the Village and is said to be navigable 50 Leagues further. A Detchment of 1 Offr & 30 Men are Quartered here where we arrived the same Day; distant from the Mouth of the River of that Name 2 Leagues. The high Grounds mentioned, skirt along the South Side of the Kaskaskia River, come opposite the Village and continue along Northerly, in a Chain nearly paralel to the East Bank

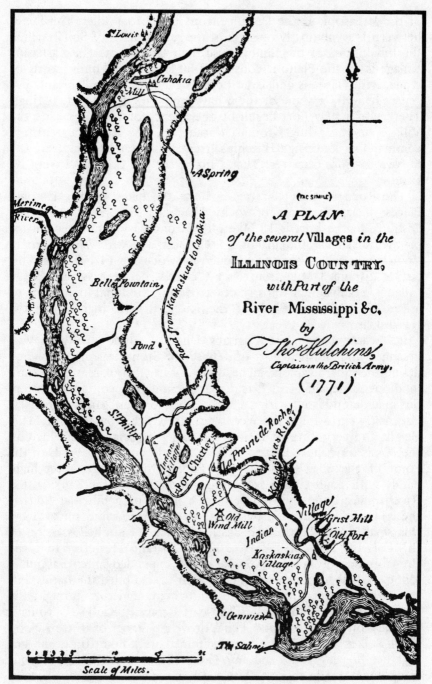

(FAC SIMILE)

A PLAN

of the several Villages *in the*

ILLINOIS COUNTRY,

with Part of the

River Mississippi &c.

by

Tho. Hutchins,

Captain in the British Army,

(1771)

Hutchins' plan of the villages in the Illinois country, 1771

of the Mississipi, at the Distance from it of 2 to 3 Miles. This Space between is level mostly open, & of the richest Kind of Soil in which the Inhabitants of the Illinois raise their Grain &ca. The Kaskaskia Village is on the Plain, it consists of 80 Houses well built mostly of stone, with Gardens and large Lots to each, whose Inhabitants live generally well, & some of them have large Stocks of Cattle & Hogs. There was a new Fort begun by the French of Logs, opposite the Village on the riding Ground, t'other side the River but entirely commanding it. Ensign Hutchins I sent by Water to compleate the Survey to Fort Chartres; That I might see the Country I went by Land.

The Road to Fort Chartres is along the Plain, passing in some Places, near the Chain of rocky Heights above mentioned. The Distance to the Fort is 18 Miles. The Road passes thro' the Village of the Kaskaskia Indians of 15 Cabbins and afterwards thro' a French one called Prairie de Roché in which are 14 Families. This last is distant 3 Mile from Fort Chartres; between is the Village called L'Etablishment mostly deserted, and the Inhabitants gone to Misere on the West Bank of the River, a little higher than the Kaskaskias.

20th arrived at Fort Chartres where I found one of a well imagined and finished Fort of 4 Bast[n] of Stone Masonry, designed defensible ag[t] Musquetry; The Barracks are also of Masonry, commodious & elegant. This Place is large enough to contain 400 Men, but may defend itself with a Third of the Number against Indians, if Care is taken to mow the Weeds near it, which grow to 10 & 11 F[t] Height and very rank. It is now in Danger of being undermined by the Mississipi, whose Eastern Bord is already within 26 Yards of the Point of the S. W. Bastion. The Bank I found thirty Feet high, Sandy with small Gravel (very uncommon Soil for the Banks of the River, that are mostly Mud or fat Clay) and perpendicular; so that the crumbling occasion'd by Frost, would demolish in a little Time this small Space before the Bastion. When we took Possession of this Fort the River was above 100 Yds Distance, & before that, the French who foresaw its Approach had expended much Labour & Money to try to prevent it; They fascined and piled the Banks, but the Torrent soon got Passage behind them. Had they brought the Banks to a large Slope, retired those of a gravelly Kind so as to have an Eddy on them in Flood Time; drove a Number of Button Wood short Stakes in the Slope, which immediately take Root, and got together floating Trees and any Thing else of that Kind the Floods bring down, made those fast at the Point where the Stream divides to come by the Fort & round the Island opposite to it; thus [they] might have averted the Strength of the Current towards the western Bank, and by stopping the Rubbish that comes along with the

Floods have formed a Bar at the Point; The gravelly Banks would not have resisted the Flood, an Eddy would have laid upon them; nor would there have been any Ressistance to the Current at Bottom, whose Effect would have thereby been diminished. Upon these Principles I gave Instructions to Lieu^t Pitman Assis^t Engineer of this Post to proceed. The Ruin of the Fort was inevitable next Spring without doing something. But a Part at least may be saved at a small Expence to lodge the Garrison till other Measures are resolved on. The Sickly State of the Troops did not allow of getting any Number to work during my Stay, nor was the Water low enough or the Heats abated to make much Work otherwise advise-able. This being the Case I proceeded the 28 to view the Country upwards; our own Boatmen being sickly and much fatigued I went by Land, accompanied with Lieu^t Pitman & Ensign Hutchins, to Kyahokie—45 Miles distant from The Fort, & the upper most Settlement on our Side. In the Route we pass le Petit Village, 5 Miles from the Fort, a Place formerly inhabited by 12 Families now only by one since our Possession. The abandoned Houses are most of them well built and left in good Order, the Grounds are favour-able near the Village for Grain, particularly Wheat; and extensive cleared Land, sufficient for the Labour of 100 Men to cultivate. We turn off here to the Eastward and in 2 Miles come on the high Ground, when we keep on till within 3 miles of Kyahokie, when we return to the Plain to get to that Village. Here are 43 Families of French who live well, & so might three Times the number as there is a great Quantity of arable clear Land of the best Soil near it. There is likewise 20 Cabbins of Peioria Indians left here. The Rest and best Part are moved to the French side 2 Miles below Pain Court. It is reckoned the Wheat thrives better here than at Kaskaskias owing probably to its being more Northerly by almost a Degree. At This Place we endeavoured to hire 3 Men & a Canoe as we said to view the Missouri but our Intention was as far as the Illinois River. we could not prevail by Intreaty or Money to get such a Number or even a Canoe to go with us; An Invitation came from Mr St Ange the French Commandant in the Illinois to go to Pain Court with Promise to be assisted in our Progress upwards. We went to Pain Court the 30th where we staid next Day, were civally treated by Mr St Ange and the other Gentlemen, but, thro a little Jealousy, were dissappointed in going upwards, & returned to Kyahokie the 31st in the Evening.

The Village of Pain Court is pleasantly situated on a high Ground which forms the W. Bank of the Mississipi. it is 3 Miles higher up than Kyahokie—has already fifty Families supported chiefly from the rice & seems to flourish very quick.

At This Place M^r Le Clef the principal Indian Trader resides who takes so good Measures, that the whole Trade of the Missouri, That of the Mississipi Northwards, and that of the Nations sur la Baye, Lake Michigan, and St Josephs, by the Illinois River are entirely brought to Him. He appears to be sensible, clever, & has been very well educated; is very active, and will give us some Trouble before we get the Parts of this Trade that belong to us out of His Hands.

We found it impractiable to go further upwards, without waiting for a Boat from the Fort, which would have been a long Time of coming, & otherwise might have given Jealousies that would have occasioned greater Dissappointment, as Mr le Clef is readily served by the Indians he has planted within 2 Miles of Him. We returned to Fort Chartres the 2nd of Septr by the same Route we came. Some Days were employed in visiting and directing Lieu^t Pitman in the Work he was set about, and Composing Instructions regarding his viewing the Country towards the Illinois River, and likewise that on the other Hand to the Ohio and the old Post of Massiac. I found myself no longer usefull at Fort Chartres, & returned to Kaskaskias the 6th.

The next Day viewed the Country round this Village, in order to fix a Situation for the principal Post in Case of the Demolition of Fort Chartres by the Curr^t of the Mississipi, which will most probably will hapen in 3 Years Time perhaps in less. viewed that part to the Nor'wrd of the small River, as also along the Bank of the great one upwards to search for a rising Ground, and a Shelter for Craft; which now lays at the Village, thro' want of such at The Fort. We discovered nothing to Purpose. The Afternoon, we cross'd the small River, with much fatigue and a Foot visited the Situation of the Fort begun by the French as mentioned already. We found it a very good one accessible only on the East Side; the West by which we went up narrow; steep and easily defended. It commands the Town, the River below, overlooks the Plain towards the Mississipi, which does not seem 3 Miles across in a Streight Line, and has a fair Chance at being a healthy Spot, at least an airy one, as it is high Placed, on dry Ground, & near good Water.

Our Possession of the Illinois is only usefull at present in one aspect. It shows the Indian Nations our superiority over the French to whom, they can thence perceive, we give Law. This is dearly bought by the Expence it is to us, and the Inconvenience of supporting it. The French carry on the Trade all round us by Land & by Water; 1st Up the Mississipi, & to the Lakes by the Ouiascoasin, Foxes, Chicagou, and Illinois Rivers; 2^{ndly} Up the Ohio to the Wabash Indians & even the small Quantity of Skins or Furs that the Kaskaskias and Peiorias (who are on our side) get by hunting is carried under our Nose to Misere and Pain Court. A Garrison at the Illinois River & a Post at La Baye will partly prevent the first; and one at Massiac will as has been said, stop their Intercourse with the People on the Wabash, who consist of several Nations. Coop'd up at Fort Chartres only, we make a foolish Figure; hardly have the Dominion of the Country, or as much Credit with the Inhabitants as induce them to give us any Thing for Money, while our neighbours have Plenty on Trust.

9th Septr we were prepared to descend the Mississipi but that night I was seized with a Fever which continued with unremitting violence untill the 16th at Night.—17th being much better, I pursued my Route down the Mississipi the 18th tho' but in a weakly State of Body.

. . . .

George Rogers Clark renders his version of the conquest of the West during the American Revolution in plain frontier prose. The then 28-year-old Virginia surveyor recalls the campaign leading to the final surrender of the "Hair Buyer," Lieutenant Governor Henry Hamilton, and the British garrison at Vincennes on the morning of February 25, 1779. His desire to proceed to attack Detroit was thwarted by the lack of supplies and by the diversion of his Kentucky volunteers to Indian raids, a circumstance that left him short of manpower. Clark's subsequent activity during the war was largely defensive action designed to keep the British out of the Illinois country. For further accounts of Clark, see James Alton James, *The Life of George Rogers Clark* (Chicago, 1928), as well as James' article, "Illinois and the Revolution in the West," published in the *Transactions of the Illinois State Historical Society*, XV (1910), pp. 63-71. A more recent interpretation of Clark can be found in John E. Bakeless, *Background to Glory: The Life of George Rogers Clark* (Philadelphia, 1957). A valuable source of primary material on the Clark expedition is *The George Rogers Clark Papers, 1771-1781*, edited by James and published by the Illinois Historical Library in 1912.

The Conquest of Vincennes

GEORGE ROGERS CLARK

I ordered Major Bowman to mount his company and part of another on horses to be procured from the town, and taking with

From George Rogers Clark, *The Conquest of the Illinois*, Milo M. Quaife, ed. (Chicago, 1920), pp. 50-53, 58-61, 128-143, 150-151. Footnotes in the original have been omitted.

him a few townsmen to inform their friends of what had happened, to proceed without delay to Cahokia and if possible gain possession of the place before the following morning. I gave him no further instructions on the subject, leaving him free to exercise his own judgment. He gave orders for collecting the horses, whereupon a number of gentlemen came to inform me that they were aware of the design. They pointed out that the soldiers were much fatigued, and said they hoped I would not reject their offer to execute whatever I might wish to have done at Cahokia. The people there were their friends and relatives and would, they thought, follow their example. At least, they hoped, they might be permitted to accompany the detachment.

Conceiving that it might be good policy to show them that we put confidence in them (which, in fact, I desired for obvious reasons to do), I told them I had no doubt Major Bowman would welcome their company and that as many as chose might go. Although we were too weak to be other than suspicious and much on our guard, I knew we had sufficient security for their good behavior. I told them that if they went at all they ought to go equipped for war. I was in hopes that everything would be settled amicably, but as it was the first time they had ever borne arms as freemen it might be well to equip themselves and see how they felt, especially as they were about to put their friends in the same situation as themselves.

They appeared to be highly pleased at this idea, and in the evening the Major set out with a force but little inferior to the one with which we had entered the country, the Frenchmen being commanded by their former militia officers. These new friends of ours were so elated over the thought of the parade they were to make at Cahokia that they were too much concerned about equipping themselves to appear to the best advantage. It was night before the party moved and the distance being twenty leagues, it was late in the morning of the sixth before they reached Cahokia. Detaining every person they met, they entered the outskirts of the town before they were discovered. The townsmen were at first much alarmed by this sudden appearance of strangers in hostile array and being ordered even by their friends and relatives to surrender the town. As the confusion among the women and children over the cry of the Big Knives being in town proved greater than had been anticipated. . . . Major Bowman told them not to be alarmed; that although resistance was out of the question he would convince them that he would prefer their friendship to their hostility. He was authorized to inform them that they were at liberty to become free Americans as their friends at Kaskaskia had done. Any who did not

H. W. Beckwith's topographical map
of George Rogers Clark's route

care to adopt this course were free to leave the country except such as had been engaged in inciting the Indians to war.

Cries of liberty and freedom, and huzzahs for the Americans rang through the whole town. The gentlemen from Kaskaskia dispersed among their friends and in a few hours all was amicably arranged, and Major Bowman snugly quartered in the old British fort. Some individuals said the town had been given up too tamely, but little attention was paid to them. A considerable number of Indians who were encamped in the neighborhood (Cahokia was an important center of Indian trade) immediately fled. One of the townsmen who was at St. Louis some time later wrote a letter to me excusing himself for not paying me a visit. By July 8, Major Bowman had everything settled agreeably to our wishes. All of the inhabitants cheerfully took the oath of allegiance, and he set about repairing the fort and regulating the internal police of the place.

The neighboring villages followed the example set by Kaskaskia and Cahokia, and since we made no strict inquiry concerning those who had been engaged in encouraging the Indians to war, within a few days the country appeared to be in a state of perfect harmony. Friendly correspondence which was at once commenced between the Spanish officers and ourselves added much to the general tranquility and happiness. . . .

Being now in position to procure all the information I desired, I was astonished at perceiving the pains and expense the British had incurred in inciting the Indians. They had sent emissaries to every tribe throughout that vast country, even bringing the denizens of Lake Superior by water to Detroit and there outfitting them for war. The sound of war was universal, there being scarcely a nation among them but what had declared and received the bloody belt and hatchet.

Vincennes I found to be a place of infinite importance for us to gain.

. . . .

Vincennes was never absent from my mind. I had reason to suspect from some things I had learned, that Mr. Gibault, the priest, had been inclined to the American interest previous to our arrival in the country. I had no doubt of his fidelity to us. Knowing he had great influence over the people, and that Vincennes was also under his jurisdiction, I sent for him and had a long conference on that subject. In response to my questions he stated that he did not think it worth my while to cause any military preparation to be made at the Falls for an attack on Vincennes although the place was strong and there was a great number of Indians in the neighborhood. He said that Governor Abbott had left the place a few weeks since on some errand to Detroit. He thought that when the inhabitants should be fully informed of what had happened at the Illinois and the present happiness of their friends there, and should be fully acquainted with the nature of the war, their sentiments concerning it would undergo a great change.

. . . .

Crossing a deep narrow lake in the canoes and marching some distance we came to a copse of timber called Warriors Island. We were now in full view of the fort and town which were distant about two miles and with not a shrub between us and the place. Every one feasted his eyes and forgot that he had suffered anything . . . . Now came the real test of our ability. The plain between us and the town was not a perfect level, and the sunken ground was covered with water full of ducks. We observed several men out on horseback shooting ducks about half a mile away and sent off several of our active young men to decoy and capture one of them in such a manner as not to alarm the rest. The information we obtained from this person was similar to that received from those we had taken on the river, with the exception of the news that the British had that evening completed the wall of the fort and that there were a large number of Indians in the town. Our situation was now sufficiently critical. We were within full view of a town which contained upwards of six hundred men, counting soldiers, inhabitants, and Indians, with no possibility of retreat open to us in case of defeat. The crew of the galley, although numbering less than fifty men, would have constituted a reinforcement of great importance to our little army. But we would not permit ourselves to dwell on this. We were now in the situation I had been laboring to attain. The idea of being taken prisoner was foreign to almost all of our men. In the event of capture they looked forward to being tortured by the savages. Our fate was now to be determined, probably within the next few hours, and we knew that nothing but the boldest conduct would insure success. I knew that some of the inhabitants wished us well, while many more were lukewarm to the interest of the British and Americans alike. I also learned that the Grand Chief, the son of Tobacco, had within a few days openly declared in council with the British that he was a brother and friend of the Big Knives. These circumstances were in our favor. Many hunters were going back and forth and there was little probability of our remaining undiscovered until dark. Accordingly I determined

Courtesy of the Illinois State Historical Library

George I. Parrish's painting of the George Rogers Clark expedition

to bring matters to an issue at once, and writing the following address to the inhabitants sent it off by the prisoner we had just taken:

To the Inhabitants of Vincennes—

Gentlemen: Being now within two miles of your village with my army determined to take your fort this night, and not being willing to surprise you, I am taking the measure of requesting such of you as are true citizens and desirous of enjoying the liberty I bring you to remain quietly in your houses. If there are any that are friends of the King of England I desire them instantly to repair to the fort and there join his troops and fight like men; and if any that do not repair to the garrison shall hereafter be discovered they may depend upon being severely punished. Those, on the other hand, who are true friends to Liberty may expect to be well treated. I once more request that they keep out of the streets, for every person found under arms upon my arrival will be treated as an enemy

I entertained conflicting ideas as to what would be the result of this letter. I knew, however, that it could do us no damage, but that it would encourage our friends, cause those who were lukewarm to take a decided stand, and astonish our enemies. I felt sure that they would suppose our information to be valid and our forces so numerous that we were certain of success; that they would suppose our army to be from Kentucky, and not from the Illinois, as it would be deemed impossible for troops to march from the latter place; and would think that my name had been employed by way of subterfuge (this they firmly believed until the next morning, when I was pointed out to them by a person in the fort who knew me well) or that we were a reconnoitering party who only employed this stratagem in order to gain time to effect our retreat. This latter idea I knew would soon be done away. Several gentlemen sent their compliments to their friends under borrowed names which were well known at Vincennes and who were supposed to have been in Kentucky. The soldiers were all given instructions that when speaking of our numbers their common conversation should be of such character as to induce a stranger overhearing it to suppose we had nearly a thousand men. We anxiously watched the messenger until he reached the town and in a few minutes we could perceive with the aid of our glasses a stirring about in every street and large numbers running or riding out into the commons, intent as we supposed upon viewing us. This proved to be the case, but to our great surprise nothing occurred to indicate that the garrison had been alarmed. Neither drum nor guns were heard. This led us to suppose that the information obtained from our prisoner was false and that the enemy was already aware of our presence and prepared to meet us. Every man among us had been impatient for the moment which was now at hand. Shortly before sunset we advanced, displaying ourselves in full view of the crowds in the town. We were plunging headlong either to certain destruction or to success. No middle ground was even thought of. I said but little to the men, aside from emphasizing the necessity for obedience. I knew they did not need encouraging and that anything might be attempted with them that it was possible for such a number of men, perfectly cool, properly disciplined, pleased with the prospect before them, and greatly attached to their officers, to perform. All declared themselves convinced that implicit obedience to orders would alone insure success, and that they hoped anyone who should violate them would immediately be put to death. To a person in my situation such language as this from the soldiers was exceedingly agreeable.

We advanced slowly in full view of the town, but as it was a matter of some consequence to make ourselves appear as formidable as possible, on leaving our place of concealment we marched and countermarched in a fashion calculated to magnify our numbers. Every person who had undertaken to enroll volunteers in the Illinois had been presented with a stand of colors and these, ten or twelve in number, they had brought along with them. We now displayed these to the best possible advantage, and since the plain through which we were marching was not perfectly level but was dotted with elevations rising seven or eight feet above the common level and running in an oblique direction to our line of march towards the town, we took advantage of one of these to march our men along the low ground so that only the colors (which had been fixed to long poles procured for the purpose) could be seen above the height. While we lay on Warriors' Island our young Frenchmen had decoyed and captured several hunters with their horses; I therefore caused our officers, mounted on these, to ride in and out in order more completely to deceive the enemy. In this manner we advanced, directing our march in such fashion that darkness fell before we had proceeded more than half way to the town. We then suddenly altered our direction and crossed some ponds where they could not suspect our presence. About eight o'clock we gained the heights in the rear of the town. There being still no enemy in sight, I became impatient to solve the mystery. I ordered Lieutenant Bailey with fourteen men to advance and open fire on the fort while the main body moved in a different direction and took possession of the strongest part of the town. The firing now commenced against the fort, but since drunken Indians often saluted it after nightfall, the garrison did not suppose it to be from any enemy until one of the men, lighting his match, was shot down through a porthole. The drums now sounded and the conflict was fairly joined on both sides. I sent reinforcements to assist in the attack on the garrison, while other dispositions were being made in the town.

We now found that the garrison had known nothing of our approach. Having finished the fort that evening, they had indulged in games for a time and then retired just before the arrival of my letter. As it was almost time for roll call when its terms were made known many of the inhabitants were afraid to show themselves outside their houses and not one had dared to inform the garrison. Our friends, meanwhile, had rushed to the commons and other convenient places from which to view the pleasing sight afforded by our approach. The garrison had noticed this action and inquired the reason for it, but a satisfactory excuse had been offered and since a portion of the town lay between our line of march and the fort we had not been seen by the sentinels on the walls. Some time before this Captain W. Shannon and another man had been captured by one of their scouting parties and brought to the fort that same evening. This party had discovered some signs of us at the Sugar Camp and, supposing it to be a party of observation which intended to land on the height some distance below the town, Captain La Mothe had been sent to intercept them. When the people were asked the reason of their unusual excitement they had said they were looking at him.

Several persons whose loyalty was under suspicion had been imprisoned in the fort, among them Mr. Moses Henry. Under the pretense of carrying some provisions to him Mrs. Henry went and whispered to him the news of our arrival and what she had seen. This Mr. Henry conveyed to his fellow prisoners. It gave them much pleasure, particularly Captain Helm, who amused himself greatly during the siege and I believe did much damage. We had a scanty supply of ammunition since most of our stores had been put on board the galley. Though her crew were small such a reinforcement would have been invaluable to us at this juncture. Fortunately, however, at the time it had been announced that all of the goods in the town were to be seized for the King's use (the owners were to receive bills of credit in return), Colonel Le Gras, Major Bosseron, and others had buried the greater part of their powder and ball. This ammunition was immediately produced and we found ourselves well supplied by these gentlemen. The Tobacco's son, being

in town with a number of his warriors, immediately mustered them
and indicated a desire to join us, saying that by morning he would
have a hundred men. I thanked him for his friendly disposition but
told him we were already strong enough and desired him to refrain.
I said we would discuss the matter in the morning, but since we
knew there were a number of Indians hostile to us in and about the
town some confusion might result if our men should mix in the
dark. I expressed the hope that we might be favored with his
counsel and company during the night and this proved agreeable to
him.

The garrison was now completely surrounded and the firing
continued without intermission (except for about fifteen minutes
shortly before dawn) until nine o'clock the following morning. Our
entire force, with the exception of fifty men kept as a reserve in
case of some emergency, participated in the attack, being joined by
a few young men. I had acquainted myself fully with the situation
of the fort and town and had detailed information concerning each
of them. The cannon were on the upper floors of strong block-
houses located at each angle of the fort eleven feet above the
ground, and the portholes were so badly cut that our troops lay
under their fire within twenty or thirty yards of the walls. The
enemy did no damage except to the buildings of the town, some of
which were badly shattered, while their musket fire in the dark was
employed in vain against woodsmen who were sheltered behind the
palings of the houses (the gardens of Vincennes were close to the
fort and for about two-thirds of the way around them were fenced
with good pickets firmly set in the ground and about six feet high.
Where these were lacking breastworks for the troops were soon
made by tearing down old houses and garden fences, so that the
troops within the fort enjoyed but little advantage over those
outside; and not knowing the number of the enemy, they thought
themselves in a worse situation than they actually were), river
banks, and ditches, and did us no damage except for the wounding
of a man or two.

Since we could not afford to lose any of our men, great pains
were taken to keep them sufficiently sheltered and to maintain a
hot fire against the fort in order to intimidate the enemy as well as
to destroy them. The embrasures for their cannon were frequently
closed, for our riflemen finding the true direction would pour in
such volleys when they were open that the artillerymen could not
stand to the guns. Seven or eight of them were shot down in a short
time. Our men frequently taunted the enemy in order to provoke
them into opening the portholes and firing the cannon so that they
might have the pleasure of cutting them down with their rifles.

Fifty rifles would be leveled the instant the port flew open, and had the garrison stood to their artillery most of them, I believe, would have been destroyed during the night as the greater part of our men, lying within thirty yards of the walls, and behind some houses, were as well sheltered as those within the fort and were much more expert in this mode of fighting. The enemy fired at the flash of our guns, but our men would change their positions the moment they had fired. On the instant of the least appearance at one of their loopholes a dozen guns would be fired at it. At times an irregular fire as hot as could be maintained was poured in from different directions for several minutes. This would be continually succeeded by a scattering fire at the portholes and a great uproar and laughter would be raised by the reserve parties in different parts of the town to give the impression they had only fired on the fort for a few minutes for amusement, while those who were keeping up a continuous fire were being regularly relieved.

Conduct such as this kept the garrison in a constant state of alarm. They did not know what moment they might be stormed or sapped as they could plainly see that we had thrown up entrenchments across the streets and we frequently appeared to be busily engaged on the bank of the river, which was within thirty feet of the wall. We knew the location of the magazine and Captain Bowman began some work designed to blow it up when our artillery should arrive. Knowing that we were daily liable to be overpowered by the numerous bands of Indians on the river in case they should again heartily join the enemy (as to the likelihood of which we were yet uninformed) we resolved to lose no time, but to gain possession of the fort as soon as possible. Unless the vessel should arrive sooner, we determined to undermine the fort the following night and fixed upon the spot and the plan of executing this work, which we intended to begin the next day.

The Indians belonging to the different hostile tribes had left the town and neighborhood but Captain La Mothe still hovered about, waiting an opportunity to make good his way into the fort. Parties of our men attempted in vain to surprise him, although a few of his men were captured, among them one Maisonville, a famous Indian partisan. Two lads who had captured him led him to a position in the street and fought from behind him as a breastwork, supposing the enemy would not fire at them for fear of killing him. An officer who discovered them at this amusement ordered them to untie him and take him away under guard. This they did, but were so inhuman as to remove part of his scalp on the way, but did him no other harm. Since almost all of those who were most active in the department of Detroit were either inside the fort or with Captain

La Mothe I became uneasy for fear he would not fall into our hands since I knew he would retire if he could not effect his purpose in the course of the night. Perceiving that unless some unforeseen accident should occur the fort must inevitably be ours, and that a reinforcement of twenty men, although considerable to them, could not be of any great moment to us in the present posture of our affairs, and knowing that we had weakened them by killing or wounding many of their gunners, I concluded after some deliberation to risk the reinforcement in preference to his going again among the Indians. I knew the garrison had at least a month's supply of provisions and if it could hold out he might in the course of this time do us great damage.

Shortly before dawn the troops were withdrawn from the fort, except for a few observation parties, and the firing totally ceased. Orders were given that in case La Mothe should approach not to alarm or fire on him without the certainty of killing or capturing the whole party. Within less than a quarter of an hour he passed within ten feet of an officer and small party of men who were lying concealed. Ladders were thrown over the walls of the fort and as they mounted them our party raised a shout. Many of them fell from the top of the wall, some inside and some outside the fort, but as we did not fire on them they all got over to the great joy of their friends. This was readily perceived by us but I had no doubt that on consideration they must be convinced that it was a stratagem of ours to let them into the fort and that we were so strong as to feel little concern for them.

While getting into the fort our men hallooed and made sport of them, at the same time withholding their fire, and our most blatant soldiers frequently told them of our stratagem and our reason for suffering them to enter the fort. This, on reflection, they must have believed; but we knew that their knowledge of it could now do us no damage while it would serve to intimidate them. Notwithstanding, the garrison appeared much elated over the recovery of a valuable officer and party.

The firing immediately recommenced with redoubled vigor on both sides and I do not believe that more noise could possibly have been made by an equal number of men. Their shouting could not be heard amid the discharge of the muskets, and a continual line of fire around the garrison was maintained until shortly before daylight, when our troops were withdrawn to positions that had been prepared for them sixty to one hundred yards from the fort. Scarcely could a loophole be darkened by the garrison when a rifle ball would pass through it, and for them to have stood to their cannon would have entailed the useless destruction of their men. In this respect the situation of the two parties was much the same. It would have been imprudent in either to have wasted men unless some decisive stroke should require it.

Thus the attack continued until nine o'clock on the morning of the twenty-fourth. Learning that the two prisoners they had brought in the day before had a considerable number of letters with them I supposed it to be an express whose arrival we were expecting about this time and which I knew to be of the greatest importance to us as we had not received any message since our arrival in this country. Not being fully acquainted with the character of our enemy I was afraid these papers might be destroyed. To prevent this I sent a flag of truce to the garrison to demand of Governor Hamilton that he should not destroy the papers, throwing out some threats in case he should do so in the event his garrison should fall into my hands. He answered that they were not disposed to be awed into anything unbecoming British subjects. The firing was warmly renewed for a considerable space of time and we were obliged to take pains to prevent our men from exposing themselves unduly. Having refreshed themselves during the flag of truce, they were greatly animated and frequently expressed the desire to storm the fort and put an end to the post at once. This, however, would have been at this time a piece of rashness. Our troops warmed to their work and poured a heavy fire into the fort through every crack that could be discovered. Several of the garrison were wounded and it was quite impossible to stand near the embrasures.

Towards evening a flag of truce appeared.

. . . .

One reason that I had for not wishing to receive the garrison until the following morning was that it was late in the evening before the capitulation was signed, and in view of the number of prisoners we should have in comparison with our own small force I felt the need of daylight to arrange matters to our advantage. Knowing that we could now prevent any misfortune happening, as we could now dispose our troops so as to render the fort almost useless for defense, I thought it prudent to let the British troops remain in it until morning. We should not have been so suspicious as to take so much precaution, but I must confess I could not help but doubt the honor of men who could condescend to encourage the barbarity of the Indians. Although almost every man had conceived a very favorable opinion of Governor Hamilton (and I believed that what affected myself made some impression on the whole) I was happy to find that while he stayed with us he never deviated from that conduct that became an officer in his situation.

On the morning of the twenty-fifth arrangements were made for receiving the garrison, and about ten o'clock it was surrendered with due formality and everything was immediately arranged by me to the best possible advantage. On first viewing the interior of the fort and its stores I was astonished at its being surrendered in the manner it had been. However, it was a prudent and lucky circumstance which probably saved the lives of many men on both sides since on the preceding night we had inclined to attempt to undermine it and I found it would have required great diligence on the part of the garrison to have prevented us from succeeding. I found, too, on further examination, that our information concerning the interior arrangements was so good that in all probability the first hot shot after the arrival of our artillery would have blown up the magazine. This would at once have put an end to the siege since the situation of the magazine and the quantity of powder it contained were such that its explosion must have destroyed the greater part of the garrison.

. . . .

4: The Territory

Arthur C. Boggess, writing for the Chicago Historical Society, probes the question of why Illinois attracted so few settlers during the territorial era. In *The Settlement of Illinois, 1778-1830* (Chicago, 1908), Boggess, then a professor of economics at Baldwin-Wallace College, points out that two obstacles account for the failure of the territory to attract new inhabitants: the confusion and delay in establishing land offices, and the reluctance of the Indians to relinquish land claims until after the War of 1812. For those who did come to Illinois, life at times was rough going. Added to the problems of disease and changing weather conditions were the risks of a lawless frontier. One account of frontier violence, *The Outlaws of Cave-in-Rock* by Otto A. Rothert, first published in 1923, centers on the Harpe brothers and their families, whose outrages rival the exploits of any outlaws of the legendary wild West. The "Literary Review" of New York's *Evening Post* commented: "As a whole this book is of decided historical value. Here, accurately and graphically treated, is an important phase of pioneer life, a dark and bloody aspect, perhaps, but of decided value in getting the atmosphere of the time" (May 3, 1924). The final selection in the special accounts of the Illinois Territory is a paper read by David McCulloch before the 1901 meeting of the Illinois State Historical Society, entitled "Old Peoria." Beginning with a description of the topography and also the naming of Peoria during the territorial period, the author then jumps back in time to tell of the earliest French visitors to the area. The narrative starts with Father Jacques Gravier, successor to Father Allouez (who in turn had taken Marquette's place) at the Kaskaskia mission.

Special Accounts

The Territory of Illinois

ARTHUR C. BOGGESS

Probably nothing affected settlement in Illinois from 1809 to 1818 more profoundly than did changes in the land question, for

From Arthur C. Boggess, *The Settlement of Illinois, 1778-1830* (Chicago, 1908), pp. 99-111. Footnotes in the original have been omitted.

during this period Congress passed important acts relative to land sales, and this was also the period of the first sales of public lands in the territory. It seems strange that such sales should have been so long delayed, yet the settlement of French claims, although begun by the Governor of the Northwest Territory at an early day, and continued by commissioners authorized by Congress and appointed in 1804, was incomplete when Illinois became a separate territory, and the United States government adhered to its policy of selling no land in the territory until the claims were finally adjudicated. When a list of decisions reported by the commissioners to Congress late in 1809 was confirmed in the following May, and the next year a long list of rejected claims arising chiefly from the work of professional falsifiers, was reported, it seemed probable that the work was nearing completion, but a final settlement was still delayed, and the longsuffering Illinois squatters were bitterly disappointed when, in February, 1812, in accordance with a resolution presented by the Committee on Public Lands, Congress made provision for the appointment of a committee to revise the confirmations made by the Governor years before. The first legislature of Illinois met in the succeeding November, and adopted a memorial to Congress in which it was pointed out that the establishment of a land-office in the territory, several years before, had led to the opinion that the public land would soon be sold, and that because of this opinion those who constituted the majority of the inhabitants of the territory had been induced to settle, hoping that they would have an opportunity to purchase land before they should have made such improvements as would tempt the competition of avaricious speculators. The fulfillment of this hope having been long deferred, many squatters had now made valuable improvements which they were in danger of losing, either at the public sales of land or through the designs of the few speculators who had bought from the needy and unbusinesslike French most of the unlocated claims. For the relief of the squatters a law was desired that would permit actual settlers to enter the land on which their improvements stood, and requiring persons holding unlocated claims to locate them on unimproved lands lying in the region designated by Congress for that purpose. It was also hoped that as Congress had given one hundred acres of land to each regular soldier, as much would be granted to each member of the Illinois militia, since the militiaman had not only fought as bravely as the regular, but had also furnished his own supplies. If such a donation was not made it was hoped that a right of preëmption would be given to the militia, or failing even this, that they might be given the right, legally, to collect from anyone entering their land, the value of their improvements. In proof of the

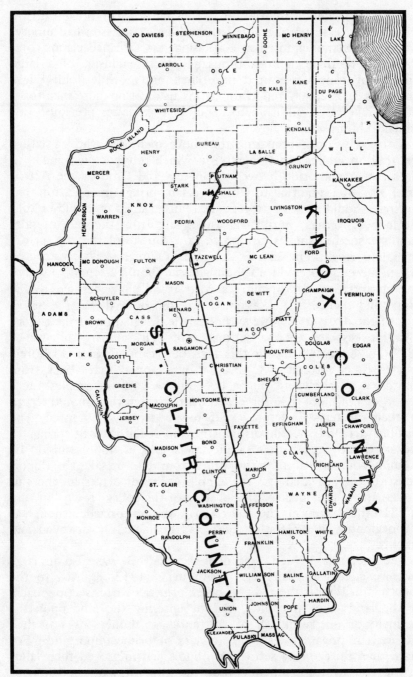

The counties of Illinois in 1790

fact stated in the memorial, that speculators had bought many French claims, it may be noted that William Morrison had ninety-two of the claims granted at Kaskaskia, his affirmed claims comprising more than eighteen thousand acres, exclusive of a large number of claims measured in French units, while John Edgar received a satisfactory report on claims aggregating more than forty thousand acres, in addition to a number of claims previously affirmed to him.

A few days after preparing the above memorial, the legislature prepared an address to Congress, in which reference was made to the arrangement made between Congress and Ohio by the Act of April 30, 1802, granting to Ohio two salt springs on condition that the state should agree not to tax such public lands as should be sold within her borders, until after five years from the date of sale. Illinois wished in similar fashion to gain control of the salt springs on Saline creek. The Illinois delegate in Congress was instructed that if the bargain could not be made, he should attempt to secure an appropriation for opening a road from Shawneetown to the Saline and thence to Kaskaskia. It was also desired that the Secretary of the Treasury should authorize the designation of the college township reserved by the Ordinance of 1787 and by the Act of 1804, and because "labor in this Territory is abundant, and laborers at this time extremely scarce," it was hoped that slaves from Kentucky or elsewhere might be employed at the salines for a period of not more than three years, after which they should return to their masters. Each prayer of this address was granted. The enabling act and the Illinois constitution ceded the salt springs to the state and agreed that public lands sold in Illinois should be exempt from taxation for five years from date of sale; the Illinois Constitution provided for the employment of slaves at the salt works; an act provided for the location of the college township; and in 1816 the making of the desired road was authorized, although at the beginning of 1818 the route had been merely surveyed and mapped.

The memorial which preceded the address was also in large measure successful. An act of February, 1813, granted to the squatters in Illinois the right of preëmpting a quarter section, each, of the lands they occupied, and of entering the land upon the payment of one-twentieth of the purchase money, as was then required in private sales. This act was of prime importance. For more than thirty years settlers in Illinois had improved their lands at the risk of losing them. Since the appointment, in 1804, of commissioners to settle the French land claims, the settlers had been expecting the public land, including those they occupied, to be offered for sale; thus it was inevitable that anxiety concerning the right of preëmption should increase as the settlement of claims neared completion, and contemporaries record that the inability to secure land titles seriously retarded settlement; now, however, the granting of the right of preëmption, before any public lands in Illinois were offered for sale, ended the long suspense of the settlers. . . .

Year after year the settlement of land claims dragged on, thus delaying the sales of land. . . .

The long delay in opening the land-offices in Illinois was fatal to an early settlement of the region, because the old states had public lands which they offered for sale at low rates, thus depriving Illinois of a fair chance as a competitor. . . .

In 1816 various classes of claimants were given increased facilities and an extension of time for locating their claims in Illinois. The business of satisfying claims was to linger for years, but with the opening of the land-offices it ceased to be a potent factor in retarding settlement.

One writer says of Illinois: "The public lands have rarely sold for more than five dollars per acre, *at auction.* Those sold at Edwardsville in October, 1816, averaged four dollars. Private sales at the land-office are fixed by law, at two dollars per acre. The old French locations command various prices, from one to fifty dollars. Titles derived from the United States government are always valid, and those from individuals rarely false." At this time emigrants were going in large numbers to Missouri, and the Illinois river country, not yet relieved of its Indian title, was being explored.

Reports concerning the sales of public lands give the quantity of land sold in Illinois toward the close of the territorial period, the figures for 1817 and 1818 being as follows:

			Total balance due:—	
	Acres in 1817.	Acres in 1818.	Jan. 1, 1818.	Sept. 30, 1818.
Shawneetown,	72,384	216,315	$291,429	$ 637,468
Kaskaskia,	90,493	121,052	209,295	406,288
Edwardsville,	149,165	121,923	301,701	451,499
	312,042	459,290	$802,425	$1,495,255

The percentage of debt showed a marked increase in the first nine months of 1818. There were received in three-quarters of 1817 and 1818, respectively:

	1817.	1818.
At Shawneetown	$32,837	$112,759
At Kaskaskia	41,218	68;975
At Edwardsville	41,426	78,788

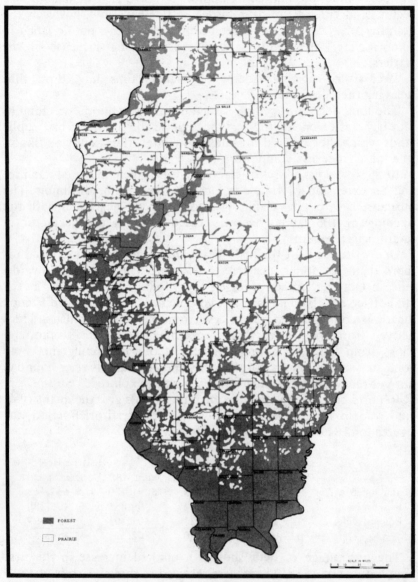

The distribution of forest and prairie in Illinois, 1820

During this same period the receipts at Steubenville, Marietta, and Wooster, Ohio, decreased, showing that Illinois was beginning to surpass Ohio as an objective point for emigrants wishing to enter land.

The Indian question was interwoven with the land question during the territorial period. In 1809 the Indians relinquished their claim to some small tracts of land lying near the point where the Wabash ceases to be a state boundary line. No more cessions were made until after the war of 1812. Although the population of Illinois increased, during the territorial period, from some eleven thousand to about forty thousand, the increase before the war was slight, and thus it came about that during the war the few whites were kept busy defending themselves from the large and hostile Indian population. So well does the manner of defence in Illinois illustrate the frontier character of the region that a sketch of the same may be given. When, in 1811, the Indians became hostile and murdered a few whites, the condition of the settlers was precarious in the extreme. Today the term city would be almost a favor to a place containing no more inhabitants than were then to be found in the white settlements in Illinois. Moreover, few as were the whites, they were dispersed in a long half-oval extending from a point on the Mississippi near the present Alton southward to the Ohio, and thence up that river and the Wabash to a point considerably north of Vincennes. This fringe of settlement was but a few miles wide in some places, while so sparse was the population near the mouth of the Ohio that the communication between northern and southern Indians was unchecked. Carlyle was regarded as the extreme eastern boundary of settlements to the westward; a fort on Muddy River, near where the old Fort Massac trace crossed the stream, was considered as one of the most exposed situations; and Fort La Motte, on a creek of the same name above Vincennes, was a far northern point. The exposed outside was some hundreds of miles long, and the interior and north were occupied by ten times as many hostile savages as there were whites in the country, the savages being given counsel and ammunition by the British garrisons on the north. Under conditions then existing, aid from the United States could be expected only in the event of dire necessity. Stout frontiersmen were almost ready to seek refuge in flight, but no general exodus took place, although in February, 1812, Governor Edwards wrote to the Secretary of War: "The alarms and apprehensions of the people are becoming so universal, that really I should not be surprised if we should, in three months, lose more than one-half of our present population. In places, in my opinion, entirely out of danger, many are removing. In other parts, large settlements are about to be totally deserted. Even in my own neighborhood, several families have removed, and others are preparing to do so in a week or two. A few days past, a gentleman of respectability arrived here from Kentucky, and he informed me that he saw on the road, in one day, upwards of twenty wagons conveying families out of this Territory. Every effort to check the prevalence of such terror seems to be ineffectual, and although much of it is unreasonably indulged, yet it is very certain the Territory will very shortly be in considerable danger. Its physical force is very inconsiderable, and is growing weaker, while it presents numerous points of attack."

To the first feeling of fear succeeded a determination to hold the ground. Before the middle of 1812, Governor Edwards had established Fort Russell, a few miles northwest of the present Edwardsville, bringing to this place, which was to be his headquarters, the cannon which Louis XIV. had had placed in Fort Chartres; and two volunteer companies had been raised, and had "ranged to a great distance—principally between the Illinois and the Kaskaskia rivers, and sometimes between the Kaskaskia and the Wabash—always keeping their line of march never less than one and sometimes three days' journey outside of all the settlements"—which incidentally shows what great unoccupied regions still existed even in the southern part of Illinois. As the rangers furnished their own supplies, the two companies went out alternately for periods of fifteen days. Sometimes the company on duty divided, one part marching in one direction and the other in the opposite, in order to produce the greatest possible effect upon the Indians. Settlers on the frontier—and that comprised a large proportion of the population—"forted themselves," as it was then expressed. Where a few families lived near each other, one of the most substantial houses was fortified, and here the community staid at night, and in case of imminent danger in the daytime as well. Isolated outlying families left their homes and retired to the nearest fort. Such places of refuge were numerous and many were the attacks which they successfully withstood.

Rangers and frontier forts were used with much effect, but the great dispersion of settlement and the large numbers of Indians combined to make it wholly impossible to make such means of defence entirely adequate. In August, 1812, the Governor wrote to the Secretary of War: "The principal settlements of this Territory being on the Mississippi, are at least one hundred and fifty miles from those of Indiana, and immense prairies intervene between them. There can, therefore, be no concert of operations for the protection of their frontiers and ours. . . . No troops of any kind have yet arrived in this Territory, and I think you may count on hearing of a bloody stroke upon us very soon. I have been extremely reluctant to send my family away, but, unless I hear shortly of more assistance than a few rangers, I shall bury my papers in the ground, send my family off, and stand my ground as long as possible." The "bloody stroke" predicted by the Governor fell on the garrison at Fort Dearborn, where Chicago now stands. Some regular troops were subsequently sent to the territory, but the war did not lose its frontier character. One of the most characteristic features was that troops sometimes set out on a campaign of considerable length, in an uninhabited region, without any baggage train and practically without pack horses, the men carrying their provisions on their horses, and the horses living on wild grass. Unflagging energy was shown by the settlers, several effective campaigns being carried on, and by the close of 1814 the war was closed in Illinois.

Extinction of Indian titles to land was retarded by the war and also by the policy of the United States, which was expressed by Secretary of War Crawford, in 1816, as follows: "The determination to purchase land only when demanded for settlement will form the settled policy of the Government. Experience has sufficiently proven that our population will spread over any cession, however extensive, before it can be brought into market, and before there is any regular and steady demand for settlement, thereby increasing the difficulty of protection, embarrassing the Government by broils with the natives, and rendering the execution of the laws regulating intercourse with the Indian tribes utterly impracticable." Some progress, however, was made in extinguishing Indian titles during the territorial period after the close of the war. In 1816, several tribes confirmed the cession of 1804 of land lying south of an east and west line passing through the southern point of Lake Michigan, and ceded a route for an Illinois-Michigan canal. At Edwardsville, on September 25, 1818, the Peoria, Kaskaskia, Michigamia, Cahokia, and Tamarois ceded a tract comprising most of southern and much of central Illinois. The significance of this cession would have been immense had it not been that it was made by weak tribes, while the powerful Kickapoo still claimed and held all that part of the ceded tract lying north of the parallel of 39°—a little to the north of the mouth of the Illinois river. This Kickapoo claim included the fertile and already famous Sangamon country, in which the state capital was eventually to be located, and squatters were pressing hard upon the Indian frontier, yet the Indians still held the land when Illinois became a state.

During the territorial period, Illinois gained the long-sought right of preëmption; the French claims ceased to retard settlement; some progress was made in the extinction of Indian titles, and the sale of public land was begun. The new state was to find the Indian question a pressing one, and some changes in the land system were yet desired, but the crucial point was passed.

The Outlaws of Cave-in-Rock

OTTO A. ROTHERT

A flatboat had come down the river and its passengers, not realizing they were near the famous rendezvous of outlaws, landed about a quarter of a mile above the Cave at the foot of a small bluff, later known as Cedar Point. Among the travelers on board were a young man and his sweetheart who, while their companions were making some repairs to the boat, strolled to the top of the cliff and there sat down upon a rock. The view from that point is still beautiful and was probably even more so in primeval days. While the two lovers were sitting on the edge of the cliff with their backs to the wild woods behind them, leisurely considering the landscape, or the life before them, the two Harpes quietly approached from the forest and, without a word of warning, pushed the lovers off the cliff. They fell on a sandy beach forty feet below and, to the surprise of all, escaped unhurt. The Harpes returned to the Cave, and, as already stated, boasted, but without the expected effect, of the prank they had played.

Shortly after this, two families, carrying a supply of tools and provisions, were floating down the Ohio in a flatboat, intending to settle in Smithland, but when they came near Cave-in-Rock they were captured and robbed by the outlaws. The two or three passengers who were not killed in the battle preceding the robbery, were brought ashore. The Harpes, seeing an opportunity to give their fellow criminals an exhibition of brutality, stripped one of the captives, tied him to a blindfolded horse and led the animal to the top of the bluff over the Cave. By wild shouts and other means the

From Otto A. Rothert, *The Outlaws of Cave-in-Rock* (New York, 1970), pp. 92-105, 117-122. Footnotes in the original have been omitted.

Courtesy of the Illinois Department of Conservation

Cave-in-Rock on the Ohio River

horse was frightened and at the same time forced to run toward the edge of the cliff, and before long the blindfolded animal with the naked man tied on its back ran off the bluff and fell a distance of more than one hundred feet to the rough and rocky shore below. Then the Harpes pointed to the mangled remains of man and horse as evidence of another triumph over law and order. . . .

It is probable that their hasty departure took place some time in May, 1799. . . . A few days later—July 22, 1799—they murdered a young son of Chesley Coffey, on Black Oak Ridge, about eight miles northwest of Knoxville. One version has it that the boy was hunting strayed cows and while in the woods was slain by the Harpes, who took his gun and the shoes he wore, and left his body lying under a tree. Another account is that "Young Coffey was riding along the road one evening to get a fiddle. These terrible men smeared a tree with his brains, making out that his horse had run against the tree."

. . . .

The Harpes continued their course northward. . . . On July 29, on the spur of a mountain since known as Brassel's Knob, they met James and Robert Brassel. James Brassel was afoot and carried a gun; Robert was on horseback and unarmed. The Harpes, who were riding good horses, pretended to be in a hurry, but seeming to have a desire to comply with the custom of civilized travelers, slowed up and saluted the men with the question: "What's the news?" The Brassels related in detail an account of the murder of William Ballard and young Coffey. The Harpes replied that they had not only heard of these tragedies, but that they were now in pursuit of the men who had committed the crimes. They further asserted that they were going to wait for the rest of the pursuing party which was coming on behind, and requested the Brassels to join them when the reinforcements arrived. To this the two innocent brothers willingly agreed. They had no more than done so when Big Harpe, accusing them of being the Harpe brothers, seized James Brassel's gun, threw it on the ground and immediately began tying his hands and feet. Robert, suspecting that he and his brother had fallen into the hands of the dreaded Harpes themselves, jumped from his horse and attempted to obtain his brother's gun in an effort to rescue him. In this he failed and, realizing that his only hope of escape was flight, he ran into the woods, leaving his horse behind. He was pursued by Little Harpe, whom he succeeded in outrunning, and, although shot at, he was unhurt.

Robert continued his flight about ten miles when he met a Mr. Dale, who, with two or three other men and Mrs. Dale, was traveling toward Knoxville. He persuaded them to return with him to the place where he had left his brother. The men had only one gun among them for their protection; nevertheless they tried to help the bewildered man. When they reached the spot in the woods a short distance from the road where Robert had left his brother, they were horrified to find that James was not only dead, but that his body had been "much beaten and his throat cut." His gun was broken to pieces. The tracks indicated that the two Harpes had gone toward Knoxville, from which direction they were coming when they overtook the Brassel brothers. After the pursuers had followed the tracks a few miles, they were much surprised to find themselves running upon the Harpes coming back. At the time the two Brassels were attacked by the Harpes the outlaws were alone and had with them nothing but their guns. But now, on their return, they were accompanied by their women and children, heavily loaded with clothing and provisions, apparently prepared for a long journey and for battle and siege.

When this fierce procession of men and women on horseback came in sight, one of Dale's men suggested that if the approaching cavalcade showed no signs of fight, no effort to arrest them should be made. This immediately met with the approval of the majority. No attempt to fight was made. The murderers, in the words of

Colonel Trabue, "looked very awful at them" and then passed on. The pursuers, too, continued their journey for a while in silence, lest any words they should utter might be overheard and mistaken by the Harpes as a threat. Robert Brassel complained bitterly of the lack of courage displayed by the men he had relied upon to help capture or kill the murderers of his brother.

. . . .

Robert Brassel resumed his pursuit of the Harpes and was soon joined by William Wood and others. When they arrived near the farm of John Tully they met Nathaniel Stockton and a number of neighbors looking for Tully, who they supposed was lost in the woods. The search continued and "near the road they found Mr. Tully, killed, and hidden under a log." The company buried him and some of the men agreed they would pursue the murderers.

. . . .

The night after the Harpes murdered Tully "they passed by old Mr. Stockton's going toward their father's-in-law, old Mr. Roberts."

"The half-faced camp" — a frontier lean-to

Courtesy of the Illinois State Historical Library

A point of great human interest is the concise and vivid description of the two Harpes given in the affidavit prepared by Colonel Trabue: "The big man is pale, dark, swarthy, bushy hair, had a reddish gun stock—the little man had a blackish gunstock, with a silver star with four straight points—they had short sailor's coats, very dirty, and grey greatcoats."

. . . .

The Harpes traveled up Marrowbone Creek and, about twenty-five miles south of Colonel Trabue's home, stopped at an out-of-the-way place on which John Graves and his thirteen-year-old son were cultivating a crop and making preparations for the rest of the family to join them.

The Harpes arrived at their cabin late in the evening and got permission to spend the night. "Early in the morning, probably before the Graveses awoke, they, with Graves' own axe, split the heads of both open and threw the bodies of both in to the brush fence that surrounded the house." "There they lay," writes Draper, in one of his note books, "until some one, seeing so many buzzards around, made an investigation and discovered what had taken place." . . .

From the Graves cabin they traveled north twenty miles or more into Russell County to the home of old man Roberts, the reputed father of the two women Big Harpe claimed as wives. The only reference to this "old Mr. Roberts" is in Colonel Trabue's affidavit sent to the Governor of Kentucky in August, 1799. Local tradition has nothing to say about Roberts—when he came or left, or where his cabin stood. Evidently he was still living in Russell County in 1802, for in November of that year Reverend Jacob Young, a Methodist preacher, met "a brother-in-law of the infamous Micajah Harpe," who, although his name is not stated in the preacher's autobiography, must have been a son of the "old Mr. Roberts" in order to qualify for the connection. At any rate, two of the Harpe women were doubtless invited by their father to remain with him. If, however, such an invitation was not extended, the women would have appealed to him for help had they been inclined to reform, and he, as many other fathers would have done, might have consented to make an effort to lead them from the vile associations into which they had fallen. What these two daughters might and should have done they failed to do. They clung to their companions in crime and with them fled westward south of Green River toward Mammoth Cave and Russellville.

While on the way the Harpes killed a little girl and a negro boy.

Writers do not agree as to just where and when these two murders took place. It is likely they were enacted while the Harpes were going to Logan County and that they led up to a third child-murder even more inhuman. The first of these tragedies, as briefly related by Breazeale, is that "they met with a negro boy going to mill, dashed the boy's brains out against a tree, but left the horse and bag of grain untouched." The other recorded by Collins is equally brief: "One of their victims was a little girl found at some distance from her home, whose tender age and helplessness would have been protection against any but incarnate fiends."

They soon reached Logan County. There, according to T. Marshall Smith, they discovered, about eight miles from Drumgool's station, now Adairville, the two Trisword brothers, who with their wives, several children, and a few black servants, were camping for the night. The next morning before sunrise, while the emigrants were still asleep, the Harpes and two Cherokee Indians made a wild attack on the tent occupied by the travelers and killed the entire party except one of the men, who ran for help. When the rescuing party arrived upon the scene it found the ground covered with the bodies of the dead, some of them badly mangled. While several of the men were occupied burying the dead, others were looking for evidence of the direction the outlaws had taken.

. . . .

In the meantime, however, the cunning Harpes were working their way northward. They stopped a few hours about three miles northeast of Russellville, on the Samuel Wilson Old Place, about half a mile up Mud River from what is now Duncan's bridge over Mud River on the Russellville and Morgantown road. There the Harpes watered their horses at the same spring that quenched the thirst of the hundreds of people who a few weeks before attended the Great Revival conducted by the Reverends John and William McGee and James M'Gready. . . . The Harpes doubtless knew or inferred from the condition of the place that it had been used recently for religious purposes.

The Harpe men had no patience with their children and often reprimanded the three women, declaring that the crying infants would some day be the means of pursuers detecting their presence. They frequently threatened to kill them. To protect their babies, the mothers many a night went apart, carrying their children sufficiently far away to prevent their cries being heard by the unnatural fathers. But the long-feared threat was at last carried out.

It is a strange sequence of events that on this same camp ground and almost immediately after the Great Revival, one of the Harpes killed his own child in the presence of its mother. A large maple tree still marks the spot near which this deed was enacted.

The details of this murder as given today by tradition are practically the same as those published by T. Marshall Smith: "Big Harpe snatched it—Susan's infant, about nine months old—from its mother's arms, slung it by the heels against a large tree by the path-side, and literally bursting its head into a dozen pieces, threw it from him as far as his great strength enabled him, into the woods." This terrible tragedy is briefly referred to by Hall and Breazeale, both of whom state that Big Harpe, just before his death, declared he regretted none of the many murders he had committed except "the killing of his own child."

. . . .

The pursuit continued in this manner for a mile or so, when, not finding the outlaws, the footmen again mounted their horses, and all went on together. But a short time elapsed before Squire McBee discovered the ruffians on a distant hill-side, a strip of low land intervening—both on foot with guns in hand, Big Harpe having a horse by his side, and both holding a parley with a person on horseback [corrected by Draper to *afoot*] whom they had apparently just met. McBee exclaimed 'there they are,' pointing towards them, and at the same time putting spurs to his horse dashed over the low ground and made for the spot. Big Harpe instantly mounted and darted off in one direction, and Little Harpe on foot in another, while the other individual rode [corrected by Draper to *ran*] rapidly towards McBee, and when within sixty or eighty yards suddenly dismounted [Draper eliminated 'dismounted'] and betook himself to a tree. Seeing this bellicose demonstration on the part of an armed man, McBee in the excitement of the moment, drew up his gun, loaded with two balls, and 'blazed away' at that part of the body exposed to view, both bullets taking effect, one passing through the right thigh, and the other the right arm. At this moment Steigal recognised the wounded man as a settler living up Pond River some two or three miles; and perceiving some of the rest of the party in the act of levelling their pieces, Steigal exclaimed 'don't shoot, it's George Smith!" The unfortunate man, who knew Squire McBee, now calling him by name apologised for his singular conduct by saying, that he was nearly bereft of his senses, expecting every moment that the Harpes would kill him, and when he *treed* he had not recovered from his fright and was totally unfitted to perceive the folly and madness of the act. Little Harpe, he said, had met him with his gun in one hand, and a kettle in the other, going after water; and made enquiries about the settlements, speaking in an elevated tone, evidently that his brother might hear from the camp, not more than eighty rods distant, and come to his aid—such at least was the effect, intentional or not, for Big Harpe rode up and dismounted, and had been there but a few moments when McBee and his party unexpectedly made their appearance. Smith desired Squire McBee to assist him home, which with pleasure he consented to do after the Harpes were secured. He redeemed his promise, and in time Smith recovered both from his fright and his wounds [corrected by Draper to read: 'Smith hobbled home by himself and in due time etc.'].

. . . .

The fleeing outlaw was closely pressed, Christian, Steigal, and Grisson each giving him a shot in the pursuit—Christian's alone taking effect, wounding him in the leg. Harpe, discovering that Leiper was considerably in advance of the others, and supposing his gun empty, concluded to take advantage, as he thought, of the circumstance, and get a fair shot at his dangerous adversary. He accordingly stopped his horse, and while renewing his priming, Leiper took unerring aim, and fired—and the same powder which the outlaws had a few days previously given Tompkins, now sped the ball that mortally wounded Big Harpe. Though badly shot through the spine of his back, the wounded ruffian, determined to sell his life as dearly as possible, levelled his gun at Leiper; but even that deserted him in his hour of need—it snapped! and he threw it away in disgust. As Leiper and Christian were rapidly advancing upon him, Steigal and Grisson having lagged far behind, Harpe drew a large tomahawk and brandished it furiously to keep off his pursuers, at the same time urging on his jaded horse as well as he could. Leiper and Christian kept close at hand, repeatedly calling upon him to surrender, when he would again brandish his toma- hawk in savage defiance. He finally agreed to surrender himself if they would stop their horses; accordingly they all reined up, Leiper and Christian dismounted and made some demonstrations towards loading; perceiving which, Harpe suddenly dashed off. Leiper's horse, which had been standing by his side, though not held by him, now took fright and darted off after Harpe's horse. Seeing the accident, Christian instantly mounted his steed and quickly over- took the runaway horse, returned him to Leiper, and both without loading renewed the pursuit. They easily followed the trail through a small canebrake of thick growth, and just as the fugitive was emerging from it they overhauled him, not more than half a mile distant from where he had taken French leave. His horse was walking quite leisurely, and Harpe's wonted daring and bravery seemed to have forsaken him; and, faint from the loss of blood, he had either lost his tomahawk or thrown it away. They rode up and pulled him from his horse without resistance. . . .

The dying outlaw, as he lay stretched upon the ground, begged for water, and Leiper took a shoe from one of Harpe's feet, and with it procured some for him near by. McBee now told him that he was already dying, but they should hasten his death; time, however, would be given him for prayer and preparation for another world— to which he made no reply, and appeared quite unconcerned. . . .

Steigal, after reminding Harpe how unfeelingly he had murdered his wife and only child, drew a knife, and exhibiting it to him, said in plain terms that he intended to cut his head off with *that!* 'I am,' said the dying outlaw faintly, 'but a young man, but young as I am I feel the death-damp already upon my brow. . . .' Steigal stepped forward and pointed the muzzle of his gun at the head of the expiring outlaw, who conscious of the intention, and desirous at least of procrastinating it dodged his head to and fro with an agility unexpected to the beholders, manifesting pretty plainly a strong disrelish 'to shuffle off this mortal coil.' Perceiving this, Steigal observed, 'very well, I believe I will not upon reflection shoot him in the head, for I want to preserve *that* as a trophy;' and thereupon shot him in the left side—and Harpe almost instantly expired without a struggle or a groan. Steigal, with the knife he had so menacingly exhibited to Harpe, now cut off the outlaw's head. Squire McBee had with him a wallet in which he had brought his provisions and provender—in one end of this, Steigal placed the severed head, and some articles of corresponding weight in the other, and then slung it behind him across his horse, and all commenced their return. Thus died Big Harpe, long the terror of the west, and his decapitated body was left in the wilds of Muhlenberg county, as unsepulchred as his merited death was unwept and unmourned.

. . . .

Old Peoria

DAVID McCULLOCH

As this paper has to do chiefly with this older village, a brief reference to the topographical features of the locality may be useful to a proper understanding of what is to follow. Peoria Lake, in early times known as Lake Pimiteoui, in reality consists of two lakes, the combined length of which is about seventeen or eighteen miles. The upper lake, which consists of a mere widening of the river, begins at the foot of an island opposite the city of Chillicothe. The land on its westerly shore rises gradually from the water's edge, and for a considerable distance slopes back into a gently rolling prairie, varying in width from two to three miles, where it is bounded by the ordinary wooded bluffs. This is LaSalle Prairie. For one half the distance from Chillicothe to Peoria the course of the lake is to the southwest. Near the village of Mossville it changes its course to almost due south, in which direction it continues to flow for a distance of about six miles. At the distance of five miles from this change of course the lake contracts into a narrow and deep channel through which it flows for the distance of nearly one mile. This is known as the "Narrows." At its southern extremity this narrows is spanned by a wagon road bridge. Near its northern extremity it was formerly crossed by a ferry. At the bridge the lake or river resumes its southwesterly course, and at that point again expands in width forming a lower lake about three miles in length, and as wide as the upper lake at its widest part. At the mouth of this lower lake LeVille de Maillet was located, about one-half of it being above, and one-half below the present location of another wagon road bridge crossing the river close to the mouth of the lake at the foot of Bridge street in the city of Peoria. This is called the lower bridge. Near the upper end of the village site, Fort Clark was erected in the year 1813. Near the center of the village had been a French fort, which is not to be confounded with Fort Clark, nor with a still older fort at the Old Village.

The new village had two streets running parallel with the river, the first of which closely hugged the declivity of the river bank, which at that point was about thirty feet higher than low water mark, as it was known before the construction of the Copperas Creek Dam in the Illinois river. At Main street, in the now city of Peoria, this break of the embankment was one hundred and ten feet from the upper side of Water street as it now exists. Following this

From David McCulloch, "Old Peoria," *Transactions of the Illinois State Historical Society*, VI (1901), 42-43, 47-50. Footnotes in the original have been omitted.

declivity of the river bank to the northeast, it gradually increases in height, until at Caroline and Mary streets, a distance of nearly one and one-half miles, it reaches its greatest altitude, the same being about fifty feet above low water mark. Soon after passing Mary street it begins to curve to the northwest, forming the southern bank of a small creek which takes its rise in Springdale Cemetery about one and one-half miles to the north. This little stream comes down through a charming little vale, known as Birket's Hollow, and at its mouth there is a point of low land covering several acres extending out into the lake several hundred feet further than the regular shore line. This point was formerly known as Plum Point. South of Plum Point is a little cove or bay formerly known as Turtle Bay now partly filled up, on the margin of which several ice houses are located, while the high ground in their rear is occupied with railroad tracks, the buildings of the Peoria Pottery Company, the Peoria Steam Marble Works, with many dwellings and business houses.

The government surveyors located the "Old Village" near the foot of Caroline street in the city of Peoria, directly facing Turtle Bay. Charles Ballance, Esq., a lawyer and surveyor was here at the time of the survey and had abundant opportunity for testing the accuracy of this location, for many of the former French inhabitants were still living at that time and continued to live long afterwards. Mr. Ballance had also much to do with the litigation concerning the French Claims and could have learned the facts as to the location of the Old Village if he had suspected the accuracy of this location. He wrote a history of the city of Peoria about the year 1870, in which he not only confirms the location of the Old Village as given by the surveyors, but further says that the "Old Fort" was located about one hundred and fifty feet north-east of the buildings of the Peoria Pottery Company, which would place it on prominent ground at the curvature, and at the highest point of the river bank as already mentioned.

Commencing at that point and extending back to the bluffs a distance of about one-half mile, and to the south-west about four or five miles, varying in width from one-half miles to a mile and a half and surrounded by a vast amphitheatre of wooded bluffs two hundred feet high, was a beautiful prairie on which the city of Peoria now stands.

When the first American settlers came to Peoria the narrows were by the Indians called Cock-a-Mink, evidently a corruption of Ke-kauk-kem-ke, a word which Governor Reynolds says was used by the Indians to designate a straight, and was the same which they applied to the river connecting Lakes Erie and St. Clair. It has its equivalent in the French word *detroit.* So fitting was this latter name to the locality that the early settlers called a village which they had laid out just above the narrows, by the name of "Detroit," while on the easterly side of the river just opposite was a country postoffice called "Little Detroit."

The first settlers also found the name "Opa," attached to the locality about Peoria which is evidently a corrupt abbreviation of the French term *"au pied du Lac"* or *"au pied"* (the foot.) The name "Opa" was by the American Fur Company given to their station established in the year 1818, at Wesley City three miles below the lake, and the city of Peoria barely escaped being afflicted with that name instead of its present euphonious title.

. . . .

Little can be gleaned from the official records as to the manners, customs and mode of life of these ancient villagers, but it may be assumed they differed little from those inhabiting the other French villages. They raised cattle and hogs, cultivated wheat and corn, they were hunters and trappers, sending their surplus products down the lakes and in return obtaining articles of merchandise brought by the traders.

. . . .

In September, 1698, Gravier is found at Mackinaw, where he met Montigny, St. Cosme and Davion, three priests of different order, on their way to establish missions near the mouth of the Ohio. On their way and when near Chicago, these three men met with Father Pinet, who had charge of a mission there, and Father Buineteau, who had charge at the Immaculate Conception. These two missionaries preceded the three newly arrived ones and reached Peoria Lake some days in advance of their arrival. On the 15th day of November these new comers reached a place called the Old Fort, a rock about one hundred feet high on the bank of the river, where LaSalle had built a fort which he had abandoned. This was evidently Fort St. Louis. There they found the Indians had gone about twenty-five leagues lower down. In his account of this expedition, St. Cosme writes as follows: "From Chicago to the fort they reckoned thirty leagues. Here navigation begins which continues uninterrupted to the Fort Permavevvi, where the Indians now are. We arrived there on the 19th of November (four days from the Old Fort)." There they overtook Pinet and Buineteau, who were on their way south, and also found Marest in charge of the mission at that place. On November 22d they were obliged to break the ice for two or three arpens to get out of the lake of (Pimiteoui). As Tonti was a member of this party, if the fort here mentioned had been Fort Creve Coeur, it is reasonable to suppose it would have been so called. Any one who has seen the ice form in Lake Peoria could be easily convinced that the place of their moorage was in Turtle Bay, opposite the site of the "Old Fort" at Peoria.

In a letter of Buineteau written in January, 1699, from the Illinois Country, he speaks of the wonderful talent of Father Gabriel Marest who had been laboring there for several months. Pinet and Buineteau had accompanied the St. Cosme party down the river, and during their journey they had passed three or four villages, one of which was that of Rouenzas, the most considerable of the Illinois chiefs. Marest was probably not far from Cahokia when Buineteau wrote.

Gravier having returned from Mackinaw, he set out on September 8, 1700, for the gulf to ascertain the condition of affairs in that region. In the account of his trip, written February 16, 1701, he says, "I arrived too late at the Illinois du Detroit of which Father Marest has charge, to prevent the transmigration of the village of the Kaskaskias, which was too precipitously made on vague news of the establishment on the Mississippi. I do not believe that the Kaskaskias would have separated from the Peorias and their Illinois du Detroit had I arrived sooner. God grant that the road from Chicago to the Strait (du Detroit) be not closed and the whole Illinois Mission suffer greatly." These passages mark the time, the place and the occasion of the separation of the Kaskaskias from the Peorias, after which time the mission of the Immaculate Conception became located on the Mississippi. In a letter written by Father Mermet from Kaskaskia in 1706, he mentions the Illinois of Detroit, otherwise the Peorias—where Father Gravier had nearly lost his life on two occasions. The conclusion from these statements is that the separation of the Kaskaskias from the Peorias took place at the Detroit or Narrows of Peoria Lake in September or October A.D. 1700. Mermet went with the Kaskaskias, leaving the Peorias for the time being without a missionary. Gravier continued his journey to the gulf, from which point he wrote the foregoing account, in which mention is also made of a church in the village but not of a fort.

On April 29, 1699, soon after the visit of the St. Cosme party to Lake Peoria, Father Marest wrote a letter to another of the same order in which he describes the village as being one-half league in length with a chapel at each end, one of which had been recently erected to accommodate the increasing number of converts. This was the year before the separation of the Kaskaskias from the Peorias. This separation may have taken place when the Kaskaskias were on their annual hunt, but it is possible both tribes may have been located there at that time. From other sources it is learned that the population of the village numbered from one to three thousand, but the time allowed will not permit a discussion of that point.

In the summer of 1705, Gravier was again among the Illinois where he was attacked by an Indian who shot five arrows at him, one of which left its point embedded in the tendons of his elbow, which afterwards resulted in his death, but not until after a visit to Paris and his return to America. Father Mermet in a letter dated March 2, 1706, gives a minute account of this transaction. Concerning the condition of the affairs of the Illinois he says: "It is good from this village (Kaskaskia) except that they threaten to leave us at the first word. It is bad, as regards both spiritual and temporal matters among the Illinois of Detroit—otherwise the Peorias—where Father Gravier nearly lost his life on two occasions, and he is not yet out of danger." After suffering for three months at that place, but having learned the Indians were hostile to his leaving, Gravier planned a secret departure at night, but when he was about ready to embark he was greatly surprised to learn that his house was surrounded by about 200 Indians who had taken down a portion of his palisade in order to get in. But through the interposition of a friendly chief he was permitted to proceed, and after arriving at Kaskaskia was sent to Mobile whence he sailed for France.

The mission house surrounded by a palisade may possibly be all that is meant by the word fort in these early narratives.

On November 9, 1712, Father Marest wrote to Father German, another Jesuit, a long account of the Missions among the Illinois in the course of which he says: "I worked with these missionaries (Pinet and Buineteau), and, after their deaths, I alone remained charged with all the labors of the mission until the arrival of Father Mermot. Previously I was in the large village of the Peorias, where Father Gravier, who had returned there for the second time received a wound which caused his death."

Having planned a journey to Mackinaw, in which it would be necessary to go by way of the village of the Peorias, Marest on Friday of Easter Week in 1711, set out on foot from Kaskaskia, stopping one night at Cahokia. After several days travel during which he endured intense suffering in his feet, he reached the Illinois river 25 leagues below the village of the Peorias. There he dispatched one of his Indians to inform the Frenchmen at the village of his sad plight, and after two days, was met by them and taken into their canoes.

Up to this time we have heard of no Frenchmen residing at

Peoria, and it is a question whether these were such. He hoped they, on their return, would take him with them to his destination at the Straits of Mackinac, but, there having been as yet no spring rains, they could not go by the river, so he proceeded on his way to St. Joseph, going partly by water and partly by land. It is to be fairly inferred that the reason why the Frenchmen could not go likewise was that they were traders and were waiting for a rise in the upper streams so they could carry their furs and peltries by water to the lake. They may not therefore have been residents but merely temporary traders at Peoria Lake.

After the lapse of several months Marest returned by the same route he had gone. In describing his entrance into the village he says: "The greater part of the men ascended to the fort, which is placed upon a rock on the bank of the river." Here occurs a grave enigma. Marest had said in the first part of his letter that there were then only three villages of the Illinois, one at Kaskaskia, one twenty-five leagues distant (Cahokia) and a third one hundred leagues distant. This one at which he halted on his return must therefore have been the same village at which he had stopped on his way north. Yet there is not a rock on the shores of Lake Peoria nor on the river bank for miles above and below upon which a fort could have been erected. The statement that the fort was placed upon a rock on the bank of the river raises a doubt which is very difficult of solution. May not the word translated *rock* admit of a wider interpretation than the English word "rock," so as to include a "mound" or "hillock" such as that upon which Fort Creve Coeur had been erected by La Salle? It must be admitted this passage is enveloped in obscurity.

For the next ten years little is heard of the Peorias. That they were sorely beset by hostile tribes is very apparent. Soon after the return of Marest to Kaskaskia, Father de Ville was sent to them as a missionary, but how long he remained does not appear.

In the beginning of October of the year 1721, Father Charlevoix made a voyage down the Illinois River and found a village on the west bank of Lake Peoria, which he terms a second village of the Illinois, the first having been found at the rock; but his estimate of distances and the courses of streams is so very unreliable as to render its exact location impossible. His description of the surrounding scenery, however, corresponds quite well with that at the old French village of Peoria. The most important statements made by him are that the village was called Pimiteoui, the same name the lake had borne from the time of LaSalle; that the Peorias were then at war with neighboring tribes, and that he found there four French Canadians apparently living with the Indians. If there had been more he would have certainly mentioned them, for he was sorely in need of their assistance. There the chief of the village invited him to a conference at a house where one of the missionaries had lodged some years before, and where probably they used to hold council. This account was written on the spot, at Pimiteoui. Nothing is said about a church or a fort or the number or character of the inhabitants.

It is a matter of history that during the next year, 1722, the Peorias, being harrassed on all sides by their enemies, took their departure from the Illinois country and followed the Kaskaskias. We, therefore, hear nothing further of the mission at Peoria.

But information of a very popular kind comes from another source. The company of the Indies, the successor of the celebrated company of the west, having assumed jurisdiction over the Illinois Country, Philip Francis Renault, the director of its mines, pushed his explorations as far as Peoria. On June 14, 1723, two years after Charlevoix's visit, "in order to make his establishment upon the mines," as its preamble declares, he obtained a grant from the Commandant of Illinois as well as from the chief director of the company, of a tract of land described as follows: "One league in front at Pimitoui on the River Illinois, facing the east and adjoining the lake bearing the name of the village, and on the other side to the banks opposite the village, for a half league above it with a depth of five leagues, the point of the compass following the Illinois River down the same upon one side and ascending by the river of Arcary which forms the middle through the rest of the depth."

This is the origin of the famous Renault claim which has been several times before Congress for confirmation, but which has always failed. If not wholly impossible, it is at least exceedingly difficult of location; the latest claim of the Renault heirs being that it commences at the foot of the lower lake, and extends three miles down the river to a point about a mile below the mouth of the Kickapoo, which stream they claim forms its middle line for the greater portion of the depth. The historical significance of the grant lies in the fact that the village of Pimiteoui, which Charlevoix had mentioned by that name, was situated on Lake Pimiteoui, or Peoria, and not on the river below it; that the River Arcary, (called in other English and French copies of the grant Arescy and Arcoury; in the deed from Darneille to Russell Cartineaux; in the Commissioners report Coteneau and Mallet's River; in the report of Edward Coles Gatinan, and in recent times Red Bud and its Indian equivalent, Kickapoo) was none other than the Kickapoo, for there is no other stream in that vicinity of sufficient length to answer the call of the grant.

From the time of this grant until the year 1765, a period of forty years or more, a gap occurs in the history of "Old Peoria" which has never yet been filled. It is very evident that at the date of Renault's grant there were few, if any, Frenchmen residing at the village. What influence that grant may have had in attracting a French population is not known, but it is certain that within that period of forty years, such a French population had centered there as to make it one of the principal trading posts in the Mississippi Valley.

Original Narratives

In December 1778, when the Virginia legislature organized its claim in the Ohio Valley, Governor Patrick Henry outlined the problems and responsibilities facing the new Illinois County Lieutenant-Commandant, John Todd, in a letter of appointment. Unfortunately, the letter is about the only thing Henry gave Todd, and conditions in the territory degenerated into administrative chaos.

Patrick Henry's Letter to John Todd

To Mr. John Todd, Esq.   *Williamsburgh, Dec. 12, 1778.*

By virtue of the act of General Assembly which establishes the county of Illinois, you are appointed County Lieutenant-Commandant there, and for the general tenor of your conduct I refer you to the law.

The grand objects which are disclosed to your countrymen will prove beneficial, or otherwise, according to the nature and abilities of that remote country. The present crisis, rendered so favourable by the good disposition of the French and Indians, may be improved to great purposes; but if, unhappily, it should be lost, a return of the same attachment to us may never happen. Considering, therefore, that costly prejudices are so hard to wear out, you

From Patrick Henry, "Letter of Instruction to John Todd, 1778," in Ninian Edwards, *History of Illinois from 1778 to 1833; and the Life and Times of Ninian Edwards* (Springfield, 1870), pp. 5-7.

will take care to cultivate and conciliate the affections of the French and Indians.

Although great reliance is placed on your prudence in managing the people you are to reside among, yet, considering you as unacquainted in some degree with their genius, usages and manners, as well as the geography of the country, I recommend it to you to advise with the most intelligent and upright persons who may fall in your way, and to give particular attention to Col. Clark and his corps, to whom the State has great obligations. You are to coöperate with him on any military undertaking, when necessary, and to give the military every aid which the circumstances of the people will admit of. The inhabitants of Illinois must not expect settled peace and safety while their and our enemies have footing at Detroit and can intercept or stop the trade of the Mississippi. If the English have not the strength or courage to come to war against us themselves, their practice has been and will be to have the savages commit murder and depredations. Illinois must expect to pay these a large price for her freedom, unless the English can be expelled from Detroit. The means for effecting this will not perhaps be in your or Col. Clark's power, but the French inhabiting the neighbourhood of that place, it is presumed, may be brought to see it done with indifference, or perhaps join in the enterprise with pleasure. This is but conjecture. When you are on the spot, you and Col. Clark may discover the fallacy or reality of the former appearances. Defense, only, is to be the object of the latter, or a good prospect of it. I hope the French and Indians at your disposal will show a zeal for the affairs equal to the benefit to be derived from establishing liberty and permanent peace.

One great good expected from holding the Illinois is to overaw the Indians from warring on the settlers on this side of the Ohio. A close attention to the disposition, character and movement of the hostile tribes is therefore necessary. The French and militia of Illinois, by being placed on the back of them, may inflict timely chastisement on those enemies whose towns are an easy prey in absence of their warriors. You perceive, by these hints, that something in the military line will be expected from you. So far as the occasion calls for the assistance of the people composing the militia, it will be necessary to coöperate with the troops sent from here, and I know of no better general directions to give than this: that you consider yourself as the head of the civil department, and as such having command of the military until ordered out by the civil authority, and to act in conjunction with them.

You are, on all occasions, to inculcate on the people the value of liberty, and the difference between the state of free citizens of this

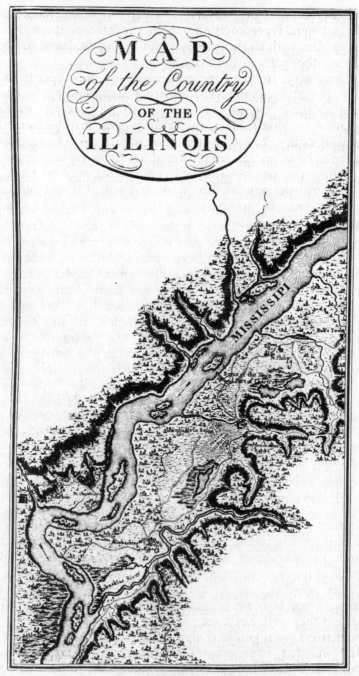

A 1796 map of the Illinois country

Commonwealth and that slavery to which the Illinois was destined. A free and equal representation may be expected by them in a little time, together with all the improvement in jurisprudence and police which the other parts of the State enjoy.

It is necessary, for the happiness, increase and prosperity of that country, that the grievances that obstruct those blessings be known, in order to their removal. Let it therefore be your care to obtain information on that subject, that proper plans may be formed for the general utility. Let it be your constant attention to see that the inhabitants have justice administered to them for any injury received from the troops. The omission of this may be fatal. Col. Clark has instructions on this head, and will, I doubt not, exert himself to quell all licentious practice of the soldiers, which, if unrestrained, will produce the most baneful effect. You will also discountenance and punish every attempt to violate the property of the Indians, particularly on their land. Our enemies have alarmed them much on that score, but I hope from your prudence and justice that there will be no grounds of complaint on that subject. You will embrace every opportunity to manifest the high regard and friendly sentiments of this Commonwealth towards all the subjects of his Catholic Majesty, for whose safety, prosperity and advantage you will give every possible advantage. You will make a tender of the friendship and services of your people to the Spanish Commandant near Kaskaskia, and cultivate the strictest connection with him and his people. The detail of your duty in the civil department I need not give; its best direction will be found in your innate love of justice, and zeal to be useful to your fellow-men. Act according to the best of your judgment in cases where these instructions are silent and the laws have not otherwise directed. Discretion is given to you from the necessity of the case, for your great distance from Government will not permit you to wait for orders in many cases of great importance. In your negotiations with the Indians confine the stipulation, as much as possible, to the single object of obtaining peace from them. Touch not the subject of lands or boundaries till particular orders are received. When necessity requires it presents may be made, but be as frugal in that matter as possible, and let them know that goods at present is scarce with us, but we expect soon to trade freely with all the world, and they shall not want when we can get them.

The matters given you in charge being singular in their nature and weighty in their consequences to the people immediately concerned, and to the whole State, they require the fullest exertion of your ability and unwearied diligence.

From matters of general concern you must turn, occasionally, to others of less consequence. Mr. Roseblove's wife and family must not suffer for want of that property of which they were bereft by our troops. It is to be restored to them, if possible; if this can not be done, the public must support them.

I think it proper for you to send me an express once in the month, with a general account of affairs with you and any particulars you wish to communicate.

It is in contemplation to appoint an agent to manage trade on public accounts, to supply Illinois and the Indians with goods. If such an appointment takes place, you will give it any possible aid. The people with you should not intermit their endeavors to procure supplies on the expectation of this, and you may act accordingly.

(Signed)   P. Henry

Brigadier General Harmar's letter to the Secretary of War, dated November 24, 1787, describes the French, English, and Spanish settlements in Illinois, and comments at length on the Indian situation. Harmar, the military commander of the Northwest Territory, had been sent by Congress on an inspection tour of the territory in the wake of complaints to that body of deteriorating conditions in the West. This document was published in Volume Two of *The St. Clair Papers* (New York, 1881). Arthur St. Clair served as Governor and Commander in Chief of the Northwest Territory from 1787 to 1802. More details about Harmar's visit can be found in F. E. Wilson, *Arthur St. Clair: Rugged Ruler of the Old Northwest* (Richmond, 1944).

Americans and Indians, 1787

JOSIAH HARMAR

Brigadier-General Harmar to the Secretary of War
Fort Harmar, November 24th, 1787.

Sir:—In my last letter [from Post Vincennes, 7th of August], after having published in French and English the Resolve of Con-

From Josiah Harmar, "Letter to the Secretary of War, November 24, 1787," in William H. Smith, ed., *The St. Clair Papers* (Cincinnati, 1882), pp. 30-35. Footnotes in the original have been omitted.

gress respecting the intruders upon the public lands at Post Vincennes, together with my orders relative thereto, and after having
sent messages to the several Indian chiefs on the Wabash to assemble at the Post, and hear what I had to say to them, as there was no
probability of these chiefs coming in in less than a month, I
informed you that it was my intention to employ that time in
visiting Kaskaskia, in order that I might be enabled to render a
statement of affairs in that part of the United States.

Accordingly, I marched on the 9th of August, from the Post with
a subaltern (Ensign McDowell) and thirty men, through the prairies,
and arrived at Kaskaskia on the 16th of the same month. Our march
was very fatiguing, as the weather was excessively warm and water
very bad and scarce on our route. I was accompanied by two
Indians—Pachan, a Miami chief, and his comrade, who hunted and
supplied the party with meat (Buffalo and deer), both on the march
and on our return. These prairies are very extensive natural meadows, covered with long grass. One in particular which we crossed
was eight leagues in breadth. They run, in general, North and South,
and, like the ocean, as far as the eye can see, the view is terminated
by the horizon. Here and there a copse of woods is interspersed.
They are free from bush and underwood, and not the least vestige
of their ever having been cultivated. The country is excellent for
grazing, and abounds in buffalo, deer, bear, etc. It is a matter of
speculation to account for the formation of the prairies. The
western side of the Wabash is overflown in the spring for several
miles.

On the 17th I was visited by the magistrates and principal
inhabitants of Kaskaskia, welcoming us upon our arrival. Baptiste
du Coigne, the chief of the Kaskaskia Indians, paid me a visit in the
afternoon, and delivered me a speech, expressive of the greatest
friendship for the United States, and presented me with one of the
calumets, or pipes of peace, which is now sent on. Some of the
Pioria Indians likewise visited me. The Kaskaskias, Piorias, Caho-
kias, and Mitcha tribes compose the Illinois Indians. They are
almost extinct at present, not exceeding forty or fifty total. Kaskaskia is a handsome little village, situated on the river of the same
name, which empties into the river Mississippi at two leagues
distance from it. It is one hundred and five miles up the Mississippi
from the mouth of the Ohio. The situation is low and unhealthy,
and subject to inundation. The inhabitants are French, and much of
the same class as those at Post Vincennes. Their number is one
hundred and ninety-one, old and young men.

Having but very little time to spare, I left Ensign McDowell with
the party at Kaskaskia, and on the 18th, set out accompanied by
Mr. Tardiveau and the gentlemen of the village, for Cahokia. We

gained Prairie du Rocher, a small village five leagues distant from Kaskaskia, where we halted for the night. On the 19th we passed through St. Philip, a trifling village three leagues distant from Prairie du Rocher, and dined at La Belle Fontaine, six leagues further. La Belle Fontaine is a small stockade, inhabited altogether by Americans, who have seated themselves there without authority. It is a beautiful situation, fine fertile land, no taxation, and the inhabitants have abundance to live upon. They were exceedingly alarmed when I informed them of their precarious state respecting a title to their possessions, and have now sent on a petition to Congress by Mr. Tardiveau. On the same day we passed another small stockade, Grand Ruisseau, inhabited by the same sort of Americans as those at La Belle Fontaine, and arrived at Cahokia that evening. Cahokia is a village of nearly the same size as that of Kaskaskia, and inhabited by the same kind of people. Their number was two hundred and thirty-nine old men and young. I was received with the greatest hospitality by the inhabitants. There was a decent submission and respect in their behavior. Cahokia is distant from Kaskaskia twenty-two French leagues, which is about fifty miles.

On the 21st, in consequence of an invitation from Monsieur Cruzat, the Spanish commandant at St. Louis, we crossed the Mississippi, and were very politely entertained by him. After dinner we returned to Cahokia. St. Louis (nicknamed *Pancour*), is much the handsomest and genteelest village I have seen on the Mississippi. It is about four miles distant from Cahokia, and five leagues above it, the river Missouri unites with the Mississippi. The inhabitants are of the same sort as before described, excepting that they are more wealthy. About twenty regular Spanish troops are stationed here. On the 22d, I left Cahokia to return to Kaskaskia. Previous to my departure, at the request of the inhabitants, I assembled them, and gave them advice to place their militia upon a more respectable footing than it was, to abide by the decision of their courts, etc., and if there were any turbulent or refractory persons to put them under guard until Congress should be pleased to order a government for them. Exclusive of the intruders already described, there are about thirty more Americans settled on the rich fertile bottoms on the Mississippi, who are likewise petitioning by this conveyance.

On the 23d, I passed by the ruins of Fort Chartres, which is one league above the Prairie du Rocher, and situated on the Mississippi. It was built of stone, and must have been a considerable fortification formerly, but the part next to the river had been carried away by the floods, and is of no consequence at present. I staid about a quarter of an hour, but had not time to view it minutely, as it was all a thicket within. Several iron pieces of cannon are here at present, and also at the different villages. This evening I returned to Kaskaskia.

. . . .

On the 27th I left Kaskaskia, after having received every mark of respect and attention from the inhabitants, in order to set out for the Post. We marched by a lower route. Several of the French, and the Kaskaskia chief, with his tribe (about ten in number), accompanied us, and we arrived safe at Post Vincennes on the afternoon of the 3d of September. I made the distance by the lower route to be about one hundred and seventy miles.

On the 5th the Piankishaw and Weea Indians arrived at the Post from up the Wabash, to the number of about one hundred and twenty. Every precaution was taken. We had a fortified camp, two redoubts were thrown up on our right and left, and the guard in front intrenched. The troops were all new clothed, and made a truly military appearance. The Indians saluted us by firing several volleys on the Wabash, opposite our camp. Their salute was returned by a party of ours firing several platoons. I was determined to impress upon them as much as possible the majesty of the United States, and at the same time that they were informed that it was the wish of Congress to live in peace and friendship with them, likewise to let them know that if they persisted in being hostile that a body of troops would march to their towns and sweep them off the face of the earth. On the 7th, I invited them to camp, and made the inclosed speech to them. The Indians admired the troops. I believe they had never seen such a sight before. On the 8th, they answered my speech, and, in strong figurative language, expressed their determination to preserve perfect peace and friendship with the United States, as long as the waters flowed, etc. They utterly disavowed any knowledge of the murder that had been committed, and assured me that inquiry should be made for the prisoner. They presented me with a number of calumets and wampum, which I now have the honor of transmitting, inclosed in a rich otter skin; they will be delivered by Mr. Coudre. Mr. Coudre has acted as volunteer for a considerable time in the regiment, and has conducted himself with propriety. If a vacancy should happen in the Connecticut quota, I beg leave to recommend him to your notice.

On the 9th, the young warriors were drinking whiskey and dancing before our tents all the morning, to demonstrate their joy. On the 10th, I made them several presents from the commissioner's goods, to no great amount. On the 12th, the chief part of them left the Post for their different villages up the Wabash. They returned highly satisfied with the treatment they received. Indeed, it was a proper tour of fatigue for me. I found it politic to pay the greatest attention to them. They are amazingly fond of whisky, and destroyed a considerable quantity of it. I trust that you may find this conference with the Indians attended with very little expense; I question whether the whole, whisky, provisions, and presents, will cost the public more than one hundred and fifty dollars. Their interpreter is a half Frenchman, and married to a Weea squaw. He has very great influence among them. I judged it necessary to pay extraordinary attention to him.

I have the honor to acknowledge the receipt of several letters from you, which I shall fully answer by the next conveyance, particularly one of the 2d of August, inclosing me a brevet commission of brigadier-general.

After finishing the conference with the Indians, and obtaining the inclosed petitions of the inhabitants of Post Vincennes to Congress, relinquishing their charter, and trusting to the generosity of that honorable body, I judged it expedient to leave a garrison at the Post, as it would have been impolitic, after the parade we had made, to entirely abandon the country. Accordingly, Major Hamtramck commands there. His command consists of Captain Smith's company, fifty-five, and part of Ferguson's company, forty; total, ninety-five. I have ordered him to fortify himself, and to regulate the militia, who are to join him in case of hostilities.

Having arranged all matters to my satisfaction, as we had a long and tiresome voyage before us, I began to think of winter quarters. Accordingly, on the 1st of October I marched by land with the well men of Captains Zeigler's and Strong's companies (total, seventy-one), for the Rapids of the Ohio. I gave orders to Major Wyllys to command the fleet, and to embark for the Rapids the next morning, with the late Captain Finney's and Mercer's companies, and the sick of the other companies, and a brass three-pounder. I omitted mention of my taking into our possession some ordnance and ammunition (public property) at Louisville and at the Post. At the former we got a brass six-pounder with several swivels; at the latter, from Mr. Dalton, two brass three-pounders. I thought it best that the public property should be under our own charge.

We marched along what is called Clarke's Trace, and arrived on the 7th of October at the Rapids of the Ohio. I was mistaken, in a former letter, concerning the distance; it is about one hundred and thirty miles. We saw no Indians, nor signs of Indians.

. . . .

John Bradbury, a Scots-born English botanist, was commissioned in 1809 to undertake a research expedition to study American plant life. He arrived in the United States that summer and visited Thomas Jefferson at Monticello. On Jefferson's advice, he established his headquarters at St. Louis and from there explored the Missouri River. Although he had intended to return home in 1812, the outbreak of war with the United States imposed a four-year stay in New York. Before leaving for England after the war's end, Bradbury came to Illinois, and his remarks about the trip were published as part of an appendix to his *Travels in the Interior of America*, printed in Liverpool in 1817. Recommended reading on conditions in the territory on the eve of statehood is Solon J. Buck, *Illinois in 1818* (Springfield, 1918).

Illinois on the Eve of Statehood

JOHN BRADBURY

Salt, the most useful article at present, is found in various places, but as yet only in a state of solution, and has mostly been indicated by the excavations made by wild animals before the country was discovered by the whites. These animals, and in particular the herbivorous kind, have a strong predilection for salt; they resorted in immense numbers to every place where a salt spring existed, and not only drank the water, but licked up all the earth in its vicinity, that was impregnated with saline particles. Some of these excavations are of a surprising extent, when the means by which they have been effected is considered. The salt spring called the Ohio Saline, about twenty miles from the mouth of the Wabash, is several acres in extent, and from six to ten feet in depth. On viewing these, and contemplating the length of time necessary for such a mass to be carried away in the stomachs of animals, the mind is struck with astonishment. The existence of salt on the Kenhawa was not pointed out by these indications. On sinking a well, the persons employed came to a red sandstone rock before they had obtained a sufficiency of water, and perforated the rock, when the salt water immediately issued up with great force. This rock is now found to extend for several miles on both sides of the river. Wherever it is perforated salt water is found beneath, and several works for the manufacture of salt are already established.*

From John Bradbury, "Remarks on Illinois and the Western Territory," Reuben G. Thwaites, ed., *Early Western Travels* (Cleveland, 1904-07), V, 275-294. Bradbury's own descriptive footnotes have been retained.
*In passing down that river I had an opportunity of seeing the manner in which they construct their wells for the salt water, which, on account of its singularity, I shall

Iron ore is found in many places, but chiefly in the neighbourhood where foundries have been established. About fourteen miles
west of the Ohio Saline, in the Illinois Territory, there is a lead
mine, which was discovered by a gentleman from Tennessee, of the
name of Guest. It is not yet worked, but seems to promise well.
Some small excavations have been made, and a quantity of galena
found. It appears to have no connection or affinity with the mines
of St. Genevieve, not only on account of the distance being about a
hundred and fifty miles, but from the marked difference in the rock
which is the matrix of the ore, and in the substances which are
concomitant with it. The rock in this mine is of that species of
limestone called kettonstone, or compact limestone of Kirwan, and
consists of very small accreted round granulations. The ore is mixed
with very beautiful fluor spar, of several colours, as blue, brown,
yellow, and pellucid. The caves yielding salt petre are still more
abundant than those of Upper Louisiana, or rather they are better
known, and some of them are of surprising extent. They abound
chiefly on Green, Tennessee, and Cumberland rivers.

The country is generally calcareous; but many rocks of freestone

---

describe. They first ascertain by boring at what depth they shall come to the rock, and
afterwards look out for a hollow tree which must be at least from three to four feet in
diameter. This they cut down carefully for fear of splitting, and saw off such a length as
will reach from the surface of the ground to the rock. If the hollow of the tree is not large
enough to allow room sufficient for a man to work within, they enlarge it. A well is next
dug, and when so deep that there is danger of the earth falling in, the trunk is put down,
and sunk to the surface of the rock. After the influx of fresh water is prevented by
calkings round the edges at the bottom of the trunk, the perforation is made, and the salt
water immediately rises to the surface. Besides the use here mentioned, hollow trees were
applied to other purposes, being cut across in different lengths, and used by the first
settlers as tubs to hold grain, &c. Any portion so cut off is called a gum, a name probably
arising from the almost exclusive application of the gum trees to these purposes; for
although many species of trees are liable to become hollow, yet none are so perfectly
hollowed as the gum tree (*liquid-amber styraciflua*). These trees, as I am informed, are
often found so completely hollow as to leave the sound part not more than an inch in
thickness, and the inside surface perfectly smooth.

Having mentioned the Kenhawa, I must observe, that on arriving at the falls of that
river, ninety miles from the Ohio, I found a boat going from thence to Kenhawa
Court-house, with some goods that had been brought over the Alleghanies. A passage was
cheerfully granted to me, during which I enquired for the burning well, and expressed a
wish to see it. The boatman informed me it was four miles from the river, and it would not
be convenient for them to wait until I visited it, but promised to show me what would
equally gratify my curiosity. Accordingly, near the edge of the river, and about fifteen
miles farther down, they landed, and conducted me to where there was a hole dug in the
sandy bank of the river, about a foot in diameter. From this hole a flame issued at least
two feet high. Several stones were placed round the margin, on which some other boatmen
had set their kettles to cook their meat. I had noticed for several miles above a vein of iron
ore appearing at the surface, about the height of the highest floods, and in almost every
part of the bank great quantities of ochre. The same appearances continued to the distance
of several miles below. From noticing this circumstance, I was led to form a conjecture on
the formation of the gas that supplied the flame, and was persuaded that there is a vast
body of iron ore, which, from the appearance of so much ochre, is in a continued state of
oxydization, and produces a constant decomposition of water, with the oxygen of which
it unites, and consequently a quantity of hydrogen is evolved—May not this be the
cause?—*Bradbury*.

occur. One producing excellent flags may be observed near the place where the battle was fought at Point Pleasant, on the Kenhawa.

Near the mouth of Cabin Creek, about six miles above Limestone, on the Ohio, there is a hill almost covered with detached petrified casts of marine shells, in which a great many species may be observed.

In the state of nature, this country was almost wholly covered with trees, many of which are of great magnitude. More than one hundred species are found, and the timber is of various qualities, affording to the farmer, ship-builder, carpenter, cooper, and cabinetmaker great opportunities of selecting what is most suitable for their different purposes.

. . . .

The price of land is so much varied by quality and situation, that no certain data can be given. Near the large towns, land is as dear as near the cities in the eastern states, and in the most populous towns, the lots sell at a very high price. . . . The lands belonging to the United States government are sold at one uniform price, viz. two dollars per acre, with five years to pay it in, or one dollar, sixty-four cents cash. There are but few European families, who have been accustomed to sedentary employments, that could submit to the fatigues incident on clearing a forest, and converting it into arable land. To such, a resource is always open, as opportunities are never wanting to purchase from the *Backwoodsman* what he calls *his improvement.* He is alarmed at the approach of population, and is anxious to remove farther back into the woods. The improvement consists in a log house, a peach, and perhaps an apple, orchard, together with from ten, to thirty or forty acres of land, inclosed, and partially cleared. For this, seldom more than from fifty to a hundred dollars is asked, exclusive of the value of the land, which in most cases belongs to the United States, and may be purchased at the land office on the usual terms. Besides the land belonging to the United States, there are large tracts in the hands of speculators, from whom it may sometimes be purchased upon as good terms as from the government, and as liberal in point of credit; but in this case, care should be taken to examine if the title is good. Many of the speculators are anxious to sell, as the land-tax, although comparatively light, becomes heavy on very extensive purchases: it amounts to one dollar, twenty cents, per annum, on one hundred acres of first-rate land; one dollar on one hundred acres of second-rate; and sixty cents on third-rate. These sums are nearly in the proportion of 14/20 of a penny per acre for first-rate; one halfpenny per acre for second rate; and 7/10 of a halfpenny per acre for third-rate. Some districts of upland may be purchased of the speculators at half a dollar, or 2s. 3d. per acre: these would answer well for sheep. No land tax is expected until five years after the purchase, when land becomes liable. They have two modes of clearing land; one by cutting the trees round, so as to kill them, and afterwards clearing away the underwood, the quantity of which is very small: this mode is called *girdling,* and is only resorted to by those who, to use their own phrase, are *"weak-handed."* The other mode is by cutting down the trees, dragging them into heaps, and burning them. This operation is almost always the subject of what they term a *frolic,* or in some places a *bee.* It is necessary to remark, that in the early part of the settlement of a country like this, a great number of things occur necessary to be done, which require the united strength of numbers to effect. In those parts, money cannot purchase for the new settler the required aid; but that kind and generous feeling which men have for each other, who are not rendered callous by the possession of wealth, or the dread of poverty, comes to his relief: his neighbours, even unsolicited, appoint a day when as a *frolic,* they shall, for instance, build him a house. On the morning of the appointed day they assemble, and divide themselves into parties, to each of which is assigned its respective duty; one party cuts down the trees, another lops and cuts them to proper lengths, a third is furnished with horses and oxen, and drags them to the spot designed for the scite of the house: another party is employed in making *shingles* to cover the roof, and at night all the materials are ready upon the spot; and on the night of the next day, he and his family sleep in their new habitation. No remuneration is expected, nor would it be received. It is considered the performance of a duty, and only lays him under the obligation to discharge the debt by doing the same to subsequent settlers. But this combination of labour in numbers, for the benefit of one individual, is not confined to the new comer only, it occurs frequently in the course of a year amongst the *old settlers,* with whom it is a continued bond of amity and social intercourse, and in no part of the world is *good neighbourship* found in greater perfection than in the western territory, or in America generally.

As the climate has already been spoken of, I shall only observe, that here, as in Upper Louisiana, the shortness and mildness of the winter is of immense advantage to the farmer. In parts where the winter is five or six months long, a great portion of time must necessarily be employed in providing food for the cattle during that season. Here very little time or land is necessary to be devoted to that purpose. The greatest part of the farmers scatter the seeds of pumpkins in the fields when planting the corn: no farther care is required, except throwing the pumpkins into the waggon when ripe. These, with the tops of the Indian corn, cut off when the ears are formed, give sufficient food for all the stock during winter. The pumpkins are raised with so little trouble, that they sell for a dollar per waggon load, and generally weigh from thirty to fifty pounds each, although some have been raised to exceed two hundred pounds. Cattle and hogs eat them with avidity.

The vine flourishes in this region, and the wheat can scarcely be surpassed, either for quality or abundance. With the exception of beans (*vicïa faba,*) and cauliflower, the culinary vegetables of Europe are raised in as much perfection as in England. In addition to these, they cultivate in their fields, amongst other crops, water melons, musk-melons, squashes, and sweet potatoes, (*convolvulus batatus.*) Cucumbers and beans (*phaseolus,*) grow in much greater perfection than in England. The fruits are excellent, and in great abundance, particularly peaches and apples.

Very little of the agricultural labour falls on the women, who employ themselves in their domestic manufactures, in which they are both expert and industrious. Almost all grow some flax, and south of latitude 39° they have what they call a *cotton patch.* * Few are without sheep. By these means the women are furnished with three staple articles, out of which they spin sufficient to produce almost all the clothing and other articles necessary for a family. Some have looms, and weave it themselves; others employ weavers, who follow that business as an occupation.†

In the towns, many of the trades or manufactories are already established, that are calculated to furnish articles of the first degree of necessity; and some of those which produce articles necessary in a more advanced state of refinement. Amongst the first, are masons, stone-cutters, brick-makers, smiths, carpenters, wheelwrights, cabinet-makers, saddlers, boot and shoe makers, ship and boat builders, nailors, coppersmiths and brass-founders, wire-drawers and wire-makers, screw and hinge makers, gunsmiths, cutlers, machine makers, clock and watch makers, curriers, glovers, distillers, butchers, bakers, brewers, stocking makers, rope makers, coffee-mill makers, and a great number of others. There are also glass manufactories, cotton and woolen manufactories, iron foundries, potteries, floor-cloth manufactories, steam engine makers, glass cutters, silversmiths, looking-glass makers, printers, bookbinders, &c. &c. There is

*Cotton does not become an object of culture as a crop north of 36°.—*Bradbury.*

†The manufacture of their woolens is much facilitated by the establishment of carding machines: almost generally throughout the United States, some proprietors have two or three machines.—*Bradbury.*

no part of the world where labour finds a better market than in the western country; this results from a state of things that will not admit of a speedy change. A very moderate sum of money enables a man to procure one or two hundred acres of land; the savings of two or three years will enable a working man to effect this, if he is prudent, and although he can only cultivate a small part of it, and perhaps for the first two or three years, not more than will maintain his family, yet the accumulation of property by the regular and rapid advance in the value of his land, forms more than an equivalent to the savings of the labourer or mechanic. From this cause there is a continued tendency in the labourers to turn to farming, as soon as they have acquired a little property: they are well aware that, by undertaking to bring *wild land* into a state of cultivation, they must undergo some hardships, and suffer some privations, but the state of ease, security and independence which will assuredly follow, makes ample amends.

That produce of every kind, of the nature of provisions, will for a very long time remain low, may be presumed by attending to the following circumstances: first the distance from a foreign market, causing a great expense in exportation: secondly, the great predominance of scattered population employed in farming, over that which is condensed in towns, or otherwise employed: and thirdly, the vast extent of land remaining west of the Alleghanies yet unoccupied; this will appear from the following statement of the area and population, in which all that part attached to the Atlantic States is excluded. The population is taken as it stood in the census of 1810, since when, although there has been a great increase, yet it makes no very sensible difference when the extent of the country is considered.

	Area in Square Miles.	Population.
Ohio State	43,860	230,760
Indiana State	39,000	24,520
Illinois Territory	52,000	12,282
Michigan Territory	34,820	4,762
North West Territory	106,830	1,000
Kentucky State	40,110	406,511
Tennessee State	43,200	261,727
Mississippi Territory	88,680	40,352
Missouri Territory	985,250	20,845
	1,433,750	1,002,759

By this statement, it appears that in 1810, there was only one inhabitant in near one and a half square miles, or, (as there are six hundred and forty acres to the square mile) one inhabitant in every nine hundred acres; not one-tenth of these are residents in towns, nor one-fifth have any employment but agriculture.

The average population of England and Wales is one hundred and ninety-two to the square mile. In Lancashire there are four hundred inhabitants to the square mile, which allows but little more than an acre and a half to each individual.

Wages in the Western Country, to a labourer or husbandman, are about fifteen dollars, or £3. 7s. 6d. per month, and his board, washing, &c. Carpenters, masons, and other handicraft men, average about one dollar and twenty-five cents per day, equal to 5s. 7 1/2 d. or one dollar and board. Shoemakers have about 4s. sterling for making a pair of shoes, and for a pair of boots about 11s. In the present state of things, flour, and other produce that is transferable to a foreign market, is higher than usual, but when not affected by a scarcity in Europe, will fall to the usual price, which is pretty near the following statement.

	American Money			Eng. Money	
	Dols.	Cents.		Shils.	Pence.
Flour, *per barrel*	4	0	or	18	0
Indian corn meal, *per 100 lbs.*	0	40	—	1	9½
Potatoes, *per bushel*	0	31	—	1	4½
Beef, mutton, and veal, *per lb.*	0	5	—	0	2½
Pork, *per lb.*	0	4	—	0	2
Bacon, *per lb.*	0	8	—	0	4½
Venison, *per lb.*	0	4	—	0	2
Fowls, *each*	0	12½	—	0	7
Ducks, *each*	0	25	—	1	1½
Geese, *each*	0	62½	—	2	10
Turkies, *each*	0	75	—	3	4½
Cheese, *per lb.*	0	10	—	0	5¼
Butter, *per lb.*	0	14	—	0	7¼
Cider, *per barrel*	3	0	—	13	6
Whiskey, *per gallon*	0	40	—	1	9½
Peach brandy, *per gallon*	0	80	—	3	7
Maple sugar, *per lb.*	0	10	—	0	5¼

By a comparison of this table with the rate of wages, it will appear, that an industrious working man may support a family with great ease in this country.

Mellish, in his description of these parts, gives a statement of the prices of provision and labour, which he closes with the following observations.

"From this list of prices, taken in connexion with the value of labour, it will be seen, that an ordinary workman can procure for a day's work, fifty pounds of flour,—or twenty pounds of beef,—or three bushels of potatoes,—or twenty-seven pounds of pork,—or eight fowls,—or four ducks,—or two ordinary geese,—or one very large turkey."

. . . .

In regard to the manners of the people west of the Alleghanies, it would be absurd to expect that a general character could be now formed, or that it will be for many years yet to come. The population is at present compounded of a great number of nations, not yet amalgamated, consisting of emigrants from every state in the Union, mixed with English, Irish, Scotch, Dutch, Swiss, Germans, French, and almost from every country in Europe. In some traits they partake in common with the inhabitants of the Atlantic States, which results from the nature of their government. That species of hauteur which one class of society in some countries show in their intercourse with the other, is here utterly unknown. By their constitution, the existence of a privileged order, vested by birth with hereditary privileges, honours, or emoluments, is for ever interdicted. If, therefore, we should here expect to find that contemptuous feeling in man for man, we should naturally examine amongst those clothed with judicial or military authority; but we should search in vain. The justice on the bench, or the officer in the field, is respected and obeyed whilst discharging the functions of his office, as the representative or agent of the law, enacted for the *good of all*; but should he be tempted to treat even the least wealthy of his neighbours or fellow citizens with contumely, he would soon find that he could not do it with impunity. Travelers from Europe, in passing through the western country, or indeed any part of the United States, ought to be previously acquainted with this part of the American character, and more particularly if they have been in the habit of treating with contempt, or irritating with abuse, those whom accidental circumstances may have placed in a situation to administer to their wants. Let no one here indulge himself in abusing the waiter or hostler at an inn: that waiter or hostler is probably a citizen, and does not, nor can he, conceive that a situation in which he discharges a duty to society, not in itself dishonourable, should subject him to insult: but this feeling, so far as I have experienced, is entirely defensive. I have travelled near ten thousand miles in the United States, and never received the least incivility or affront.

The Americans in general are accused by travellers of being inquisitive. If this be a crime, the western people are guilty; but for my part I must say that it is a practice that I never was disposed to complain of, because I always found them as ready to answer a question as to ask one, and therefore I always came off a gainer by this sort of barter; and if any traveller does not, it is his own fault. As this leads me to notice their general conduct to strangers, I feel myself bound in gratitude and regard to truth, to speak of their hospitality. In my travels through the inhabited parts of the United States, not less than two thousand miles was through parts where there were no taverns, and where a traveller is under the necessity of appealing to the hospitality of the inhabitants. In no one instance has my appeal been fruitless, although in many cases the furnishing of a bed has been evidently attended with inconvenience, and in a great many instances no remuneration would be received. Other European travellers have experienced this liberal spirit of hospitality, and some have repaid it by calumny. These calumnies have reached them: they are well acquainted with what Weld and a person who calls himself Ashe have said of them.* In respect to their moral character, my experience reaches chiefly to the western, middle, and some of the southern states. In the western states, I noticed that very few of the houses in which I slept had either locks or bolts on the doors, and that the jails were in general without a single tenant.

It has already been observed that no people discharge the social duties, as respects the character of neighbours, better, and I believe no country, having a population equal to the United States, can exhibit the records of their courts containing fewer statements of crimes committed against the laws.

. . . .

*As the book published by this Ashe contains numberless statements, bearing in themselves such evidences of being void of truth as to deprive him of all claim to veracity, and as it has already sunk into the oblivion it merits, the malignant falsehoods propagated by him, respecting America and the American people, should have remained unnoticed by me, had I not witnessed the just indignation it has excited in that country, and also found that Ashe had been received and treated with the greatest kindness by the very people whom he has so grossly libelled. His statements are too numerous, and many of them too absurd, to deserve a serious refutation; but I think it a duty due both to myself and my country to state, that his description of the American people, and the accusations he makes against them, are void of foundation. If Mr. Ashe saw any instance to warrant his observation, he must have kept the worst of company.—*Bradbury.*

Gershom Flagg, whose letter to his brother is reprinted below, was born at Orwell, Vermont, in 1792 and served in that state's militia at the Battle of Plattsburg during the War of 1812. In 1816 he came to Illinois and in two years had established a quarter-section farm near Edwardsville. In letters to relatives, including this one to his brother, he pictured the attractive economic and social conditions found in his adopted state. Partly as a result of Gershom's accounts, five of his eight brothers and sisters migrated to Illinois. The letters appeared in the 1903 edition of the *Transactions of the Illinois State Historical Society*, edited by Solon J. Buck.

Pioneer Letter

GERSHOM FLAGG

St. Louis, Dec. 7, 1817

I should have answered your letter before if I had had an opportunity for the mail did not arrive for three weeks past until the 28 Nov, at which time I was absent in the Illinois Territory. . . .

I am pleased with this Country it is the Richest soil and most handsomely situated of any I have ever seen. I have not seen the Military bounty Lands nor can I get business of surveying at present. The surveyor Genl. informs me that 3 1/2 Million of acres have been surveyed N. W. of the Illinois River & that 1/2 Million is to be surveyed N. [*MS. torn*] of the Missouri River & 2 Millions between [the] Rivers Arkansas & St Francis. If [you sh]ould purchase any Patents let them [be] in the Illinois Territory for the Missouri is not so good. . . . I am told by the Surveyors that the Land is Rich handsome & well watered but poorly timbered. I am not anxious about your purchasing any for I do not expect it will be settled soon & if it does not the land will not be so valuable as it otherwise would be.

I am told that one half of the Lands are Prairie and the other timbered. The timbered Land will be very valuable and the Prairie the reverse so that it is like a Lottery you have about an equal chance to draw a great prize & it must be some prize because the Land is to be fit for cultivation. Some say that the Prairie that has no timber upon it will be returned unfit for cultivation to the General Land Office. But I think this will not be the

From Solon J. Buck, ed., "Pioneer Letters of Gershom Flagg," *Transactions of the Illinois State Historical Society*, XV (1910), 139-184. All but one footnote in the original have been omitted.

case.* If you should purchase any you will be good enough to let me know the No. &c. as soon as convenient.

. . . .

As you may wish to know something of the Country in which I live I will write a few lines respecting it. The Territory of Illinois contains nearly all that part of the United States Territory east of the Mississippi and N. W. of the Ohio & Wabash Rivers. The late law of Congress enabling the people to form a Constitution & State Government makes the boundaries on the S. & W. Ohio & Missisippi Rivers on the East by Indiana State N by 42° 30′ N. Lat. The conjunction of the Ohio & Missisippi Rivers is in Lat. 37° N so that this Territory is 350 miles in length. The face of the Country is very level without any mountains and but few hills. It is not exceeded by levelness [or] richness of soil by any in the United States. The prairies are very large while the timbered land is confined almost wholly to the intervales and low rounds. Where ever the land is high and dry enough for the fire to run in the spring & fall the timber is all destroyed. The Soil is of such an alluvial nature that the water courses cut out deep chanels from 6 to 20 feet deep generally. Where this is the case the streams do not overflow

We have all kinds of soil from midling poor to the very best. It produces Corn & Wheat better than any other Country I have seen. It also produces hemp, flax, Mellons, Sweet potatoes, Turnips & all kinds of vegetables except Irish Potatoes as good as any other Country. Cotton is raised sufficient for domestic use a very small piece of ground produces enough for a family.

We have plenty of Apples Peaches &c in places. Grapes & of several kinds and several kinds of Wild plumbs & Cherries in profusion also Dew Berries Black berries Strawberries. The bottom Prairies are covered with Weeds of different kinds and grass about 8 feet high. The high Prairies are also thickly covered with grass but finer & not so tall. The prairies are continually covered (in the summer season) with wild flowers of all colors which gives them a very handsome appearance. These high Prairies are smoother than any intervale & not a stone, log, or anything but grass & weeds to

*This low opinion of the value of prairie land was almost universal among the early pioneers. They were inclined to believe that land upon which trees did not grow could be of little value for agricultural purposes. Thus in 1786 James Monroe, afterwards president of the United States, wrote of the Northwest: "A great part of the territory is miserably poor, especially that near Lakes Michigan and Erie, and that upon the Mississippi and the Illinois consists of extensive plains which have not, from appearances, and will not have, a single bush on them for ages. The districts, therefore, within which these fall will never contain a sufficient number of inhabitants to entitle them to membership in the confederacy." There were, however, certain real obstacles to the occupation of the prairies by the early settlers, most important of which were: lack of water; lack of wood for buildings, fences, and fuel; and difficulties of transportation.

be seen for miles excep[t] where they border the timber there is generally a thicket of plumb bushes, hazel grape vines, &c &c. The Roots of the grass are very tough it generally requires 3 yoke of Oxen or six horses to plough up the prairies & the plough must be kept at a keen edge by filing often, the steel not being hardened, but this is all that is to be done excep[t] fencing to raise a crop. After one year the ground is mellow and requires but a light team to plough it. The Timber in this Country is very different from any you have seen. The most Common timber is White, Black, Spanish, post, Chincopin, Pin, and Burrh Oak, Walnut Black & White, Basswood, Cherry Button wood Ash, Elm, Sassafras, Sumach, Elder, Honey locust, Mulberry, Crab Apple Thorn of different kinds Red-bud, Pecon, Hackberry Maple, Cotton Wood, Pawpaw which bears a fruit larger than an apple. The timber is not so good as I have seen, generally, the fire kills & checks the growth every year. When the fire gets into high thick grass it goes faster than a horse can Run & burns the Prairie smooth.

The situation of this Territory is good for trade having the advantage of Water carriage on all sides the Missisipi on the West the Ohio & Wabash S. E. & the Kaskaskia and Illinois in the interior of the Territory. The Illinois which is about 400 miles in length heads near Lake Michigan. A branch of the Illinois heads within 4 miles of the head of Chicago a short River which empties into Lake michgon [*sic*]. In freshe[t]s boats pass this portage the waters being connected. They are made shallow for the purpose. I have seen them at St. Louis landing. I think there will be a canall cut to connect the waters of Illinois & Chicago at no distant period. From information the expense would not be great. One hundred thousand acres of Land is appropriated for this purpose. This done we have a water communication from almost any part of the Territory to the states of Indiana Ohio & Pensylvania on either side of those stat[e]s. Also with New York by the way of Lake Erie & an easy Communication with the Ocean by New Orleans. One steam Boat Run from St. Louis to Louisville Kentucky the last season and another from St. Louis, to New Orleans. One of them came up to St. Louis the 1st January last and returned but the Ice generally covers the River in January & February That is, drifting ice, for the Missisipi was not shut over last winter at St. louis tho' it sometimes is. The Missouri was frozen over last winter. There are 8 or 10 steam boats on the Ohio and Missisipi Rivers and more building there was two built in Cincinnati last summer, & one at the Rising Sun and one at New Albany below the falls of Ohio. The Trade from St. Louis to Orleans is very considerable there are in St. Louis between 40 & 50 mercantile Stores.

We have a great plenty Deer, Turkies, Wolves, Opossoms, Prairie hens, Eagles, Turky Buzzards, Swans, Geese, ducks, Brant, sand hill Cranes, Parokites & with many other small Animals & birds. Gray squirrels are as thick here as I have ever seen stripeid [*sic*] ones in Vermont. There is more honey here in this Territory I suppose than in any other place in the world, I have heard the Hunters say that they have found 8 or 10 swarms in a day on the St. Gama & Illinois Rivers where there are no settlements (Truly this must be the Land of Milk & honey.) The Climate is not so hot as might be expected there is almost a continual breeze blowing from the large prairies like the breezes on large Lakes & ponds. The country is so open that it is considerable cold in Winter the ground freezes very hard There being generally but little snow. The past summer has been very hot more than common I am told. The Thermometer on the hottest day stood at 98°. I learn from the News Papers that the Weather has been very hot in different parts of the United States.

The Stock of this Country consists principally of horses horned Cattle & hogs. Sheep will do very well here if they can be kept from the Wolves but this cannot well be done in the newsettled parts the wolves are so very numerous. Hogs will live & get fat in the Woods & Prairies. I have seen some as fat upon Hickorynuts, Acorns, Pecons & Walnuts, as ever I did those that were fat[t]ed upon Corn. All that prevents this country being as full of Wild hogs as of Deer is the Wolves which kill the pigs when the sows are not shut up til the pigs are a few weeks old. There are places in this Territory where Cattle & horses will live all winter & be in good order without feeding, that is upon the Rivers. Most of the people cut no hay for their Cattle & horses but this is a foolish way of theirs they either have to feed out their Corn or their Cattle get very poor. Cattle & horses do very well in this Country they get very fat by the middle of June. They do not gain much after this being so harrassed by swarms of flies which prevent their feeding any in the heat of the day. They are so bad upon horses that it is almost impossible to travel from the 15 June til the 1st Sept unles a horse is covered with blankets. Where ever a fly lights upon a horse a drop of blood starts. I have seen white horses red with blood that these flies had drawn out of him. As the Country becomes settled these flies disappear.

. . . .

We have had a very severe winter [1819] and considerable snow and this spring we have had several severe storms. Two men have been found dead in the Prairie supposed to have chilled to death by the cold weather and snow. I was one of the Jurors who examined the body of one of the men who was found dead and it appeared that after being out in the open Prairie for about 24 hours great part of which time it either Rained or snowed accompanied with a very Cold Wind he fell from his horse so benum[b]ed with cold that he never strugled but went to sleep for the last time. I began to plough the first day of March but have only ploughed 16 acres the ground having been frozen for several days past until yesterday.

We have pretty tight times here. Most of the People are in debt for Land and many otherwise more than they can posably [sic] pay. Our *wise Legislator* [sic] have taken the matter into serious consideration and *made a Bank without any Specie* to Redeem their notes and have stopt all Executions until the first of November next and after that time if the creditor will not endorse on the back of the Execution that he will receive the amount in State Paper The Execution is stopped for three years longer. This money is to be loaned out (The capital Stock of which is three hundred thousand dollars) to individuals by their giving real estate in security. The notes are to be given for one year but to be renewed every year on paying ten per cent so that it will be ten years before the borrower finishes paying.

Corn now sells at 12½ cents per Bushel Pork at 2½ and 3 dollars Wheat 50 cents Whiskey at 25 cents per gallon by the Barrel flour is 3 and 3½ dollars per Barrel.

Lewis Curtis of Burlington has set up his business in St. Charles on the Missouri River 20 miles from St Louis and 30 from here. Although Money is very scarce in this country there was 26 thousand dollars taken in the Land office at this place during the sale in Jan. Last and that mostly Specie. I have Recd a letter from Eliza a few days ago dated June 8th. You will please to give my respects to all my friends and acquaintance. I have enjoyed [good ?] health since I wrote you last and re[main] your most affectionate Brothe[r].

Gershom Flagg

Even at the end of the territorial stage of development, Indian problems still existed in some parts of the future state. A flavor of Indian-American relations is found in the two addresses which conclude this section of original narratives, one by the territorial governor, Maryland-born Ninian Edwards, the other by a Potawatomi chief. The editor of the second document, Milo M. Quaife, taught at Wayne State University, was Superintendent of the Wisconsin State Historical Society, and wrote and edited a number of significant books on the Midwest. From 1924 to 1947 he served as Secretary and Editor of the Burton Historical Collection, Detroit Public Library.

'To the Chiefs and Warriors of the Pottawottamies'

NINIAN EDWARDS

Illinois Territory, July 21, 1811.

To the Chiefs and Warriors of the tribes of Pottawottamies, residing on the Illinois River and its waters, in the Territory of Illinois.

My Children, you are now met together, by my desire, on a very important occasion. You are now to be asked to do an act of justice. Should you refuse, it may once more involve the red and white brethren in all the horrors of bloody war. On the other hand, if you should perform what justice itself calls for, it will brighten the chain of friendship, which has for a long time united the red people with their white brethren of the United States.

My Children, ever since Wayne's treaty, our Great Father, the President of the United States, has faithfully fulfilled all his treaties with you. He has endeavored to make his red and white children live as one great family, loving and obliging one another, and he has always strictly forbidden his white children from doing any harm to their red brethren.

My Children, for a long time the bloody tomahawk and scalping-knife have been buried. The sun of peace has shone upon us, blessing us with his light and giving gladness to our hearts. The red people have enjoyed their forests and pursued their game in peace; and the white people have cultivated the earth without fear. But, my children, these bright prospects are darkened. A storm seems to be gathering which threatens destruction, unless it should be dissipated by that justice which you, as good men, ought to render.

From Ninian Edwards, *History of Illinois from 1778 to 1833; and the Life and Times of Ninian Edwards* (Springfield, 1870), pp. 45-47.

My Children, while we trusted to treaties with you—while we believed our red brethren to be friendly—some of our people, fearing no danger, have been plundered of their property and deprived of their lives by some of your bad men.

My Children, last year a perogue was cut loose on the Mississippi and a considerable quantity of goods was taken out of it, and carried off, by some of your people. A great many horses have been stolen from this Territory, both during the last and the present year, many of which have certainly been carried off by some of your people. Other horses have been stolen from the neighborhood of St. Charles, in Louisiana. I demand satisfaction for these outrages.

My Children, on the 19th day of July, last year, in the district of St. Charles, and Territory of Louisiana, a party of Pottawottamies stole several horses. On the next day they were pursued by the white people, who lost their trail and quit the pursuit. On that night those Pottawottamies fell upon those white men, in their camp, killed four of them, wounded a fifth, and carried off several horses and other property. Among those Indians were Cat Fish, O-hic-ka-ja-mis and Mis-pead-na-mis. I demand that these bad men, and all others who were of the party, together with the property they stole, shall be delivered up to Capt. Levering and his party, or that you yourselves shall deliver them and the property to me.

My Children, on the 2d day of last June, on Shoal creek, in St. Clair county, in this Territory, three of your bad men went to the house of a Mr. Cox, plundered his property, took two guns, two mares and colts, and a stud horse, barbarously killed his son, and took his daughter a prisoner. A few days after this outrage, near the Mississippi, in the same county and Territory, others of your bad men killed a man by the name of Price, and wounded another by the name of Ellis. I demand that these bad men, together with all the property they took off, shall be delivered to Capt. Levering, or that you shall deliver them and the property to me.

My Children, the blood of those innocent men who have been wounded and murdered cries aloud to the Great Spirit for vengeance. The hearts of their relations and brethren bleed with sorrow. The fire of revenge flames in their hearts, and they thirst for blood.

My Children, I have found it almost impossible to prevent the white people from rushing to your towns, to destroy your corn, burn your property, take your women and children prisoners, and murder your warriors. But I told them that those who have done the mischief were bad men; that you would disapprove their conduct, and deliver them to me as enemies both to you and your white

Courtesy of the Illinois State Historical Library

Governor Ninian Edwards

brethren. I commanded your white brethren not to raise the tomahawk or go to war with you, and they obeyed me.

My Children, now open your ears to hear my words, and let them
sink deep into your hearts. If you wish for peace with us, you must
do us justice. If you disapprove those murders and other outrages
that have been committed, you must deliver up the offenders; for if
you harbor among you such deadly enemies to us, you cannot be
our friends, and you ought not to expect our friendship.

My Children, Gov. Harrison demanded some of those bad men,
when they were within his Territory, and they fled to the Illinois
River and took up shelter among you. I now demand them and you
must not say they are fled elsewhere. They murdered our people—
they are our enemies—and if you have protected them and they

belong to your bands, you must find them and deliver them up, or we must consider you as approving their horrid deeds and as being our enemies.

My Children, liars and bad advisers are among you; they profess to be your friends, and they deceive you; they have their interest in view and care not what becomes of you, if they can succeed in their designs. Avoid such people.

My Children, you can remember when such men persuaded you to make war upon your white brethren of the United States. They promised you great assistance, but they left you to fight your own battles, and you found it necessary to sue for peace. At that time you were stronger than you now are; the woods were then full of game of all kinds; large numbers of you could collect together and traverse the country without fear of wanting meat. But this cannot now be done.

My Children, when we were at war with you, we were then weak; we have now grown strong—have everything necessary for war, and are your near neighbors. Our Great Father's dominions extend over vast countries, bounded by the great waters; his great towns and cities are hardly to be counted; and his white children are thick and numerous like the stars of the sky.

My Children, your Great Father, the President of the United States, has nothing to fear from wars, but he wishes to be at peace with you, because he loves you and wishes to make you happy. You ought to try to merit his kindness and avoid his resentment.

My Children, your Great Father asks nothing but justice from you. Suffer not bad advisers to persuade you to refuse it. In kindness, none can exceed him; but if you should be determined to treat him and his white children as enemies, storms and hurricanes, and the thunder and lightening of heaven, cannot be more terrible than will be his resentment.

My Children, Capt. Samuel Levering will deliver you this talk; he is authorized, by me, to demand of you the property that has been stolen, and those bad men who committed the murders, and all who were of the party. You will confer with Capt. Levering, and come to as speedy a determination as possible.

My Children, let justice be done, let all cause of quarrel be removed, and let us live like brothers.

Your affectionate father,

Ninian Edwards

'To Cover the Bones of Our Tribe'

POTAWATOMI CHIEF

My Father,—We have listened to what you have said. We shall now retire to our camps and consult upon it. You will hear nothing more from us at present.

It might be inferred from the attention with which the proposition was received, that they were not averse to it, though the cautious reply we have quoted furnished nothing from which an opinion, either favourable or unfavourable, could be drawn. This led us to expect their formal reply of the 19th with increased interest. It was delivered by the same person who had spoken before, and as this speech evinces a cast of retrospection which is not usual, and a hesitancy between following the policy of selling their lands adopted by their forefathers, or stopping short;— together with a boldness of sentiment, tempered by a fear to offend, and finally, by a negative to the proposition, which was afterward reversed, we shall present it entire.

My Father,—We meet you here to-day, because we had promised it, to tell you our minds, and what we have agreed upon among ourselves. You will listen to us with a good mind, and believe what we say.

My Father,—You know that we first came to this country, a long time ago, and when we sat ourselves down upon it, we met with a great many hardships and difficulties. Our country was then very large, but it has dwindled away to a small spot; and you wish to purchase that! This has caused us to reflect much upon what you have told us, and we have, therefore, brought along all the chiefs and warriors, and the young men and women and children of our tribe, that one part may not do what the others object to, and that all may be witnesses of what is going forward.

My Father,—You know your children. Since you first came among them, they have listened to your words with an attentive ear; and have always hearkened to your counsels. Whenever you have had a proposal to make to us—whenever you have had a favour to ask of us, we have always lent a favourable ear, and our invariable answer has been "Yes." This you know!

My Father,—A long time has passed since we first came upon our lands; and our people have all sunk into their graves. They had sense. We are all young and foolish, and do not wish to do any thing

From Milo Milton Quaife, ed., *Pictures of Illinois One Hundred Years Ago* (Chicago, 1919), pp. 124-128.

Courtesy of the Illinois State Historical Library

Potawatomi Indian

that they would not approve, were they living. We are fearful we shall offend their spirits if we sell our lands; and we are fearful we shall offend you, if we do *not* sell them. This has caused us great perplexity of thought, because we have counselled among ourselves, and do not know how we can part with the land.

My Father,—Our country was given to us by the Great Spirit, who gave it to us to hunt upon, and to make down our beds upon, when we die. And he would never forgive us, should we now bargain it away. When you first spoke to us for lands at St. Mary's,* we said we had a little, and agreed to sell you a piece of it; but we told you we could spare no more. Now, you ask us again. You are never satisfied!

My Father,—We have sold you a great tract of land, already; but it is not enough! We sold it to you for the benefit of your children, to farm and to live upon. We have now but little left. We shall want it all for ourselves. We know not how long we may live, and we wish to leave some lands for our children to hunt upon. You are gradually taking away our hunting grounds. Your children are driving us before them. We are growing uneasy. What lands you have, you may retain for ever; but we shall sell no more.

My Father,—You think, perhaps, that I speak in passion; but my heart is good towards you. I speak like one of your own children. I am an Indian, a red-skin, and live by hunting and fishing, but my country is already too small; and I do not know how to bring up my children, if I give it all away. We sold you a fine tract of land at St. Mary's. We said to you then, it was enough to satisfy your children, and the last we should sell; and we thought it would be the last you would ask for.

My Father,—We have now told you what we had to say. It is what was determined on, in council among ourselves; and what I have spoken is the voice of my nation. On this account, all our people have come here to listen to me; but do not think we have a bad opinion of you. Where should we get a bad opinion of you? We speak to you with a good heart, and the feelings of a friend.

My Father,—You are acquainted with this piece of land—the country we live in. Shall we give it up? Take notice it is a small piece of land, and if we give it away, what will become of us? The Great Spirit, who has provided it for our use, allows us to keep it, to bring up our young men and support our families. We should incur his anger, if we bartered it away. If we had more land, you should get more, but our land has been wasting away ever since the

*Ohio.

white people became our neighbours, and we have now hardly enough left to cover the bones of our tribe.

. . . .

My Father,—We all shake hands with you.* Behold our warriors, our women, and children. Take pity on us, and on our words.

*This, it will be perceived, is a figurative expression, much used.

Part II

THE PRAIRIE YEARS, 1818-1860

Introduction

In point of fact, Illinois hardly deserved its instant statehood. Although it was the second largest state in size in 1818, it had the fewest people—just under 35,000—concentrated predominantly in the southern tip of the state. The northern and central counties contained about 12,000 Indians and a few white traders. There were no roads to speak of; travel was restricted to muddy paths that were still often patrolled by outlaws. Climate in the southern region—known as the American Bottom—was notoriously unhealthy as a result of the low-lying, swampy terrain. Potential settlers were warned of the malaria, typhus, pneumonia, and milk sickness that awaited them in the hot, fly-infested cabins of the unsettled territory. Only two settlements, Shawneetown and Kaskaskia, could claim any resemblance to established communities. The former, a nest of some thirty log houses on the junction of the Ohio and Wabash rivers, was a commercial center for pioneers spread out northward along the Wabash. Directly across the state, Kaskaskia served a similar function for an estimated 15,000 settlers who were thinly scattered along the tributaries of the Kaskaskia and Mississippi rivers.

Nevertheless, there were some advantages in moving to Illinois in 1818: the settler could acquire land without rent or taxes; there was timber for cabins, furniture, fences, and fuel; the land was productive and game was plentiful. And, to ease the plagues of insects, disease, and summer's heat, there was corn whiskey—plenty of it—at 20 cents a gallon, or it could be home-brewed to yield two gallons per bushel of corn.

The first state government was as primitive and simple as frontier life itself. Governor Shadrach Bond had barely mastered the basics of grammar. Until a permanent structure was built at Vandalia in 1820, the capitol was a rented, low-ceilinged Kaskaskia dwelling no more elaborate than a farmhouse. Money was a chronic problem: efforts to raise revenue by means of a land tax and a lottery failed, and the treasury was in constant need of funds. Equally vexing to the new government was the slavery question. Southern-born residents, led by Governor Bond and Justice Joseph Phillips, tried to legalize the institution in Illinois in order to provide the heavy labor force necessary for such ventures as the salt works near Shawnee-town. But a new governor, Virginian Edward Coles, aided by Morris Birkbeck and his colony of English farmers at Albion, turned back the effort in an 1824 popular referendum by a vote of 6,640 to 4,972.

Birkbeck and his countrymen had come to Illinois to prove the practicability of an experiment which the Southern-born settlers had rejected out of hand—that the prairie could be profitably farmed. In contrast to the Southern frontiersman, who believed that there was something inherently wrong with soil that could not support timber, Birkbeck argued that prairie soil, once broken, was the richest in America. Many people from regions outside the South listened to Birkbeck. Beginning in the 1830s, Yankee settlers, attracted by the relatively cheap price the government was asking for the attractive grassland, migrated to the prairie in sizable numbers. Some came by stage from Detroit to Chicago; some floated down the Ohio and then up the Mississippi by steamboat; but most came via the Great Lakes over the newly completed Erie Canal.

The Yankee migration transformed Illinois from a slowly grow-ing, crude frontier society to an expanding community alive with new towns, colleges, newspapers, and internal improvements. And as news of the booming West reached the eastern cities, European arrivals there set their hopes on opportunities offered in the Prairie State. Partly as a reflection of the changing demography, the capital was moved north from Vandalia to Springfield in 1837.

However, not all were welcome in Illinois. When Black Hawk and 1500 Sauk braves and their families returned to the state in 1831 in search of land on which to plant corn, the frontiersmen's instinc-tive distrust of the Indian quickly turned to panic. The governor raised an army of some 3,000 men (one of whom was young Captain Abraham Lincoln) to hound the families into Wisconsin and, finally, to a slaughter at the Battle of Bad Ax on the east bank of the Mississippi River.

The Mormons met with much the same fate: violence and expul-sion. Although Joseph Smith and his Latter Day Saints were ac-cepted upon their arrival at Quincy from Missouri in 1839, local reaction to their presence grew rapidly hostile. The causes of the mounting alarm were the remarkable growth of a virtually autono-mous community with its own standing army at Nauvoo, its unusual religious beliefs, and—after 1841—rumors of polygamy. Added to these alarming developments were increasing reports of counterfeiting and lawlessness at the Mormon city, which by 1844 was the largest municipality in the state. The crisis came that year when Smith ordered the destruction of a hostile Nauvoo newspaper. Seeking to avoid an open clash between his Nauvoo Legion and the militia called by Governor Ford to maintain order, Smith went to the county seat at Carthage to answer charges brought against him by the editor of the destroyed newspaper. A few days later he and his brother Hyrum were murdered by a mob in the Carthage jail. After a bitter organizational struggle, the Mormons at Nauvoo elected to leave the Prairie State. A small number stayed on for a short time under the leadership of the Smith family before moving to Independence, Missouri, but most followed the next prophet, Brigham Young, westward in search of a new Zion in the Rockies.

By the time of the Mormon expulsion, Illinois had passed out of the frontier stage of development. Gone were the primitive log settlements (such as the one re-created at Salem); as visitors noted, they were being replaced by bustling brick towns and prosperous prairie farms. Illinoisans themselves wrote of new railroads and colleges as they looked with optimism toward the approaching decade of the 1850s. A new constitution, adopted in 1848, reformed and modernized the structure of state government. Chicago was a boom city beyond belief. No one anticipated civil war, at least not until Lincoln and Douglas sounded the tocsin on the slavery issue in their forensic exchange during the 1858 senatorial election.

1: Pioneer Life

In the opening chapter of *The Frontier State, 1818-1848*, another book in the series commemorating the centennial of Illinois statehood, Theodore Calvin Pease discusses the land and its people. He portrays the Indian tribes, the frontier hunter, English colonists, and the arrival of the permanent settlers. With the coming of prairie farmers, who were first attracted to the state by the English agricultural experiments at Albion near the Wabash, Pease detects signs of civilization and the coming end of the frontier stage of development. A noted authority on early Illinois history, Pease is the author of *The Story of Illinois* (1925) and *George Rogers Clark and the Revolution in Illinois, 1763-1787* (1929), and editor of *Illinois Election Returns, 1818-1848* (1923) and *The Laws of the Northwest Territory* (1925). Besides being a professor of history at the University of Illinois, Pease was the director and president of the Illinois State Historical Society and editor of the *American Archivist*. The second selection, by Edward Everett Dale, concerns eating habits on the frontier. Dale received his doctorate from Harvard in 1914 and taught at the University of Oklahoma, where he was head of the history department between 1924 and 1942. He has written a number of books on the American Southwest, including *A History of Oklahoma* (Norman, Okla., 1924), *Cow Country* (1942), *The Indians of the Southwest* (1949), and *The Vanquished Prairie* (1973).

N. Dwight Harris' monograph on slavery in Illinois appeared in 1904 and it remains the only thorough treatment of that subject. The work is essentially a revision of his doctoral dissertation at the University of Chicago in 1901. His narrative picks up the story of the Illinois blacks after the 1824 defeat of an effort to introduce slavery into the state by means of a special constitutional convention. Although the defeat of that convention movement made the state theoretically "safe from slavery for all time," in Harris' words, the condition of the Illinois black was actually little changed from the days when slavery had been tolerated. Masters who already owned slaves could keep them, slave-buying and -selling continued, and even free blacks were not allowed by law to testify against whites in court. Indentureship, a modified form of slavery limited by contract to definite periods of time, served in many parts of the state as a substitute for slavery until the late 1830s. Nor were Illinoisans receptive to criticisms of the "peculiar institution" where it was permitted to exist in the South. Antislavery agitation never got off the ground, except in a handful of northern and central counties; the results of abolitionist activity, Harris concedes, "were not over-propitious." Another unattractive aspect of pioneer life is discussed by Professor Donald F. Tingley, of Eastern Illinois University, in his article on anti-intellectualism on the Illinois frontier. Tingley has also published " 'The Robin's Egg Renaissance': Chicago and the Arts, 1910-1923," *Journal of the Illinois State Historical Society*, LXIII (1970), 35-55. And in the *Transactions of the Illinois State Historical Society* of 1905, James Haines portrays the everyday life of pioneer settlers in terms of dress and amusements. Haines came to Illinois from Ohio in 1823 at the age of five, along with his parents and ten brothers and sisters. They settled in Tazewell County near Peoria.

Special Accounts

The Prairie State

THEODORE C. PEASE

Change and evolution sound the keynote of frontier Illinois. For the first thirty years of statehood its politicians sprang up, flourished, changed sides, and left the state to seek new careers with a rapidity that is the despair of the chronicler. Pioneers passed over its territory in waves with varying manners, ideals, and habits of life. Civilization first of simple, then of more complex, gradations sprang up with amazing rapidity behind and among the frontiersmen. The half savage frontiersman and the college-bred lawyer, the woman of the backwoods and the fine lady rubbed elbows in the little village where the frame house was rapidly replacing the log cabin. Into communities without religion came numerous denominations striving to supply the lack of spiritual life. Churches were organized, were torn by quarrels and secessions, and yet reached out for better education. Above all, this community ready and eager to go up and possess the land continually had to fight politically in the hope of obtaining from its landlord, the federal government, better and better terms for the acquisition of its land.

. . . .

From Theodore C. Pease, *The Frontier State, 1818-1848* (Chicago, 1918), pp. 1-3, 6-9, 12-19, 22-24. Footnotes in the original have been omitted.

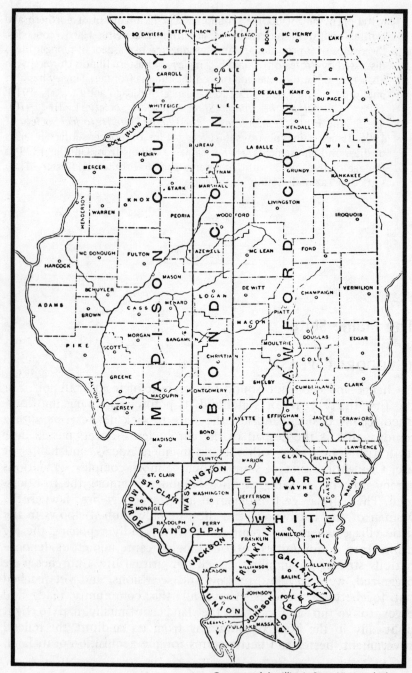

Courtesy of the Illinois State Historical Library

The county boundaries of Illinois in 1818

On the day when Illinois was both territory and state its population of some 35,000 lay in two columns on opposite sides of the
state, resting on the connection with the outside world furnished by
the Mississippi, the Ohio, and the Wabash rivers respectively. The
population clustered in the rich river bottom, gift of the Mississippi,
where Illinois history began, and in the neighborhood of the United
States saline in Gallatin county. It tended always to make settlements on water courses for the sake of securing timber, water, and
easy communication. Away from the rivers lay an unpopulated
region in the interior of southern Illinois, where the traveler to St.
Louis or Kaskaskia who preferred to cut across by road from
Vincennes or Shawneetown rather than pole up the Mississippi,
could still stage tales of robbers, murders, and hairbreadth escapes.
On the east population had crept north, clinging closely to the
Wabash, as far as the present Edgar county. On the west settlements
had reached the southern part of Calhoun county and were pushing
up the creeks into Greene and Macoupin; they had also followed
the Kaskaskia and its south-flowing tributaries, so that settlements
lay in Bond, Clinton, and Washington counties. Elsewhere there was
wilderness.

To the north of the area of settlement lay another world distinct
and independent from that to the south. The Kickapoo Indians still
inhabited central Illinois, and the Sauk and Foxes, chastised in the
War of 1812, but still morose, occupied a little of the territory
northwest of the Illinois river—the Military Bounty Tract—though
this had for some time been surveyed and allotted in military
bounties to soldiers of the War of 1812. The main strength of the
Sauk and Foxes in Illinois, however, lay in the territory near the
junction of the Rock and the Mississippi, where Fort Armstrong on
Rock Island had lately risen to overawe them. In the territory east
of them lay villages of Winnebago and Potawatomi. Among them in
northern Illinois and on the Illinois and the Wabash rivers wandered
the fur traders of the American Fur Company; these came south
down the lake in their Mackinaw boats each fall, dragged their boats
over the Chicago portage to the Des Plaines river, went into winter
trading posts along the Illinois from which trading expeditions were
sent out during the winter, and carried their harvest of furs to
Mackinac in the spring. Besides Fort Armstrong there lay in this
district Fort Edwards on the Mississippi, Fort Clark at the present
site of Peoria, and Fort Dearborn; though as Indian dangers waned
and Indian cessions were consummated, the forts were successively
abandoned.

. . . .

It is not easy to describe, or even to divide into classes, the newcomers who were sweeping over the land of Illinois. On the outskirts of settlement was a fringe of hunters leading a half savage life in the forests, supporting their families by the products of the hunt and by the produce of a few acres of cornland planted among the girdled forest trees. Their life was a series of retreats before the advance of civilization, and they were ever ready to sell their improvements to a newcomer and to push out one stage further into the wilderness.

It is possible to differentiate this first class from later comers only in degree, since the men of the whole frontier were more or less migrating. The men who succeeded the hunters came also from the south for the most part, yet they were in various degrees more civilized in their habits, laid less emphasis on hunting and more on building, making improvements, and clearing land for the corn-fields. They very often possessed hogs and cattle which furnished to the little towns a continually increasing amount of raw products to be traded for store goods and to be freighted in flatboats or

A pioneer cabin

Courtesy of the Illinois State Historical Library

keel-boats down the Ohio and Mississippi as articles of commerce. This produce of the farm was not only corn, ginseng, beeswax, salted pork, tallow, hides, and beef, the last named sometimes bought by the storekeepers on the hoof and slaughtered for market, but also various rough wool and flax fabrics. Important in the frontier market were such items as deer skins and venison hams, distinctly the products of the rifle rather than of the hoe.

The habit of some writers to classify these southern men as hunter pioneers and to contrast them with the New England and northern farmers who settled the prairies of the north is misleading unless the contrast is carefully limited and defined. The settlers of the south hunted, as did white men everywhere in the wilderness where there were no game laws. They enlarged their cornlands by clearing the forest instead of cultivating the prairies because, in the decade in which they settled the state, farmers preferred such lands, chiefly because the forested lands offered greater accessibility to wood and water, partly because they lacked the capital necessary for breaking up and fencing the prairie, and partly because the scarcity of markets offered no temptation to raise grain that could not be sold. Without a heavy ox team breaking the prairie was almost impossible, and without improved transportation produce could not be carried to market.

. . . .

Besides this class of so-called hunter pioneers the community had a set of young men of education, of legal training, and of good address, who aspired to the leadership of the community. Frequently they had a few hundreds or thousands to invest in land speculations. Some of them married into the well-to-do French families. They were men of more finished manner than the average pioneer, and their wives and daughters speedily gave the community a touch of sophistication. Doubtless it was for this class the stores advertised the finer goods such as silks, crêpes, and other fabrics of similar character, and kept the choicer wines, liquors, and groceries.

The conditions in the towns are more or less truthfully mirrored in the contemporary newspapers. In the towns, when the state was young, the rising brick and frame houses contrasted sharply with the log cabins of the territorial days; yet the stage of civilization must not be overestimated, for even in 1821 Shawneetown had no courthouse, jail, church, or school. The towns were disorderly places at best, a Shawneetown Sunday being a byword. Frequently they were rendered unhealthy by pools of stagnant water and by the lack of all sanitation. In 1822 the trustees of Shawneetown had to pass an ordinance providing for the removal of dead animals and for the laying of sidewalks.

. . . .

In the Illinois of 1818 Shawneetown seemed to hold a favorable position as the gateway, a fact which had been recognized by the United States government by the designation of the town as a port of entry. It was the natural Illinois *entrepôt* for the eastern part of the state and for the country up the tributaries of the Wabash. One rival to its trade near at hand, however, was the New Harmony settlement of Frederick Rapp, which in 1823 maintained a store in Shawneetown for the sale of its goods, woolen cloths, cottons, hats, shoes, stockings, leather, flour, wine, whisky, brandy, beer, etc., as well as a line of eastern goods from Philadelphia. Rapp's failure to buy as well as sell made him unpopular, however, with the resident merchants.

. . . .

The history of the development of Illinois between 1818 and 1822 would be incomplete without mention of a concerted scheme of colonization that, running in channels completely different from those which carried the ordinary course of settlement, was to influence the development of the state out of all proportion to the numbers engaged in it. This enterprise was the settlement of English Prairie in Edwards county by Morris Birkbeck and the Flowers. At its inception the motive force in the movement was the discontent with economic and political conditions in England that affected men of the comparatively affluent classes. For example, Morris Birkbeck by his industry and ability had raised himself to the position of a tenant farmer, farming on long lease a holding of 1,500 acres in the hamlet of Wanborough; yet he was not a freeholder and therefore not entitled to the vote; he chafed at the social and political inferiority which thus marked him, as well as at the heavy taxes and tithes levied on him by the parliament in which he had no voice and by the church in which he was not a communicant. He aspired, to use his own words, to leave his children citizens of "a flourishing, public-spirited, energetic community, where the insolence of wealth, and the servility of pauperism, between which, in England, there is scarcely an interval remaining, are alike unknown." The United States seemed to him the realization of his political ideals; and except for his detestation of slavery he looked on its institutions and the assumed political and social virtues of its republic and citizens through glasses of rose tint. No less attractive perhaps was the opportunity it afforded him of becoming a free-

Courtesy of the Illinois State Historical Library

A painting of Park House, Albion, Illinois

holder at a rate comparable to English rental values. George Flower, son of Birkbeck's friend, Richard Flower, who had been sent to the United States in search of land, had conceived a romantic affection for the prairies of which he had read in Imlay's *Topographical Description of the Western Territory of North America.* When at last he and Birkbeck crossed the Wabash into Illinois and attained the Boltonhouse prairie, depressed as they had been by the mighty forests through which they had journeyed, the broad expanse of meadow stretching for miles embayed in the surrounding timber seemed to them the manor park that they coveted, and they hastened to acquire as much of it as their funds would permit.

In presenting their design of a colony to the English public by the publication of Birkbeck's letters, the promoters strove to induce men of their own social status—tenant farmers possessed of capital and desirous of becoming landholders—to take up land from them or in their vicinity. As a complement this necessarily required the establishment of a class comparable to English agricultural laborers or cottagers; and in fact the enemies of the enterprise later insinuated that while holding great tracts for wealthy emigrants who never came, the promoters refused to sell smaller tracts to poorer men. The accusation was made that they had founded a rich man's settlement. The first settlers to come, however, were mechanics and laborers, who had not been concerned in the original enterprise but who were attracted by Birkbeck's books.

Birkbeck, who remained on the ground over winter with the uncertain labor obtainable from the backwoodsmen—half hunters, half farmers—who surrounded him, was not able to get accommodations completed for newcomers. Food for the first year had largely to be procured from the nearby Rapp community at New Harmony in Indiana. The newcomers and such wealthier immigrants as followed fared well or ill, according to their ability to work for themselves and to make the best of backwoods conditions. Men without large capital or enterprise missed the agricultural laboring class of England and the presence of women servants, and they were described by persons not well disposed to the enterprise as for the time reduced to squalid wretchedness. Attacks inspired by the "borough managers," so the leaders believed, and by men interested in eastern lands who enlisted in their behalf the sharp pen of Cobbett—sometimes known as Porcupine Cobbett—spread the tales of the wretchedness and woe existing at English Prairie. They made the most of expressions of pleasure by Birkbeck at the absence of all religious observance on the frontier and used them to brand the enterprise as irreligious; this accusation was met by the building of churches, in one of which Unitarian and in the other Episcopal services were installed by Flower and Birkbeck, respectively.

. . . .

By 1819 there were 400 English and 700 Americans in the settlement. They had established comfortable homes and large farm structures, had discovered the futility, in default of labor, of extensive grain farming, were turning their attention to the raising of cattle, sheep, and hogs, and were making progress. Practical farmers with money and industry were doing well, and good laborers imported by the leaders were acquiring lands of their own. The leaders had perhaps totally abandoned their desire of a cluster of manors in southeastern Illinois, as they discovered that the English agricultural laborers they imported also caught the land fever. Men of narrower views believed they saw in the lack of labor a justification of negro slavery and a necessity for it. Men like Birkbeck were able to accept the facts as they were and at the same time to foresee an Illinois of free farmers, neither masters nor servants.

The enterprise had done much for Illinois. It had brought the prairie into notice if not into vogue. Against the agriculture necessarily practiced by the farmer of small means—a cornpatch among trees girdled by the ax, growing larger year by year—it had set the utility of prairie land either for grazing or for grain when broken as it could be by men able to afford a six-ox team. Through the numerous books of Birkbeck, the Flowers, and others, it had brought Illinois into notice not only in England but in the eastern United States and in continental Europe as well. More important still, it had in Morris Birkbeck brought to the state a leader whose services in the struggle with slavery were past all estimate.

Almost equally important was Birkbeck's influence in the advancement of scientific agriculture. The call for the formation of an agricultural society appeared October 8, 1819, in the *Edwardsville Spectator*. It was signed "A Farmer of Madison" and hence may very possibly have originated with Edward Coles. At the meeting for organization held on November 10, the society elected Birkbeck president and Coles first vice president, and it speedily drew the support of the prominent men of the state. It offered premiums not only for wheat, corn, hay, and fine livestock, but also for hemp, flax, cotton, homespun cloth—the premium for this last was in 1823 awarded to Governor Bond—tobacco, castor oil, wool, malt liquor, salt, and cheese. Agricultural societies, with some emphasis on the policy of non-importation due to the hardness of the times, were founded in Madison and Bond counties; and these were affiliated with the state society.

. . . .

If it is difficult to describe frontier Illinois in its physical aspects since it is impossible to describe it in its mental and spiritual; the evidence is even more fragmentary and more subject to bias in the observers. . . .

Some general characteristics can be positively described. English observers, friendly or hostile, commented on the open and unabashed manner of the people. In the Illinois frontiersman there was none of the self-conscious awkward rusticity of the English peasant. The instillation of the doctrine of liberty and equality undoubtedly had so far borne fruit as to make the conviction of his own dignity apparent in the conversation of every man. The interpretation put upon this attitude and the form it took naturally varied with the attitude of the observer. If he expected his money to buy him obsequiousness he was disappointed and had to complain often of a positive bad faith and trickiness which at times may well have been a desperate attempt on the part of the native to vindicate an affront to his dignity. If the traveler met all men with an open friendliness, he generally encountered in return a real kindliness and courtesy. If the frontiersman was appealed to as a man for help and sympathy he usually responded in liberal measure. If he was hired as a servant, little good could be expected from him.

. . . .

How far social distinctions divided the frontier state into classes, it is difficult to say. Most observers remarked that, the backwoods pioneer being omitted, the various classes did not vary nearly so much in intellectual grasp as in England. "In this remote part of America, judges, generals of militia, colonels, captains, and esquires, are not generally men of property or education; and it is usual to see them employed in any common kind of labour. Yet I have seen men among them that possess very good abilities; far from ignorant, and much better informed than could be expected from their appearance." So far as wealth and its means of display were concerned, however, the basis for social distinction existed. When Shawneetown was a village of one brick and several frame houses amid a cluster of log cabins, it boasted one jewelry store which at least advertised a surprisingly wide selection. Advertisements of silks, satins, broadcloths, muslins, cambrics, and silk gloves, among plaids and cheap stuffs and offerings of fine groceries and Madeira wine as well as of whisky by the barrel prove the existence of such distinctions. To take action against the importation of such luxuries, societies were formed between the years 1819 and 1821. The political aspirations of the well-to-do men doubtless induced them, especially at elections, to keep such distinctions in the background. Nevertheless the society of afternoon teas and great dinners must have lived side by side with the simple society whose social events were the dance after the corn husking or barn raising and the gathering at the county seat on court day or at the camp meeting, the last two probably partaken of by rich as well as by poor. Woods mentions husking, raising, reaping, rolling, picking, sewing, and quilting frolics; and they were much more common than their mention in the contemporary literature of the frontier might lead one to suppose.

. . . .

Such systematic education as the state afforded was supplied by private schools and for a price, for the state during the first decade made scarcely any use of its endowment from the federal government. Some of the schools were of about the grade of grammar schools; and girls' schools where needlework, painting, and similar subjects were taught for an extra charge were not uncommon. Frequently board was offered also. Charges for tuition varied from three dollars and fifty cents to seven dollars a quarter, according to subjects taught, needlework in girls' schools usually being an extra.

There was not wanting, however, more ambitious establishments. One at Salu was kept by a New England schoolma'am. The Reverend Mr. Desmoulin had a school in Kaskaskia in which he taught Latin and French. At Ebenezer they advertised for a preceptor who was qualified to teach Greek, Latin, and the higher mathematics. At Galena in 1829 a school (Aratus Kent's) purported to teach Latin and Greek. One public school at Alton was free to the children of parents residing in the corporation, for Alton had been incorporated with an endowment of one hundred lots for religious and educational purposes.

The foundations of collegiate education were laid before the end of the period. In 1827 the indefatigable John Mason Peck opened a seminary at Rock Spring as a theological training school, equipping it with the books and other property that he had collected in the east. It was intended primarily for the education of ministers, but in addition it offered courses in literature and the sciences. At a meeting at Rock Spring, January 1, 1827, Peck was appointed superintendent and agent to obtain funds. It was decided that a farm for student labor be operated and that subscriptions be solicited for buildings payable in provisions, cattle, labor, books, or building materials. Contribution entitled a subscriber to send his children or wards without charge for rent or for the use of the library. The school was to have a theological professor and one for mathematics, natural philosophy, and languages.

Religion came to be the most universally pervasive intellectual force of the frontier. As might be expected, on the frontier the first tendency was toward a disregard of religious observances. The emigrant from the older settled regions left behind him the machinery and the establishment of sectarian religion. Until that machinery could be set up again on the frontier he lived without formal worship and often for the time at least the sense of the need of it passed out of his life. In cases where observance had been due to social convention there was no doubt a welcome feeling of freedom and restraint.

Normally the frontiersman was unreligious. Birkbeck noted with relish the absence of ceremony at baptism or funeral and the tolerance of all backwoods preachers alike, whether they raved or reasoned. Sunday was a day for riot and disorder. Other observers looked with horror on such a state of things, did their best to set up at least stated regular worship, and noted an improvement in morals as a result. Yet for years the riot and license of a Shawneetown Sabbath was a shocking thing to a prim New England bride. Further, if one may believe the early preachers of both Baptists and Methodists, deistic and atheistic belief flourished on the frontier among even the better classes. Evidence is not lacking to corroborate the frequency of this attitude of mind, which accentuated the sharp line drawn among men between the religious and the irreligious, the good and the wicked. The latter term connoted those who did not fall in with the beliefs and practices of the denominationally pious. The idea of the sheep and goats divided by observances and beliefs, possibly also by such habits as profane swearing and drinking, persists in the pioneer narratives. "A man of good character," wrote Fordham, "is an acquisition; not that there is a small proportion of such men, but because the bad are as undisguisedly bad, as their opposites are professedly good. This is not the land of Hypocrisy. It would not here have its reward. Religion is not the road to worldly respectability, nor a possession of it the cloak of immorality."

Into this western wilderness containing many who had grown accustomed to the lack of religious food, many who openly professed diabolism, and many who yearned for religious observances, the organizations of the Protestant denominations threw themselves.

. . . .

Food of the Frontier

EDWARD E. DALE

Though food is the most fundamental of all human needs it varies widely among the different peoples of the world and is subject to numerous curious taboos and prejudices. "What's one man's poison . . . is another's meat or drink" seems to have a large element of truth. The Comanche and Kiowa Indians never ate the wild turkeys which swarmed along the streams of their homeland in

From Edward E. Dale, "The Food of the Frontier," *Journal of the Illinois State Historical Society*, XL (1947), 38-62. Reprinted by permission of the Illinois State Historical Society.

such abundance, but they were very fond of dog stew, roasted
terrapins, or the broiled entrails of buffalo and cattle. The French
consider snails a great delicacy though the late Will Rogers often
asserted that he himself "would really prefer grasshoppers."

Diet and dietary habits are, moreover, national or regional in
their nature, and various peoples seem to be characterized by a
certain article or articles of food. We have the rice of China,
spaghetti of Italy, caviar of Russia, tortillas of Mexico, and sauer-
kraut and sausages of Germany. In our own country it is the same.
It is commonly said that you "never know beans until you go to
Boston." Baked beans, brown bread, and codfish cakes, however,
are common throughout all New England, just as are fried chicken,
spoon bread, and beaten biscuits in the South. Virginia has Smith-
field ham and hominy grits, the Northwest coast has grilled salmon.
Texas has borrowed from Mexico hot tamales and chile con carne
while beefsteak, apple pie, and ice cream are so universal as to be
virtually national in scope.

. . . .

One of the first tasks of virtually every frontier settler was to
plan and plant a garden in order to furnish his family with an ample
supply of vegetables. These were of many kinds, including beans,
peas, squashes, pumpkins, radishes, mustard, lettuce, carrots, beets,
onions, turnips, cabbage, potatoes, sweet potatoes, cucumbers, melons, and several others. Tomatoes, formerly called "love apples,"
were in early days thought to be poisonous but were occasionally
grown as ornamental plants because of the beauty of the bright red
fruit. It was some years before it was learned that they are a
wholesome article of food and they became a commonly grown
vegetable on the American frontier.

Pending the growth of a garden, the pioneer settler must depend
upon such native products as were available for fresh vegetable food
but these were often of considerable variety. The Indians consumed
quantitites of wild onions of which they were very fond, but these
were seldom eaten by the white settlers. Yet, there were many wild
products which were widely utilized, including several kinds of
"wild greens" such as lamb's quarter, "poke salad," dandelions, and
two or three varieties of dock. Boiled with a piece of salt pork, any
of these furnished a tasty and satisfying food and, while the pioneer
had never heard of vitamins, such wild pottage was regarded as
conducive to health and in addition furnished a welcome change
from the dry or salt food which had been the ordinary diet of the
winter months.

Once garden vegetables were available the pioneer usually had an

The interior of a pioneer cabin

ample supply of fresh vegetable food throughout the summer and early autumn. Mustard, spinach, turnip tops, cabbage, and collards took the place of the "wild greens." Green peas, commonly called "English peas," were boiled with new potatoes with the addition of a lump of butter and half a cup of milk into which had been stirred a spoonful of flour. String beans and potatoes were also boiled together with a slab of salt pork. Potatoes were cooked in a variety of ways and sweet potatoes were roasted in the ashes or boiled. In some cases, raw sweet potatoes were cut in thick slices and fried for breakfast. Squashes were baked in the shell or cut into pieces and stewed with the addition of a little sugar. Turnips and cabbage were boiled with salt pork. Radishes, lettuce, and spring onions were eaten raw and mature onions fried in butter or pork fat. Also onions, boiled beets, and raw cucumbers were sliced and covered with vinegar, and boiled beets were often sliced and buttered.

The pioneer settlers usually put away large quantities of vegetables for winter use. Green corn was boiled, cut from the cob, and dried in the sun. Beans and peas were shelled when dry and put in sacks to be hung from the rafters of the smoke house. Potatoes, sweet potatoes, turnips, beets, cabbage, and pumpkins were stored in a "root cellar" or merely piled up in heaps in the field or garden and covered, first with hay, then with a thick layer of earth to prevent their freezing. Slices of peeled pumpkin were commonly dried in the sun and long strings of onions hung up in the smokehouse, shed room, or cellar. Remote from markets, and with virtually no "money crop," the pioneer could concentrate each summer on the problem of providing an adequate supply of food for his family during the coming winter.

Lack of fruit proved a considerable hardship to many pioneer settlers, especially on the western prairies, though this was true to a somewhat less degree even in the wooded regions of the earlier frontier. Orchards and vineyards are of comparatively slow growth, usually requiring some years to come into full bearing. In the meantime, the settler must depend upon wild fruits and berries, or such fruit substitutes as could be grown in a single season. In the forested areas, wild grapes and plums of several varieties were abundant. In addition, there were often blackberries, dewberries, strawberries, raspberries, gooseberries, currants, papaws, and persimmons. These were eaten fresh, stewed, or made into pies and cobblers during the time they were in season, and made into preserves, jams, or jellies for winter use if sugar or even syrup could be had, but the supply of sugar was often very scanty. The wild berry bushes or vines were also dug up and transplanted to a plot of ground in the garden to form a "berry patch." In addition, virtually every settler sought to "put out an orchard" just as soon as possible.

. . . .

Virtually every pioneer settler was more or less a hunter and the same was true of all his sons above the age of ten or twelve years. Venison was often a staple article of food in the frontier home, and deer hams were hung up and cured for winter use. Fried quail, rabbit, and squirrel commonly appeared on the table, as did squirrel stew, pigeon or quail pot pie, and roast duck, goose, or turkey. Gradually the game disappeared, however, due to the ever-growing influx of settlers, but by the time it had become scarce the domestic animals had increased sufficiently to provide an ample supply of meat. After this, hunting declined as a serious business and became more of a sport or avocation. Yet in the absence of fresh meat during the greater part of the year, an occasional mess of quails, or squirrels, or a wild turkey made a most acceptable addition to the pioneer's ordinary fare. After the first few years, however, the staple meat of the frontier settler and his family was pork and its various products as ham, bacon, and sausage.

Pigs were "earmarked" when quite young so that each man might distinguish his own animals from those of his neighbors. Ranging at large in the woods, they fattened largest on the "mast" which was the general term for nuts and acorns. Perhaps this took a long time, but in the language of the Arkansas settler: "What is time to a hog?" It was customary, however, if at all possible, to call them up each evening and feed them a little corn or slops from the kitchen. This was designed, in the frontier vernacular, to "ha'nt 'em home"— attach them to the dwelling of their owner. This enabled him to see them each day, and also the additional food kept them growing faster and in a thriving condition. If sufficient corn had been grown, those designated for slaughter were confined in a pen for six weeks or more in the autumn and fed liberally on grain until they were fat enough to be butchered.

"Hog killing time," usually late in November, was a more or less gala occasion, especially for the children of the family. The meat was cut into hams, shoulders, and "middlings" or sides. These were carefully trimmed and "salted down" in barrels or large wooden boxes. The scraps trimmed away were ground into sausage which was seasoned with salt, pepper, and sage, and stuffed into long narrow sacks made of cloth to be hung in the smokehouse. Some preferred to pack the sausage in stone jars and pour melted lard on top of it. Others made the sausage into cakes which were fried, packed in jars, and covered with melted lard. The more usual method, however, was to pack it in sacks, but in the absence of material to make them it might be wrapped in cornhusks and hung in the smokehouse or "shed room." Hog killing also involved "rendering out" the lard, and the making of "souse" or head cheese. The liver, heart, backbones, and spareribs were eaten fresh and were often shared with some of the neighbors. Since people killed hogs at different times this mutual exchange of a surplus usually provided everyone in the community with fresh pork at intervals during a period of several weeks.

Methods of cooking fresh pork varied. Backbones were usually boiled, spareribs cut across three of four times and either fried or sprinkled with salt, pepper, and flour and baked in the oven. Pigs' feet were cleaned and boiled until very tender. They were then cut in two and either pickled in hot vinegar to which spices had been added, or dipped in batter and fried in hot fat. Sausage would keep for weeks or months. It was sliced in thick round slices or made into cakes and fried for breakfast. Many a man reared on the frontier can still remember the savory "sagey" odor of frying sausage which greeted him upon awakening in the morning and which proved the chief incentive to his rolling out of his warm bed into the icy cold of his sleeping quarters in the upstairs of a frontier farm home.

After some weeks, when the pork packed in barrels or boxes had thoroughly "taken salt," it was removed, and surplus salt was washed off, and the cut sides of the hams and shoulders rubbed with a mixture of black pepper and molasses. The meat was then hung up in the smokehouse and thoroughly smoked with hickory wood or chips. Sometimes the "side meat" was smoked to form bacon, but a part of it was often left in salt to be used as dry salt pork. The cured hams and shoulders would keep indefinitely though the bacon or "middlings" sometimes tended to get strong before the end of the following summer.

. . . .

On the frontier, beefsteak was almost never broiled. It was cut in slices, pounded with a mallet or the edge of a heavy plate or saucer, and then rolled in flour and fried in hot suet. Large cuts containing some bone were boiled, or sprinkled with flour and baked in the oven. After being served at one meal, what was left was sliced and served cold, or cut into small pieces and stewed with chopped potatoes and onions to form Irish stew or hash. With such an abundant supply of pork, ham, and bacon, together with some fresh beef from time to time, and the occasional use of game, it is not surprising that meat constituted a large part of the diet of the average pioneer settler. In fact, so much was consumed as to give rise to the old folk tale of the illiterate Irishman who had newly come to America and asked a friend to write a letter for him to send to his family in the Old Country. "Tell them," said he, "that here in America we have meat three times a week." "Why not say three times a day?" asked his friend. "Faith, no! It's no use to tell them that," was the answer. "They wouldn't believe it but would swear I was lyin'. Make it three times a week and maybe they might believe me."

Few frontier families considered a dessert necessary to the completion of a meal, except on Sunday or in case "company" was present. At other times the syrup pitcher was placed on the table three times a day and each meal was likely to be "topped off" with sorghum or some other form of syrup. Sorghum mills were usually more numerous than gristmills, and many settlers would grow a patch of sorghum which, when ripe, was cut and hauled to the mill to be ground and the juice settled down into sorghum "on the shares."

Despite the frequent absence of any form of dessert, the average pioneer housewife was skilled in making pies, cakes, and gingerbread. Cobblers were also made from peaches, blackqerries, or sweet potatoes, and fried pies known in the North as "turnovers" were common during the winter season. These were made by lining a saucer with "pie dough" which was not too rich and placing dried apples or peaches which had been stewed and crushed to a pulp on one side. The edge of the dough was then moistened all around so that the edges would stick together and the flap of dough folded over the fruit and the edges firmly pressed together. These half-moon shaped "pies" were then fried to a rich brown in deep fat and served hot. Properly made, they were delicious even if a somewhat heavy food. Children were usually very fond of them and were happy when one or two were placed in their lunch baskets or the "dinner buckets" that they carried to school.

. . . .

Faced with the necessity of improvising, the frontier housewife often showed rare ingenuity in matters of food. Lacking fruit, she baked a vinegar pie. This was made by mixing half a cupful of vinegar with a quart of water and adding sugar to taste. A lump of butter the size of an egg was then melted in a pan and a heaping teaspoonful of flour stirred into it. To this was added the tangy vinegar mixture, a little at a time, stirring it vigorously all the while until it had boiled sufficiently long to begin to thicken. The mixture was then poured into a piepan lined with a rich crust and additional strips of dough were "criss crossed" over the top. Bits of butter were sprinkled over these crossbars, and the pie was then baked in a hot oven. It came out with the crust a deep brown and the filling reduced to the consistency of jelly. To serve a considerable number of persons the quantity of the mixture was merely increased and baked in a long pan. This formed something in the nature of fruit cobbler and was sometimes called "vinegarone."

"Butter roll" was made of a rich biscuit dough which was rolled thin and sprinkled thickly with sugar and small lumps of butter. It was then rolled up and baked to a rich brown in a hot oven. Pies were also made from rhubarb, pie melons, squash, pumpkin, green tomatoes, green grapes, and even the fleshy acid leaves of the wild sheep sorrel. Nearly always, however, the housewife was faced with the problem of a shortage of sugar and, in many cases, honey, sorghum, or some other form of syrup, must be used as a substitute. Fortunately, there was usually an ample supply of milk, butter, and eggs and these helped vastly in preparing good meals even when other resources were pitifully scanty.

In few parts of America did frontier conditions persist for more than one or two generations. With the steady growth of population, the trails over which the pioneer emigrants journeyed west were widened to broad highways. Attractive farm homes replaced the former log cabins or sod houses. Towns and cities grew up. Differentiations in the social classes began to appear. Gradually the old order disappeared, and in its place came civilization, and the sophistication that is associated with urban life, while new frontier regions appeared farther west. One by one these, too, disappeared until about the dawn of the present century we came to the end of a great historic movement, and the frontier and pioneer conditions in America vanished forever.

. . . .

Antislavery in Illinois

N. DWIGHT HARRIS

The triumph of the Anticonventionists in Illinois was generally regarded, both in the North and South, as an antislavery victory, and the prevailing opinion seems to have been that a strong anti-

From N. Dwight Harris, *The History of Negro Servitude in Illinois, and of the Slavery Question in that State, 1719-1864* (Chicago, 1904), pp. 50-53, 125-129, 136-139, 144-145. Footnotes in the original have been omitted.

slavery party existed within the State. The population at once increased rapidly through immigration, so that the number of inhabitants rose from 55,211, in 1820, to 71,309, in 1825, and attained the remarkable figure of 157,575 by 1830. Within the same ten years thirty-four new counties were organized, of which twenty-nine were settled chiefly by Eastern men and but five by men of Southern sympathies.

One might naturally infer from this, that a strong antislavery party would be evolved from the anticonvenition party as a nucleus, or at least a powerful antislavery sentiment created during the decade from 1820 to 1830, which would have brought about the dissolution of the indenture system. Nothing of the kind occurred. No antislavery movement of any sort grew out of the contest of 1823-1824.

With the vote in August, 1824, the organization of the Anticonventionists fell to the ground. The discussion of slavery in the papers ceased. People generally stopped talking about it, and it played no vital part in the selection of a United States Senator in 1826, or in the popular elections of 1826, 1828, and 1830. The subject of slavery seems to have been dropped by common consent. The Anticonventionists, joyous over their victory, felt no desire to carry the matter further, since the State was safe from slavery for all time. The Conventionists were anxious to see the topics of slavery and convention sink as rapidly as possible into oblivion. They desired to regain popularity and to be free from the taint of association in the scheme to make Illinois a slave State. So the subject was allowed to fade quietly out of mind, no word even being raised against the holding of negroes as indentured servants.

The courts sustained masters in their right to hold slaves, and the Legislature showed little disposition to repeal the "Black Laws" of 1819. In 1825 the freeing of negroes who had lately come within the State was made possible under certain conditions, but no law was enacted which altered in any way the existing contracts for personal service. In fact, the disposition was to strengthen rather than to weaken the position of the master.

In 1827 and 1829 laws were passed forbidding negroes to act as witnesses in the courts against any white person, and prohibiting them from suing for their freedom.

. . . .

Here and there able and good men were won to the [abolitionist] cause, but the abolition following was extremely small before 1836.

It remained for the "Alton Observer" to stimulate and unify the scattered elements, and for the first time, to create something like a general antislavery sentiment within the State. The paper had been running hardly a year before the effect of Mr. Lovejoy's work was apparent, and requests for the formation of a State antislavery society began to pour in upon him from various portions of Illinois. The final outcome, as has been shown, was the organization of the Illinois Antislavery Society, in October, 1837, at Upper Alton, with a membership of fifty-five.

There were then five county societies in existence, only one of which—the Adams County Society—was founded before 1837. These five societies—four county and one State—might be called Mr. Lovejoy's legacy to the abolition cause, for from this little nucleus were to come the antislavery agitation and the Abolition and Liberty organizations of the future.

After the death of Mr. Lovejoy there was a temporary cessation of effort on the part of the abolitionists.

. . . .

Meanwhile the Illinois Antislavery Society was taking definite steps toward the organization of the abolition movement within the State. It held its first annual meeting in Farmington, in October, 1838, and chose officers and a board of managers for the ensuing year. Ninety-nine delegates were present, representing sixteen Illinois counties, and including two representatives from the Iowa and Wisconsin Territories. The Rev. Chauncey Cook was selected as a travelling agent for the society, and two thousand dollars was voted to meet the expenses of the coming year. The "Genius of Universal Emancipation" was adopted as the official organ of the society, and the executive committee was requested to evolve a plan for the promotion of the abolition work.

The plan proposed involved the organization of antislavery societies in every county, which should be auxiliaries of the State society. They were to hold quarterly meetings, engage lecturers, circulate antislavery pamphlets and petitions to Congress, raise funds, and agitate the subject generally. In addition, district societies were to be formed in every town or neighborhood, which should hold their meetings monthly and work along the same lines as the county associations of which they were to be auxiliaries. Antislavery newspapers and almanacs were to be circulated as far as possible. Great stress was laid on individual effort, and finally, a model constitution for district societies was suggested by the committee in their plan.

Weak in numbers, deficient in effective organization and working facilities, cramped by great financial weakness, and faced on all sides by a stern opposition, the Illinois abolitionists labored on,

hopefully and earnestly, to carry out during the year that followed—October, 1838, to October, 1839—the proposed scheme of
organization and agitation. During that time three county and
sixteen district societies were formed, nineteen in all. Of these, nine
at least were formed directly by the agency of the Illinois Antislavery Society. About three hundred and fifty members were
added to the ranks of antislavery adherents. Of these, some two
hundred and sixty were won over through the labors of the agent of
the State society, Rev. Chauncey Cook.

. . . .

The abolitionists thus early recognized the hopelessness of accomplishing much by antislavery agitation in "Egypt"; and consequently we find their efforts directed hereafter largely to Central
and Northern Illinois.

In the year 1841 we find increasing activities, although the lack
of sufficient funds was still severely felt, especially by the editors of
the "Genius of Liberty." On the 24th of February a special meeting
of the Illinois Antislavery Society was held at Lowell. There was a
good attendance and the best of feeling animated the delegates.
Great interest was shown in the topics discussed, and some of those
present averred that this was the most enthusiastic abolition meeting ever held (up to that time) in the State.

Here the ground was taken that slavery was to be removed
through laws on the subject, and therefore, that it was inconsistent
and suicidal for abolitionists to vote for proslavery men for legislative and executive offices. Here, too, for the first time, the agitation
of the temperance question along with slavery was discussed.

The society then recommended its executive committee to accept the offer of the LaSalle County Antislavery Society to transfer
the control of the "Genius of Liberty" from its own hands to those
of the State society, and to make that paper the official organ of
the Illinois Antislavery Society. This the committee proceeded to
do at its next meeting, on July 5, and the "Genius of Liberty" bore
the name of this committee at its head from July, 1841, till April,
1842.

. . . .

The attention of the Illinois abolitionists throughout this year
seems to have centred largely upon the two topics of petitions to
Congress and of repeal of the "Black Laws" in Illinois. In the
annual report of the executive committee, made at the annual
meeting in June, 1841, we learn that two hundred copies of the
minutes of the last annual meeting, in which both subjects are urged

by resolutions, had been distributed in the State, and that five hundred copies of the form of petitions to the State Legislature to repeal the "Black Code" had been printed also, and in large part distributed. In addition, the "Genius of Liberty" urged continually the repeal of the "Black Laws," and asked for any information that would expose the evils arising from these enactments, and in July a petition advocating the abolition of slavery in the United States, and signed by seventy-one Illinois abolitionists, was read in the Senate.

. . . .

The beginnings of an agitation attempted by these men were not over-propitious. Nor was their organization thorough and effective, owing largely to a lack of means. But their efforts were earnest, sincere, progressive, and their work met with at least one promising result—it awoke among the people of Illinois a lively interest in the question of slavery, it started an impulse, vigorous, sympathetic, and zealous, in favor of the negro and freedom, which refused to be silent, and which prepared Illinois to assume a prominent rôle in the great antislavery conflict that followed.

Anti-Intellectualism on the Illinois Frontier

DONALD F. TINGLEY

Many histories describing the social and cultural conditions on the frontier and in Illinois might lead the unwary reader to believe that there was a great movement for improvement of the educational opportunities for the people and that there was considerable intellectual activity and respect for things of the intellect. A closer examination seems to indicate that actually there was on the frontier a deep-seated anti-intellectual attitude on the part of most of the pioneers and Illinois in its formative years was no exception to

From Donald F. Tingley, "Anti-Intellectualism on the Illinois Frontier," from *Essays in Illinois History in Honor of Glenn Huron Seymour* (pp. 3-17), edited by Donald F. Tingley. Copyright © 1968 by Southern Illinois University Press. Reprinted by permission of Southern Illinois University Press. Footnotes in the original have been omitted.

this. Scrutiny of the life of the people who moved beyond the fringes of civilization leads one to believe that it would be surprising if it had been otherwise.

For purposes of this paper the frontier is loosely defined, following Pease, as the first thirty years of statehood. By this time the frontier had passed on for the most part and doubtless in the more densely settled areas, particularly where New Englanders had come in, the attitudes described here had weakened somewhat but the anti-intellectualism was probably still predominant. . . .

Richard Hofstadter in his excellent work on the subject defines anti-intellectualism as "a resentment and suspicion of the life of the mind and of those who are considered to represent it; and a disposition constantly to minimize the value of that life." Certainly all of this is present on the frontier of Illinois.

. . . .

In the various memoirs and reminiscences of the period most writers divide prominent persons into three groups: those of little education, those with a good English education, and those with a classical education. The first group probably had little or no formal education but may have been self-taught to some degree. The second had probably the equivalent of a common-school education while the last group had some college education although they were not necessarily graduates of a college. . . .

There were a number of people in the state during these early years who had some literary pretensions. Governor John Reynolds in his later years wrote history, an autobiography, a plea for education, and a number of other things. Governor Ford wrote a history of the state that is a classic. James Hall carried on many literary projects while John Russell wrote some poetry. There were some literate editors who produced decent newspapers for a brief season but these were few. The intellectual historian always has to face the problem of finding the climate of opinion by an analysis of the record left by the most articulate people. His raw material has to be what was left by these people, but he is in the position of often being drawn in the wrong direction by assuming that the great inarticulate mass believed as the articulate did. It would seem that the general population of Illinois was not impressed with the intellectuals during the frontier period because, although the literary output was impressive, there was little support for the writers and the historian could be easily misled. There is little evidence of a wide readership and certainly James Hall, the most prolific writer, had to pull back from Illinois to Cincinnati where the intellectual climate was better in order to find a market for his writing.

It seems to have been generally the case with immigrants coming to the United States, and with those moving from place to place within the country, that the motivating factor was largely economic. The colonists, by and large, came to the new world seeking a better living. So it was later that the pioneers came to Illinois seeking cheaper land, a place where they would not have to compete with slave labor, or simply to get a fresh start in a new country. Frontier life was hard and their preoccupation was quite naturally with the material rather than with the intellectual or the aesthetic. Governor John M. Palmer recalled many years later that when he came to Illinois in the 1830's all he heard men talk of was entry of land, improvements on public lands, the breaking up of the prairies, and such practical matters. Morris Birkbeck said he was shocked to hear Americans calling a beautiful piece of scenery in the countryside disgusting because it could not be plowed.

Even the advocates of education thought it to be important almost solely for material advantage. One of the early settlers said that many parents were unwilling to have their children study arithmetic on the grounds that it was unnecessary to farmers, and grammar was of no use to anyone "who could talk so as to be understood by everybody." John Reynolds, who always stood for free schools, stated the case for such schools in highly materialistic terms. The mechanic or day laborer would profit by an education because he would know better how to do his job and while working on the streets, for example, would be a more competent judge of tools and their use. If he was employed to make fences, drive a team, or do other farm work, it would be to the advantage of both employee and employer if he were educated. Reynolds reiterates often the proposition that the educated laborer will be more regularly employed than his uneducated fellow worker, and that the educated farmer will be a better farmer and make a better living. An education presumably would teach him the proper seeds to plant, the time to sow and plant his fields, as well as the best management of a dairy. Reynolds wrote, "It is impossible to obtain for this noble branch of industry the high standing and general usefulness to which it is entitled, without education."

. . . .

According to most observers this deep-seated doubt about the value of education was shared by most of the people. Mrs. Christina Tillson was shocked and amused at the ignorance of her neighbors when she moved to Hillsboro about the time of statehood. She found that they were not only unimpressed with education, but that they actually felt that it was a waste of time and money. Here again, the economic factor was important because books not only cost a lot of money but, if read, consumed a lot of time. While visiting one of her neighbors she noted that the only literature was "an old almanac, begrimed and greasy, hanging against the wall." The husband of the family said,

> "twant so bad for men to read, for there was a heap of time when they couldn't work out, and could jest set by the fire; and if a man had books and keered to read he mought; but women had no business to hurtle away their time, case they could all us find something to du, and there had been a heap of trouble in old Kaintuck with some rich men's gals that had learned to write. They was sent to school, and were high larnt, and cud write letters almost as well as a man, and would write to the young fellows, and, bless your soul, get a match fixed up before their father and mother knowed a hait about it."

Mrs. Tillson reported that these sentiments were shared by at least nine-tenths of the people in the neighborhood. This fear of moral decay brought on by education is found also in John Reynolds who felt that bad company, society, and books might "sow the seeds of passion in the breast of a tender, kind-hearted, and hitherto honest girl." This problem was doubtless limited largely to the female sex but was a pressing worry. Reynolds was especially worried about the evil effects of the wrong kind of books on the young ladies for young girls could be led astray by reading "wild and vicious novels on the subject of love" and be so corrupted that "the crazy girl is often ready to run off with and marry the first wild fiddler she meets."

The schools that were in existence, while better than none, inspired scant respect. In spite of the fact that the legislature had been passing bills since 1823 to provide for free tax-supported schools, few of these had been established and in the 1840's the subscription school was still the most common. Anyone who felt called upon to teach or, as Julian Sturtevant put it, anyone who was otherwise unemployed, would announce that he was starting a school and sign up students, often taking his tuition payments in produce. There was no guarantee of the instructor's education or fitness to teach. Sturtevant says that there also was no assurance of his moral character, perhaps lending some reason to accept Reynolds' concern about the moral deterioration of the students. The teacher usually boarded around the neighborhood. If he knew enough to read, write, and teach a little arithmetic, he could get along well enough because, as Governor Ford pointed out, this was thought to be sufficient in the early days as the professional men usually came from some other area and the preachers sprung from the people to whom they ministered.

In any case the lot of the teacher was not an enviable one and doubtless not many wanted to become teachers unless there was no other way to make a living. James Flint, a Scottish traveler in America, observed that the teacher was "anything but that object of reverence which becomes his office." Flint believed that most children were actually taught to despise the learned person, and remarked of the children he saw, "It gives no pleasing sensations to hear them swearing, at an age when they ought to be learning to know one letter from another." Not only was there doubt about the benefits of an education but it was particularly difficult to persuade people that the state should provide this education. A society to promote education was formed in 1840 and a convention was held in 1844 in Peoria to petition the legislature to provide for education. Ultimately some progress was made in this direction, but it was in the face of massive indifference if not actual opposition.

There was always on the frontier a strong primitivism, the tendency to settle problems in a direct way with a maximum of muscle and a minimum of reason, and this violence involved everyone from the lowliest citizen to those most prominent in political life. In 1827, in the legislature meeting in Vandalia, the defeated candidate for state treasurer, Abner Field, started a brawl which involved, among others, John Reynolds, later governor of Illinois, and Thomas Reynolds, later governor of Missouri. Field threatened John Reynolds with a knife and the latter retreated, "receiving a kick in the posteriors." Thomas Reynolds then took up a chair to defend himself from the knife but he too fled, making a "strait shirt tail" out of the legislative hall. The fight, later continued in the hotel, could hardly be described as a deliberative and intellectual discussion of the issues involved in legislative problems.

Brawls and violence went on everywhere. The *Autobiography* of Peter Cartwright, Methodist circuit rider, is filled with accounts of how he beat up and outwitted the camp-meeting bullies who threatened to break up his evangelistic meetings. Even a preacher had to be handy with his fists if he was to gain the respect of the people. Governor Ford describes the class of illiterate citizens who were called the "butcher knife boys" or the "half horse and half alligator men." These had a great propensity for fighting and held a balance of power in politics even down through the 1840's. Gangs and mobs were common in all parts of the state and often were able to defy the authorities and had to be dealt with by vigilante groups that brought some counties to the brink of small civil wars.

The people of the frontier drank great quantities of whiskey which contributed to the violence of the times. Candidates for public office were expected to furnish large amounts of liquor for the voters, leasing all the saloons or "groceries" in a town for weeks before the election. On Saturdays the candidates would appear in the town for a rally and after the stump speeches the drinking began. By evening the populace would be wild with drink, and there would be much swearing, boasting, fighting, and cheering of the candidates. Often court days in the towns were hardly better. The fighting was vicious, involving the attempt to gouge out the eyes of the opponent or to bite off his nose or ears. Travelers in Illinois noted the constant swearing of the people. James Flint, for example, commented that he had heard in a few months on the frontier more swearing than he had heard in his whole previous life. This boisterous frontier life was largely antagonistic to the intellectual life. It was primitive and nonintellectual at best and in most instances actively anti-intellectual.

. . . .

Taking the definition of anti-intellectualism to be a general distrust of the affairs of the mind and of education in general, it will be seen that this condition existed on almost every level of human activity in frontier Illinois. The question of why the attitude existed still remains. The natural equalitarianism of the frontier was unquestionably a factor. On the frontier every man was as good as another as long as he could prove it by the standards of the area and this took the form of proving it with fists more often than with the intellect. It was a highly materialistic society intent on rapid improvement of its economic status which could be accomplished best with brawn and a bit of native shrewdness. Education helped little.

The human ego causes everyone to justify and apologize for what he is, and every man seems to feel the need to prove that his own background is the best. Few men came to the frontier with education or wealth but many, in spite of this, became successful in politics, business, or law. This must prove that education was not necessary and at best was only a frill or luxury which was all right as long as those who had formal education did not try to appear superior.

On the Illinois frontier there were still more complicating factors. There was often rivalry between the educated and the noneducated, the intellectual and the nonintellectual, but often, however, this was a clash between older cultures. Ford points out that most of the southerners who came into Illinois were likely to be very poor and badly educated while, on the other hand, the New Englanders who came were richer and better educated. This happened because the richer people from the South were likely to be slave owners and therefore went to the newer slave states where their slave property could be taken along. In Illinois, of course, the institution of slavery was illegal. Thus, according to Ford, the average New Englander saw only the worst examples of the southerner and thought of them all as "a long, lank, lean, lazy, and ignorant animal, but little in advance of the savage state." The southerner thought of the Yankee, on the other hand, as a "close, miserly, dishonest, selfish getter of money, void of generosity, hospitality or any of the kindlier feelings of human nature." One traveler in the West recounted a story that the coonskin was the most common kind of currency in use; this worked very well until the Yankees began sewing raccoon tails on catskins, thus debasing the medium of exchange. On the religious scene it might appear to be a quarrel between the intellectual and the nonintellectual, but it was also a struggle between the dogmas of the southern, noneducated Methodist or Baptist preacher and his Presbyterian or Congregational counterpart from New England who was sure to be a man with a college education. Thus while it was anti-intellectualism it was also a reaction of the poor against the rich, the Methodist against the Calvinist Congregationalist, the southerner against the Yankee. Which of the factors was most important in fostering anti-intellectualism on the Illinois frontier? It would have to be a guess. Doubtless, John Reynolds, or Peter Cartwright, or any of the nameless thousands who shared their feelings could not have told. The historian can only say that anti-intellectualism was one of the major characteristics of the frontier mind.

Everyday Scenes

JAMES HAINES

It is not the present population of central Illinois whose social life and scenes I wish to portray before you, but that of the pioneer population emigrating to and dwelling there in the early settlement

From James Haines, "Social Life and Scenes in the Early Settlement at Central Illinois," *Transactions of the Illinois State Historical Society*, X (1905), 35-57.

of central Illinois. There was great variety too and disparity in this new-comer population. Gathered as it was from many and widely distant states of the older portions of the union, it would necessarily partake somewhat of each locality whence it came. Dress, manners, language and occupation gave token of the land and race furnishing the supply of individuals to form the mass of population whose social life I wish to describe.

. All were common in dress, some rude in manner, few boisterous, mostly quiet in speech and slow in movement, very little refined as now gauged, no learning from books outside the bible, hymn, song music, and school books. Intercourse between inmates and close relatives, frank, laconic, abrupt, good natured; with acquaintances only and strangers, inquisitive, genial, tolerant and leading to more intimacy. These characteristics I recall of men mostly. Women conformed in milder degree of each phase of speech, manner and action.

Necessary labor was fairly well performed but little love for it was displayed, except by the women, whose greatest and constant toil was feeding the hungry—cooking, housekeeping, nursing the children and sick—where as ever from first history they were always present, active, patient, successful and pleasing. All females of age to work found constant, useful employment about their cabin homes at the time and place which I am trying to illustrate.

Sheep were raised as much for their wool as for their flesh. Flax and cotton were cultivated too. All these home-grown materials combined to furnish a fairly full supply of home-made clothing for winter and summer. The hunter contingent for the population furnished a useful share of material for the clothing department as well as food supply. Preparation of the clothing material fell largely to the womankind, and after the web was produced, cutting, fitting and making the garments for all the family was entirely their work, except moccasins, shoes and boots, which were made by the males of the family, or hired cobblers.

All home-grown cotton had to be ginned by a rude home-made gin of my elder brother's invention and had to be carded by hand-cards as there was no power-driven machinery for that purpose then known to us. Thus production of cotton yarn for cotton cloth became tedious and a heavy draft on labor of the household, and was early abandoned by the new comers. But it was soon afterward quite easily obtained from St. Louis, Mo., by keel boats, Mackinaw boats and pirogues—very large canoes. Home-made cotton yarn was never used by the population I am writing of for warp or length-wise thread of cloth or web, but only for woof, or filling, as many generally designated then. Hence wool and flax became of

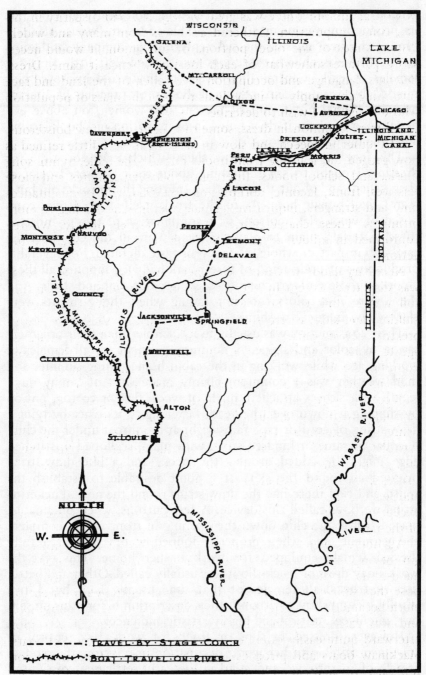

Travel by stagecoach and riverboat in Illinois

general use as material for all our clothing and nearly all labor for its production was woman's work. This added to "house affairs," care of children, nursing the sick, entertaining company, and going to meetings—as church gatherings were called—left little time for females of early Central Illinois to "cultivate and improve their minds" by reading and study of books or practice of literary pursuits. Would not a jury of present day women, on above evidence, excuse them if they failed in examination in "book-larnin" and "the higher education?"

This jury would surely allow them—which I do not—time for dressing. I ought to say something about their dresses—frocks, as then called, and about their dressing—putting these frocks on; but I fear I shall bungle here. As to the frock itself, first: It was composed of wool, flax, cotton, or a combination of two or more of these materials, plain or plaid, relieved with all the colors of the rainbow, in part or whole, as fancy or taste dictated. For vegetable productions of prairie and of forest bark had well supplied all these colors to these embryo chemists seeking color, tint and shade. And these were *fast* colors too, not fading when the garments were cleansed by frequent washings.

Their construction was usually much simpler than their ornamentation by color and stripe. A common garment for all females of working age while working in the cabin home during summer and mild weather was a common, plainly made skirt of "rainy day" length with sleeves attached, made of wool, flax or cotton, put on by slipping it down over the head, fastening to its place by tying a draw-string of cord or tape fairly tight at the throat under the chin. A collar of same or kindred stuff, with plain, scalloped or stitched edge might be added around the neck, and a like draw-string inserted all round the skirt at a point desirable to establish the waist; and tied there like the draw-string round the neck. Puckering string we boys called this device. A few buttons, when obtainable, placed below the chin down the opening in front would complete the garment, and when properly donned would present a fully dressed female equipped for work in her home. This was the work-a-day dress or frock-slip it was usually called. Other and better dresses—frocks, all females of that time usually had, but I feel wholly incompetent to attempt their description before this present day, intelligent, critical and highly artistic audience.

However, dressed in slips or frocks of wool, flax, cotton or tow-linen suitable to her work, occupation or position, the pioneer female of mature age and mind in the early settlement of Central Illinois was the peer of any of her sex in truth, purity, virtue and morality. Great Caesar himself could have sanely and safely chosen a wife there and then, without fear she would fall below his high requirement—"Must be beyond suspicion."

*   *   *   *   *

More intimate association between parents and children in the old pioneer days than now and sharing with them by the parents in all important matters of family and life interests increased the kindred ties of blood, affection and love. This strengthened the force of parental control—convincing the children of that over-mastering power the parental tie, especially as manifested in the mother's love. Children were not spoiled "by sparing the rod" however, as some stings in my memory recall.

Demonstrations not unfrequently witnessed then of the forces of these sentiments call to mind what the same great poet wrote to parental affection near the period we are now considering:

> "Some feelings are to mortals given
> With less of earth in them than heaven,
> And if there be one human tear
> From passion's dross refined and clear—
> A tear so limpid and so meek
> It would not stain an angel's cheek,
> 'Tis that which pious parents shed
> Upon duteous childhood's head."

Perhaps I have given more space and more fatigue to my helpless hearers in praising the female branch of my subject and "magnifying their office" in all good works of the heart and the affections than is justly their due. But I had a mother and five sisters all older and better than I, and it is all from the precious memory of their good deeds, constant care and tenderness for me—the baby of the large family—their innate truth, purity, and active watchful charity and love unfailing for me, that I have been able—inspired—to write this all-too-feeble and faulty tribute to the woman-kind in the early settlement of Central Illinois.

Amusements.

Amusements of the time I write about were quite equally distributed between male and female. While the women cultivated the joys and pleasures of the hearth and home and were themselves the authors of their happiness, they fully shared in all their delights and enjoyment. Men had the hunt, the chase, the horse-race, foot-race, the jolly meetings at rude elections, school meetings, muster-meetings, cabin raisings, road making and road repairing, pitching horse shoes—instead of quoits, town-ball and bull-pen—quite all to themselves. Women of that day attended none of these rough and exerting sports of men. Foot-ball had not yet come to pollute the purer taste of that day to its brutal grade of barbarity and cruelty.

I had five brothers, all older than I, making me as above stated the baby of the whole family of eleven children. From memory of their work, amusements, conduct, characters, I draw my descriptions of all other like population of the territory and time I try to illustrate before you.

My brothers were all tender, kind, considerate, helpful to all my wants and needs; physical, mental, moral and social. Like conditions and relations I know prevailed in many other families of that time and country, and hence I believe these noble sentiments and worthy characteristics dominated and controlled largely all the population male and female.

One marked characteristic of all gatherings of these people was interest in each other and care for each other's well fare and comfort, showing a bond of union and of good will. The affection and love manifested by children for their parents, brothers and sisters, and by the parents for their children, as I have tried to show, existed so generally among the pioneer population, and the good effect it produced on the children in early Central Illinois as compared with conduct of children in the same territory now, lead to the belief there was a latent power ruling in the family then that does not wholly dominate it now. As I call to my memory to give me the clue to this potent ruling force echoes of its name and office come to my ears and kindle response in my heart and impel the tongue to speak, the pen to write, words of the grand poet so often called on in this paper.

> "Love rules the court, the camp, the grove,
> And men below and saints above;
> For love is heaven and heaven is love."

In all gatherings of both sexes of this people while there was levity, jollity, frankness and liberal affection manifested there were few or no sallies or attempts at flirting with the true, pure feelings of the heart, now called *flirting*.

I recall no such word then in use; perhaps because no such trivial practice then existed to require such odious name. Independent, manly and honorable, the males could not stoop to such trifling conduct, while the females were too pure, too true, too worthy to ask aid from falsehood and deceit. Neither sex feared recognition of all their good qualities and honest claims of merit and had no fear on this point, only the fear of doing wrong and being unworthy of true love and its just reward.

Male Dress and Business Habits.

Having written freely about female dress, male attire should also have some attention now:

All males of work age dressed nearly alike. Male apparel too, at the time I am writing about, was made almost wholly by the females, the wearers' associates. The common working boy and man, during summer and mild weather, in field, prairie or forest, wore no more than three articles of dress at one time. Hat of plaited rye, oats or wheat-straw; shirt and pants of cotton, flax or tow-linen cloth. All made in simplest, plainest manner, indeed so uniform in style as to claim the title of fashion. Comfort and utility absolutely controlled material, make, and fit of all male garments, whether for summer or winter, hot or cold weather, home or wear abroad. Traveling or local cobblers were utilized for supply of boots and shoes for males and females of all ages. Almost the sole thought controlling change of apparel for male wearers was to suit the weather and work engaged in. Attending meetings of church or other interests had little influence as to dress. Greater cleanliness of apparel was desired when going away from home among strangers.

There was very little time spent in what deserves the name of business as now understood, either private or public. Trade, barter and exchange of commodities and swapping work in corn-planting and harvest time, for work back in corn-husking and hay-making time was the only commerce known in very early times. Honest, faithful memory, discarding day book and ledger, held all accounts and recorded balances of money and labor due; and merciful, charitable memory forgot all debts of debtors too poor to pay.

So simple and domestic were all the ways and wants of that early country life. Loafing was yet unknown. That came with earliest saloons for sale of intoxicating liquors, in small towns. They were called groceries, or doggeries then. Road-making, efforts to secure schools or aid church interests, to regulate militia musters and drills, to select the best candidates for elective offices of county, state and nation required only a small portion of time, at command of the ordinary citizen.

As to the last duty, selecting candidates for offices of all kinds and grades, serious attention and ample time were always given and the best, wisest and most competent men were always sought and selected, differing diametrically from the custom of the present-day population of the same district in this most important duty of citizenship in a republic like ours.

The voting citizens of that time seemed more intelligently concerned about a wise use of the ballot. The close of the revolutionary war and the achievement of our independence of England and all other foreign powers, was much fresher in the memories of the voters of that day than now. And the value of liberty, newly and blood bought, seemed greater to them than to us. The war of 1812 with England had been lately fought in defense of this inestimable liberty, and they had helped to win the victory that would make liberty a permanent possession of our whole country. Hence the revolutionary war and the war of 1812 that demonstrated our ability to defend and maintain our dearly bought rights were the leading and constant themes of thought and discussion. Nobler and more patriotic themes than now absorb and control the whole thought, aim and struggle of our active, strenuous, commercial, money-grabbing voting population. They talked of, admired and sought to imitate the pure patriots, great statesmen and generals who won our independence and established free government by the people for the greatest republic the world has ever known. Pure, noble thoughts and desires indulged by a people will make them strive to achieve and secure their high aspirations and ideals. Such were the early settlers of whom I write.

Elective officers and rulers of our State and its organized counties in these early days have made and left a history that proves the ballot of that time and territory was not only highly esteemed but honestly, wisely and successfully used to secure happiness and prosperity to the vast population that has won third place in our union, for Illinois.

*   *   *   *   *

Social Singing.

Some one esteemed for wisdom said or wrote: If he were allowed to write the songs of a people any one else might make their laws. A large share of the amusements and entertainments indulged in and practiced by the early population of Central Illinois consisted in social singing of play or forfeit songs, illustrating the evening entertainment of home and fire-side, for girls and boys. Singing of well-known hymns to familiar tunes used at church and religious meetings enlisted the aged also of both sexes. So it often happened after the light and frolic plays of the youth had ended in sale and redemption of all play-forfeits and pawns in affection and hilarity, some elder witness of the youthful jollity would raise a tuneful voice of psalmody, reciting in solemn melody the words of some "Hymn, devout or holy psalm," in which all, young and old, would join to make a benediction to close the evening's entertainment.

I wish to enlarge somewhat on this branch of old fashioned early-time youthful entertainment. Each play or individual entertainment was introduced by a song or words in jingling rhyme sung in chorus by all taking part in the play. These words explained and carried forward, as it were, the movement and progress of the play to its own close, when another song for like purpose would start and carry forward another play.

OLD PLAY AND FORFEIT SONGS.

We are marching down towards Old Quebec
  Where the drums are loudly beating,
The Americans have gained the day
  And the British are retreating.

The wars are o'er and we'll turn back
  No more forever to be parted;
We'll open the ring and choose a couple in
  Because they are true-hearted.

2

King William was King James' son
And for the royal race he run,
Upon his breast he wore a star,
That always points to the compass far.

Go choose you east, go choose you west,
Go choose the girl that you love best,
If she is not here to take a part,
Go choose another with all your heart.

Down on this carpet you must kneel
Sure as the grass grows in the field,
Salute your bride and kiss her sweet,
And then arise upon your feet.

3

O, Sister Phoebe, how merry were we
That night we sat under the Juniper tree,
  The Juniper tree, heigho.
Put this hat upon your head
  To keep your head warm
And take a sweet kiss,
  It will do you no harm—
It will do you much good—heigho.

Real tea and coffee of commerce could not be used at meals during the early period of which I write. Their supply was limited to that brought with new comers from home lands till improved transportation from St. Louis, supplied them for common use in Central Illinois. Herbs and roots from forest and prairie, supplied the only tea generally used by pioneers. Dr. Wm. S. Maus, my father-in-law, told this anecdote about early use of tea. The family doctor in early days stood next to the preacher in respect and esteem—even in preference at births. Dr. Maus practiced widely and had to make long rides on horseback to reach patients in need of his services, hence was often hungry. The custom was universal to ask the doctor to "stay and eat something" before leaving his patient, and equally customary for him to accept offered hospitality. Usually just before the meal was "set up" inquiry came from the cook: "What kind of tea do you like best, doctor? We have both kinds, in plenty, sage and sassafras."

Liberality of supply, frank heartiness in offering—even pressing food on table guests were prominent and pleasing graces at all meals. No suggestion of stint or stinginess ever appeared in manners, act, or words of gracious host or hostess. Greed of gain, that insidious poison that kills all real enjoyment of food bounties, lest hospitality exhaust the supply and want may follow, had not touched or stung the broad liberality of the big generous hearts of that day.

The Spinning Wheel.

One gentle touch on young memory's valve and the old light of pioneer days streams in showing the interior of a log cabin home complete, of that day.

An elder wife—perhaps grandmother in person—sits at the small spinning wheel driving it rapidly by intermittent pressure with her right foot on the treadle, with eye and mind intent on drawing out and twisting the fine linen thread from the flax-covered distaff of even size and continuous length, while a younger wife or unmarried girl drives a big wheel to furious motion and loud hum with the wheel-pin in her right hand dashing backward to draw the roll of carded wool to proper size as the whirring spindle unites and hardens it into yarn-woof for the loom. And ever as she returns in gentle pace from the utmost stretch of the yarn she jogs with her foot the sugar-trough cradle close to her line of retreat to reunite the baby's broken slumber. Meantime the low sound of gently simmering cabbage and bacon—perchance fresh venison, fruit of the hunter's skill—from the singing iron pot on the wood fire, joins with the hum of wheel and lullaby song of the spinner. Rare fragrance from the boiling pot fills the cabin area with appetizing odors reminding all its occupants of approaching meal time. The spinner hastens her humming wheel to complete the half dozen cuts—her stint for the dinner hour, eighteen cuts or hanks being a big day's work.

When at noon the simple meal is set up and all the family gather at the table to discuss the "creature comforts" of a log cabin dinner, the graceful, health-giving exercise of the big wheel over a puncheon floor and the rugged sprinting demands of the chase or long plodding guidance of the plow, all prove their power to win a vigorous appetite. Not strictly a "dinner of herbs" yet it had the Bible element to sweeten it—"love therewith."

Prairie Fires.

The great annual growth of tall thick prairie grass covering vast areas of surface when killed by autumn frosts and dried to tinder by Indian summer suns was liable to accidental and malicious fires each year. A conflagration of this abundant material forming a continuous line of many miles in length driven by a high wind would make the solid earth tremble and quiver beneath the feet as if the embattled charging columns of flame had weight equal to their brilliant light. A low sullen roar, like distant Niagara, accompanied its march as if Pluto, from his fiery regions, lent it subterranean music. Flame, light, motion and sound combined to make a spectacle and scene, in night time, unequalled in beauty and grandeur.

Often alarm for safety of property, home and human life, added excitement to the absorbing manifestation of power and splendor. Billowy swaying clouds of black smoke, lifting skyward would suddenly explode into flame, lighting the whole landscape and heaven above, beyond the brightness of noonday even if the hour was midnight. All combustible substance melted and vanished before this besom of heat and flame. Its progress was swift as the wind. The fleetest horse could hardly escape it by utmost strain of speed. Birds of the air and wild beasts of the prairie and grove, fled before its withering, scathing march with cries, screams and howls of fright and terror, sometimes overtaken and burned to cinder despite their wings and fleetness of foot.

Early inhabitants, from experience, had learned to guard against danger and loss from prairie fires, by plowing wide and numerous furrows round fields, cabins, stables, stacks of hay, grain, fodder and all exposed property. But sometimes great sheets of flame driven by strong winds would be torn from the line of fire and leap over protecting plowed spaces and kindle in hay stack or thatch of stable or shed, threatening cabin-roof and all property and life, home and surroundings. If instant sufficient help were not present, all might be swept away in one fell swoop of fire and devastation. Sometimes such fiery visitation came in the darkness of night and neighboring homes were added to the smoking ruins of the same fire. To skillfully fight and rescue life, homes, and property from the ravages and loss by prairie fires, offered quite as wide opportunity to bravery and heroism of that time, as did fear, danger and suffering from tomahawk and scalping knife. And there were many men of that day, and not a few women too, ever present to act the brave hero and fearless heroine in time of need.

. . . .

Original Narratives

In 1819, Ferdinand Ernst, the wealthy promoter of a colony of German settlers at Vandalia, visited the settled parts of the new state. His account of the journey, first published in 1820 in Hanover, Germany, and later in E. P. Baker's English translation in the *Transactions of the Illinois State Historical Society* of 1903, did much to arouse the interest of his countrymen in Illinois. The opportunities for growth and prosperity he described were very appealing for those in the economically depressed Rhine Valley, and within a decade thousands of Germans flocked to the Prairie State to make a fresh start.

Travels in Illinois in 1819

FERDINAND ERNST

Toward noon of the 29th of July, (1819), I came upon the so-called English meadow where the Englishmen, Birkbeck and Flower, have been established for three years. These men, who have selected a region not remarkable for its fruitfulness and appear to show, on the other hand, but little industry in the cultivation of the land, have, nevertheless, already attracted to themselves such a colony of people that a little town, New Albion, is being built, and in spite of the very unfavorable local circumstances this region will soon be well populated.

Birkbeck's "Notes on a Journey in America, Etc.," I have at all times found to be in conformity with the truth, but his "Letters from Illinois," the accounts asserted will appear to every unpreju-

From Ferdinand Ernst, "Travels in Illinois in 1819," *Transactions of the Illinois State Historical Society*, VIII (1903), 155-159. Only one footnote in the original has been retained.

diced farmer not sufficiently well founded, to say nothing of a man who investigated and tested the matter on the spot for an economic purpose and found in the broad meadow lands not a single acre either of Indian corn (maize) especially necessary in the first year of culture, nor of wheat; but many hundreds of these are introduced into the accounts. Likewise there has come to my notice not a single fruit farm so essential from an economic standpoint, and in this climate so wholesome; yet the peach begins to bear fruit in the third year and can therefore be cultivated quickly and easily.

It was not possible to go from here directly across the Little Wabash to Kaskaskia. Therefore I saw myself obliged to continue my wanderings southward to the confluence of the great and Little Wabash whither a very fine road leads toward Carmi. This city lies upon the Little Wabash about 30 English miles above its union with the great Wabash. It conducts rather lively trade in wares which on account of the shorter and very fine road, arrive here for the most part by land from Shawneetown.

Before one reaches Carmi the road leads through several very well cultivated farms where the eye is delighted by luxuriant fields of maize. Here is the strip where, in the year 1813, a fearful hurricane produced terrible devastation. The road leads through a forest in which all trees have, from seven to ten feet above the ground, been twisted like willows, and their tops often cast to the ground in the opposite direction. Upon the Ohio this hurricane picked up a boat and threw it on land far from the bank. I traversed almost the entire continent of America, in width about one English mile and in direction from west to east.

Not far from Carmi the road leads into a meadowy expanse (Big Prairie) in which, on account of its great fertility, a considerable number of settlers have already located.

Many of these so-called prairies are found in the State of Illinois, and one could probably assume that they amount to a half of the entire area. According to the nature of their fertility they are covered with tall or short grasses and shrubs and, indeed, no more inviting thing can be imagined for a stranger than to settle here and to live and move in this abundance of nature. He needs to do nothing more than to put the plow once into these grassy plains, which are for the most part quite level, and his fields are splendid with the richest fruits and the most abundant harvests. How much easier is here the beginning of a planter than in the dense forest on the Ohio! In proof of this I venture to bring forward the fact that of all lands which till now have been offered for sale in the State of Illinois not a spot remains unsold where good water and timber are found together in fertile plains. But, alas, the good water is all too scarce in the southern part. The rivers have here no strong current, which circumstance, along with many others, produces each year many fevers; but one finds that this evil decreases in the same degree in which the land is brought under more extensive cultivation. A number of these evils as flies, mosquitoes, etc., likewise disappear with increased cultivation.

The flies become exceedingly troublesome to the traveler on horse in the great plains during the summer months of July, August and September; yes, it is even asserted that these insects in very hot weather are able to kill a horse in a short time. There are two kinds of these flies; the little green ones and the large horse fly. The first are the size of a common fly, the second often as large as a hornet. Since they almost always attack the head, neck and breast of the horse, a covering of canvas suffices to protect these parts. If one, in addition to this, uses the precaution of traveling, for the most part, before sunrise and after sunset then this nuisance is of but slight significance.

What the flies are to the horses, the mosquitoes are to man. The mosquito is probably nothing more than the European gnat; at least I have found no difference between the mosquitoes in the States north of the Ohio and our gnat. Their bite is by no means more painful; their size, form and the fact that they make their appearance only in wet places and in the night time; all these things they have in common with the gnat. They are found in large numbers upon the low lands of the rivers and in uncultivated swampy regions. Everything that I have ever heard or read, be it good or bad, concerning these insects as well as everything concerning America is, for the most part, somewhat exaggerated.

Upon the other side of the Little Wabash one finds much forest and fewer settlements. The nearer one comes, however, to Kaskaskia the more the grass lands with alternating forests increase, which often form the most lovely views. If there were not too great lack of water here then these regions could be considered among the most beautiful and pleasing.

On the other bank of the Kaskaskia (Okaw), a very important river here, lies the town Kaskaskia where at present the seat of the State government is located. It was founded more than 50 years ago by the French Canadians and is nevertheless not very important; it appears, likewise, not to have a very healthy location, since it lies in the valley of the Mississippi (American bottoms) which is recognized as very unhealthful in every part. Yet, this evil which proceeds from the overflowing of the Mississippi and from the damp ground improves gradually with time. It has been observed that from year to year this valley dries out more, and at present, is very seldom overflowed by the river, and that only in the lower parts. Kaskaskia has not been inundated for 30 years. In the Catholic church at that place I found a rather large congregation assembled. The young, well dressed minister edified us in the French language with such rare eloquence and such an excellent pronunciation that I was greatly surprised because it was quite unexpected to me.

After dinner I had the honor of being invited to tea at the home of Governor Bond where I, for the first time in the new world, found myself in a company of distinguished ladies. On the whole I was shewn great attention and agreeable kindness. That which stands the stranger in good stead—who is usually too little acquainted with the language of the land and its customs—is the banishment from higher and lower society of all so-called etiquette and unnecessary compliments. The American never greets one by taking off the hat, but by a cordial grasp of the hand. One steps up to the most distinguished persons with covered head. He is urged little, or not at all, to eat and drink according to the measure of his appetite. Nevertheless in all companies the greatest order and decorum prevails, and great respect and attention is shown the ladies present.

As in a free state, the distinction of classes does not come into consideration, so is this also the case here between the Governor and his guests.

From here I took a walk to the Mississippi, 1 1/2 English miles distant. This powerful stream, which collects all the waters of the great rivers of North America in its monstrous bed, was at that time very low; nevertheless its swiftly flowing waters inspired astonishment in me. Its water is turbid and the beauty of the stream is greatly diminished by the many tree trunks projecting here and there in its bed. By high water the stream tears these trees out of its banks and leaves them resting upon shallow places until a higher flood carries them farther. Nevertheless it often happens that the trunk with its roots weighed down with earth, sinking down to the bottom of the river, remains lodged there sticking in the mud; then the trunks having become lighter through the loss of their branches rise and project out of the water like posts driven in. A short time ago they had an example of the dangerous effects of such a tree, pointed through the breaking off of its top, when a steamboat received one in its side and sank in a short time.

In order to avoid this danger they are now beginning to provide steamboats with a double bottom, so that when the first is penetrated the second will furnish the desired security. Those tree trunks, dangerous to navigation, the Americans call logs, or snags.

All towns founded by the French have usually a common pastur-

ing place as well as several other pieces of ground held in common.
Upon this common pasture before Kaskaskia I saw for the first time
in America that beautiful green grass plot which Europe produces
so perfectly in so many varieties, delighting the eye, and the
existence of which, as is well known, is due simply to the teeth of
the cattle pasturing upon it.

Edwardsville, July 30, 1820.

At Kaskaskia begin the so-called American bottoms which form
the valley of the Mississippi. Immediately above Kaskaskia the
valley stretches out seven miles, as far as the village of Prairie du
Rocher, and is shut in upon the east by steep rocky walls from
which frequently the finest springs gush forth. The river is fringed
completely with forests, then up to the foot of the rocks extend
level grassy plains the fruitfulness of which exceeds anything which
one can imagine.

Here I saw fields of maize in which grain had been grown for 30
years and that, too, without any fertilizer. They left nothing to be
desired for the stalks grow luxuriantly to the height of 15 feet. This
soil consists of very rich black slime mingled with sand which is at
times dun colored and, on account of the superfluity of humus,
very light. The hills above the steep rocks are adorned, in part, by
forest, in part by beautiful green sward. The valley hereby receives a
very pleasing setting as that, on the whole, it produces one of the
most charming regions of the State of Illinois.

Above Prairie du Rocher the steep overhanging rocky walls lose
themselves in the high hills. Here I saw the beginning of the destruction which the above mentioned tornado produced, and how it had
taken its way, by Harrisonville, over the Mississippi. But its strength
appeared not to have been so destructive as on the Wabash. On the
27th of July I crossed the Mississippi to St. Louis, a city situated
upon the right bank of the river on elevated ground the substratum
of which consists of rock. In these rocks (limestone) are found most
remarkable impressions—for example, perfect impressions of feet,
hands, bows and arrows of the Indians—so that one is inclined to
believe this stone was in earlier times such a soft mass that it could
receive such impressions, whereupon then these hard masses of
stone have been formed by nature and time. There is such a stone at
(New) Harmony which the colonists of that place, at great cost,
caused to be transported thither, 180 English miles on account of
its strangeness.

A fine spring which gushed from the rocky bank, together with
the elevated region free from forest, was presumably the inducement for the first settling of the city of St. Louis. Its founding falls

within the period in which Philadelphia was established. Only since the mouth of the Mississippi and the surrounding region came into possession of the United States has St. Louis entered upon a period of prosperity. Therefore one cannot reproach this important place with its relatively advanced age. At present the city is expanding upon the heights of the river bank outside the district at present occupied, and this part will soon excel in beauty the distant part which was a failure in the very outset. One finds here various quite handsome buildings, and the inhabitants are employed on every hand in the construction of new houses; hence, the many sawmills in the vicinity among which is one driven by steam.

St. Louis is situated in 38° 39′ north latitude, and may easily have 4,000 inhabitants. The surrounding region inland is meadow land which is, however, not so fertile as are usually the lands in the State of Illinois. This city is the seat of the territorial government of the Missouri territory. The motion to be advanced to a state and to have its own constitution met with difficulties in Congress, since Congress wished to impose the condition that slavery should be abolished in the state of Missouri. Now one finds most every day in the newspapers paragraphs concerning this subject, the majority of which are almost always zealously opposed to the introduction of slavery in the state of Missouri. Everywhere much is being written now concerning the possibility of getting rid of slavery as an acknowledged evil in the entire compass of the free states, so that people in general actually entertain the hope of seeing even the southern states soon freed from this plague.

The left bank of the river is quite liable to cave and wash, while upon the right bank are stones and rock which ward off these effects of the swift current. This washing away of the bank often amounts to 10 or 12 feet in a year, so that not seldom whole plantations are lost thereby. Two small towns, Illinoistown and Jacksonville, which are located opposite St. Louis, run the risk of finding their grave in the Mississippi in the course of time.

In general, one may assume that all river banks in America are unhealthy places of abode, and especially the banks of the larger rivers. This year the ague is found in St. Louis more frequently than is usual. They attribute this to the great heat of this summer because all kinds of fevers appear more frequently this year.

When I had returned across the Mississippi and found myself again in the State of Illinois, I turned up stream to travel through this valley as far as the mouth of the Missouri.

A few miles from Illinois City I found the mill of Mr. Jarrott, a Frenchman, which has in its construction the peculiar feature that the water wheels run while lying in the water, and turn the shaft which projects upward from them. It is said that through this discovery the movement of these wheels is not hindered even in the case of from 7 to 10 feet of backwater.

Several small towns are found located in this valley, which, however, are not especially prosperous, and, too, on account of the unhealthy location. For example, St. Marie, just opposite the mouth of the Missouri, has, indeed, four or five houses, but without a single occupant. It is greatly to be regretted that this region, so fruitful and so admirably located for trade, is so unhealthy. But every year the ground, here and there swampy, is becoming firmer and drier, and one may yield to the hope that even here time will remedy this evil.

In another town, by the name of Gibraltar, three miles farther up, I found a good many inhabitants, and they were employed in building.

From Gibraltar I took the road to Edwardsville. One finds between here and the bluffs some large farms, and, what was still more agreeable to me, everybody was in good health.

Towards evening of the 27th of July I reached Edwardsville, a pretty town about six or seven miles from the bluffs of the Mississippi and 25 miles from St. Louis. This fertile region is covered with fine farms, and where one has opportunity of admiring the astonishing productiveness of the soil. I found the maize from 12 to 15 feet high on an average. The gardens which have sufficient age for fruit settings are luxuriant with peach trees and other fruit trees. The peach is a kind of fruit which flourishes admirably here; the seedling producing fruit in four years, and, almost without exception, bears every year afterward so full that its branches have to be propped. Peach brandy and dried peaches are very common here.

On the other hand I have seldom in all America found the plum tree except in (New) Harmony; but there are apples in great quantities, excellent in all old orchards, and I have met with many fine varieties among them. Moreover the gardens produce melons, especially watermelons, in great quantity and of unusual size—the latter are regarded as a more healthful food than the others. That all other kinds of garden fruits will thrive here may be supposed from what has been said. The pumpkin at times reaches the gigantic size of 3 feet in diameter. Brown and red cabbage I have found nowhere in America, and the ground seems to be too rich for potatoes and many other growths. Potatoes, for example, cannot be planted until very late, often not until July; early planted ones almost never thrive. Maize wheat and oats grow excellently, barley and rye I have not found.

Here, in Edwardsville, I met again my traveling companion, Mr. Hollmann, and it may not be disagreeable to the reader to receive some report of his journey. I shall therefore give here a brief extract from his diary.

"On the 11th of July, (1819) I, in company with ten travelers on horse, crossed the Wabash and entered the State of Illinois. If the traveler from the coast of the Atlantic Ocean to this point has grown weary of the endless journey in the forests then he believes himself transferred to another region of the world as soon as he crosses the Wabash and beholds those great prairies alternating with little wooded districts. Yet, this is one of the largest prairies and, on account of the scarcity of wood, not very well adapted to cultivation.

"After a journey of 22 miles through these prairies were ached the tavern; it was full of travelers. Nevertheless each one was served well enough, the horses were well cared for, and only with respect to the lodgings was the comfort not great. Each one had to prepare his own bed upon the floor as well as he could, and even here the American shows a peculiar ease which is the result of his noble freedom. Everything is done without ado and without ceremony. This manner of living, which was to me at first very strange and disagreeable, soon received my entire approval—little by little one feels himself free among free, honest people. The character of the Americans, which at first was so little agreeable to me, is, nevertheless, on the whole, good. This opinion may be due to the fact that my living with them has, little by little, changed my judgment, or that the people themselves here are better than in the eastern states.

"The road leads through prairies where one all day long sees no house, no, not even a tree, so that protected from the burning heat of the sun, one could rest in its shade. In the middle of this prairie, 24 miles wide, an axle of my wagon broke, whereby I got into no small difficulty. My mounted traveling companions could not help me and had to leave me; but two pedestrians, who had made the journey afoot from Baltimore in this manner, proved friends in need. They went back three miles to get a tree trunk which we had seen lying there by the road. With great difficulty we then took the wagon to the next house. These honest Americans repaid me evil with good. They had been in our company for some time, and at the crossing of the river I did not wish to permit them to take a place in my wagon.

"When we arrived at the next tavern the remaining traveling companions had already sent for a wheelwright, and thus through the kind aid of my comrades it was possible for me to continue the journey with them on the next morning. Toward noon the heat became oppressive and the flies so intolerable that we resolved to make a halt. Not until towards 6:00 o'clock did we continue our journey. Traveling at night time in these prairies is very much to be preferred. One can, without the aid of the moon, find the beautiful level road, and the horses are not tormented by either heat or flies.

"The landlord at the next tavern received us with the remark that tavern keeping was only a secondary matter with him, and he requested of his guests that they accommodate themselves to his wishes, and whoever would not consent to this might travel on. The company of travelers regarded the words of the landlord as very strange, but resolved to put up here as the next tavern was quite a distance off, and men and horses were very tired. After supper the landlord with his family began to pray and sing so that the ears of us tired travelers tingled. Many of the travelers would have gladly requested them to desist from this entertainment if the landlord had not taken the above precautions upon our entrance. After prayers the landlord related to me that he had often been disturbed in his religious exercises, and even been shamefully ridiculed by travelers; he therefore had been obliged to make that condition upon the reception of guests. He was a Quaker.

"On the 23d of July I entered Edwardsville. The most remarkable curiosity which met me here was the camp of the Kickapoo Indians who were now sojourning here in order to conclude a treaty with the plenipotentiaries of the United States, whereby they renounced all their rights and claims to the lands on the Sangamon, Onaquispasippi, and in the entire State of Illinois; ceding the same to Congress, and to immediately vacate the State of Illinois. Their color is reddish-brown; their hair is cut to a tuft upon the crown of the head and painted various colors. Very few are clothed, in summer a woolen covering, in winter a buffalo skin, is their only covering. They seem to be very fond of adornments, as of silver rings about the neck and arms. They likewise carry a shield before the breast."

Vandalia, Sept. 10, 1819.

Immediately after I had joined my traveling companion, Mr. Hollmann, in Edwardsville, we visited our countryman, named Barensbach, whose farm was about four miles from the village, to ask him to show us the lands which are to be sold at public auction, at the land office in Edwardsville, on the first of August this year. He granted our request not only with the greatest readiness, but to this excellent man we owe for many other courtesies and much information. His experience and his advice we have found at all times very helpful. So greatly is he respected in this entire region that we have almost never heard his name mentioned by the inhabitants without its being accompanied by great praise. In spite of his disinclination for every public service they have called him to the important office of judge.

The 24 townships which are to be sold lie between this place and Edwardsville on Shoal creek and Sugar creek and Silver creek. There are many good lands among them, and we would certainly have purchased land at this auction if it had been possible to get anything really as good in the vicinity of the town of Vandalia, that is now about to be laid out.

According to the Constitution of the State of Illinois this town is to be the seat of the government of the State, and the lots will be publicly sold on the 6th of September of this year. In the vicinity of this town is a large amount of fine lands; but everyone is full of praise for those which lie about 60 to 80 miles northward upon the river Sangamon. The Indians have concluded their treaty with Congress, and the latter is now in full possession of these so highly prized regions. In consideration of all this we regarded it more advisable to wait, and resolved for the present to settle in the town Vandalia, and then from here purchase land in time. In order to use the interval to as good advantage as possible, we began to build a little house here from logs, after the manner of the Americans—the logs are laid one upon another, the ends let down into grooves. As soon as the building was far enough advanced so that my companion was able to finish it alone, I started upon a journey to view the wonderful land upon the Sangamon before I returned to Europe. On the 27th of August I, accompanied by a guide, set out upon this little journey. We were both mounted, and had filled our portmanteaus as bountifully as possible with food for man and horse, because upon such a journey in those regions one can not count upon much. A fine, well-traveled road leads thither from Edwardsville. In order to reach this we rode out from Vandalia across Shoal creek, and then northward into the prairie. We left the forests about the sources of Sugar and Silver creeks to the south, and in the vicinity of the groves about the sources of the Macoupin we came upon this road. We now touched upon points of timber on some branches of this river, and then came into that great prairie which extends from the Illinois river through the greater part of the State from west to east and disappears about the source of the Okaw (Kaskaskia) and upon the banks of the Wabash. This great prairie is the dividing line of the waters flowing southward to the Mississippi and northward to the Sangamon but is, however, of no considerable height (elevation). East of the road are some lakes or swamps from which the two branches of Shoal creek receive their first water. The entire region south of this prairie elevation is especially distinguished by the elevation of the prairie and by the smoothness and fertility of the land; however, no spring or river water is to be found anywhere in it. In general the few springs which may possibly be there occur only in the bordering timber. The banks of the rivers are very high and hilly, upon these alone are found the patches of forest. All rivers here have but little soil and form many stagnant bodies of water, while in dry seasons the rivers dry up almost completely, and thereby are produced those vapors which make the air unhealthy.

As soon as one arrives upon the elevation and northern side of this prairie, the grass of the prairie changes and the ground becomes visibly better. The river banks decline in a gentle slope from the prairie to the water, and are likewise covered with woods, which also shows the greater fertility of the soil. We find here in the State of Illinois almost the same variety of woods that are found in Ohio; and I found, in addition to the soft maple, the sugar tree which, in its leaves differs but little from it. The inhabitants regard the latter as far better for the production of sugar.

On Sugar creek, where we passed the second night, we found, right at the point of the timber, a family who had not yet finished their log cabin. Half a mile farther three families had settled near an excellent spring, and here we passed the night. Upon this little stream, which about 15 miles to the north of its source empties into the Sangamon, about 60 farms have already been laid out and indeed all since this spring of 1819. They have only broken up the sod of the prairie with the plow and planted their corn, and now one sees these splendid fields covered almost without exception with corn from ten to 15 feet high. It is no wonder that such a high degree of fruitfulness attracts men to bid defiance to the various dangers and inconveniences that might, up to this time, present themselves to such a settlement. And one can therefore predict that possibly no region in all this broad America will be so quickly populated as this. Nevertheless, one must regard as venturesome daredevils all settlers who this early have located here for they trespassed upon the possessions of the Indians, and ran the risk of being driven out or killed during the great annual hunt of the Indians,* if that treaty at Edwardsville had not fortunately been

*Every autumn the Indians within the entire circuit of their possessions hold a grand hunt. They then set fire to the dry grass of the prairie, and the flame with incredible rapidity spreads over all the country. Before it all wild game flees, having been frightened from their safe retreats, and fall victim to the fatal shot of the red hunters. This destructive custom of burning off the prairies is the reason that timber is confined to the area of streams and a few other places. The heat of the fire not only prevents entirely further extension of the forests but even diminishes their area. Upon these annual hunts the Indians forcibly eject all white settlers from their territory.

made. But now how many will migrate hither since everything is quiet and safe here! Let us consider these present farmers in respect to their property right upon these their plantations. How extremely dangerous is their position in this regard! The land is not even surveyed, and therefore cannot be offered for sale for three or four years. And then, when offered for sale, anyone is at liberty to outbid the present settler for his farm which is already in cultivation. If now all these considerations and actual dangers could not restrain men from migrating to this territory, this then is the most convincing proof of its value and that it is justly styled "the beautiful land on the Sangamon."

From Sugar creek we turned immediately westward with the intention of reaching the point where the Sangamon empties into the Illinois and there crossing the former to the north bank. We crossed Lake creek, then the two branches of Spring creek, both of which flow in the open prairie—a thing which I had never before seen here in America. On the other side of Spring creek is a camping ground of the Indians, whence the prairie rises to gentle hills where we found two fine springs shaded simply by a few trees. The water of these brooks flows swift and clear through the luxuriant prairie, the high grass of which often reaches above the head of the horseman. From these two little brooks rises a plain which extends to Richland creek.

Here we passed the night at the home of farmer Schaffer, who was just then employed in breaking up more prairie. It was a pleasure to me to see that this first plowing produced arable ground like the best clover field. I advised him to plant at least a small part to wheat which from appearances must undoubtedly be the best and most suitable grain for this soil. He, however, asserted that maize planted upon it the next spring would be more profitable. Nevertheless, he promised to make a trial with wheat; but he had already intended this year's corn field for the wheat. Maize, turnips and melons were the products which he expected this year upon the first breaking up of the prairie.

That this region leaves nothing to be desired with respect to health was sufficiently demonstrated to me by the healthy appearance of its inhabitants.

Further on in the prairie we again found some springs, and continuing westward, about noon reached another small river upon which we found three or four farms. The timber on this river bank consisted almost exclusively of sugar trees, and gave those people the most promising prospect of a harvest of sugar the coming spring. From all reports which we gathered it appeared to us that no one upon the bank of the Illinois river had ever been to the mouth of the Sangamon; prevented from doing so by the difficulty of penetrating the intervening woods and underbrush; but they estimated the distance at about 25 or 30 miles.

Since the heat was oppressive and the flies unendurable we were obliged to give up further progress to the Illinois river, we therefore turned again to the Sangamon, and toward noon reached its forest. Here, also, we found three farms, but we could not pass the river as it was very high. This river (the Sangamon) is rather large, and must be navigable the greater part of the year for medium sized vessels. It differs very advantageously from all the other rivers of western America in that its clear water even in this dry time maintains a moderate height, and it is uncommonly well stocked with fish.

We were now obliged to proceed farther up the river, and between the mouths of Sugar and Spring creeks we found a crossing where there was a canoe in which we crossed and let the horses swim alongside. The bank of the river is here about 50 feet high, measured from the surface of the Sangamon, where a broad plain is formed—a grand spot for the founding of a city. Below, upon the river bank, I found a very good clay for pottery and tile work. As soon as we had left the timber of the Sangamon, upon the other bank we came into another large prairie where a not insignificant hill covered with timber attracted our attention. It was the Elkhart (Grove.) This place is renowned on account of its agreeable and advantageous situation. A not too steep hill about two miles in circuit provided with two excellent springs, is the only piece of timbered land in a prairie from six to eight miles broad. Its forest trees show great fertility of the soil.

I found on it sugar trees from 3 to 4 feet in diameter, and the farmer settled here, Mr. Latham, had 30 acres enclosed by the wood of the ash. This hill is lost toward the Sangamon, as well as northward toward the Onaquispasippi in alternating hills without forest, which, to me, judging from the kinds of which grass they bore, seemed very well adapted to sheep grazing or vineyards. Eastward, at the foot of the hill, is a level, rich prairie. Here Mr. Latham had planted 30 acres of corn this spring which thrived beyond all expectation. From this soil I took a small sample which seems to consist of loam and an insignificant admixture of sand. In the surrounding prairie the two springs reappear which were lost in the ground at the edge of the forest.

Towards the south there are several springs in the prairie, some which form little waterfalls often three or four feet high. All these circumstances make the Elkhart not only a beautiful, but—from an agricultural point of view—a very valuable possession. For whoever owns the woodlands of the Elkhart controls at the same time the greater part of the large and rich prairie surrounding it, where, on account of the scarcity of wood, it would be difficult to establish a farm. This farm is, up to the present time, the one situated farthest north in the whole State of Illinois—except, perhaps, in the military lands on the other side of the Illinois river. However, it will not remain so much longer, since 15 miles farther, where formerly stood the Kickapoo Indian capital, some corn fields have been laid out, and a farm will be established there towards spring.

We continued our journey northward and soon reached the charming banks of the Onaquispasippi. (Satz). Alas! this river was likewise too high to be crossed on horseback. Here a rather passable road runs northward to Fort Clair, (Clark) on Lake Peoria. The soil northward on (of) the Sangamon has far more sand in it than in the remaining part of the State; and the only thing that might be feared would be that, on that account, its exceptional fertility in time might decrease. But this point of time is certainly very far off. The Onaquispasippi is still a more beautiful river than the Sangamon, for it has all the characteristics of the latter but in a higher degree. It is likewise navigable for medium sized vessels.

In this prairie I found many rattlesnakes; but all small, of gray color, and of one species. During my entire journey I have heard of no fatality produced by their bite. Unable to get across the river we were obliged to forego examination of the locality of Kickapoo town, and we started on our return journey. We had, however, seen enough to be able to assert that this region is one of the most important in the State of Illinois; or rather, will become such in a short time. One of the greatest obstacles that may retard the rapid population of this district is the scarcity of wood; yet, there is sufficient timber for a moderate population, and the stock of forest will soon greatly increase now that the destructive prairie fires will be stopped. Likewise the rivers Sangamon and Onaquispasippi can greatly facilitate the importation of this article. These two rivers will not only open up a market for all produce in the direction of St. Louis and New Orleans, but their proximity to the Illinois river will in time furnish this region with another very promising prospect by the lakes to New York City by means of the canal now in progress connecting that city and Lake Erie.

It is, also, a very easy thing to unite the Illinois with Lake Michigan by a 12-mile canal—even now, in the case of high water, the transit there is now made. By means of this canal then, inland navigation would be opened up from New York to New Orleans, a distance of 3,000 English miles. Such an internal waterway not only does not exist at the present time in the whole world, but, it will never exist anywhere else. Besides, this State enjoys the navigation of its boundary and internal rivers amounting to 3,094 miles, and all are placed in communication with each other through the

Mississippi. In short, I do not believe that any one State in all America is so highly favored by nature, in every respect, as the State of Illinois.

The entire length of the Sangamon is still unknown; yet we know that it is navigable for at least 300 miles from its union with the Illinois. About 60 miles from its mouth it separates into two arms of which the southern one bears the name Mooqua, which, in the language of the Kickapoo Indians signifies "wolf's face." This arm is up to the present time the best known, and its borders are already rather well occupied with farms. Above the source of the Sangamon is found a rock 50 feet high which has a fissure in its middle. In this fissure the Indians placed tobacco, maize, honey and other products of the land as a thanks offering to the Great Spirit.

The Indians, for the most part, cultivate some maize, and are great reverers of this useful grain. As soon as the first ripe ears of maize are brought to the chief he institutes a grand feast where music and dance delight the company, and where the pipe of peace is industriously smoked. The benefits of the maize to the white settlers are manifold. As soon as the ears have attained some maturity it furnishes a good healthy food. The ears are either boiled in water, or roasted by the fire. From its meal, bread is prepared, and they make a porridge from it which with milk is an excellent dish. Besides this it is fed to all cattle, especially horses and pigs. Even its dry stalks are carefully preserved in stacks to serve as fodder for horses and cattle during the winter.

After an extremely tiresome day's journey we reached, about 11:00 o'clock at night the first farms on Shoal creek where we spent the night. Here the ague was raging, especially among those who had come here this year from the eastern states. This sickness is owing very much to the manner of life of these people; for they live in part upon dried venison, water melons, etc., and often expose themselves to wet weather. Such a manner of life must of necessity produce sickness. The wholesome effect of quinine is striking in the treatment of these fevers. I had brought a quantity of it with me from Baltimore, and this remedy very soon helped everyone to whom I administered it.

On the 5th of September I arrived at Vandalia. This place, in accordance with the Constitution, is to become the seat of government of the new State. It is 50 miles from Edwardsville, and about 60 from the Wabash; so that it is located about in the middle of the State. Its situation is well chosen, upon a bank of the Kaskaskia, 50 feet high, and richly provided with wood for building, and with good spring water, as well as with a vicinage of excellent land. The river, which is navigable to this point, here describes a sharp curve which amounts very nearly to a right-angle, coming from the east and going to the south.

The plan of the town is a square subdivided into 64 squares, and the space of two of these squares in the middle is intended for public use. Every square, having eight building lots, contains 320 square rods; each building lot is 80 feet wide 152 feet deep. Each square is cut from south to north by a 16-foot alley; and the large, regular and straight streets, 80 feet wide, intersect each other at right-angles.

Only four weeks ago the Commissioners advertised the sale of these lots (it will take place tomorrow), and there is already considerable activity manifested. Charles Reavise and I were the first who began to build. How difficult it was at that time to penetrate the dense forest which embraces the entire circuit of the future city. At present there are several passable roads leading hither. Now the most active preparations are being made for the construction of houses, and we are daily visited by travelers. But how it will have changed in 10 or 20 years! All these huge forests will have then disappeared and a flourishing city with fine buildings will stand in their place. A free people will then from this place rule itself through its representatives and watch over their freedom and well-being.

. . . .

Another insight into daily life during Illinois's first years as a state is provided by Philadelphia-born lawyer James Hall. Residing in Shawnee-town between 1820 and 1828, he left for Vandalia to become state treasurer and one of that town's most influential citizens. In addition to carrying on a prosperous legal practice, he assumed the editorship of the second newspaper to appear in the state, the *Illinois Gazette*. He was later editor of the *Illinois Monthly Magazine*, the state's first literary magazine, which he founded in 1830.

Shawneetown and the Saline Reserve, 1828

JAMES HALL

Shawnee Town occupies a beautiful situation on the western bank of the Ohio, nine miles below the mouth of the Wabash, and one hundred and twenty miles above the junction of the Ohio and

From James Hall, *Letters from the West; Containing Sketches of Scenery, Manners, and Customs; and Anecdotes Connected with the First Settlements of the Western Sections of the United States* (London, 1828), pp. 220-223, 228-233.

Mississippi. Its distance from Pittsburgh, by water, is about a thousand miles, and from New Orleans about eleven hundred. The town stands on a level plain, and embraces a view of the river of four or five miles in each direction.

There was formerly a village of Shawnee Indians at this spot, but it was forsaken before the whites attempted a settlement, and no vestige of it now remains but two small mounds. A few cabins were afterwards built by the French traders; but these had also disappeared, and the ground was covered with bushes, when the present town was established. As recently as the year 1808, there was not a house on the ground; in February 1812, an office for the sale of public lands was established at this place; and in March 1814, an act was passed by Congress, providing that two sections of land adjoining Shawnee Town should be laid out into town-lots, streets, avenues, and outlets, and sold in the same manner as other public lands. The town now contains about one hundred houses, of which five or six are of brick, several of frame, and the remainder of log. It has twelve stores, at which a large and active trade is carried on, besides a number of shops of a smaller description; two excellent taverns, an independent bank, and a branch of the state bank; a land office, a post office, two printing offices; and furnishes employment to carpenters, cabinet makers, blacksmiths, tailors, shoemakers, bakers, and other mechanics, of whom a number are settled here.

The ground, as is usually the case in bottom lands, is higher on the edge of the river, where the town stands, than at some distance back, and the town is often insulated, when not actually overflowed. The waters begin to swell in February or March, and continue rising for several weeks. The greatest rise, from the lowest to the highest point, is about fifty feet. The greatest floods of which we have any account, were in 1813 and 1815, when the water covered all the streets, and entered the lower apartments of the dwellings, reaching nearly to the second floors. Since that time the inhabitants have not been expelled by the conquering element, although the water annually covers the plain in the rear of the town, and advances in front to their very doors. The inconvenience and alarm occasioned by the inundations are not so great as might be supposed. The alarm is little, and that little is imaginary, because the irruption is not sudden, nor accompanied with any violent current, or destructive consequence; and the inconvenience is temporary, as the waters subside in a few days, and the soil being sandy, and its surface uneven, no moisture remains. A small deposit of decayed vegetable matter is left, but not enough to corrupt the atmosphere: and even this, before the weather becomes warm, loses its deleterious quality by evaporation, or yields its juices to the vegetable kingdom. When the river first begins to swell, it usually rises as much as three or four feet in twenty-four hours; but as the volume of water increases, its velocity becomes greater, while the widening of the banks affords it room to expand, and the rise becomes daily less perceptible. At length it begins to fill the bayoux, backs up the channels of the tributary streams, and at last spreads over the banks, covering the bottoms for miles. This gradual process affords ample time to the inhabitants to secure their cattle, and to retreat if necessary. . . .

Before the introduction of steam-boats upon this river, its immense commerce was chiefly carried on by means of *barges*—large boats, calculated to descend as well as to ascend the stream, and which required many hands to navigate them. Each barge carried from thirty to forty boatmen, and a number of these boats frequently sailed in company. The arrival of such a squadron at a small town was the certain forerunner of riot. The boatmen, proverbially lawless and dissolute, were often more numerous than the citizens, and indulged, without restraint, in every species of debauchery, outrage, and mischief . . . and these towns were filled with the wretched ministers of crime. Sometimes, the citizens, roused to indignation, attempted to enforce the laws; but the attempt was regarded as a declaration of war, which arrayed the offenders and their allies in hostility; the inhabitants were obliged to unite in the defence of each other, and the contest usually terminated in the success of that party which had least to lose, and were most prodigal of life and careless of consequences. The rapid emigration to this country was beginning to afford these towns such an increase of population as would have ensured their ascendancy over the despots of the river, when the introduction of steam-boats at once effected a revolution.

The substitution of machinery for manual labour, occasioned a vast diminution in the number of men required for the river navigation. A steam-boat, with the same crew as a barge, will carry ten times the burthen, and perform her voyage in a fifth part of the time required by the latter. The bargemen infested the whole country, by stopping frequently, and often spending their nights on shore; while the steam-boats pass rapidly from one large port to another, making no halt but to receive or discharge merchandise, at intermediate places. The commanders of steam-boats are men of character; property to an immense amount is intrusted to their care; their responsibility is great; and they are careful of their own deportment, and of the conduct of those under their control. The number of boatmen is therefore not only greatly reduced, in proportion to the amount of trade, but a sort of discipline is introduced among them, while the increase of population has enabled the towns to maintain their police.

During the reign of the bargemen, Shawnee Town, and other places on the river, were described as presenting the most barbarous scenes of outrage, and as being the odious receptacles of every species of filth and villainy. These accounts were probably exaggerated; but that they were true to a certain degree, is readily conceded. But the disorderly character acquired by these towns in the manner I have related, is unjustly attributed to them now, when the fruitful cause of their worst vices has been removed, and when wholesome regulations ensure protection to the peaceable and industrious. Shawnee Town is now a quiet place, exhibiting much of the activity of business, with but little dissipation, and still less of outbreaking disorder.

The Saline Reserve Commences a few miles from Shawnee Town, and embraces a tract of ninety thousand acres. There are a number of wells of salt water, the nearest of which is seven and the farthest fourteen miles from town. The Indians resorted to these Salines, for the purpose of making salt, previous to their discovery by the whites; earthen vessels, of different sizes, used by them in the manufacture, have been found in large numbers by the persons employed in digging wells. Some of these are large, and display no small ingenuity of workmanship; they are generally fractured; but one or two have been found entire. Gigantic bones of quadrupeds have also been disinterred, resembling the huge remains which have been dug from the *Licks* in Kentucky. Previous to the erection of the Illinois Territory into a state, the Saline was leased to individuals by the United States; but at the reception of this state into the Union, this valuable tract was granted to it in perpetuity, with a restriction that it should not be leased at any time for a longer term than ten years. There are now five salt works in operation in the hands of different individuals, at the whole of which an aggregate of immense amount in bushels of salt are manufactured annually, which sells at from thirty-seven and a half to fifty cents a bushel, at the works, or in Shawnee Town. It is sold by weight, the bushel being estimated at sixty pounds; about one hundred and twenty gallons of water yield sixty pounds of salt. The large tract of land reserved is devoted solely to the purpose of making salt, no part of it being leased for tillage; the object of this regulation is to preserve a supply of timber for fuel. Beds of stone-coal have recently been discovered near the furnaces, but they have not yet been brought into use. The constitution of this state, while it prohibited slavery, allowed the salt makers to hire slaves within the Saline boundary, until the expiration of the year 1825. While this privilege, which was suggested by the scarcity of labourers in a new country, continued to exist, the labour of salt making was performed by negroes, hired from the people of Kentucky and Tennessee. A temporary suspension of operations has been caused by the change from the old to the new order of things. What will be the ultimate effect of the new system is bare matter of conjecture; the better opinion seems to be that the change will be beneficial.

The following selection describes the hard life awaiting settlers on the Illinois frontier. So severe were conditions in the winter of 1830-31 that the following spring and summer parts of the state, especially in the southwest, were critically short of food for both animals and humans. The scarcity reminded many then of the famine which had plagued Pharaoh's Egypt, hence, some believe, the designation of that part of Illinois as "Little Egypt." For more on the origins of the nickname, see Robert P. Howard, *Illinois: A History of the Prairie State* (Grand Rapids, 1972), pp. 162-165. Eleanor Atkinson, an Indiana native, wrote for the *Chicago Tribune* from 1889-91 under the pen name Nora Marks. She was the author of numerous historical novels, the best known of which include *Boyhood of Lincoln* (1908) and *The Story of Chicago* (1910).

The Year of the Deep Snow

ELEANOR ATKINSON

In 1830 winter set in unusually early. Cold rain began to fall by the 20th of December . . . occasionally changing to snow or sleet, until the earth was saturated and frozen. The day before Christmas the rain turned definitely to snow, falling in large, soft flakes that soon covered the earth to the depth of 6 inches. The most was made of this by the young people in holiday frolics of snow-balling, coasting and riding in hastily contrived bob-sleds. The wildest

From Eleanor Atkinson, "The Winter of the Deep Snow," *Transactions of the Illinois State Historical Society*, XIV (1909), 49-55. Footnotes in the original have been omitted.

imagination could not have dreamed that this first fall of snow was merely the overture to a winter of continuous storm. The first white mantle still lay unsullied on the frozen prairie, in a profound hush of nature, when the meteorological opera opened with a crash on the 30th of December.

A furious gale, bitter cold, a blinding, swirling blur of snow, and leaden, lowering skies, combined to make this storm a thing to paralyze that prairie country. It seems to have continued for days, unabated—a wonder, at first, then a terror, a benumbing horror as it became a menace to life of men and animals. The food was in the fields, the fuel in the woods, the cattle huddled and perishing of cold and starvation, in the open. How long this first storm continued is unknown. In one sense it did not end at all; it merely changed in character, from time to time, for the next sixty days. All accounts of the winter in Illinois agree with Dr. Sturtevant's that the storm began in the last days of December. The data was impressed upon his mind by anxiety for the fate of Dr. Edward Beecher.

This first president of the new college had been in Vandalia, trying to get a charter for the institution from the legislature. He was returning from the capital in the Christmas holidays, when overtaken by this storm. Dr. Beecher, with a fellow traveler, Mr. Charles Holmes, took refuge for some days in the house of a settler on the prairie. When the storm abated its first fury, it seemed impossible to cover the remaining distance of 40 miles to Jacksonville, for the snow lay 3 feet in depth over the prairie. It seems probable, from the depth of snow, that they were detained until after the storm of January 14 and 15 which, as Dr. Hildreth reports, had visited the entire length of the United States. A driving rain, freezing as it fell, formed a crust on top of this snow, not quite strong enough to bear a man's weight. On top of this crust 3 more inches of snow fell, as light and fine as ashes and as hard as sand. Then a bright, cold sun shone on the dazzling landscape, to threaten the eyesight. To add to these difficulties a strong, northwest wind arose, to fill the air with flying snow, so stinging, blinding and choking that men could not long make headway against it. But Dr. Beecher was reared on Litchfield hill, Connecticut, and was not easily dismayed by weather. He and Mr. Holmes hitched a horse to a light, improvised sleigh and, in some incredible way, accomplished the perilous task of crossing that 40 mile prairie, where the horse broke every step through ice crust and 3 feet of snow, and in the face of the blizzard. There is no record of any other men having performed such a feat in Illinois, that winter. That many must have attempted such journeys and perished, is proven by the finding of the bodies of strangers in many places when the snow went off in the spring.

In Jacksonville Dr. Sturtevant had been forced to abandon his cabin in the town and to camp out in one of the unfinished college buildings. There Dr. Beecher was forced to remain with him until March, when he returned to Boston. And the two, with other New Englanders in the place, gave of all their experience to help the marooned settlement battle with the elements. It was impossible to break roads in the New England fashion. There were no traps of ravines and forests, few fences, even, to catch and hold the drifts. The wind was a steady, fierce gale, day and night, for many weeks, and the snow drifted before it all winter. It snowed almost daily, up to the middle of February. Often it was not easy to determine whether new snow was falling or only old surface snow being driven before the icy blast. For nine weeks snow covered the ground to the average depth of four feet. No morning dawned for many days at a time when the thermometer registered less than 12 degrees below zero.

"The situation of the people," says Dr. Sturtevant, "was somewhat alarming. It was not at first apparent that sufficient food and fuel could be got to keep everybody from starving and freezing." The shocks of grain were entirely under frozen snow, the lower limbs of trees were lying on the surface, making it impossible to drive teams into the groves. A road was finally made from College Hill to the town, by driving repeatedly through one track until the snow was rounded up and packed down like a turnpike. Such roads were opened all over the country and were kept open only by ceaseless vigilance and labor. Food and fuel were got, somehow; famishing deer and small game were easily obtained, but crops were lost, much of the live stock perished, and many kinds of small game were very nearly exterminated. Mail was interrupted for weeks at a time, carriers being unable to make the trip to Springfield.

In Sangamon county experiences of pioneers were identical. In Springfield and New Salem snow lay four feet in depth on the level. There was the same ice-crust; the same incessant, biting gale; the daily fresh falls of snow; the deer breaking through the crust with their sharp, bounding little hoofs and falling easy victims to hunters, wolves and dogs. It took a man an entire day to dig enough corn out of frozen shocks to keep a few cattle alive for two or three days. Stake-and-rider fences, corn shocks, low out buildings were buried; streams could be traced only by half submerged and snow-burdened lines of woods. All the familiar features of the landscape were obliterated in that smother and blur of snow. It was beyond human power to do more than to keep at bay the twin spectres of

cold and starvation. Many and ingeneious are the devices described
to ward away freezing and famine.

One cannot but admire the scholarly detachment and stoic self-
control of the newspapers of Illinois of that day. Statecraft was the
thing of permanent interest—speeches by Webster and Clay, political
moves by General Jackson, continued to engage the editorial mind.
Weather was a thing that today is, and tomorrow is cast into the
limbo of things forgotten. The entire country had been in the grip
of that pitiless winter for two months, before the *Illinois Intelligencer* of Vandalia, condescended to notice it. Then, in an editorial
paragraph of two sticks full of type, the subject was summed up
and dismissed:

"The newspapers that reach us from every direction, are filled
with accounts of severely cold weather, and immense falls of snow.
In no part of the continent has this been felt more severely than in
Illinois. We have had an extraordinary season. The cold has been
intense and uninterrupted. The whole country has been blocked up
with snowbanks, that have covered the earth since December.
Several travelers have perished on the prairies near here. Such a
winter has never been known in this region."

The Edwardsville *Advocate* shows a still greater restraint of style,
an economy of adjectives that is commended to our yellow press:
"We have issued no paper for the last two weeks, owing to the
excessively cold weather, and our office being too open to resist the
rude attacks of the northern blasts." It was a relief to discover, in
Missouri, a newspaper that betrayed interest, if not excitement, in
that phenomenal weather. But now for northern Illinois.

Eighteen Thirty-one, it should be remembered, was the year
before the Black Hawk War. Chicago was only a frontier fort and
trading post, whose first newspaper did not appear until nearly
three years later. The region between the Desplaines river and the
Mississippi was held by the Sacs and Foxes, and the only permanent
white settler appears to have been John Dixon, at Dixon's Ferry, on
Rock river. The mining town of Galena had communication with
the outer world only over the Mississippi. In southern Wisconsin, at
the point that is now Portage City, Ft. Winnebago was encompassed
by the wilderness. But for the circumstances that there was, at Ft.
Winnebago, a somewhat willful little lady, recently come from the
east as the bride of John H. Kinzie, United States Indian agent at
the post, and determined on a visit to her unknown mother-in-law
in Chicago, the record of that winter and spring in northern Illinois
would be meager, indeed. The bride took the journey, and lived to
tell of the dangers she had passed through; to tell of them in the

lifetime of people who shared its perils; to tell the story graphically, for she had the gift of literary expression. Juliette M. Kinzie was Chicago's first author, and some of us trail a long way behind her "Wau Bun" today. So much for the authenticity of this account.

The continuation of the wedding journey was planned for the Christmas holidays. But in Wisconsin, too, winter set in early and with severity. There was rain and wind and snow; then sleet and bitter cold and snow again. The storm of December 30 must have fallen on the frontier fort with greater fury than it did farther south, for early in January the snow was reported to lie five and six feet deep in the lead mining regions—an unheard of, unbelievable depth. The mail-carrier and dispatch-bearer to Chicago, had to lie over in an Indian lodge on the prairie for three weeks, and went nearly blind from the sun and flying snow.

Young Mrs. Kinzie had all the pluck of inexperience. She insisted on making the start to Chicago, in sledges lined with buffalo robes; but the commanding officer of the fort flatly forbade any such foolish undertaking threatening, at last, that if they started he would order the sentinels to fire on them. The station was storm bound all winter. Early in March the snow suddenly went off in a great flood. By the 8th the marshes and water courses were fringed with green, promising an early and genial spring. The start was made on horseback, with servants, an Indian guide, and a camping outfit on pack ponies. The journey to Chicago was usually made in five or six days; but it was necessary to go out of the way, somewhat, to cross the Rock river at Dixon's ferry, for the Indians were all gone on the hunt, and there would be no canoes at the usual crossings. Young Mrs. Kinzie consented to wear a habit of heavy military broadcloth, but kept her kid gloves, and blithely donned the latest confection in straw bonnets, a part of her wedding finery.

The first day a canoe was upset, and the bride was tumbled into an icy stream. Her riding habit froze stiff and stood upright until it was thawed by the camp fire hastily built. The ground froze so hard that night that it was difficult to drive tent pins. In the morning a dazzling white blanket lay on the prairie, as if winter had taken a fresh start, and they rode all day in a freezing sleet. It took the party five days to reach Dixon's Ferry. On the 15th of March water left in a coffee-pot froze solid over night. They crossed a wide marsh, frozen as hard as iron, in an arctic gale. Another snow-storm impenetrable to the eye as a fog at sea made even the Indian guide lose all sense of direction, and they wandered from their course in the blizzard.

When still fifty miles from Chicago, their food gave out. In the nick of time one lone Pottawatomie lodge was found, but game had been made so scarce by the terrible winter that the Indians had nothing to share with them but wild artichokes. Presently some ducks were shot, for a hurricane swept down from the north, and myriads of waterfowl that had migrated northward only two weeks before, fled southward from a land of famine. The leaden sky above ice-locked streams was black with them, screaming before the blast. The little band of travelers were sobered by the sight. Their own escape from the perils of that frigid plain was by no means certain.

Setting up their tents in the doubtful shelter of a belt of woods, trees crashed around them all night long, while the world seemed rocked in the tempest. Fifty forest giants lay around their tents in the morning, and it was with difficulty that the horses picked their way out, over prostrate trunks. They were dazed to find themselves and their animals uninjured. The fury of the storm was over, but the weather was intensely cold. Mrs. Kinzie beat her feet against her saddle, until they were bruised, to keep them from freezing. Streams that had been in flood were frozen over again, but not thickly enough to bear the weight. They had to break up the ice and swim the horses across. They were over the east fork of the Desplaines no more than an hour, fed and sheltered in a white man's cabin, when the ice broke up again, with thunderous crashes, and the floods fell, the wild, ice-blocked torrent carrying forest trees down with it. One hour's delay and the already exhausted little party would have been marooned, and must have perished on a prairie that was an arctic desert. The time is not definitely stated, but the journey is figured out from the narrative as having taken thirteen or fourteen days.

Nor was this incredible weather yet ended for northern Illinois. Leaving his wife with his mother, John H. Kinzie, after a three weeks' visit, started back to Fort Winnebago in the second week of April. He was overtaken by a storm, so severe and prolonged, that he and his men had to lie over in an Indian lodge for three days. In Chicago, young Mrs. Kinzie records that only twice, during the two months of her stay (until late in May), did the sun shine out through the entire day. The weather continued inclement beyond anything that had ever been known at Fort Dearborn. Some young men who went out to the Calumet region in April to hunt were given up for lost. They were saved from freezing to death only by having two blankets apiece with them, and by taking refuge in an empty cabin on the marsh.

In southern Illinois there was the same sudden thaw, in early March, causing the waters to rise "higher than they had been since

Noah's flood." But the temperature fell again, not so low that another freeze was recorded, but the snow-turnpikes that had been made along main-traveled roads, remained long after the great body of snow had melted—shining ribbons of white across the green spring prairie. Dr. Hildreth at Marietta says that a belt of clouds encircled the western states for six months after the "great eclipse" of the sun in February, making a cold, dark, stormy summer. Corroboration of that was received from Kentucky. Inquiry of the Nautical Almanac Bureau in Washington as to that eclipse, resulted in the information that it was only the annular eclipse, and of no importance. Peculiar meteorological conditions attending it probably made it appear as a "great eclipse" at Marietta.

Of the high floods of the spring of 1831, there is very convincing proof in the fact that Lincoln had engaged to meet Denton Offutt in Springfield, as soon as the snow should go off, to take a boat load of merchandise, that Offutt was to have ready at Beardstown, down to New Orleans. When the snow did go off travel by land was impracticable, so Lincoln, John Hanks and John D. Johnston came down the Sangamon in a big canoe. Offutt had been unable to procure a flat boat in Beardstown. The water promised to remain so high, however, that Lincoln and his two relatives took timber out of the woods and built a boat at Sangamon Town, seven miles north of Springfield.

They had a misadventure there in launching a dug-out that nearly ended in a drowning. Thus, in the middle of April, the Sangamon is described as "fairly booming," "running with the speed of a mill-race" and with such a roaring sound that the voices of the men on shore failed to carry to the men struggling in the flood. Lincoln straddled a log, paid out with a rope tied to a tree, and rescued two men from perilous perches in the branches of a drifted giant of the forest. This flood, says Miss Tarbell, in a footnote to her "Life of Lincoln," followed the "Winter of the Deep Snow," from which early settlers of Illinois calculated time. Nicolay and Hay give two pages to the deep snow of 1831 and the subsequent flood.

If further proof were needed that there was an exceptionally severe season in Illinois, ample evidence is readily forthcoming from neighboring states. In Indiana "the weather was steadily and severely cold. The snow fell from 12 to 18 inches in February, and the temperature to 18 and 20 degrees below zero, at the settlement of Indianapolis, by far the coldest weather ever known. On the 11th of April, the steamboat Robert Hanna arrived, the only steamboat that ever came up to that point on the White river."

Missouri keeps up its reputation by "showing" real weather.

There was sleighing in St. Louis on New Year's day, and the river was closed by ice both above and below the city. In February the weather was so severe that public and private charity was taxed to prevent suffering and death. The files of the *Missouri Intelligencer* of Columbia for 1831 yielded an abundance of evidence. In the issue of Christmas day, 1830, mention is first made of the severity of the weather. On January 8, 1831, the following occurs: "We are informed that the snow in the upper counties of Missouri is 41 inches deep, and, what is very remarkable, the falling was accompanied by frequent and tremendous peals of thunder and vivid blue streaks of lightning. It was an awful scene, indeed."

The issue for January 15th is only a half-sheet. The little settlement was cut off from the world. "Have no news. Last three mails brought only one Washington paper, no paper from Jefferson City. (Distance about thirty miles). St. Louis *Times* reports eight to 10 inches of snow in last storm. Here it was not less than 20 inches, and most of it remains, for the weather has been intensely cold." February 5, report from Rock Spring, Ill. (near Alton), dated January 19, says: "Have had northern winter for four weeks. Snow lies three feet deep on the level in Morgan and Sangamon county. Around Vandalia it is one glaze of ice. Still snowing." February 12—On Monday, 9 or 10 more inches of snow; Wednesday, two or three more; five degrees below zero. The St. Louis *Times* quotes eastern papers as having accounts of 18 inches of snow at Baltimore. February 19—Accounts of snow-storms in Kentucky, Tennessee, New York, etc. Severity of temperatures and great depth of snow, extending from Missouri to Maine, presents an extraordinary winter. Another "old-fashioned" snow storm gripped Missouri on the 14th. March 5—An extract from the Illinois *Pioneer,* Rock Spring (near Alton), announces the general thaw and adds this: "French settlers along the river say that about fifty years ago the winter was as severe as this one." May 21—Many and long-continued rains are mentioned.

Those rains were the special grievance of Kentucky. As Colonel Waterson once plaintively remarked, after a Democratic defeat: "Nothing but weather and elections." On May 10, 1831, there was an extensive and violent hail storm in several counties, with hail stones three inches in circumference. July 22d, a tremendous electric storm did incredible damage to property. Finally the Ohio river was frozen over solid, from December 11, 1831, to January 8, 1832. When the ice broke up, nine steamboats were destroyed. In February, 1832, there was the greatest flood ever known, with violent gales that capsized steamboats.

Dr. Hildreth at Marietta confirms the fact that inclement weather extended over the entire year of 1831. He says: "There were 160 cloudy days, fifty-seven more than in 1830. Fruit trees were three weeks late in blossoming. Heavy rains commenced falling late in June and continued all summer. Crops were beaten down and destroyed." The Mississippi was so swollen that the largest steamboats were able to come up to St. Louis in mid-summer. The steamboat Yellowstone went up to the mouth of the Little Missouri, above Bismarck, N.D., 600 miles farther than any steamer had navigated before, returning to St. Louis safely, in the middle of July. Throughout July there were heavy rains in the Mississippi bottoms that destroyed crops and washed away bridges. On the 30th of June, a destructive tornado, accompanied by hail and torrents of rain, was reported from Port Gibson, Miss. Late in October the St. Louis mail coach, in crossing the Elm river, was overturned by the force of the swollen current, and sunk in 10 feet of water. At Marietta, O., there were only eight or ten days of Indian summer, instead of three or four weeks, and winter set in with vigor, late in November. By December 4, the rivers were full of ice. On the 10th the Ohio could be crossed by the heaviest teams. The Mississippi was reported frozen over solid for 130 miles south of the mouth of the Ohio and there was skating in New Orleans. The winter was very severe, but less snow fell than in 1831, only six or eight inches.

. . . .

Two descriptions of Chicago, one written in 1823 by William H. Keating, the other published a decade later by Charles J. Latrobe, portray Chicago as an unimpressive village surrounded by Indian tribes with "no cheering prospects." The city was not to come into its own until the frontier had passed. Keating, a professor of chemistry at the University of Pennsylvania, accompanied Major Stephen H. Long on his exploratory expedition to the upper Mississippi in 1823. Latrobe, a London-born mountain climber, came to America in 1832 and, after a stop at New York City, journeyed on to Chicago. A full discussion of Chicago during those years is found in the first volume of Bessie Louise Pierce, *A History of Chicago*, 3 volumes (New York, 1940).

Fort Dearborn and Chicago, 1823

WILLIAM H. KEATING

Fort Dearborn is situated in the State of Illinois, on the south bank, and near to the mouth of Chicago river; the boundary line between this state and that of Indiana strikes the western shore of Lake Michigan ten miles north of its southernmost extremity, and then continues along the shore of the lake until it reaches the forty-second and a half degree of north latitude, along which it extends to the Mississippi. The post at Chicago was abandoned a few months after the party visited it. Its establishment had been found necessary to intimidate the hostile and still very powerful tribes of Indians that inhabit this part of the country; but the rapid extension of the white population to the west, the establishment along the Mississippi of a chain of military posts which encloses them, and at the same time convinces them of the vigilance of the government, and of the inevitable destruction which they would bring upon themselves by the most trifling act of hostility on their part, have, it is thought, rendered the continuance of a military force at this place unnecessary. An Indian agent remains there, in order to keep up amicable relations with them, and to attend to their wants, which are daily becoming greater, owing to the increasing scarcity of game in the country.

We were much disappointed at the appearance of Chicago and its vicinity. We found in it nothing to justify the great eulogium lavished upon this place by a late traveller, who observes that "it is the most fertile and beautiful that can be imagined." "As a farming

From William H. Keating, *Narrative of an Expedition to the Source of St. Peter's River ... 1823 ... under the Command of Stephen H. Long, U.S.T.E.; Compiled from Notes on Major Long, Messrs. Say, Keating and Calhoun* (Philadelphia, 1824), I, 163-167. Footnotes in the original have been omitted.

Courtesy of the Illinois State Historical Library

Chicago in 1831

country," says he, "it unites the fertile soil of the finest lowland prairies with an elevation which exempts it from the influence of stagnant waters, and a summer climate of delightful serenity." The best comment upon this description of the climate and soil is the fact that, with the most active vigilance on the part of the officers, it was impossible for the garrison, consisting of from seventy to ninety men, to subsist upon the grain raised in the country, although much of their time was devoted to agricultural pursuits. The difficulties which the agriculturist meets with here are numerous; they arise from the shallowness of the soil, from its humidity, and from its exposure to the cold and damp winds which blow from the lake with great force during most part of the year. The grain is frequently destroyed by swarms of insects. There are also a number of destructive birds of which it was impossible for the garrison to avoid the baneful influence, except by keeping, as was practised at Fort Dearborn, a party of soldiers constantly engaged in shooting at the crows and blackbirds that committed depredations upon the corn planted by them. But, even with all these exertions the maize seldom has time to ripen, owing to the shortness and coldness of the season. The provisions for the garrison were, for the most part, conveyed from Mackinaw in a schooner, and sometimes they were brought from St. Louis, a distance of three hundred and eighty-six miles up the Illinois and Des Plaines river.

The appearance of the country near Chicago offers but few features upon which the eye of the traveller can dwell with pleasure. There is too much uniformity in the scenery; the extensive water prospect is a waste unchecked by islands, unenlivened by the spreading canvas, and the fatiguing monotony of which is increased by the equally undiversified prospect of the land scenery, which affords no relief to the sight, as it consists merely of a plain, in which but few patches of thin and scrubby woods are observed scattered here and there.

The village presents no cheering prospect, as, notwithstanding its antiquity, it consists of but few huts, inhabited by a miserable race of men, scarcely equal to the Indians from whom they are descended. Their log or bark-houses are low, filthy and disgusting, displaying not the least trace of comfort. Chicago is, perhaps, one of the oldest settlements in the Indian country; its name, derived from the Potawatomi language, signifies either a skunk, or wild onion; and each of these significations has been occasionally given for it. A fort is said to have formerly existed there. Mention is made of the place as having been visited in 1671 by Perrot, who found "Chicagou" to be the residence of a powerful chief of the Miamis. The number of trails centering all at this spot, and their apparent antiquity, indicate that this was probably for a long while the site of a large Indian village. As a place of business, it offers no inducement to the settler; for the whole annual amount of the trade on the lake did not exceed the cargo of five or six schooners, even at the time when the garrison received its supplies from Mackinaw. It is not impossible that at some distant day, when the banks of the Illinois shall have been covered with a dense population, and when the low prairies which extend between that river and Fort Wayne, shall have acquired a population proportionate to the produce which they can yield, that Chicago may become one of the points in the direct line of communication between the northern lakes and the Mississippi; but even the intercourse which will be carried on through this communication, will, we think, at all times be a limited one; the dangers attending the navigation of the lake, and the scarcity of harbours along the shore, must ever prove a serious obstacle to the increase of the commercial importance of Chicago. The extent of the sand banks which are formed on the eastern and southern shore, by the prevailing north and northwesterly winds, will likewise prevent any important works from being undertaken to improve the post of Chicago.

Chicago, 1833

CHARLES J. LATROBE

I have been in many odd assemblages of my species, but in few, if any, of an equally singular character as with that in the midst of which we spent a week at Chicago.

This little mushroom town is situated upon the verge of a perfectly level tract of country, for the great part consisting of open prairie lands, at a point where a small river whose sources interlock in the wet season with those of the Illinois, enters Lake Michigan. It however forms no harbour, and vessels must anchor in the open lake, which spreads to the horizon to the north and east, in a sheet of unbroken extent.

Fort Dearborn . . . is a small stockaded enclosure with two block-houses, and is garrisoned by two companies of infantry. It had been nearly abandoned till the late Indian war on the frontier made its occupation necessary. The upstart village lies chiefly on the right bank of the river above the fort. When the proposed steam-boat communication between Chicago and the St. Joseph's river, which lies forty miles distant across the lake, is put into execution, the journey to Detroit may be effected in three days, whereas we had been upwards of six on the road.

. . . .

The Pottawattomies were encamped on all sides,—on the wide level prairie beyond the scattered village, beneath the shelter of the low woods which chequered them, on the side of the small river, or to the leeward of the sand hills near the beach of the lake. They consisted of three principal tribes with certain adjuncts from smaller tribes. The main divisions are, The Pottawattomies of the Prairie and those of the Forest, and these are subdivided into distinct villages under their several chiefs.

The General Government of the United States, in pursuance of the scheme of removing the whole Indian population westward of the Mississippi, had empowered certain gentlemen to frame a Treaty with these tribes, to settle the terms upon which the cession of their Reservations in these States should be made.

A preliminary council had been held with the chiefs some days before our arrival. The principal Commissioner had opened it, as we learnt, by stating, that, as "the Great Father in Washington had heard that they wished to sell their land, he had sent Commissioners to treat with them." The Indians promptly answered by their organ,

From Charles J. Latrobe, *The Rambler in North America*, 2d ed. (London, 1836), II, pp. 203-216. Footnotes in the original have been omitted.

"that their Great Fathers in Washington must have seen a bad bird which had told him a lie, for that far from wishing to sell their land, they wished to keep it." The Commissioner, nothing daunted, replied: "that nevertheless, as they had come together for a Council, they must take the matter into consideration." He then explained to them promptly the wishes and intentions of their Great Father, and asked their opinion thereon. Thus pressed, they looked at the sky, saw a few wandering clouds, and straightway adjourned *sine die,* as the weather is not clear enough for so solemn a council.

However, as the Treaty had been opened, provision was supplied to them by regular rations; and the same night they had had great rejoicings,—danced the war-dance, and kept the eyes and ears of all open by running howling about the village.

Such was the state of affairs on our arrival. Companies of old warriors might be seen sitting smoking under every bush; arguing, palavering, or "powwowing," with great earnestness; but there seemed no possibility of bringing them to another Council in a hurry.

Meanwhile the village and its occupants presented a most motley scene.

The fort contained within its palisades by far the most enlightened residents, in the little knot of officers attached to the slender garrison. The quarters here consequently were too confined to afford place of residence for the Government Commissioners, for whom and a crowd of dependents, a temporary set of plank huts were erected on the north side of the river. To the latter gentlemen we, as the only idle lookers on, were indebted for much friendly attention; and in the frank and hospitable treatment we received from the inhabitants of Fort Dearborn, we had a foretaste of that which we subsequently met with everywhere under like circumstances, during our autumnal wanderings over the Frontier.

. . . .

Next in rank to the Officers and Commissioners, may be noticed certain store-keepers and merchants resident here; looking either to the influx of new settlers establishing themselves in the neighbourhood, or those passing yet further to the westward, for custom and profit; not to forget the chance of extraordinary occasions like the present. Add to these a doctor or two, two or three lawyers, a land-agent, and five or six hotel-keepers. These may be considered as stationary, and proprietors of the half a hundred clap-board houses around you.

Then for the birds of passage, exclusive of the Pottawattomies, of whom more anon—and emigrants and land-speculators as numerous as the sand. You will find horse-dealers, and horse-stealers,—rogues of every description, white, black, brown, and red—half-breeds, quarter-breeds, and men of no breed at all;—dealers in pigs, poultry, and potatoes;—men pursuing Indian claims, some for tracts of land, others . . . for pigs which the wolves had eaten;—creditors of the tribes, or of particular Indians, who know that they have no chance of getting their money, if they do not get it from the Government agents;—sharpers of every degree; pedlars, grog-sellers; Indian agents and Indian traders of every description, and Contractors to supply the Pottawattomies with food. The little village was in an uproar from morning to night, and from night to morning; for, during the hours of darkness, when the housed portion of the population of Chicago strove to obtain repose in the crowded plank edifices of the village, the Indians howled, sang, wept, yelled, and whooped in their various encampments. With all this, the whites seemed to me to be more pagan than the red men.

You will have understood, that the large body of Indians, collected in the vicinity, consisted not merely of chiefs and warriors, but that in fact the greater part of the whole tribe were present.

. . . .

Far and wide the grassy Prairie teemed with figures; warriors mounted or on foot, squaws, and horses. Here a race between three or four Indian ponies, each carrying a double rider, whooping and yelling like fiends. There a solitary horseman with a long spear, turbaned like an Arab, scouring along at full speed;—groups of hobbled horses; Indian dogs and children, or a grave conclave of grey chiefs seated on the grass in consultation.

It was amusing to wind silently from group to group—here noting the raised knife, the sudden drunken brawl, quashed by the good-natured and even playful interference of the neighbours; there a party breaking up their encampment, and falling with their little train of loaded ponies, and wolfish dogs, into the deep black narrow trail running to the north. You peep into a wig-wam, and see a domestic feud; the chief sitting in dogged silence on the mat, while the women, of which there were commonly two or three in every dwelling, and who appeared every evening even more elevated with the fumes of whiskey than the males, read him a lecture. From another tent a constant voice of wrangling and weeping would proceed, when suddenly an offended fair one would draw the mat aside, and taking a youth standing without by the hand, lead him apart, and sitting down on the grass, set up the most indescribable whine as she told her grief. Then forward comes an Indian, staggering with his chum from a debauch; he is met by his squaw, with her child dangling in a fold of her blanket behind, and the sobbing and weeping which accompanies her whining appeal to him, as she hangs to his hand, would melt your heart, if you did not see that she was quite as tipsy as himself.

Here sitting apart and solitary, an Indian expends the exuberance of his intoxicated spirits in the most ludicrous singing and gesticulation; and there squat a circle of unruly topers indulging themselves in the most unphilosophic and excessive peals of laughter.

It is a grievous thing that Government is not strong-handed enough to put a stop to the shameful and scandalous sale of whiskey to these poor miserable wretches. But here lie casks of it for sale under the very eye of the Commissioners, met together for purposes, which demand that sobriety should be maintained, were it only that no one should be able to lay at their door an accusation of unfair dealing, and of having taken advantage of the helpless Indian in a bargain, whereby the people of the United States were to be so greatly the gainers. And such was the state of things day by day.

The British novelist Charles Dickens had been taken in by exaggerated promotional literature on the possibilities of financial investment in the city of Cairo, and he had lost a considerable sum of money in the abortive Cairo City and Canal Company. His views on the state may well have been colored by this unfortunate experience. In any event, following a visit to the United States in 1842, he published *American Notes*, the humorous and rather contemptuous travelogue in which he describes the uncomfortable travel accommodations and the "desolate kind of waste" to be found in the Prairie State. *Charles Dickens: His Tragedy and Triumph*, 2 vols. (1953), by E. Johnson is a major study of the man and his work.

The Looking-Glass Prairie, 1842

CHARLES DICKENS

I may premise that the word Prairie is variously pronounced *paraaer, parearer,* and *paroarer.* The latter mode of pronunciation is perhaps the most in favour.

We were fourteen in all, and all young men: indeed it is a singular though very natural feature in the society of these distant settlements, that it is mainly composed of adventurous persons in the prime of life, and has very few grey heads among it. There were no ladies: the trip being a fatiguing one: and we were to start at five o'clock in the morning punctually.

I was called at four, that I might be certain of keeping nobody waiting; and having got some bread and milk for breakfast, threw up the window and looked down into the street, expecting to see the whole party busily astir, and great preparations going on below. But as everything was very quiet, and the street presented that hopeless aspect with which five o'clock in the morning is familiar elsewhere, I deemed it as well to go to bed again and went accordingly.

I woke again at seven o'clock, and by that time the party had assembled, and were gathered round, one light carriage, with a very stout axletree; one something on wheels like an amateur carrier's cart; one double phaeton of great antiquity and unearthly construction; one gig with a great hole in its back and a broken head; and one rider on horseback who was to go on before. I got into the first coach with three companions; the rest bestowed themselves in the other vehicles; two large baskets were made fast to the lightest; two

From Charles Dickens, *American Notes for General Circulation*, II (London, 1842), pp. 177-184.

large stone jars in wicker cases, technically known as demi-johns, were consigned to the "least rowdy" of the party for safe-keeping; and the procession moved off to the ferry-boat, in which it was to cross the river bodily, men, horses, carriages, and all, as the manner in these parts is.

We got over the river in due course, and mustered again before a little wooden box on wheels, hove down all aslant in a morass, with *"merchant tailor"* painted in very large letters over the door. Having settled the order of proceeding, and the road to be taken, we started off once more and began to make our way through an ill-favoured Black Hollow, called, less expressively, the American Bottom.

The previous day had been—not to say hot, for the term is weak and lukewarm in its power of conveying an idea of the temperature. The town had been on fire; in a blaze. But at night it had come on to rain in torrents, and all night long it had rained without cessation. We had a pair of very strong horses, but travelled at the rate of little more than a couple of miles an hour, through one unbroken slough of black mud and water. It had no variety but in depth. Now it was only half over the wheels, now it hid the axletree, and now the coach sank down in it almost to the windows. The air resounded in all directions with the loud chirping of the frogs, who, with the pigs (a coarse, ugly breed, as unwholesome-looking as though they were the spontaneous growth of the country), had the whole scene to themselves. Here and there we passed a log hut: but the the wretched cabins were wide apart and thinly scattered, for though the soil is very rich in this place, few people can exist in such a deadly atmosphere. On either side of the track, if it deserve the name, was the thick "bush;" and everywhere was stagnant, slimy, rotten, filthy water.

As it is the custom in these parts to give a horse a gallon or so of cold water whenever he is in a foam with heat, we halted for that purpose, at a long inn in the wood, far romoved from any other residence. It consisted of one room, bare-roofed and bare-walled of course, with a loft above. The ministering priest was a swarthy young savage, in a shirt of cotton print like bed-furniture, and a pair of ragged trousers. There were a couple of young boys, too, nearly naked, lying idle by the well; and they, and he, and *the* traveller at the inn, turned out to look at us.

The traveller was an old man with a grey grizzly beard two inches long, a shaggy moustache of the same hue, and enormous eyebrows; which almost obscured his lazy, semi-drunken glance, as he stood regarding us with folded arms: poising himself alternately upon his toes and heels. On being addressed by one of the party, he drew nearer, and said, rubbing his chin (which scraped under his horny hand like fresh gravel beneath a nailed shoe), that he was from Delaware, and had lately bought a farm "down there," pointing into one of the marshes where the stunted trees were thickest. He was "going," he added, to St. Louis, to fetch his family, whom he had left behind; but he seemed in no great hurry to bring on these incumbrances, for when we moved away, he loitered back into the cabin, and was plainly bent on stopping there so long as his money lasted. He was a great politician of course, and explained his opinions at some length to one of our company; but I only remember that he concluded with two sentiments, one of which was, Somebody for ever; and the other, Blast everybody else! which is by no means a bad abstract of the general creed in these matters.

When the horses were swollen out to about twice their natural dimensions (there seems to be an idea here, that this kind of inflation improves their going), we went forward again, through mud and mire, and damp, and festering heat, and brake and bush, attended always by the music of the frogs and pigs, until nearly noon, when we halted at a place called Belleville.

Belleville was a small collection of wooden houses, huddled together in the very heart of the bush and swamp. Many of them had singularly bright doors of red and yellow; for the place had been lately visited by a travelling painter, "who got along," as I was told, "by eating his way." The criminal court was sitting, and was at that moment trying some criminals for horse-stealing: with whom it would most likely go hard: for live stock of all kinds being necessarily very much exposed in the woods, is held by the community in rather higher value than human life; and for this reason, juries generally make a point of finding all men indicted for cattle-stealing, guilty, whether or no.

The horses belonging to the bar, the judge, and the witnesses, were tied to temporary racks set up roughly in the road; by which it is to be understood, a forest path, nearly knee-deep in mud and slime.

There was an hotel in this place, which, like all hotels in America, had its large dining-room for the public table. It was an odd, shambling, low-roofed out-house, half-cowshed and half-kitchen, with a coarse brown canvas table-cloth, and tin sconces stuck against the walls, to hold candles at supper-time. The horseman had gone forward to have coffee and some eatables prepared, and they were by this time nearly ready. He had ordered "wheat-bread and chicken fixings," in preference to "corn-bread and common doings." The latter kind of refection includes only pork and bacon. The former comprehends broiled ham, sausages, veal cutlets, steaks, and such other viands of that nature as may be supposed, by a tolerably wide poetical construction, "to fix" a chicken comfortably in the digestive organs of any lady or gentleman.

On one of the door-posts at this inn, was a tin plate, whereon was inscribed in characters of gold, "Doctor Crocus;" and on a sheet of paper, pasted up by the side of this plate, was a written announcement that Dr. Crocus would that evening deliver a lecture on Phrenology for the benefit of the Belleville public, at a charge, for admission, of so much a head.

Straying upstairs, during the preparation of the chicken fixings, I happened to pass the doctor's chamber; and as the door stood wide open, and the room was empty, I made bold to peep in.

It was a bare, unfurnished, comfortless room, with an unframed portrait hanging up at the head of the bed; a likeness, I take it, of the Doctor, for the forehead was fully displayed, and great stress was laid by the artist upon its phrenological developments. The bed itself was covered with an old patch-work counterpane. The room was destitute of carpet or of curtain. There was a damp fireplace without any stove, full of wood ashes; a chair, and a very small table; and on the last-named piece of furniture was displayed, in grand array, the doctor's library, consisting of some half-dozen greasy old books.

Now, it certainly looked about the last apartment on the whole earth out of which any man would be likely to get anything to do him good. But the door, as I have said, stood coaxingly open, and plainly said in conjunction with the chair, the portrait, the table, and the books, "Walk in, gentlemen, walk in! Don't be ill, gentlemen, when you may be well in no time. Doctor Crocus is here, gentlemen, the celebrated Dr. Crocus! Doctor Crocus has come all this way to cure you, gentlemen. If you haven't heard of Dr. Crocus, it's your fault, gentlemen, who live a little way out of the world here: not Dr. Crocus's. Walk in, gentlemen, walk in!"

In the passage below, when I went downstairs again, was Dr. Crocus himself. A crowd had flocked in from the Court House, and a voice from among them called out to the landlord, "Colonel! introduce Dr. Crocus."

"Mr. Dickens," says the colonel, "Doctor Crocus."

Upon which Dr. Crocus, who is a tall, fine-looking Scotchman, but rather fierce and warlike in appearance for a professor of the peaceful art of healing, bursts out of the concourse with his right arm extended, and his chest thrown out as far as it will possibly come, and says:

"Your countryman, Sir!"

Whereupon Doctor Crocus and I shake hands; and Doctor Crocus looks as if I didn't by any means realise his expectations, which, in a linen blouse, and a great straw hat, with a green ribbon, and no gloves, and my face and nose profusely ornamented with the stings of mosquitoes and the bites of bugs, it is very likely I did not.

"Long in these parts, Sir?" says I.

"Three or four months, Sir," says the Doctor.

"Do you think of soon returning to the old country?" says I.

Doctor Crocus makes no verbal answer, but gives me an imploring look, which says so plainly, "Will you ask me that again, a little louder, if you please?" that I repeat the question.

"Think of soon returning to the old country, Sir?" repeats the Doctor.

"To the old country, Sir," I rejoin.

Doctor Crocus looks round upon the crowd to observe the effect he produces, rubs his hands, and says, in a very loud voice:

"Not yet awhile, Sir, not yet. You won't catch me at that just yet, Sir. I am a little too fond of freedom for *that*, Sir. Ha, ha! It's not so easy for a man to tear himself from a free country such as this is, Sir. Ha, ha! No, no! Ha, ha! None of that till one's obliged to do it, Sir. No, no!"

As Doctor Crocus says these latter words, he shakes his head, knowingly, and laughs again. Many of the bystanders shake their heads in concert with the doctor, and laugh too, and look at each other as much as to say, "A pretty bright and first-rate sort of chap is Crocus!" and unless I am very much mistaken a good many people went to the lecture that night, who never thought about phrenology, or about Doctor Crocus either, in all their lives before.

From Belleville, we went on, through the same desolate kind of waste, and constantly attended, without the interval of a moment, by the same music; until, at three o'clock in the afternoon, we halted once more at a village called Lebanon to inflate the horses again, and give them some corn besides: of which they stood much in need. Pending this ceremony, I walked into the village, where I met a full-sized dwelling-house coming down-hill at a round trot, drawn by a score or more of oxen.

The public-house was so very clean and good a one, that the managers of the jaunt resolved to return to it and put up there for the night, if possible. This course decided on, and the horses being well refreshed, we again pushed forward, and came upon the Prairie at sunset.

It would be difficult to say why, or how—though it was possibly from having heard and read so much about it—but the effect on me was disappointment. Looking towards the setting sun, there lay, stretched out before my view, a vast expanse of level ground; unbroken, save by one thin line of trees, which scarcely amounted to a scratch upon the great blank; until it met the glowing sky, wherein it seemed to dip: mingling with its rich colours and mellowing in its distant blue. There it lay, a tranquil sea or lake without water, if such a simile be admissible, with the day going down upon it: a few birds wheeling here and there: and solitude and silence reigning paramount around. But the grass was not yet high; there were bare black patches on the ground; and the few wild flowers that the eye could see, were poor and scanty. Great as the picture was, its very flatness and extent, which left nothing to the imagination, tamed it down and cramped its interest. I felt little of that sense of freedom and exhilaration which a Scottish heath inspires, or even our English downs awaken. It was lonely and wild, but oppressive in its barren monotony. I felt that in traversing the Prairies, I could never abandon myself to the scene, forgetful of all else; as I should do instinctively, were the heather underneath my feet, or an iron-bound coast beyond; but should often glance towards the distant and frequently-receding line of the horizon, and wish it gained and passed. It is not a scene to be forgotten, but it is scarcely one, I think (at all events, as I saw it), to remember with much pleasure, or to covet the looking-on again, in after-life.

We encamped near a solitary log-house, for the sake of its water, and dined upon the plain. The baskets contained roast fowls, buffalo's tongue (an exquisite dainty, by-the-way), ham, bread, cheese, and butter; biscuits, champagne, sherry; lemons and sugar for punch; and abundance of rough ice. The meal was delicious, and the entertainers were the soul of kindness and good humour. I have often recalled that cheerful party to my pleasant recollection since, and shall not easily forget, in junketings nearer home with friends of older date, my boon companions on the Prairie.

Returning to Lebanon that night, we lay at the little inn at which we had halted in the afternoon. In point of cleanliness and comfort it would have suffered by no comparison with any English alehouse, of a homely kind, in England.

Rising at five o'clock next morning, I took a walk about the village: none of the houses were strolling about to-day, but it was early for them yet, perhaps: and then amused myself by lounging in a kind of farm-yard behind the tavern, of which the leading features were, a strange jumble of rough sheds for stables; a rude colonnade, built as a cool place of summer resort; a deep well; a great earthen mound for keeping vegetables in, in winter time; and a pigeon-house, whose little apertures looked, as they do in all pigeon-houses, very much too small for the admission of the plump and swelling-breasted birds who were strutting about it, though they tried to get in never so hard. That interest exhausted, I took a survey of the inn's two parlours, which were decorated with coloured prints of Washington, and President Madison, and of a white-faced young lady (much speckled by the flies), who held up her gold neck-chain for the admiration of the spectator, and informed all admiring comers that she was "Just Seventeen:" although I should have thought her older. In the best room were two oil portraits of the kit-cat size, representing the landlord and his infant son; both looking as bold as lions, and staring out of the canvas with an intensity that would have been cheap at any price. They were painted, I think, by the artist who had touched up the Belleville doors with red and gold; for I seemed to recognise his style immediately.

After breakfast, we started to return by a different way from that which we had taken yesterday, and coming up at ten o'clock with an encampment of German emigrants carrying their goods in carts, who had made a rousing fire which they were just quitting, stopped there to refresh. And very pleasant the fire was; for, hot though it had been yesterday, it was quite cold to-day, and the wind blew keenly. Looming in the distance, as we rode along, was another of the ancient Indian burial-places, called The Monks' Mound; in memory of a body of fanatics of the order of La Trappe, who founded a desolate convent there, many years ago, when there were no settlers within a thousand miles, and were all swept off by the pernicious climate: in which lamentable fatality, few national people will suppose, perhaps, that society experienced any very severe deprivation.

The track of to-day had the same features as the track of yesterday. There was the swamp, the bush, and the perpetual chorus of frogs, the rank unseemly growth, the unwholesome steaming earth. Here and there, and frequently too, we encountered a solitary broken-down waggon, full of some new settler's goods. It was a pitiful sight to see one of these vehicles deep in the mire; the axletree broken; the wheel lying idly by its side; the man gone miles away, to look for assistance; the woman seated among their wandering household gods with a baby at her breast, a picture of forlorn, dejected patience; the team of oxen crouching down mournfully in the mud, and breathing forth such clouds of vapour from their mouths and nostrils, that all the damp mist and fog around seemed to have come direct from them.

In due time we mustered once again before the merchant tailor's, and having done so, crossed over to the city in the ferry-boat: passing, on the way, a spot called Bloody Island, the duelling-ground of St. Louis, and so designated in honour of the last fatal combat fought there, which was with pistols, breast to breast. Both combatants fell dead upon the ground; and possibly some rational people may think of them, as of the gloomy madmen on the Monks' Mound, that they were no great loss to the community.

2: The Passing Frontier

Among the earliest signs of the passing of the frontier in Illinois was the appearance of a new kind of settler in the Military Tract during the 1820s and 1830s—the prairie farmer. W.V. Pooley's *The Settlement of Illinois from 1830 to 1850* chronicles the influx of the Yankee farmer, who introduced a spirit that transformed the character of the northern half of the state. "The prairie man who was primarily a pioneer of the agricultural class," he states in this book, "had now jumped into first place to the exclusion of the hunter and small farmer." Pooley's work was a revision of his 1905 doctoral dissertation at the University of Wisconsin. Theodore Pease analyzes the quickened pace of social and cultural life and the problems of urbanization, crime, and education which had appeared by mid-century. This selection is from the twelfth chapter of *The Frontier State*.

The final article in this section of special accounts is a report of the violent deaths of the leaders of the Mormon settlers in Illinois, Joseph and Hyrum Smith. George R. Gayler, an authority on Mormon history, further analyzes the political background of the assassination of the Smith brothers in "The Mormons and Politics in Illinois: 1839-1844," *Journal of the Illinois State Historical Society*, XLIX (1956), 48-66. In the spring of 1971, the Society devoted an entire issue of the *Journal* to the story of the Mormons. For further reading on the Illinois Mormons, see Robert B. Flanders, *Nauvoo: Kingdom on the Mississippi* (Urbana, 1965) and the very readable *No Man Knows My History: The Life of Joseph Smith, the Mormon Prophet* (New York, 1945), by Fawn M. Brodie.

The Yankees Arrive

WILLIAM VIPOND POOLEY

By 1840 it appears that further encroachment had been made upon the great prairies, for all of the state, with the exception of a small part on the eastern side was credited with at least two inhabitants to the square mile. At this date the Military Tract is shown as settled and the outskirts of settlement along the Illinois river extended to Chicago instead of Peoria as designated a decade before. Population was densest on the western side of the state in a belt extending from Quincy to Jacksonville and thence south into Madison and St. Clair counties. The least number of settlers was on the northern and eastern prairies.

In 1850 those parts of the state bordering the Wabash, Ohio and Mississippi rivers were all credited with not less than eighteen inhabitants to the square mile. The strip of territory along the Illinois river was equally well settled as were those counties in the extreme north.

The prairies of eastern Illinois and of the Military Tract are clearly marked by the sparseness of settlement. No part of the state had more than forty-five settlers to the square mile.

These maps give a general idea of the location of population, but in detail they are not accurate. Settlements in 1830 were entirely within the timbered tracts; by 1840 the frontier had moved farther to the north, but still the settlers clung to the timber. Not until after 1850 was the settlement of the open prairies to be really accomplished.

During the years 1831 and 1832 the beginnings of settlement were made in northern and eastern Illinois. At the first alarm of the Black Hawk War the settlers, save in a few instances where communities seemed strong enough to maintain themselves against an Indian attack, fled back to the more thickly populated portions of the state and for the time the spread of settlement ceased along the northern Illinois frontier. These settlements had been planted by pioneers of the hunter type and when the flight southward came it

From W. V. Pooley, *The Settlement of Illinois from 1830 to 1850* (Madison, Wis., 1908), pp. 273-279, 280-281, 286-288. Footnotes in the original have been omitted.

appears that the hunter-pioneers lost their opportunity for settling the woodlands along the rivers of northern Illinois.

Several causes operated to make this retreat before the Indians a permanent one. The trip through the northern portion of the state in pursuit of the fleeing Indian chief disclosed for the first time its wonderful resources as an agricultural district. Here we see the greatest effect of the war of 1832 and one overpowering the temporary compression of settlement during that year.

From 1833 until 1837 or 1838 Illinois had a wonderful growth. The last of the Indian land titles within the limits of the state were extinguished, and the Indians themselves were either induced or compelled to vacate their claims in Illinois and to cross the Mississippi, thus removing the last cause for Indian scares and reassuring the immigrants from the East that their families and homes would be safe on the Illinois frontier. Land sales were constantly taking place at the various offices of the state and the immense internal improvement system already planned and soon to be begun, led the people not only of Illinois but of the eastern states, to believe that here were to be presented numerous opportunities for rapid acquisition of wealth.

. . . .

The farmers of New England, especially the generation of young men who could see no future for themselves in their native states, began to look to the great West for a livelihood. The development of the wool industry tended also to consolidate the small farms into large ones, and those farmers seeing an opportunity to dispose of their small holdings at good prices did so with the intention of moving to a new country. In the middle states frequent reports came, telling of the wonderful opportunities in the western country. Pamphlets advertising Illinois lands flooded the states from Ohio to the sea-board. Since the subdivision of farms had, in the Middle Atlantic states, reached such a degree that the small patches of ground would no longer comfortably support families, and since renters began to see that in the space of a few years they could own farms in the West by the investment of no more capital than they paid from year to year for rent, many were more than willing to try the experiment of western life.

. . . .

Gradually the stream increased in size and by 1835 the speculation in Illinois lands was fairly under way. The stages, steamboats, hotels, taverns and places of general resort were thronged with land sellers and land buyers and in advance of the thickest of the throng

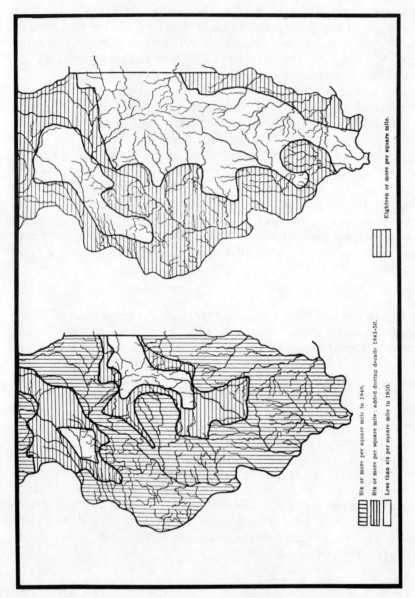

Six or more per square mile in 1840.

Six or more per square mile: added during decade 1841-50.

Less than six per square mile in 1850.

Eighteen or more per square mile.

Distribution of Illinois population in 1850

like an army of locusts seeking to devour the broad acres of the National domain, was the crowd of land speculators. Five million dollars worth of lands was entered during 1836. Even business men of sober, careful judgment, farmers and mechanics formerly wary and conservative, added their stimulus to the ever-increasing scramble for land and invested to the utmost limit which their credit would allow. Individuals who had reached their limit of credit, joined themselves together into companies and with the aid of the banks continued their financial gymnastics.

It is estimated that during the years 1835, 1836 and 1837 more than five hundred new towns were laid out in Illinois, each company believing that its town was, in the near future, to become a metropolis, the center of a thriving, populous, wealthy community.

. . . .

In this period just described (1833 to 1837) the character of the settlement of northern Illinois was fixed once for all—the prairie man who was primarily a pioneer of the agricultural class, or the third type in the succession as followed heretofore, had now jumped into first place to the exclusion of the hunter and the small farmer. Events had operated for this and the result was inevitable. While the pioneers who had occupied the Illinois river woodlands were still safely residing in the southern settlements waiting for the last echoes of the Black Hawk War to die away on the frontier, events were shaping themselves for a new immigration of a different type. Restlessness had ever been a failing of Americans and it was increased after 1830 by a combination of influences. In the previously enumerated causes may be found the reasons *for the new flow of immigration to Illinois, and in the application of steam to lake traffic may be found the influence directing this stream of immigration, which gave eastern rather than southern characteristics to northern Illinois. Illinois land was as fertile as any in the West and land was what the immigrant wanted; Chicago was the terminus of the lake route, a natural gateway to the prairies and as a consequence when the great rage for speculation broke out in the thirties and a wild rush was made to the West, Illinois received a liberal share of the new settlers.

The hunter-pioneers who were again returning to the woodlands of the upper Illinois were few in numbers; the agricultural pioneers from New England and New York were poured into Illinois in swarms by the ever-increasing number of lake steamers. As the mania for speculation increased, the army of immigrants increased also, until all the available timber of this portion of the state was taken up. The hunter was primarily a frontiersman; the new immigrant was primarily a farmer.

. . . .

Lines of transportation and communication influenced the character of the settlement of the various districts of the state. On the outskirts of the Great Prairie of eastern Illinois, in the timbered portions, were found the pioneers of the southwestern states, who had come by the southern wagon roads to this district. Later the men from Ohio and Indiana filled up the remaining spaces. They, too, to a great extent, came by various wagon roads and finding good land in this region were content to settle upon it. In the middle Illinois river counties the same thing is noticeable as in the southern portion of the Military Tract. Contact with the central Illinois counties, which were populated to a great extent by Kentuckians, influenced the population of these districts. Going farther to the north we find in the upper Illinois river counties and the valleys of the Fox and Rock rivers, the New Yorkers and New Englanders. They had come by the easiest road, over the Great Lakes, and had settled in the northern counties before the southern stream had reached the northern timber tracts. Across the state in the lead region a community with southern sympathies was planted. The Mississippi river was the highway of commerce and travel for this part of the state and the southern cities were the outlets of its commerce. As a consequence southern influences were brought to bear directly on the inhabitants of the district. Many of the settlers were southerners by birth and this fact combined with the close connection with the South by way of the river tended to give the entire region a marked southern tone.

The importance of communication is shown by the fact that the chief cities, Quincy, Peoria, Rushville, Peru, Ottawa, Joliet, Elgin, St. Charles, Rockford and Galena were on or near the rivers. Chicago and Waukegan were on Lake Michigan. Many of the small inland villages, through the influence of the railroads, grew to be of importance after 1850.

The census states that 736,931 native born Americans resided in Illinois in 1850. Of these 343,618 were natives of the state itself and 393,313 had come from other localities. Over 36,500 were New Englanders; 112,000 were from the Middle States; nearly 52,600 were from the South Atlantic States; 2,400 from Kentucky and Tennessee; 98,400 from the states of the Northwest Territory, and 9,469 were from across the Mississippi. New York sent 67,180 immigrants; Ohio, 64,219; Kentucky, 49,588; Pennsylvania, 37,979; Tennessee, 32,303; Indiana, 30,953 and Virginia, 24,697. The other states each sent less than 20,000. Not one New England state is found in the above list, the greatest number coming from any of those states came from Vermont, which sent 11,381. The representation from California was the least of all—three.

In closing the discussion it may be stated that the great pervading power which influenced the settlement of northern Illinois and built up this portion of the state with astonishing rapidity and which gave the northern character to its population was the development of steam navigation upon the lakes. It is true that the spirit of immigration pervaded the entire nation and that this factor augmented by general influences sweeping over the East and by local conditions in its various regions served as levers to start the movement westward with tremendous force; but it remained for the transportation lines of the Great Lakes to shape the course of the movement and to turn the stream into Illinois through its gateway at Chicago. In this respect the settlement of northern Illinois is typical of the development of the North Middle States in that the influence of the lines of transportation tended to reproduce in the New West hundreds of communities in sympathy with their parent states across the Alleghanies. The strong bonds of lines of transportation connecting the East and the West, tended to wipe out sectional feelings between these parts of the nation and the lack of lines connecting the North and South serves to increase this feeling between the North and the South. Sectionalism in the United States, with the increase of these transportation lines now changed rapidly from longitudinal to latitudinal.

Strictly speaking, the period from 1830 to 1850 is one of varied characteristics, but taken in the light of the solution of the problem of the prairies, it is one of beginnings only. The pioneer as yet did not understand the wide, treeless areas around him; he lacked confidence in his ability to cope with the difficulties they offered and he lacked the power to overcome these obstacles single-handed. Steam was again to be the key to the situation and during the following decade when the railroads spanned the state south and west from Chicago the line of communication with the East was completed. The market was brought closer to the consumer and to the producer, the problem of obtaining lumber and merchandise at reasonable prices was solved and most important of all, when the prairie farmer was finally able to see railroad trains cross the state day after day, he felt that no longer was he shut off from the rest of mankind when at last he swung clear of the timber and built his cabin on the open prairie.

Social, Educational, and Religious Advance, 1830-1848

THEODORE C. PEASE

Compared with the Illinois of 1818, the Illinois of 1848 was a community quickened into mental life and independence. On its accession to statehood, Illinois was intellectually provincial; its leaders came from older states, bringing with them tastes already established; and mental culture was the possession and badge of a social class. In 1848 this was in a measure still true; but Illinois colleges and schools had begun the work of democratizing education. Moreover, Illinois numbered among its citizens men like J. B. Turner and Thomas Ford whose thought, keen and original, was molded by the environment the state afforded them. Easterners came to quicken the life of the state, and their own intellectual life affected by the freedom of their new surroundings ceased to be purely eastern.

The cities growing up in the state were superimposing new and more complex social conditions on the older rural communities. The old-time Fourth of July celebration continued in vogue though sometimes under temperance or Sunday school auspices. As early as 1845, however, newspapers were descanting on the number of accidents during such celebrations and were calling for a sane Fourth. Chicago had queens of the May on May day and kept the old-fashioned New Year's custom of calls and refreshments. There were donation parties and church fairs. There were traveling circuses to carry amusement to the village, though these were condemned by the fastidious as indecent. There was dancing. There were theatricals in Chicago and other cities, amateur and professional, the latter becoming from the critic's point of view, increasingly valid. Among sports there were horse races which at least in Chicago were sometimes scenes of disorder. Of course there was hunting, sometimes in the form of community wolf drives. At Chicago there was a boxing academy in 1845. In 1840 there was even a cricket match between Chicago and Auplaine.

Chicago was growing up; by 1842 it recognized a need of shade trees, deprecated its ineffective system of checking the frequent fires, and dilated on the route northward it offered southern travelers. Moreover, it was acquiring, as had formerly Little Fort and even forgotten Salem, a reputation for bad morals; in 1842 women of evil fame scandalously accused pious men before grand juries. The

From Theodore C. Pease, *The Frontier State, 1818-1848* (Chicago, 1918), pp. 410-411, 426-439. Footnotes in the original have been omitted.

advantages which Chicago offered as a market for products and the frequency with which the farmer availed himself of them, made it appropriate for the newspapers to offer advice concerning his conduct in town. He must beware of taverns that assign him to garret rooms and set before him shinbone steak. He must never go to a house merely because a runner recommends it. He must be sure on the register to bracket his name with that of the bedfellow he chooses and to bespeak a room when he first enters.

. . . .

The crimes of the day were more numerous than those of the earlier period though in both instances they arose from the contact of the wilderness with the property rights of civilization. Robberies, at times involving large sums, were not infrequent. There was an occasional murder not the work of a gang; one notes but few cases of crimes of sex. Counterfeiting and forgery, especially of land titles, were prevalent. Gangs frequently combined several activities, making and circulating counterfeits, horse stealing, and occasional murder. The large scale operation and organization of these gangs, especially such a one as the banditti of the prairies in northern Illinois, went far beyond the ability of the slight legal machinery of the county to compass.

This being the case the citizens had occasional recourse to extraordinary means. Sometimes a mob would wreck a little hamlet, the resort of crime of all sorts, sometimes it would break up a gambling booth at a race course. Sometimes societies would be formed to put down horse stealing. Occasionally a man of doubtful life in a community who had excited the wrath of his neighbors might be visited with the extreme penalty of mob violence.

In southern Illinois, Massac and Pope counties had for years been terrorized by a powerful gang of horse thieves, counterfeiters, and robbers until in 1846 the honest portion of the citizens formed themselves into a band of regulators to torture and harass the rascals into leaving the state. Suspected persons were taken to the Ohio and held under water until willing to confess; "others had ropes tied around their bodies over their arms, and a stick twisted into the ropes until their ribs and sides were crushed in by force of the pressure" in order that information of their confederates might be gained. Such methods did not settle the matter, however, for the "Flatheads," as the outlaws were called, were too numerous and had been powerful for too long a period to be summarily disposed of. In Massac they gained the control of the county offices and in August made application to the governor for a militia force to sustain the authority of the law. "This disturbance," writes Governor Ford, "being at a distance of two hundred and fifty miles from the seat of government, and in a part of the country between which and the seat of government there was but very little communication, the facts concerning it were but imperfectly known to the governor." In the interval of inquiry that ensued, disturbances broke out more violently than ever. Regulators from Pope county and from Kentucky joined their fellows in Massac, drove out the officers, and defied the judgments of the circuit court—forcibly liberating those of their number who were arrested; they became so sweepingly tyrannical that the counties were almost as terrorized as under the outlaws. The militia, however, refused to turn out to protect officials in league with horse thieves. Thus the regulators were left undisputed masters of the county; they whipped, tarred and feathered, and drove out of the country both rascals and honest opponents. Conditions became somewhat quieter that winter through state intervention; special legislation was passed creating a court to try offenders and at the same time vesting the governor with additional powers in that region. Notwithstanding all efforts, however, spasmodic outbursts continued for years.

The struggle of the state to master its problem of education, despite its rich endowment, was marked with only a measured success. The main reliance for the education of the young was still on private schools. A report to the legislature of 1832 frankly admitted that the state policy must be one of grants in aid rather than one of forming by enactment a complete system. In Illinois finance the school, college, and seminary funds went into the state treasury to pay state expenses, the state holding itself responsible for the payment of interest for school purposes to teachers presenting proper schedules of teaching.

The absence of anything like uniformity or organization in the state's primary school system was keenly felt by those intimately connected with it. Teachers complained that parents afforded them no moral support in disciplining their children, that neighborhoods by preference employed the lowest bidders and therefore had the worst teachers. They complained of cold ill-ventilated schoolrooms, of the thousand and one different methods of teaching, use of books, and of other difficulties. The actual workings of the Illinois system under moderately favorable conditions may be gathered from the report of a school township secretary in Peoria county. His fund was $6,455.96 all loaned at ten to twelve per cent. Of the accrued interest, however, only $178.96 was collected; and this with $184.42 from the state school fund was paid to five teachers in amounts varying from $24.75 to $118.79. The schools, with two hundred and fifty pupils, ran two, four, six, eight, and eleven and one-half months respectively. With this may be compared the account of a school teacher in Tazewell, in whose school one hundred and ten scholars were registered with a maximum attendance on any day of fifty-eight. In addition to the "common school branches" this man taught astronomy, philosophy, chemistry, surveying, algebra, and bookkeeping.

Nevertheless in the thirties there was real and sometimes intelligent interest in educational problems. The demonstration of a new method of teaching English grammar by lectures would be the occasion of a newspaper invitation to the public to attend the meeting. In 1832-1833 the formation of an Illinois institute of education was undertaken to deal on the basis of educational statistics with the difficult problems of education in the state. In 1834 delegates to a state educational convention were chosen. That convention recommended the establishment of school districts by voluntary action but mainly devoted itself to recommendations regarding seminary and college funds. As early as 1837 one finds an appeal for the establishment of the office of superintendent of public instruction. Interest began to be directed in particular toward two different methods of school management and teaching—the New England system and the Prussian.

With the forties, however, the state moved on toward a unified system. Attention was called to the fact that one hundred thousand children in Illinois were said to be out of school and that 28,780 adults were accounted illiterate. The act of 1841 provided for township administration of school lands in the familiar way with an added provision that congressional townships might on vote of the people be incorporated for school purposes. The *Belleville Advocate* urged a similar organization in St. Clair county. An attempt in 1843 to secure an act allowing the taxation for schools by local vote called out a flash of the same opposition to taxation for education that had defeated the school law of 1825. O. H. Browning pleaded for it referring to what Connecticut's school system had done for that state, to which Orlando B. Ficklin retorted that taxing one class for the benefit of another was unjust—witness the fact that Connecticut had inundated the west with clockpeddlers and men who lived by their wits. In 1845 an act was passed incorporating all congressional townships as school townships and allowing voters in school districts to levy a special tax for the support of the schools. More than this, the school system of the state for the first time was given unity by the designation of the secretary of state as state superintendent of public schools. An attempt was made to secure state recognition of German schools, but in vain.

The last years of the old constitution were marked on the part of educators by a renewed interest and hopefulness in their profession. A teachers' convention called at Jacksonville in 1845 set itself to discuss education for professional, agricultural, mechanical, and commercial pursuits, differentiation of education for the sexes, the possibility of an efficient school system without a complete town-ship system, and possible state aid to colleges and seminaries in training teachers. A teachers' convention at Belvidere that same year considered the possibility of a normal school that appears to have been near akin to the teachers' institute.

The broadening interest in education perceived the possibility, and consequent necessity of teaching the blind and deaf. The bill for the establishment of the deaf and dumb asylum was passed in 1839, but because of insufficient funds, the building contract was not let until 1843; three years later the school opened with thirteen pupils. In 1847 a blind man had undertaken, at the expense of private charity in Jacksonville, the instruction of six blind children. The success of the experiment was instrumental two years later in the passage of "an act to establish the Illinois Institution for the Education of the Blind." Through the influence of the "Jacksonville crowd," that city, after much bickering in the legislature, secured both schools.

If Illinois lacked for a unified school system, it did not lack for much private effort in behalf of schools, seminaries, and colleges, a surprisingly large number of which struggled on. As early as 1830 one notes high schools and academies, sometimes free to subscrib-ers' children, sometimes combined with a young ladies' school to teach the polite accomplishments of that day. In 1833 the Convent of the Ladies of Visitation was established in connection with Menard Academy at Kaskaskia which three years later opened a commodious building to pupils. By 1842 eighteen sisters had the care of seventy pupils, twelve of whom were orphans taught free of charge. Tuition for the curriculum of literature, music, and arith-metic was one hundred and twenty-five dollars a year for boarding pupils, and twenty-five dollars for day students. In 1844 the school building was practically destroyed by the Mississippi flood, and this academy was removed to St. Louis; but Catholic day schools were maintained at Cahokia, La Salle, and other places in this state.

Every denomination was concerned with similar efforts to pro-vide instruction for its children. Cartwright advertised a school at Pleasant Plains that began with the three R's and ended with natural and moral philosophy and Latin and Greek, with promise of other sciences and "female accomplishments" as soon as suitable teachers could be found. Meanwhile, common branches were taught at the rate of five dollars for a five months' session and one might board with Cartwright for one dollar a week if paid in advance, otherwise the rate was a dollar and a quarter.

In 1835 the Jacksonville Female Academy was incorporated by the legislature, a majority voting to apply the stern republican principle of making trustees liable for debts contracted in their corporate capacity. The year 1836 saw a much larger crop of school corporations, a favorite type being the "manual labor" seminary in which the students were required to labor with their hands partly to lessen the cost of their education, partly for their health's sake. Session after session of the legislature added to the number of these schools, many of which had real life and energy. They offered studies similar to those in Cartwright's curriculum.

For children of well-to-do parents, however, outside schools held greater attractions. The Menard children went to Georgetown University or to Missouri schools. One school at Linden Wood, St. Louis, which asked two dollars and a half a week for plain tuition and board, prescribed a uniform that speaks a certain degree of luxury. Sabbath uniform dresses for summer were white dress, pink sash, handkerchief, straw bonnet trimmed with light blue ribbon, white cape, and black silk apron; for winter a crimson dress of English merino, white collar, black silk apron, and dark green cloak.

The legislature had never evidenced any intention of using immediately the college and seminary funds for establishing the schools for which they had been set aside. Popular opinion did not greatly protest. In 1840 the *Chicago Weekly Tribune* believed the time not yet ripe for a state college or university, though it did insist that the state should have a competent system of high schools and a school of education. In such a situation it was perhaps inevitable that, though deprecated by some, collegiate education would develop along sectarian lines. In 1835 an act incorporating four colleges, specified that no particular christian faith be held or taught in any, but the prohibition prevented only for the moment theological seminary training for it was soon evaded. In 1840 the state had twelve colleges, though Illinois College was the only one granting degrees.

The foundation of certain of these colleges had been laid before 1830. Shurtleff grew out of Peck's seminary at Rock Spring, which in 1831-1832 had been removed to Alton and opened there as Alton Seminary. It rejected in 1833 a character which forbade the teaching of theology by any professor; but in 1835 a somewhat objectionable compromise was accepted, a seminary being conducted side by side with the college until 1841, when the restriction was repealed. In 1836 the name of the college, in recognition of the donations of Dr. Benjamin Shurtleff, was changed to Shurtleff College.

. . . .

McKendree College, a Methodist institution, developed from Lebanon Seminary founded in 1828. At first there was strong opposition in the board of trustees itself both to abolition and to the establishment of a school of theology. The institution emphasized the manual training principle and boasted a female department. Students' board bills were payable two-thirds in produce, one-third in good bacon, pickled pork, beef, flour, or milch cows with young calves; tuition for a five months' term in the higher branches was eight dollars. The school was taken successively under the patronage of the Missouri and the Illinois conferences, and in gratitude for a donation from Bishop William McKendree it was renamed, first, McKendreean College, then, McKendree. It was incorporated with other colleges in 1835. The college had to suspend in 1845 but reopened in the next year with three professors and a principal for the preparatory department.

In 1835-1836 Bishop Philander Chase collected funds in England for an Episcopal college in Illinois; the corner stone of Jubilee College was laid in 1839 at Robins Nest, Peoria county, but a charter was not secured until 1847.

In 1837 the Presbyterians and Congregationalists laid the foundations for two small colleges. Through the Reverend Gideon Blackburn funds were obtained for a theological institution at Carlinville. He entered lands for eastern investors at two dollars an acre, keeping twenty-five cents of the surplus over government price for himself and appropriating the remainder to the purchase of lands for the college. In 1837 the future Blackburn University had in trust an endowment of seventeen thousand acres; the enterprise, however, lay dormant for twenty years, when in 1857 the college was formally incorporated.

The Reverend George W. Gale, a new school Presbyterian of New York, was responsible for the inception of the other educational venture. In order to combine study with wholesome physical labor for students he conceived the idea of buying at government prices a township of fertile western land, reserving a town site and large farm for the use of a college, and selling the remainder which carried tuition rights in the college at five dollars an acre; the surplus would endow the college. The project met with favor; in 1835 a committee inspected and purchased land in Knox county, and forty-six colonists there undertook to carry out the plan. In 1837 Knox

Manual Labor College was incorporated, and a year later forty students were enrolled at the formal opening of the academy. By 1842 there were one hundred and forty-seven preparatory students, and the collegiate department had been opened with ten freshmen.

Illinois College, the greatest educational venture of the Presbyterians and Congregationalists in Illinois, was the fruit, but a partial fruit indeed, of the imperial dream of a group of young students, the famous "Yale band." In Yale Theological Seminary, Theron Baldwin, John F. Brooks, Mason Grosvenor, Elisha Jenner, William Kirby, J. M. Sturtevant, and Asa Turner, with the magnificent enthusiasm of youth planned to be workers in an enterprise, both educational and religious, to raise the west out of intellectual darkness. Some of them were to serve as settled ministers or missionaries, some of them to give their time to seminaries and to a college that was to crown the whole educational system. At the time that this idea was taking form the Reverend J. M. Ellis, a Presbyterian missionary in Illinois since 1826, was busy with the scheme of a college in the state of Illinois at Jacksonville; and the little group, accepting it as the center of their enterprise—the seat of a new and greater Yale to be reared on the western prairies—enlisted the American Home Missionary Association in its support. Illinois College opened in January of 1830 with Julian Sturtevant as teacher in it; during the year the Reverend Edward Beecher came to be president; three years later, a brother of Asa Turner, Jonathan Baldwin Turner, arrived and began his connection with the state. In 1835-1836 there were four seniors, seven juniors, thirteen sophomores, sixteen freshmen, and forty preparatory students. In 1839 the preparatory department was abandoned as tending to lower the tone of the college. Meanwhile in 1837, Baldwin, who had served as a pastor and as editor of the *Common School Advocate*, became principal of the Monticello Female Seminary. The college had to meet the question of finance. Its founders were able to supplement local resources with contributions from the treasuries of the society in the east. A subscription of seventy-five thousand dollars was lost in the panic of 1837. Finally in 1843 the Society for Promoting Collegiate and Theological Education at the West, with Theron Baldwin as its secretary and financial agent, took Illinois College over together with Western Reserve, Wabash, Marietta, and Lane colleges. In 1846 Sturtevant urged that the property of the college be sold for Illinois bonds then at a heavy discount, but the scheme was too visionary for the trustees, and they preferred to sell for cash.

From a larger point of view the college never met the ideal of its founders, but by no fault of theirs. To begin with the scheme excited jealousy both from rival denominations and from those who believed New England was plotting to federalize the west. Hardly had Sturtevant arrived when Peter Cartwright delivered himself of a sermon, anathematizing and caricaturing Presbyterian doctrine and ridiculing learned ministers; and Sturtevant, at the time just pain- fully learning to preach without reading his sermon, was at a disadvantage. Further the jealousy between old school and new school, and new school and Congregational was to do its work. The "Yale band" had imbibed at their alma mater the theology of N. W. Taylor which was anathema to the strict Presbyterian. In 1833 Edward Beecher, Julian Sturtevant, and William Kirby were accused of heresy in the Presbytery at Jacksonville; but subsequently they were acquitted. In 1839, despite previous attempts on the part of Beecher and Sturtevant to prevent it, a Congregational church was organized at Jacksonville. Sturtevant later gave some countenance to it; and as the tide of New Englanders sweeping into the north disregarded the plan of union and organized churches of their own, distrust and suspicion deepened. The antislavery views of men like Beecher and Sturtevant were an added difficulty. Finally, in 1844, Beecher resigned, possibly from necessity. Turner followed him a few years later; but Sturtevant remained to round out a long career at Jacksonville.

The story of Illinois College leads naturally to the consideration of one of the most remarkable men intellectually in the state of that day—Jonathan Baldwin Turner. The fact that of what he offered her, his country, and especially his adopted state, cared to take only the Osage orange hedge and the agricultural college, should not blind the student to the fact that Turner's intellectual interests were far broader than either scientific agriculture or highly technical education. In 1843-1844, for example, he edited at Jack- sonville the *Illinois Statesman*; and that paper to the student of ideas is a land flowing with milk and honey in a desert otherwise relieved only by half-arid oases. From other papers one can learn only by indirection of the intellectual life of Illinois of that day; from Turner one gets the comment on it of a powerful and keenly interested mind.

It was not to be expected that Turner would compromise with the public tastes of his day. Sensational news had so little interest to him that he would not vex himself to give it to his readers. Under the head of "Crimes and Casualties" he printed: "Our paper is small, and if our readers will for the present just have the goodness to imagine a certain due proportion of fires, tornadoes, murders, thefts, robberies and bully fights, from week to week, it will do just as well, for we can assure them they actually take place." The man who, when the thunders of denominational denunciation were rolling forth against Mormonism, was moved to analyze the sect as a fascinating study in comparative religion was not likely to blind his eyes to the violence of the deeds and plans of the anti-Mormons. He urged the people of the Military Tract to abide by the law and to have pity on the helpless at Nauvoo. What would Europe think of the state, if one year she granted Smith lawmaking powers and the next made open war on him?

Because of Turner's keen, trenchant comment on politics the *Illinoisan* made fierce war on the "crack-brained, gaping, half-witted theorist Yankee," who cheerfully replied in abusive rhetoric that Milton himself might have envied. Turner's paper reflected a popular disgust with political partisanship and party manipulation on either side, declaring that the politicians on both sides were usually men who could not be trusted with any of the ordinary concerns of life. Turner was disgusted with Van Buren as a political manipulator and hoped for a time that Calhoun might lead the party to a higher plane of statesmanship, until he saw the latter's slavery drift. At the same time he regarded the possible defeat of Clay, the duelist and gambler, as a moral triumph. Further he tore to pieces mercilessly the whigs' argument for protection and other of their pet doctrines. He was keen enough to see that the democrats really stood in theory at least for certain fundamental truths as well as for certain very important measures. To the whigs he was willing to ascribe the conservative function, that of promoting steadiness and stability of progress, remarking that they necessarily had to show greater statesmanship than their opponents for this very reason.

In his consideration of the slavery question Turner steered as original a course as he did elsewhere. He was not an out and out abolitionist, and he occasionally deprecated the violence of referring to all slaveholders as kidnappers and manstealers. As to runaways he was disposed to think the proper course somewhere midway between turning all the people of Illinois into slavecatchers and enticing slaves away. As a result he had one or two tifts with the *Western Citizen*. He denounced slavery bitterly enough in his own way, as an instituituion in monstrous contrast with the nation's principles of political liberty, or an imposition on a majority of the whites for the benefit of an aristocratic ruling-class minority. He professed, however, that he could not support the liberty party on the ground that he could not vote for a man like James G. Birney who was not a tried statesman. On the exclusion from church membership of slaveholders he remarked with a full vision of the essential barrenness of "one idealism" that "no one conformity or non-conformity can make a man good or bad." His final comment, however, on the intellectual ferment that followed on the train of abolitionism in the east was, "there is always some good in all protestantism."

Religiously that was Turner's ideal. His creed was simply christianity, including belief in the atonement and in the Sermon on the Mount as containing all the doctrine necessary to man's salvation. It had, however, no place in it for heresy hunting and little for denominational organization. Baptism to him was a rite which any minister without regard to church bounds was entitled to perform for all believers. His notion of church membership ended with the association of men into voluntary societies having no control of baptism or of the Lord's Supper. He was Congregational in his belief solely from a pragmatic view of the essential flexibility of that system. There was to him no halfway house between the entire independency of the local church and the centralization of government under the vatican at Rome.

Turner emphatically was the critic rather than the exponent of the Illinois of his day. Yet he introduced into the intellectual life of the state a freshness of view, a cosmopolitanism that by the very fact that it jars no more sharply upon its surroundings shows how Illinois had traveled since the early days of statehood. Society in the state, conventionalized and stiff, posing in every intellectual attitude, original in nothing, had had a change worked in it. Men had come to think broadly in terms of general political principles; they had come to think more independently on the set forms of law, of slavery, and, as Turner exemplified, of the set dogmas and forms of church doctrine and discipline. The Illinois of 1818 like the nation it existed in was dreaming dreams and interpreting the future in terms of the past; in the Illinois of 1848, there were many men of vigorous mind who had visions of the future.

Governor Ford and the Death of Joseph and Hyrum Smith

GEORGE R. GAYLER

Between 1839 and 1844, the Mormons, under the leadership of their Prophet, Joseph Smith, succeeded in establishing at Nauvoo, Illinois, what was perhaps the most unusual *imperium in imperio* in United States history. However, the hostility of their Gentile neighbors, which had plagued the sect during trying times in Ohio and Missouri, soon manifested itself in western Illinois. Stories of theft, the introduction of polygamy, and the threat to the always delicate frontier political situation in Illinois, soon turned the Gentiles against them. For some time unpleasant "incidents" had been becoming more and more numerous. Then Joseph Smith's ruthless and unwise crushing of an opposition newspaper within Nauvoo, the *Nauvoo Expositor,* in June, 1844, served as the spark to set off a chain of events that was to culminate in the death of the Mormon leader, a "Mormon War," and the expulsion of most members of the sect from Illinois.

After Joseph Smith ordered the destruction of the *Expositor* press, a new and, to that time, most violent outbreak of opposition flared. The owners and operators of the newspaper fled to nearby Carthage, where they quickly clamored for justice. Almost immediately an attempt was made to arrest the Mormon leader and others named as instigators of the *"Expositor* Affair." David Bettisworth, agent for the county court at Carthage, was dispatched to Nauvoo to arrest those men named in the indictment.

The writ ordered Smith and the other defendants to appear before Judge Thomas Morrison of Carthage "or some other justice of the peace." The Prophet immediately pointed out that the wording of the writ placed no obligation on him to appear at Carthage; instead he declared he was ready to appear before any justice of the peace in Nauvoo. Smith stated that Bettisworth, realizing he had been out-generaled in the matter, "seemed very wrathy" and he "swore he would be damned but he would carry them [the defendants] to Carthage before [Judge] Morrison, who issued the writ. . . ." Smith wrote in his diary: "I felt so indignant at his [Bettisworth's] abuse in depriving me of the privilege of the statute of Illinois in going before 'some other justice,' that I determined to take out a writ of *habeas corpus.*" Smith promptly

From George R. Gayler, "Governor Ford and the Death of Joseph Smith," *Journal of the Illinois State Historical Society,* L (1957), 391-411. Reprinted by permission of the author and the Illinois State Historical Society.

sued for such a writ, which was just as promptly granted by the acquiescent municipal court of Nauvoo, and he was freed along with all the other defendants.

Joseph Smith's challenge to their legal authority was promptly accepted by the citizens of Hancock County and the anti-Mormon inhabitants turned to threats of force. Public meetings were held in various places giving expression to the popular indignation. The threat of a "Mormon War," reminiscent of bloody days in Missouri, appeared all too imminent.

The town of Warsaw, on the Mississippi River about twenty miles south of Nauvoo, was considered the most violent anti-Mormon neighborhood, and its local newspaper, the *Warsaw Signal*, was especially bitter in its attacks. On June 12, five days following Smith's ruthless destruction of the *Nauvoo Expositor*, the *Warsaw Signal* furiously declared:

> We have only to state that this [destruction of the *Expositor* press] is sufficient! War and extermination is inevitable! *Citizens arise, one* and *all!!!* Can you *stand* by, and suffer such *infernal devils!* to *rob* men of their property rights, without avenging them. We have no time for comment! every man will make his own. *Let it be with powder and ball!!* [*Warsaw Signal,* June 12, 1844]

Governor Ford related that Hyrum Smith was reported to have offered a reward for the destruction of this paper, though the Mormons in a public proclamation on June 17 denied the charge. In Warsaw a citizens' resolution called for all-out war of extermination. A force of 150 men was gathered, and $1,000 was voted for supplying the force. The war-like attitude within Warsaw was shown by a news item dated June 19: "Business has been almost entirely suspended, and every able bodied man is under arms and almost constantly in drill." Several other neighboring communities, including Carthage, Rushville, and Macomb, passed similar resolutions and went on a war-like footing.

Numerous rumors concerning the Mormons were circulated, and calls were made for the militia to protect non-Mormons against armed Mormon marauders who were believed to be in the area. When these rumors reached the ears of Governor Thomas Ford, he addressed an open letter to the citizens of Hancock County. In his message, published on June 12 in the *Warsaw Signal,* the Governor urged the people to be calm and avert any act that might be regretted later. But his advice was disregarded. Two days later the *Signal* issued a special edition which consisted in its entirety of a violent and abusive attack upon the Mormons.

Governor Ford's direct involvement in the affair occurred when, on June 17, he was visited at the state capital by a committee of

Hancock County citizens who hysterically urged that he call out the militia immediately. This had not been the first instance that such a demand had been made upon Ford. The preceding January, the Illinois Governor had been asked to interfere in disturbances in Nauvoo, but had refused.

. . . .

Upon his arrival at Carthage on June 21, Ford found a considerable force assembled as a *posse comitatus,* and similar forces from McDonough and Schuyler counties were also in the city. It was estimated by a local newspaper that 250 men were under arms in Warsaw, 300 in Carthage; and that the Mormons had 4,000 men under arms. "If he [Governor Ford] does not act," the *Signal* declared, "there is no need for a Governor."

Ford's first action was to organize the various elements of armed bodies of men. Next he wrote a lengthy letter to Joseph Smith on June 22. In it he stressed again his decision to arrest the Prophet and the others named on the previous arrest order, but promised at the same time a guarantee of safety for the accused. Ford next enacted an oath from members of the militiamen gathered in and around Carthage that those groups would sustain him in a strictly legal course; that the prisoners, when taken, would be free from violence.

In the meantime, a small posse led by a constable from Carthage arrived at Nauvoo for the purpose of arresting Smith and his followers. Smith was hidden by the citizens of Nauvoo, and after making no real attempt to discover the Prophet's whereabouts, the posse returned to Carthage, and reported to the Governor that the accused had fled.

. . . .

Smith dispatched a message to Governor Ford in which the Prophet indicated his decision to give himself up. He promised to appear the following day, June 24, at 2 P.M. Accordingly, Smith, and all those named in the arrest order on the charge of riot in the destruction of the *Expositor,* started for Carthage the following morning. They were met four miles out of the town by a company of sixty of the McDonough County militia; and with this armed escort (which was believed needed), they were taken to the Carthage jail. On the trip to town Joseph Smith made his last prophecy:

> I am going like a lamb to the slaughter, but I am calm as a summer's morning. I have a conscience void of offence toward God and toward all men. If they take my life I shall die an innocent man, and my blood shall

cry from the ground for vengeance, and it shall be said of me 'He was murdered in cold blood!'

The reason for Smith's apprehension, as well as the state of mind of the Carthage mob, was shown by the reception given the party upon their entrance into the village. While Smith was passing through the public square, "many of the troops, especially the Carthage Greys, made use of the following expressions: 'Where is the damned prophet?' 'Stand away, you McDonough boys, and let us shoot the damned Mormons.' 'G— D— you, old Joe, we've got you now' . . . at the same time whooping, yelling, hooting, and cursing like a pack of savages."

While these events were taking place, Governor Ford had been busy at Carthage. At the same time that Smith was being led to the city jail, Ford proposed to march to Nauvoo. The council of militia officers, to which the proposal was made, however, was of the opinion that its group was too small for such a venture, and the Governor immediately realized the wisdom of hesitancy. . . .

Governor Ford next debated a further call for militia, but delayed this action because of the season of the year. The men were needed to plant crops as the weather had just turned suitable for plowing, and "the loss of two weeks, or even of one, at that time, was likely to produce a general famine all over the country." Instead Ford decided upon an alternate maneuver. He made a sudden request upon the Nauvoo Legion for the surrender of state arms in its possession. It was believed that this would virtually have the same effect as multiplying many times Ford's own forces. It would, therefore, make the excursion to Nauvoo a much safer venture. . . .

Meanwhile Joseph and Hyrum Smith were placed in the Carthage jail. This structure was made of stone and was situated near a group of trees at the western boundary of the village. The jail contained an apartment for the jailer, cells for prisoners, and on the second story a small assembly room. At the suggestion of Governor Ford, the two prisoners were allowed the freedom of this latter room. They were permitted to have visitors at any time with no precautions made against the introduction of tools or weapons for their attempted escape. Ford did not believe the prisoners would make such an attempt, though he believed that any escape on the part of the Smiths could possibly have brought about the expulsion of the Mormons from Illinois. . . .

Unknown to Governor Ford, a plan was already being laid for the prevention of such an escape attempt; namely the cold-blooded murder of Joseph and Hyrum Smith.

By June 25 the total number of armed men in Carthage was estimated to have been 1,200 or 1,300, with 400 or 500 more under arms at Warsaw. Most of this force, technically under the Governor's command, was eager to be ordered to march on Nauvoo. The excuse given was ostensibly to search that city for a counterfeiting establishment and to overawe the Mormons with a show of force. These excuses seemed to have been calculated to draw the Governor away from Carthage so that the assassination of Smith could be carried out. Ford did not, in all probability, realize the great danger that menaced the Smiths. If he had, under no circumstances would he have allowed himself to be enticed away from Carthage.

. . . .

The Governor next made the error of relying too greatly upon his conviction that the majority of the inhabitants of Carthage, knowing his feelings toward the prisoners, would not dare make any move to harm the Smiths during his absence. All had taken an oath to prevent bloodshed, and at the last moment Ford took two final precautions. First, he ordered all troops at both Carthage and Warsaw disbanded, with the exception of three companies. Secondly, two of the remaining companies were ordered to guard the jail while the third was to accompany him to Nauvoo. Thus Ford believed he was removing any threats to the lives of the Mormon leaders. In his choice of the guards for the Carthage jail, however, the governor laid himself wide open for all time to the charge by pro-Mormons of collaborating with the assassination of the Smith brothers. The two companies making up this jail guard were composed of the Carthage Greys under the command of Captain R. F. Smith. It was well known that the most rabidly anti-Mormon contingent of the militia was this very group. In an endeavor to clear himself of censure, Ford stated in his memoirs:

> I had confidence in their loyalty and integrity; because their captain was universally spoken of as a most respectable citizen and honorable man. . . . I relied upon this company especially, because it was an independent company, for a long time instructed and practiced in military discipline and subordination. I also had their word and [of] honor, officers and men, to do their duty according to law.

Charged with failure to use the McDonough County militia, which was known to have been much less violent in its anti-Mormon feelings, and which had voted against the march on Nauvoo, Ford explained:

the militia of that county were very much dissatisfied to remain; their crops were suffering at home; they were in a perfect fever to be discharged; and I was destitute of provisions to supply them for more than a few days. They were far from home, where they could not supply themselves. Whilst the Carthage company could board at their own houses, and would be put to little inconvenience in comparison.

Ford believed he had found the solutions to most of his problems and he was especially certain that the prisoners in the jail would not be harmed. He then started with his forces to Nauvoo on the morning of Thursday, June 27. After the expedition had progressed four of the eighteen miles from Carthage to Nauvoo, the Governor was informed by one of his officers that an attack upon the jail was allegedly to be carried out during his absence. The Governor, however, was unconvinced. "I myself entertained no suspicion of such an attack, . . ." he stated. "I could not believe that any person would attack the jail whilst we were in Nauvoo, and thereby expose my life and the life [sic] of my companions to the sudden vengeance of the Mormons, upon hearing of the death of their leaders." Ford, nevertheless, at once dispatched a messenger to Captain Smith of the Carthage Greys, "to guard the jail strictly, and at the peril of his life" until he returned. The Governor then continued with his pointless expedition to Nauvoo. . . .

That the assassination of Joseph and Hyrum Smith had been carefully planned there was no doubt, and it was no credit to Governor Ford that the plan so easily succeeded. The governor had had ample warning, but he had refused to believe the stories that reached his ears.

. . . .

On the day before the assassination, the first clue that something was in the air was given to the Prophet and his brother. At 1 P.M., Constable Bettisworth, a violent anti-Mormon (who had previously been sent to arrest Smith at Nauvoo), appeared at the jail with an order demanding the prisoners be delivered into his hands. The jailer, Stigall by name, refused to recognize the order, and by so doing probably saved the lives of the two Smith brothers at the time. The first positive evidence that a plan was afoot to murder the Smiths appeared at 5:30 A.M., on June 27. Dan Jones, one of Smith's disciples and frequent visitors, reported to the Prophet that Frank Worrel, Officer of the Guard at the Carthage jail and one of the Carthage Greys, told him as Jones entered the jail that day:

We have had too much trouble to bring Old Joe here to let him ever escape alive, and unless you want to die with him, you had better leave

before sundown; and you are not a damned bit better that [sic] him for
taking his part, and you'll see that I can prophesy better than Old Joe,
for neither he nor his brother, nor anyone who will remain with them
will see the sun set today.

. . . .

Accounts of the actual assassination of Joseph and Hyrum Smith
differ, but variances for the most part are minor. Perhaps the best
and most reliable accounts are those given by Willard Richards and
John Taylor, both ardent disciples of the Mormon Prophet. These
two men were visiting Smith at the time the jail was stormed.

Richards, Taylor, and the Smith brothers were sitting in shirt
sleeves in their room when Richards glanced out the window and
spied the men, with blackened faces, advancing toward the jail. The
door to the room was immediately closed and Hyrum Smith and
Richards placed their shoulders against it, as the door unaccounta-
bly was without a lock. Finding their entrance barred, the assailants
fired a shot through the door, which forced Hyrum Smith and
Richards to leap back. While Hyrum was retreating, but still facing
the door, a second shot was fired which struck him in the face, and,
at the same time, another ball, fired through the window (possibly a
ricochet), entered his back. He fell immediately exclaiming "I am a
dead man," and expired.

When Joseph saw his brother fall he advanced to the door with a
six-shot pistol left by a previous caller. He opened the door a few
inches and fired. The first three barrels misfired, but the last three
were reported to have each wounded a man—the extent of which
was never fully ascertained. While Joseph was firing Taylor stood
next to him and parried the assailants' guns when they were thrust
into the room. The attackers hesitated for a few moments, perhaps
not knowing how fully armed the prisoners were. At that moment
Taylor decided to risk jumping from the second floor window, but
was not able to accomplish his purpose. As he reached the window
the mob again fired through the door, and Taylor was hit in the leg.
The attackers continued to fire through the now partially opened
door, and Taylor, attempting to crawl to safety in the corner of the
room was struck three more times, in the knee, arm, and hip. At the
moment Taylor fell, Joseph Smith leaped for the open window, and
as he was part way out, two balls entered his chest. He fell outward,
exclaiming "Oh Lord, my God." Upon perceiving the Prophet's leap
from the window, the mob ran outside. Smith's body was propped
up against a well by the conspirators and "they despatched him
with four balls shot through his body." Evidently satisfying themselves that the Smiths were dead, the mob dispersed, and did not

wreak their vengeance further upon the wounded Taylor or Richards. The latter survived the ordeal untouched except for a slight nick on the left ear, although his large size had made him a more than ample target.

After the object of the attack upon the jail had been accomplished, it was reported:

> The cannon fired at Carthage told the people over in Missouri and down at Warsaw that the objective had been attained. The echo came from Warsaw—a paean of congratulation—and presently from across the river in Missouri came the faint peal of bells; not tolling bells, but clamorous peals of rejoicing! [Harry M. Beardsley, *Joseph Smith and his Mormon Empire* (Boston, 1931), p. 368]

. . . .

Public opinion concerning the murder of the Smiths did not coincide with the previous general attitudes toward the Mormon Prophet and his followers. Governor Ford stated in a proclamation, published in contemporary newspapers, that "the Mormons had done all that was required or which ought to have been required of them," and called the murder a "disgrace." One publication termed the assassination one of "the most disgraceful and cold blooded murders ever committed in a Christian land," while another commented:

> It will probably never be known who shot Joseph and Hirum [sic] Smith—but their murder was a cold-blooded cowardly act, which will consign the perpetrators if discovered to merited infamy and disgrace— They [the murderers] have broken their pledges to the Governor— disgraced themselves and the State to which they belong. They have crimsoned their perfidity with blood. [*Quincy Herald*, June 27, 1844]

In October, 1844, indictments were returned against a number of men accused of the murder, and their trial convened the following May. An acquittal of the accused was a foregone conclusion. The jail guards could not (or would not) identify anyone, and witnesses refused to testify or gave contradictory evidence. No one was neutral, and no truly unbiased jury could possibly have been selected. But the Prophet, according to the Mormons, was avenged by "divine judgment."

. . . .

Original Narratives

No better firsthand description of the prophet Joseph Smith can be found than the observations of Henry Lewis, an American artist who had been living in Germany in the 1830s. The complete English translation of the original book, *Das illustrierte Mississippithal* (Düsseldorf, 1854), was published under the editorship of Bertha L. Heilbron by the Minnesota Historical Society in 1967.

The Prophet

HENRY LEWIS

["] Joseph Smith*, prophet, priest, prince of the Mormons, generalissimo of the armies of the faithful and――!! number one innkeeper of the holy city!

["] On April 26, 1844, we had the honor to be presented to this high and mighty ruler. Our party consisted of twelve young people, one of whom boasted of a long-standing and intimate friendship

---

From Henry Lewis, *The Valley of the Mississippi Illustrated,* A. Hermina Poatgieter, trans., Bertha L. Heilbron, ed. (St. Paul, Minn., 1967), pp. 248-252. Copyright by the Minnesota Historical Society and used with permission. All but two footnotes in the original have been omitted.

*Joseph, or for short, Jol Smith, the founder of Nauvoo and Prophet of the Mormons, belonged to a wandering family from the vicinity of Palmyra [New York]. His relatives were mainly known as *money diggers* (gold or treasure diggers) and usually lived a vagabond life. From his youth, Jol was a stupid and utterly untalented fellow. His father, however, maintained that he possessed a second sight by which he could find treasures located in the deepest bowels of the earth. Therefore, long before they had thought of a golden Bible, Jol was the leader on their adventuresome excursions. They usually set out at night so that no one could find the place where the treasures would be discovered. In his hand Jol carried a hat in which lay a curious stone. He sometimes looked through his stone to discover the places where gold was located. But when Jol and his father learned that the people in their vicinity had lost faith in their money digging, they pretended to have found a golden Bible. The Book of Mormon, which they made public at the same time, was only an introduction to it.

No one bothered to suppress this work, because no danger was anticipated from a book whose authors could boast neither of their honesty nor of their friends.

This book, the foundation of Mormonism, was first made public in 1830. From that time until they were driven out of Illinois and their Temple was burned (at sunrise on October 9, 1848) the believers and defenders of Mormonism spread its teachings and absurdities with an enthusiasm that would have been worthy of a better cause. The apostles of this wild madness traveled through all the states of the Union and Canada, spread the principles of their faith, and deluded hundreds into accepting Mormonism. They crossed the sea and, if one cares to believe their own assertions, made thousands of proselytes in England; in fact they sent their missionaries as far as Palestine.

Courtesy of the Illinois State Historical Library

Joseph Smith

with the 'general' and who did indeed pride himself not a little about it.

["] Conducted by this worthy, who was, by the way, considerably 'lit up,' we were ushered with repeated scrapings, countless bowings, and similar compliments into the *Mansion House'* (inn) of Nauvoo. The Prophet received us at the threshold and welcomed us within his four walls with an appearance of utter benevolence and with expressions of extreme courtesy.

["] The first impression the Prophet made on us was not at all satisfactory to me and certainly not flattering to our host. 'Is this the Mormon hero,' we thought, the far-famed founder of the new and strange sect, the Mohammed of the nineteenth century, the 'veiled Prophet' (if all the tales are true), the prince of Nauvoo? Truly this was not the man we had expected to see. But one is usually disappointed in such cases by one's preconceptions.

["] 'General Smith,' for as such he announced himself, is a tall, well-proportioned man. His figure could be called a fine one, although by no means distinguished for symmetry or grace; his gait and movements are really awkward. On that day he was dressed entirely in black, with no ornament, and with a clumsily knotted, ordinary chintz cravat tied around his throat, pressing a small collar, stiff as a board, tightly against his cheeks. His chest and shoulders are broad and muscular, although his arms and hands seem never to have been developed by physical toil, and the latter are very small for his proportions. His foot, however, is large and broad enough to make up for the symmetry disturbed by the size of the hands. His head is a long oval in shape, with a high crown, indicating a determined will; the nape bone and back of the head full, denoting powerful impulses; and the forehead low and receding, although the region which phrenologists declare to be the seat of capacity for thought stands out unusually. He said that his head had often been examined by phrenologists, but he did not believe in this science. Indeed, he entered into a long (but unintelligible) argument to prove that neither phrenology nor mesmerism had the slightest claims to be called science. His forehead is white and smooth and, notwithstanding the small facial angle, almost symmetrical. It was impossible to detect a single line of care or of thought in his face, or a single cloud on its smooth expanse. His hair is very light and fine, complexion pale, cheeks full, temperament evidently sanguine, lips thin rather than thick and definitely not indicative of boldness or determination of character, teeth white but not regular, and one of the right incisors was missing—a lack which is noticed at once and somewhat mars the expression of the mouth. But the Prophet's most remarkable feature is his eye; not because it is very large, bright, thoughtful, or restless, or particularly expressive or deep-set—for strangely enough, it does not possess any of these character-istics—but because anyone accustomed to reading character in the eye would surely see at first glance that the Prophet's eye did not belong to an ordinary man. The color is light hazel, and it is shaded by long, thick, but light lashes. His *beetle brows* are light and thick, and the general expression of the Prophet's eyes shows the utmost degree of cunning and craft, especially when he half closes them, which he often did during our conversation, as though he wanted to conceal his innermost thoughts from us. Taken all together, the general's figure and aspect are genteel, and his manners, though dignified, easy and courteous. He may be about forty years old. The Prophet's voice in ordinary conversation is soft and low, and his smile would be exceptionally agreeable if his appearance were not marred by the loss of a front tooth as soon as he opens his mouth.

We were several times on the point of advising the holy man to put himself for a few hours into the hands of our friend, the dentist *Dr.* [Edward] H[ale] of St. Louis, and have the lost tooth replaced by a little piece of ivory.

["] Our conversation with the Prophet, which extended over the greatest variety of subjects, was fortunately uninterrupted; thus we had sufficient time to observe him carefully—a fact which can hardly have escaped him. In the course of the conversation the Prophet mentioned the unusually rapid increase of the Mormon colony. 'Four years ago,' he said, 'there was hardly a habitation on the site of Nauvoo, and now the city extends over six square miles, and has a population of 25,000 souls!'—an estimate exaggerated at least by 10,000. He declared the fighting strength of the Mormons to be 4,000 men—a figure which doubtless also was exaggerated. After the exodus of his people from Mount Zion in Missouri, he himself had bought the site on which Nauvoo stands, but since he was unable to make the payments on time, part of the land went back to its former owners. For this and other reasons, a large part of the plain on the west shore of the *Point* is still unoccupied.

["] In the course of the conversation, we asked the Prophet whether, in his capacity as *mayor,* he ever experienced difficulty in keeping peace and order. This question served as an excuse to test the Prophet, for we knew very well that only the day before he had been called to quell a revolt against his person and authority, on which dangerous occasion he had conducted himself most courageously. 'Only yesterday,' he said, 'an infuriated man who sought my life held a loaded double-barreled pistol to my heart.' Thereupon he related the details of the incident as follows: A certain [Orson] Spencer, a poor, crippled, but worthy and intelligent man, brought a complaint against his brother [Augustine Spencer] for beating and otherwise maltreating him in his own house. The Prophet at once sent an official to arrest the accused, and, in the meantime, he prepared the warrant. Spencer resisted arrest without a writ from the mayor, though the arrest would have been legal in accordance with an express ordinance of the city. Thereupon an armed posse of Mormons started out, led by the Prophet and his coadjutor [Orrin P.] Rockwell. The Prophet ordered the arrest of Spencer. Instantly three men, a certain [Chauncey L.] Highbee and the two Foster brothers [Robert D. and Charles], came to Spencer's rescue. A hand-to-hand fight ensued, and the younger Foster drew his pistol, and swore that he would shoot the Prophet on the spot, calling him a villain, murderer, impostor, and tyrant. An eye-witness told us that the Prophet calmly approached the enraged man, seized the pistol by the breech, and wrenched the weapon from his grasp. In doing so, he hurt his hand somewhat on the sharp angle of the lock. The result was that the rioters were arrested and taken [before the mayor] in the Masonic Hall, [tried,] pronounced guilty, and each of them fined $100. Besides, they had to deposit considerable sums for bail, to insure their peaceful behavior during the next six months. After this verdict, the Prophet rose from his judgment seat and addressed the crowd. He said that he was not a despot, assassin, swindler, nor scoundrel, and they could be sure that he was also no coward, for the fear of man was not in him. Hy loved his people, he said, and mourned the delusions of his foes. It grieved him to have to use severity, but sooner than have his authority resisted and his laws broken, he would risk his life—yes, he would do that as long as he lived! Then he informed the offenders that they were 'blind fools' and told them to go home. The ones who had been punished obeyed humbly enough; the crowd dispersed; order was restored, and—the Prophet in triumph returned to his tavern to deal out whisky, three cents a glass!! ["] *

*Whether or not Smith sold and served whisky in his inn is a matter of dispute. A visitor of 1844 records that near the entrance "was a small and very comfortless-looking bar-room; all the more comfortless, perchance, from its being a dry bar-room, as no spirituous liquors were permitted at Nauvoo."

Mrs. K. T. Anderson reminisces about the life of women in early Rock Island in the following original narrative. She describes the appearance of the first Yankee families in the area, the greed of the lone white entrepreneur living off the Indians, the arrival of the steamboat, and the incorporation of the town of Stephenson, which was situated on the flood plain of the Mississippi. These recollections are typical of the numerous remembrances published in the early editions of the *Transactions of the Illinois State Historical Society* during the first decade of the twentieth century. Of questionable historical accuracy, they nevertheless provide a colorful source of the experiences of long-forgotten Illinois settlers. Mrs. Anderson served as a member of the Board of Directors of the Rock Island County Historical Society in 1930; she also wrote "Col. Conrad Weiser, Pioneer, Soldier, Diplomat, Judge, Provincial Interpreter," *Journal of the Illinois State Historical Society*, XXIII (1930), 604-617.

A Pioneer Woman Reminisces

MRS. K. T. ANDERSON

. . . I thrill with admiration for those who dared to leave behind home, friends and the comforts of civilization and strike out into the pathless wilds. To me there is nothing more interesting than to dwell on the stories of early times, especially those as told to me personally by some of the earliest settlers of our county. Many of these accounts are in a sense similar and yet each individual has looked back upon the life and viewed it from a different angle, so that each one's story has a value of its own. But it manifestly would be impossible to relate in this paper all the reminiscences I have enjoyed. I have therefore selected some recollections, for the most part, of pioneer women who necessarily suffered more than the men from the dangers, rigors and privations of frontier life, who contributed in their own way, just as valuable aid in the conquering of the wilds and yet whose services have received far less recognition than is their due. . . .

The only white women who lived here from the first—Mrs. Davenport and Mrs. Clark—passed to the Great Beyond years and years ago, leaving behind them not a word which would even hint their view of the life they lived at this place during the transition period from the native wilderness to the beginnings of a settlement. In order, therefore, to fill in this gap I shall have to use extracts from his own notes and letters written to a close friend in Rock

"Some Reminiscences of Pioneer Rock Island Women," Mrs. K. T. Anderson, *Transactions of the Illinois State Historical Society*, XVII (1912), pp. 63-76.

Island by Capt. W. L. Clark who died about a year ago at Buffalo, Ia., at the age of ninety-three and who was the last remaining member, living hereabouts, of the first family to settle on the mainland at or near what is now Rock Island. The family came originally from Virginia, settled first in Wabash County, later moved to Fort Edwards near Warsaw where they remained but a short time, again moving on up the river and finally landing on the mainland opposite Fort Armstrong in August of 1828. Captain Clark was a lad of five and said he well remembered when his father carried him down the gang-plank of the little steamer and stood him on the shore amidst hundreds of Indians gathered to see the boat come in. I have often wondered what the mother's emotions were as she watched the boat steam away on up the river leaving her there, the only white woman on the main land, her's the only white family, and the nearest neighbors (except for the Davenports on the island) a hundred miles away. After the family was settled in a cabin which they put up close to the river, Davenport, having heard of the family's advent sent for the elder Clark and engaged him to cut wild hay for the stock at Fort Armstrong. When this contract was completed, Mr. Clark proceeded to cut hay for his own use, for he had determined to go back to Fort Edwards and drive up some cattle which he owned there. Davenport ordered him to stop cutting hay since the fort was supplied, but when no attention was paid to his orders he became very angry for he did not want any white people to settle here since it would interfere with and finally stop his enormously profitable trade with the Indians. From now on he did all he could to try to drive the family away. He refused to sell them any clothing or provisions and with winter almost upon them, it must have been a dreary outlook. Fortunately on his last trip down the river, the captain of the steamer which had moved them to Rock Island left in charge of the family till his return in the spring a barrel of whiskey. As winter set in, the family's stock of provisions grew lower and lower till finally they were in desperate straits. About this time the soldiers in the fort learned of this barrel of whiskey and while a strict guard was maintained to prevent any intercourse with the lone family on shore, yet the soldiers discovered a way to get at the liquor through a cave under the fort, of which the officers had no knowledge. They would steal out in pairs at night, go to the Clark cabin and exchange coffee, sugar, salt, beans, rice, flour and shoes for whiskey from the barrel and in this way, much contrary to Davenport's evident expectations, they managed to live through the winter. When the trader could not drive them away by the starvation plan, he bribed Indians (with all kinds of trinkets) to annoy and frighten them. One afternoon while father Clark was away from the house, four half drunk Indians, two on a pony, came riding up to the cabin, dismounted and going into the cabin, sat down on the floor and ordered mother Clark to give them food. Being timid and entirely alone she obeyed; but in the midst of the feast father Clark unexpectedly returned and upon learning what the trouble was, he commanded the Indians to "puk-a-chee"—go away. This incensed the Indians and they jumped up to fight. Mr. Clark stepped outside the door, which was one log above the ground, and as the Indians came out, each, half drunk as they were, stumbled over the sill. Mr. Clark had in his hand a hoop-pole, with which he had been driving cattle, and he now used it with telling effect, knocking down first one and then the other of the drunken brutes till they all begged for mercy. He then marched them to the river where they washed their wounds and then mounting their ponies they were about to ride away when one of them raised a war-club to throw at Mr. Clark. Before he could do so, however, father Clark raised a fish-gig, which he had picked up, to strike at the Indian. This frightened the buck and dropping his weapon they all rode away at full speed to their Rock River village. The next day what was the family's surprise to receive a visit from Chief Black Hawk and these same four Indians. The chief interviewed Mr. Clark and after having ascertained all the facts, he filled his pipe with KinniKinnic, lit it, and after taking a few whiffs, handed it to father Clark who in turn handed it to the other Indians and so, all having smoked the peace pipe, friendship was once more restored. On another occasion an Indian whose wickiup was only about thirty feet from the Clark cabin, and who had always been peaceable and friendly, came in a half drunk condition, forced his way into the cabin and wanted to fight. Mr. Clark was at home and taking a good sized switch he thrashed the visitor till he ran howling from the house. An Indian would stand up without a tremor before a gun but he would run from a switching, for this they considered the most humiliating form of punishment, and in the breast of this Indian his disgrace rankled till he determined to have revenge. During the winter all the Indians were off on their winter hunt when Mr. Clark was called to Fort Edwards on business. As he was traveling home, walking close to the shore on the snow-covered ice, near the bluff at Fort Madison, he saw an Indian running toward a large tree. Suspecting treachery he raised his gun and commanded the Indian to come out on the ice. He obeyed and as he approached Mr. Clark he proved to be the Indian whom he had switched and who evidently had planned to wipe out his disgrace by securing his enemy's scalp. Father Clark compelled him to lay all his weapons on the ice and then march many miles before him up the river, after which he allowed him to return again for his weapons. Black Hawk, whom Mr. Clark knew very well, claimed that both of these quarrels were instigated by Davenport in an attempt to frighten away the family. But the Clarks stuck and were it not for them a settlement at this point would not have been made until several years later. But what a tragically lonely life it must have been for Mother Clark, cut off from all society and intercourse with other white families, feeling that they were looked upon as interlopers and begrudged even the meagre living they secured, living in constant dread of the Indians, with no doctor near and no one to turn to for help or sympathy in time of sickness, and with but scant communication with the outside world, for when Judge J. W. Spencer came to Fort Armstrong in the latter part of December, 1829, on his way to Galena, the commander of the garrison engaged him to carry the mail from the fort and bring one back with him on his return trip as they had received no mail for two months and were anxious to know who had been elected President of the United States. And when the mail did come one can imagine there were no great sheafs of papers, magazines and letters when newspapers were few and far between and postage on letters was 25 cents. With what joy then must this lone pioneer woman have welcomed the tide of immigration to this spot which began about 1830. The news had spread far and wide about this garden spot of the frontier and its possibilities and in far distant states, families, responding to the alluring call from this unknown land of promise, sold household goods, bade farewell to friends and relatives and turned toward the west. One old lady's narrative gave me a glimpse at what a tragedy it was in those days to break home ties. She was a little girl and child-like was wild with pleasurable excitement and anticipation in the trip before them. But when the time for departure at last came and they were all in their places in the prairie schooner that was to carry them to their destination, the last goodby had been said amidst tears and sobs and the horses had started on the ascent of the Green Mountains at the foot of which lay the farm, and the distance began to lengthen between themselves and the old grandparents watching the departing wagon, then into even her childish soul came at least a faint realization of the agony of parting and the tremendous responsibility they had assumed. She said that just before they dropped behind the last rise in the road from the top of which they could once more see the old farmhouse, they could still distinguish the old people standing in the doorway and probably straining with tear-dimmed eyes to catch one more glimpse of the departing loved ones. They never saw the grandparents or the old farm again. The family first settled in Greene county but very soon came on to a farm which they purchased and which lay in what is now the very heart of Moline. The mother, children and household goods came by boat from Alton. The steamer had what was called a "high pressure" engine and the passengers had to get off at the landing places and help "wood up" the boat. On the farm was a log cabin with a lean-to at one end in which were penned the chickens—close to the house because the wolves and foxes were numerous and troublesome. About the cabin was a snake fence made of split black walnut rails. Great flocks of wild turkeys and pigeons were all about through the woods. The Indians frequently visited the cabin and since the mother was very much afraid of the redskins, it was on the occasions of their visits that an old dog which they had brought with them from the east, proved himself a real comfort to her, a very shield and buckler of defense. In order not to be entirely helpless when the men were out in the fields, it was agreed that if the men were urgently needed at the house, the mother should run up a white flag on a pole by the door of the cabin. This signal was used on several occasions. One time when the men came running from the field they found a company of Indians on the outside of the fence. They were making a great deal of noise but they did not attempt to enter the yard for occupying the top of a primitive stile, that served instead of a gate, was the dog who with alert eye and ominous calm was taking no chances by allowing Indians to come inside the fence. Another time when the signal was used the men found a number of Indians again on the outside of the fence (out of respect to the dog) and when the father came up to the group they pointed to a barrel beside the door, in which the mother was making vinegar, and demanded "whisk." The father tried to explain that the stuff was not whiskey but they would not believe him so he thought it best to let them convince themselves. He went up to the door but could not get in till the mother had removed some of the furniture with which she had barricaded the door. When he finally gained entrance he took a gourd dipper and invited the Indians to come in and help themselves. They did so eagerly and after one taste they made all manner of wry faces and departed on their way disgusted but convinced. There was no time for play on the farm in summer and in winter the spare time was used in making axe-handles which were traded at Fort Armstrong for staple articles of food. On rare occasions the family drove three miles through the underbrush and timber to visit and trade in the little settlement that was growing up about the Clark's cabin. It must have been interesting to see those families from every walk of life and from distant states, with their preconceived ideas of what pioneer life would be like, pouring into the new settlement—into the "melting-pot"—and still more interesting to watch the process of readjustment of their ideas and views to the reality of existing circumstances. The experience of one family in particular that I have in mind, illustrates what I mean. The father, mother and five daughters determined to emigrate to Illinois. They were educated, cultured people, accustomed to wealth and all the shelter, comforts and social prestige which it gives, perhaps a little haughty, perhaps measuring people as a whole by city-fostered, sometimes false standards, and certainly totally unacquainted with even the first meaning of pioneer life. They left their home and friends in New Hampshire and traveled by boat over the Great Lakes to Chicago, then to Fort Dearborn. Here they were met by an uncle who had come all the way from Rock Island or Stephenson, as it was then called, with an ox team and prairie schooner to convey them back with him to Stephenson, since of course there were no railroads. This to them unique and humble mode of travel so outraged the sensibilities and pride of these city bred young ladies that they absolutely refused to ride in the homely conveyance and started to walk in thin shoes and fashionable but impractical clothes. One of the sisters confessed in after years that before they were halfway across the town about Fort Dearborn they would have been glad to have been in the prairie schooner for the mud was so deep that the wheels of the wagon sank almost to the hub and by the time the outskirts of the village were reached each girl was so bedraggled and footsore and their collective pride was so humbled that they all thankfully took advantage of what comfort a prairie schooner afforded. The trip was a most laborious one and often they had to stop and make a corduroy road in order to get over a boggy place. By the time they reached the end of their journey it would have been hard to find a more disheartened, homesick lot of girls. But necessity is a stern taskmaster and under trials character develops and these girls, who in the environment of their New Hampshire home might have gone on living inconsequential purposeless lives, now under the stress of new circumstances, showed their mettle and developed into the sturdy wholesome kind of pioneer women that helped to make this middle west. Among the earliest arrivals to the village of Stephenson in the spring of 1836 were Mr. and Mrs. M. J. Hartzell, a newly married couple. Mr. Hartzell had come to the settlement the previous spring expecting to return to Pennsylvania in the fall for his sweetheart, but before he could get away from Stephenson the river froze up and winter had set in, and as the Mississippi was their only highway, there was nothing to do but wait till spring. Mrs. Hartzell told me that during the whole winter she never heard a word from her betrothed husband, but her faith in his return never wavered for a moment and in the spring when he came she was ready, they were married and immediately started for the new home, going by boat down the Ohio and up our Mississippi. It required three weeks to make the journey and Mrs. Hartzell said she would never forget the beautiful scene which swept into view as the steamer rounded the bend in the river a mile below the town. Right ahead gleamed the white walls of the fort on the island. To the left were the beautiful bluffs of Iowa, to the right the park-like plain with the handful of houses that constituted the town of Stephenson. But best of all was the sight of familiar faces on shore, for everybody had dropped their work and come to the landing to see the boat come in, and among the group were friends who had emigrated from Pennsylvania the previous year. These gave the little bride a hearty welcome and helped put up a temporary cabin right by the river in which the young couple lived till a better house, which Mr. Hartzell had already begun, was ready. This house, by the way, was the first plastered house in Stephenson. The little cabin had no fireplace so they had to do their cooking outside on campfires and since a storm came up nearly every evening about five o'clock, they had to manage to get their supper out of the way before that time or be content with a cold meal. These storms seem to have been a natural phenomenon, something out of the ordinary for many of the old settlers hereabouts recall the fact of their great severity and almost daily recurrence at the same time of the day. The Hartzells many times had to seek shelter in a neighbor's cabin further away from the river. This cabin had a puncheon floor under which on at least one occasion they sought protection from the cyclonic fury of the storm. When they returned to their own cabin everything in it was soaking wet—even a big roll of muslin in a chest had not escaped. We of today with every imaginable convenience for making housework easy and attractive can hardly realize how handicapped was the pioneer housekeeper. Mrs. Hartzell's laundry was a rough plank hewn from a log, supported by two legs and run out a few feet into the river. She had no washboard but got the clothes clean by rubbing them between her hands. She had no clothes line but the low bushes about the cabin and the green sod served nicely in lieu of this. They were compelled to go to St. Louis for all food stuffs and often when their supplies arrived they were musty or mouldy. One time the boat, on which was their winter supply of flour, froze in at Keokuk and the price of flour rose to $14 per barrel. She had but few dishes and only a couple of pans and kettles and yet out of these came an almost limitless hospitality. On the first Sabbath after their arrival in Stephenson, they saw several men—strangers—

walking along evidently seeking some particular place. Mr. Hartzell went out and spoke to them and they told him they were looking for a church. There was no church in the little settlement, but Mr. Hartzell invited them into his cabin and conducted a prayer service for them. I might add that when the Hartzells new house was built the one big room was planned to be used also for church services. Here a prayer meeting was held every Thursday evening and once a quarter a circuit rider would come through, when all the furniture of this room was moved out of doors to make room for the congregation that would gather. . . .

As I mentioned before, the young couple were most hospitable, and their home became a sort of headquarters for every stranger that came to town. When they were settled in their new home Mrs. Hartzell said she felt a little better off than her neighbors because she had a new Franklin stove. After she had pictured this stove to me I failed to see how she could bake with it so she explained that she baked the bread in a kettle set in front of the open fire and when I wondered how she got it baked on top she said she heated an iron lid and covered the kettle with that. One Saturday, in preparation for the Sabbath, she had with great labor gotten eight loaves of bread baked but before evening they were all gone—to feed strangers. She had no table but used the top of a big walnut chest for this purpose. On many a Sunday she fed as high as fourteen people from its top. Even the Indians shared her hospitality, coming frequently to beg of her and never departing unsatisfied. One time, at least, the overstraining of her generosity caused her tears. She had just finished baking and it was cooling on a shelf when in came a number of Indians and demanded the bread. Being alone and naturally afraid of them she let them take all of her new bread. Another time a big brave came and begged for something to eat. She gave him his dinner in a new iron kettle and after he had devoured the last morsel of the food, he set the kettle aside with the evident intention of taking it along home with him. Thinking he would not notice the substitution, she took the new pot when he wasn't looking and put in its place an old one; but when he was ready to depart and came for his kettle he immediately noticed what had been done. He flew into a rage and nothing would pacify him but the return of the original kettle. On one occasion Black Hawk, who was a great admirer of Mrs. Hartzell's, came to their cabin to consult with Mr. Hartzell about buying the young wife and gravely offered quite a liberal number of ponies, blankets, and trinkets in exchange for her. Mrs. Hartzell as well as others told of visits to the isolated Davenport house on the island which by this time had become famous as the finest mansion between St. Louis and

Galena. One writer of that time speaks of the homestead as "surpassing in natural beauty and attractiveness, indoor spaciousness, comfort and luxuriousness, and outdoor tasteful embellishments and productiveness the far famed residence of Blennerhasset as described by Wirt." This mansion, which was the scene of the trader's murder in 1844 and which had fallen into decay, has recently been restored and is one of the show-places of Rock Island. One of my brothers helped in the work of restoration and he says the sills and timbers of the old building are sound and good for yet many a year to come. This old home was the scene of countless gay gatherings for both Mr. and Mrs. Davenport were excellent entertainers and most thoughtful and kind to those they liked. Only recently I visited an old lady who proudly exhibited to me a little brown earthenware jug of odd design which Mrs. Davenport had filled with quince preserves and sent to her once when she was ill. There was plenty of opportunity to test neighborliness during the years 1836-7 for there was so much sickness in this locality that there were not enough well people to nurse those who were ill. A pioneer doctor who began practice in this county about 1836 says that the prevailing diseases were climatic fever and ague and quinine in some form or combination was regarded as a sheet anchor. When anyone died the whole settlement was sad and their sympathy was personal and practical. The neighbors made the coffin, consulted together as to where to bury the dead, dug the lonely grave and sadly performed the last services.

Up to the time of the incorporating of the town of Stephenson, the most important centre of the hamlet was the old Barrel House, a log cabin, erected years before by Davenport and Russel Farnum as a trading post which they called Farnumsberg. This cabin was later enlarged by a story and a half addition and then occupied as a hotel by one John Barrel. Here it was that court convened, here was the postoffice, and here was the common meeting place of the village men. The men lodgers were accommodated in one large room on the second floor, which was reached by a ladder on the outside of the building. Here the only beds were ticks filled with straw and placed on the floor. A sign at the foot of the ladder admonished the lodgers to remove their boots before going upstairs. A pump in the yard, with a common basin and towel, constituted the hotel lavatory. Mein host's mother-in-law was one of the Barrel household and they say she was entirely out of sympathy with pioneer life. Her most cherished possession was a real China tea-set which I have reason to believe John Barrel at least regarded as a "white elephant." Several times during the Black Hawk war the settlers were compelled to flee from their cabins to the protection of Fort Armstrong and each time John Barrel had to drag along that precious tea set. Years afterward when the family had long been gone from this locality and when the old Barrel house was being torn down, what should the workmen find, hidden safely away under the front door step, but a large, real China teapot. Even a worm will turn and I've no doubt that John Barrel was asked once too often to carry that teapot.

. . . .

James P. Savage, an economist for a New York City investment firm, presents excerpts from some guidebooks used by mid-century immigrants to Illinois.

Do-It-Yourself Books for Illinois Immigrants

JAMES P. SAVAGE, JR.

During the period from 1840 to 1870 thousands of people from the eastern United States and from Europe flocked to the prairies of mid-America. For many it was necessary to make a long journey through unfamiliar country. Once arrived at their destination they had to adapt themselves to a strange environment. They way they lived and worked was quite different from the life and work they had left behind. At the time, however, there were many published works which they could use in planning their move, choosing a location, making the journey, and finally carving a new home out of the wilderness.

Imagine a young man from central New York state or from England or Germany, with some small capital, who decided that perhaps a golden opportunity awaited him in mid-America. He may have heard that there was land to be had in Illinois. To what sources could he have gone for information to plan his venture? Perhaps the potential emigrant first got the notion to emigrate from reading the

From James P. Savage, Jr., "Do-It-Yourself Books for Illinois Immigrants," *Journal of the Illinois State Historical Society*, LVII (1964), 30-48. Footnotes in the original have been omitted. Reprinted by permission of the author and the Illinois State Historical Society.

Emigrant's Almanack. This almanac was published in England and Scotland in 1849 and 1850 and stated its intent in the preface or "Address":

> We are anxious to promote emigration, and with that view desire to present in these pages a mass of sound and practical information on all essential points. There are many books published giving valuable accounts of various settlements and their capabilities, but we have not found one which gives, at a glance, a full view of all fields for emigration, with the necessary particulars to guide the intended emigrant. There are many inquiries presenting themselves to the mind of a person when his attention is first directed to the expediency of such a step. "Am I likely to succeed better than at home?—and where?" Before a decision is made several important questions have to be answered—as to soil, climate, mode of travel, etc. "How can I get there with the least inconvenience and the smallest amount of expense?—what must I do on shipboard?—and what steps must I take on landing?" These are but a few of the queries which naturally occur to a man of ordinary prudence before his determination is made. We seek to lay before him such information as will enable him to decide for himself.

Emphasis was placed on descriptions of the various sections of the United States: "The soil is so rich in Illinois, that, though indifferently farmed, it will produce anything in the shape of vegetation in great abundance." Information was given concerning comparative opportunities for various occupations in the different territories: "Carpenters, wheelwrights, millwrights, blacksmiths and tanners are in request. School masters and mistresses would here (in Illinois) meet with immediate and full employment, and liberal remuneration of their services. It is however, the worst country in the world for clerks and shopmen." Advice concerning the preparation for and timing of the journey to the Midwest was also included: "Those bound for Northern Ohio, Michigan, Wisconsin, or Illinois should not leave home before the 1st of April; nor should they defer their departure till after the 1st of September." There was an itemization of expenses likely to be incurred which included a section illustrating the costs of a moderately stocked Illinois prairie farm:

Cost of a Prairie Farm in Illinois

	£	s	d
A quarter section of prairie land, that is, 160 acres at 5s., $1.25 is	41	13	4
Timber, say 40 acres	25	00	0
Breaking up the prairie, at	50	00	0
Fencing into four lots, eight rails high, and stakes, 960 rods in three miles, 15,366 rails at one cent.,			

153.53 (sic) dollars, 3,840 stakes at a half cent.			
19.20 dollars	36	00	10
A comfortable log cabin such as first settlers			
generally occupy.	10	8	4
Other small buildings, etc.	10	8	4
Cost of a well with pump and buckets	3	2	6
Garden, cow yard, hog pen, and other fittings	15	00	0
	191	13	4

. . . .

In 1855 the railroad company pamphlet listed for sale "2,500,000 acres [of] selected prairie, farm and wood lands" available in "tracts of any size, to suit purchasers." It further stated that such lands might be purchased "on long credits, and at low rates of interest." The interest rate listed in the pamphlet was 2 per cent. This was extremely reasonable in view of the existence of rates as high as 50 per cent in frontier Illinois.

The pamphlet contained a discussion of the company's title to the lands, the route of the railroad, and the location of the company's land:

> The lands are situated on each side of the Road between Dunleith and Cairo on the main line, and between Chicago and Centralia, by the Chicago Branch. As it traverses north and south from end to end of the State, it passes through a great variety of climates. Lands may be thus selected in various latitudes, to suit the disposition of the purchaser. The Road passes immediately over some of the lands; others vary in distance from it from one to fifteen miles.

There was also a large double-page map with both English and German titles, showing routes to the Illinois Central lands from the East Coast.

The price of land and the terms of payment were stated clearly:

> The price will vary from $5 to $25 per acre, according to location, quality, distance from stations, villages, &c. Contracts for deeds may be made during the year 1855, stipulating the purchase money to be made in five payments, with the succeeding year's interest added in advance. The first payment to be made in two years from the date of the contract, and the others annually thereafter.

It was claimed that the land would "produce, with less labor, as large a crop as any farm in the Eastern or Middle States, valued at $100 to $150 per acre."

For the emigrant starting from New York, the pamphlet gave costs of moving to Chicago, and a list of the articles that should be brought from the East: "Agricultural tools—Small Agricultural Tools are more extensively made at the East, but Reaping, Mowing and Threshing Machines, are extensively made at the West. Spades, Shovels, &c., you [can] buy cheaper at the East, but Plows of different kinds you can buy as reasonably here." A table of prices of corn, wheat, and oats at the Chicago market during the 1854 season provided an answer to one of the most important questions of the prospective emigrant. Several testimonial letters from Illinois farmers were included describing the quality and productivity of the soil and giving some hints about prairie farming methods.

The 1859 pamphlet was somewhat similar to that of 1855, although the land offering had been reduced to 1,400,000 acres. According to this pamphlet, transportation of produce would be no problem because

> The means of intercommunication provided by nature are unsurpassed. The State is bounded on the West and South by two great navigable rivers, and for fifty miles on the Northeast by Lake Michigan; while the interior is penetrated for more than two hundred miles by the Illinois River, whose waters are connected with the Lake by the Illinois and Michigan Canal. About two-thirds of the boundaries of the State is made up of navigable rivers, amounting to about 1,000 miles in length.

. . . .

The guidebooks could be discarded. But there was one book which would have been useful in the planning stages of his venture, during his journey, and would have continued to be a valuable reference work to consult in his daily routine.

The Farmer's and Emigrant's Handbook, compiled by Josiah T. Marshall, was exactly what its author claimed it to be, "A luminous and ample Directory and Guide." First published in 1845 by D. Appleton and Company, New York, it was printed in both German and English, and within its covers was information dealing with every facet of the emigrant farmer's toil. Much of the information was taken from the writings of prominent "agriculturists," architects, veterinarians, and travelers. Reference was made to several agricultural periodicals, including *The Prairie Farmer,* the *Proceedings of the New York State Agricultural Society, The Plow,* (a monthly chronicle of rural affairs and progress in agricultural technology), and the *Southern Agriculturist.*

In his preface Marshall presented a clear statement of his purpose:

> In times past, the European emigrants, and even the settlers from the Atlantic States who removed to the West were exposed to numberless trials and disadvantages, chiefly arising from the dearth of essential information concerning the various novel circumstances in which the change of their abode and habits of life unavoidably placed them. A luminous and ample Directory and Guide; comprehensive and minute,

the result of experience and observation, has long been desired by both of the classes of persons referred to; and also by those who have been born and nurtured in the newly opened districts.

The publishers are gratified that they are enabled to satisfy the universal demand, by a volume which comprises a mass of superior materials, partly derived from the most authentic sources, and partly obtained by extensive and protracted research.

The author began by giving advice on the selection and purchase of land. He also listed the implements and supplies needed, along with their cost:

Articles Necessary for a New Settler

One span of Horses, say	$100.00
One yoke of oxen	50.00
One double wagon	50.00
One superior plough	10.00
One drag	5.00
One spade, shovel and hoe	2.50
Two log chains	8.00
One cradle, scythe, and snath	7.00
One axe	2.00
Two augers—half inch and inch	.75
One saw	1.00
Two chisels	1.00
Rake and pitchfork	1.00
One hammer and 10 lbs of nails	1.25
One cow	15.00
	$254.50

His estimates of the expenditure of time and money necessary to erect a suitable dwelling were:

Cutting, hewing, and hauling timber	4 days work
Raising, (mostly done by the neighbors)	1 day
Putting on roof and gable-ends	2 days
Cutting out doors, windows, and place for fireplace, and casing doors, and windows, and making doors	4 days
Laying floors and making a ladder to chamber	3 days
Chinking and daubing	3 days
Building chimney	3 days
In all	20 days work

Now, the cash out will be, for ten day's work hired	$ 5.00
1000 ft. of lumber for floors, etc.	10.00
20 lbs. of nails	1.00
30 lights, sash and glass, (6 lights for chamber)	1.87
2 pair butts and screws, (use wooden latches)	.25
400 split clapboards for the roof	2.50
	$20.62

But we will add for contingencies, which will make
even money,   4.38
                                                              ‾‾‾‾‾‾
                                                              $25.00

To those whose destination was the prairie he gave instructions on the first year's activities. He placed the best time to start as June, and listed the supplies the emigrant should have when he reached his destination:

Beds and bedding he should never sell, and he may as well take an extra stock of clothing of all kinds, except "finery;" a snug little bookcase well filled; together with "Town's Spelling Book," and "Webster's Dictionary;" a slate for each of the children, and a receipt for the subscription of at least two agricultural and miscellaneous papers for two years; and thus equipped, he will be prepared to begin life in the west.

General farm management was the topic of the third chapter. Seven areas were considered:

In writing on this subject, we shall divide it in the following order:
Firstly—What proportion of the farm it is proper to preserve uncleared of wood.
Secondly—The proper division of the cleared land into fields, size of fields, manner of fencing, etc.
Thirdly—The proper improvements of the soil which will include draining, manuring, etc.
Fourthly—The cultivation of various kinds of crops.
Fifthly—Seeding of land with grass seeds.
Sixthly—Raising domestic animals.
Seventhly—Necessity of barns and sheds sufficient to store all crops, and protect domestic animals from the inclemency of the weather.

Marshall included plans and instructions for building modest log shanties, log cabins, pretentious farm homes, and barns. He even provided plans for icehouses and hen houses. Where timber was scarce a substitute was suggested. Sun-dried clay molded into bricks and known as "pise" was shown to be a very sturdy and economical building material: "it is the true rural construction, cool in summer, warm in winter; and is besides susceptible, at a small expense, of the handsomest decorations by means of fresco painting, which are easily put on, and resist the vicissitudes of the seasons; it will be seen also, that they can be of very great solidity."

Every aspect of home making, animal and agricultural husbandry, and their allied pursuits was described in this book. There were treatises on the dairy, its management and produce; cookery, including pickling, soap and candle making, and cloth making and dyeing. A chapter was devoted to farriery—the treatment of diseased or wounded animals. This was followed by a discussion of diseases and accidents and the maintenance of the health of humans. However, neither in the chapter dealing with animal ailments nor in that dealing with human ailments was there mention of the procedures to be followed during a birth. To provide the farmstead with fresh vegetables and fruit, Marshall gave detailed instructions for the planting and care of gardens and fruit trees. Among other useful information there were instructions for cultivation and preparation of dyer's madder; for the curing of provisions for the English market; and for the use of hops.

To help the emigrant become a citizen (or a better one if he were already a citizen), Marshall presented a survey of the Constitution and of the naturalization and preemption laws.

Finally there was a large section of miscellaneous recipes, hints, and tables of useful data. Among the subjects discussed in the chapter on miscellany were: the preparation of potash and pearlash, byproducts of land clearance; purification of water; and the disposal of sewage. The postal rates, foreign exchange rates and commodity prices for the year were also given. Finally there was an article on prairie farming, taken from the *Union Agriculturist*.

Nearly all phases of the settler's activity were included by one writer or another. The best time for the journey and for arrival had been suggested. The emigrant had been given travel instructions to enable him to reach his destination. Costs of traveling, building, supplies, and preparing the land had been enumerated. The methods of acquiring land had been explained. Suggestions had been made as to the type and number of implements needed, and the supplies which should have been brought to the frontier. Instructions for building a dwelling, for clearing land, and for cultivating prairie land were included. The emigrant had been told which crops and what livestock would flourish, and where. He had been informed concerning educational facilities, and the religions that were practiced in the new lands. Altogether, much good advice from experienced people had been put at his disposal.

The existence of such information seems to indicate that those hardy souls who sought fortune and personal freedom in the American wilderness were not wild-eyed dreamers. Rather, they were a practical, thoughtful people, who realized the enormity of the task they were about to undertake.

That these books and pamphlets existed shows that someone recognized a need for them. The fact that many went through several editions, as noted earlier, leads to the conclusion that they were put to substantial use. Certainly the very least that can be attributed to them is that they kept before the eyes of the American public the promise of the unsettled West.

Stephen J. Tonsor, professor of history at the University of Michigan, edited the letters of a German immigrant, Adolphus von Aman, for the 1961 *Journal of the Illinois State Historical Society*. Born in Salzburg, the son of an army captain, Aman served in a Bavarian regiment during the Napoleonic Wars and in 1817 left for America. Aman wrote to his brother from his farm in White County, Illinois, where he died in 1841. Three of the letters were published in the Munich newspaper *Eos* between 1829 and 1831.

'I Am My Own Boss'

ADOLPHUS AMAN

The United States of North America, the State of Illinois
White County, Carmi, December 15, 1828

Dear Brother!

Should this letter be fortunate enough to come into your hands, which is very uncertain when one considers what expanses of land and ocean separate us, it will be like the appearance of one risen from the dead. This fact and the impermanence of my residences since my arrival is the reason that I have not written you sooner— Yes, dear brother, I am still alive and well and I hope that you are still alive, well, and happy. I fear that our mother is dead, for she was very old when I left Germany. It is for this reason that I address this letter to you. But whether or not you still live in Munich is unknown to me; a great deal may have happened to you since last I heard from you. It is very difficult for me to write you this letter in German, for I have forgotten nearly all my German and therefore I beg you to excuse my poor style.

It is impossible in this letter for me to give you my whole story and a description of my travels; therefore I will describe only my reasons for leaving military service and Germany and then tell you something of my present mode of life. Dissatisfaction with military service, especially in peace time and the wish to lead a private life in the circle of my own family compelled me to find means by which I could realize these wishes. You yourself know that it is almost impossible in Germany to obtain a position in the civil service, a position which was suitable to my character and my

From Stephen Tonsor, " 'I Am My Own Boss'—A German Immigrant Writes from Illinois," *Journal of the Illinois State Historical Society*, LIV (1961), 392-404. Footnotes in the original have been omitted. Reprinted by permission of the author and the Illinois State Historical Society.

descent. Therefore since my fatherland denied me the fulfillment of my dearest wish, I decided to turn my eyes to distant and happier realms! And I did so not in vain—I found a free and happy land called the United States of America on the western shores of the Atlantic Ocean.

The first four years after my arrival in America I spent in travels through the states of Pennsylvania, Maryland, Virginia, North Carolina, Tennessee, Alabama, and Kentucky, and in learning the art of brickmaking and the construction of houses and chimneys from this building material. In 1821 I came to the state of Illinois, where I now live, and married on the 4th of February, 1822, Sarah Rupert, a girl of German descent, who, however, cannot speak German. A short time after I married I chose a piece of land, and I now have a fine open plantation which produces everything necessary for life. I have brought four children into the world. . . .

I possess at the present time 3 horses; 21 cows, calves, and oxen; and 56 pigs. In winter and spring up to the 15th of July I am at home and work on my plantation; bring more land into cultivation; improve the old fence; feed my cattle, horses, and pigs; chop wood and bring it home with a wagon and a yoke of oxen; in winter and in spring I plow the ground and plant corn, cotton, tobacco, indigo, pumpkins, sweet-potatoes, water and musk-melons, and a great number of other garden things. In the remaining time I make bricks and build chimneys and houses in the surrounding countryside, something by which I earn a considerable amount of money.

I will give you a short description of the state of Illinois in which I live. . . . This land is flat, with the exception of a few hills, and is very fertile. The greater part of it is covered with woods. There are, however, a great number of natural meadows, (called prairies), of from three to a hundred miles long where the grass grows from 5 to 6 feet high. The woods consist of oak trees, nut trees, wild cherries, mulberries, sassafras, crab-apples, plum, and numerous other trees for which I do not know the German names. Really, this is a blessed country where every man can live in happiness and superfluity if he works and does not violate the law of the land.—Write me as soon as you can. Write me of all the news and of all the changes which have come about in the last twelve years. Give my regards to all my relatives and old friends. If you write, address your letter as follows: To Mr. Adolphus Aman in Carmi, White County, State of Illinois, The United States of America, via—(You must direct whether the letter is to go by way of London, Paris, Hamburg, or Amsterdam, and write this under the via).

My wife and children send you their heartfelt good wishes, Farewell!

In the hope of hearing from you soon I am your ever-loving brother,

Adolphus Aman.

Dear Brother!
. . . .

For the first three years I rued it greatly that I had come to America, and my only effort was to save enough money to pay my way back to Germany. In Athens after I had earned a considerable amount of money, I made up my mind to go to Florence, (a city on the Tennessee River), and there get a job as a boatman on a produce-laden boat bound for New Orleans, a trip for which I would have received 50 or 60 dollars. Providence, however, did not desire this, and I believe that it was all for my best.

On March 11, 1821, after the man named Mackle Ray, for whom I worked, had paid me, I began my journey. However, due to an indescribable error I took the wrong road and did not notice my mistake until I had traveled a day's journey. The next morning the man in whose house I had passed the night gave me directions by which I could, he said, get on the road by traveling an almost invisible trail, across various big creeks and through a heavy forest. I traveled for two or three miles until I came to a creek which was frozen over. I took off my shoes and stockings and crossed the creek. The ice was so thin that I broken through with every step. When I reached the other side, I could not find the slightest trace of a trail, and I saw that I was in a very dubious position. I stood there and thought it over for a while and finally gave up completely my resolution to go to New Orleans and then to Germany.

I decided to continue my journey on the road which I had left that morning, and in the space of 10 days it brought me to Illinois. When I arrived at Shawneetown, I attempted to change a fifty-dollar bank note in a store, but, unfortunately, the storekeeper told me that it was a counterfeit note. I wrote Mackle Ray that I would have him arrested if he did not immediately send me better money. I wrote a judge in Athens and asked him to help me get my money. I did not receive any answer from either person, and so I completely lost these fifty dollars.

And now had I gone to New Orleans in what regrettable circumstances I would have found myself when I discovered the loss of my money! You are quite right, I do have to support myself and my family with hard work, but it isn't as hard as you think. I do not regard it in so dark or melancholy a light. I am my own boss, I have no master, I work when it pleases me, and when I am tired, I rest. I am always happy with my work. It gives me great pleasure to see the work of my hands; for example, a piece of land which was previously full of trees and brush, sad and unpleasant to look upon, open now to the warming sun—it is really a pleasant sight. The same is true of a field planted to corn, if it is well cultivated, ten feet high with dark green leaves, the red and the white silks hanging from the ears and glistening through the rows. It makes me feel good to see a beautiful brick house which I have built.

There is no danger that the piece of land where I live will be sold, for there are so many better pieces of land. Should it be sold, I would not trouble myself much over it but would only go into the woods and cultivate new ground. One is not so troubled about making a living here as people are in Europe.

. . . .

In the summer of 1829 it was very dry here, as it usually is; however, in the spring there were many heavy rains. Last winter was very mild, and we had only nine inches of snow, which lasted only a week, until the 15th of March. The cattle could find enough grass in the woods. If we ever had a winter here such as the one you describe in your letter, nearly all the men and animals would certainly freeze, for the houses are rather open and without stoves; the cattle and the pigs live through summer and winter, and day and night, in the woods; and the horses have open stalls which would not protect them from the cold.

The grapes which grow here are very good and would yield an excellent wine; however, the people hereabouts don't know anything about wine-making and, moreover, do not have the time to hunt the grapes in the woods and bring them home. Storekeeper Willmann, a German, bought a great mass of grapes from some poor people for practically nothing and made them into wine. I had some of it and found it very good. A measure of wine here costs from seven to three florins. If I planted a vineyard of domesticated grapes, I could make a great deal of money. If I had a brewer and a vintner from Germany here, within five years I would be the richest man in the country.

Occasionally beer is brought here from Cincinnati in the state of Ohio and costs from 1 to 10 kr. the measure. After a week of hard work Sunday is very welcome with me. There is a great difference between a Sunday here and one in Germany. For the most part I remain at home and spend the time with the singing of David's psalms and with reading the Old and New Testament and other spiritual books. . . . There are very many good and instructive books in the English language, and I am very perplexed why those are not translated into German. I see the cause in the fact that they would find no readers in Germany, where the taste of the readers has been corrupted by light reading and novels. I know this from my own experience. After this I take a walk through the plantation and the woods. Occasionally a neighbor with his wife and children visits us. For these occasions Sarah prepares a good dinner. During these visits the various events in the settlement, discussions of farming and political events form the conversation.

Occasionally we visit a neighbor, nearly all of whom are Sarah's relatives. . . . Occasionally we ride from two to four miles to hear a sermon. We do not have any holidays here, but other days which one can describe as days of amusement; for example, the 4th of July on which the independence of the United States was declared and which is celebrated yearly. Every fourth year there is the election day of the President, the senators and representatives, the state governors, a sheriff, county commissioners, the justice of the peace, and the constables. On these days nearly everyone goes to Carmi, talks and drinks with his acquaintances, and has a good time.

. . . .

My Dear Brother,

. . . .

Life certainly would be easier in one of the older states, but it is difficult to obtain land there because of its dearness. If you were suddenly transplanted from the tumult of the city of Munich to my plantation, you would doubtless call it a wilderness. To me, however, who have been weaned from the city and its pleasures for many years, it is a friendly and home-like place and I am never more satisfied than when I am at home.

If I were of the same mind as thirteen years ago, it would bring me to distraction to have to live here without beer, without wine, without music, without the theatre, and without every other pleasure! I hope that by the first of March, 1831, my family will have a new addition. Last fall Sarah took in a nursing child named Tempe whose parents died last summer. When you retire from the army will it be possible for you to buy a small estate?

. . . .

We raise chickens, ducks, geese, etc., which are often in danger of being eaten by foxes, possums, and night-owls. Last autumn I sold six steers for 41 dollars. They weighed 2400 lbs. Had I sold them in Munich, I would have received 250 fl. for them. Next autumn I have 20 pigs, which will weigh around 3000 lbs., to sell and will get about 60 dollars for them. In Munich I might get about 500 fl. for them. (?) I now have fifteen head of calves, for I sold together with the six steers a cow and a calf, a cow and two young steers, and I slaughtered a big steer last winter. My mare, Silva, foaled last spring. Thomas, my brown, is twenty years old and still works well. Charles, a black three-year-old, I broke to the saddle and to the plow this summer. How much did your horse cost you? An ordinary horse here costs 50 dollars.

Last fall I earned 50 dollars laying bricks. This fall I will earn 65 dollars. If there were another mason in the country I would give up this business completely, for I have too much work on my plantation. I also have two young hounds, Nimrod and Venus. Without them the wild animals would take over the fields. I want to thank you for the receipt for brewing beer. I don't as yet understand it perfectly, yet I think I can make it work. At first I am going to try making only a little of it. Will an iron kettle do or must the kettle be made of copper? Since wild hops are difficult to find here, I wish that if possible you would send me some good hop seeds. We have no stoves here, only fireplaces such as they have in France. My furniture consists of four beds, a table and a chest made of walnut, which is a very beautiful brown wood, five chairs; and on the wall near the fireplace are three shelves on which the white porcelain and the coffee cups parade. N.B. The house consists of only one room. Joined to the house is another building in which I salt, hang, and smoke pork, and in which I store the flour, lard, soap, and vinegar. Over the area between these two buildings is an attic where I store my implements, tools, and other odds and ends.

. . . .

Since next fall I am going to build a new house on the other side of the plantation and make some radical changes I will still not send you a sketch of my plantation. The United States keeps only a small army in peacetime, garrisoned in the port cities and on the frontiers. The soldiers are recruited and receive eight dollars per month, together with provisions and clothing; their term of enlistment is five years, and on discharge they all receive a quarter-section of land. The United States has moreover a fairly respectable navy, which does not take second place to even the English navy. Now, dear Brother, I will close. I believe that I have answered all your questions. [There follow many greetings and regards to relatives, acquaintances, and officers; and the writer expresses the hope that by the 1st of March of 1831 he will have received another letter from Europe.]

. . . .

Daniel Harmon Brush recalls his melancholy experiences in and around Murphysboro in the mid-1840s. Born in New York, Brush migrated to Illinois with his family at the age of eight in 1820. The memoir itself, which was never intended for publication, according to The Lakeside Press, was written at Brush's Carbondale home during the years just before his death in 1890. "His story is not exciting," observes the publisher, "but it gives a good picture of how the enterprise and character of a pioneer were reflected in the growth and character of the community as they both grew up together."

Growing Up with Southern Illinois

DANIEL H. BRUSH

When I located in Murphysboro there was no store there and on April 20, 1844 John M. Hanson, who had married my wife's eldest sister, and myself agreed to commence a small mercantile business in the village.

The capital was six hundred dollars to start on. I had shelves put in the little room I had secured for a writing place, and a counter across the back end, and in this building we opened up for trade. The good people of the vicinage came and bought. To the envious and malignant clique opposed to me this was like a red flag to an angry bull. The anger of their chief was savage and his threats of vengeance upon me were dire. I knew I owed him nothing while he owed me about $80 that I never expected to recover, and I kept still and waited.

The threatened vengeance of Jenkins against me was not long in taking shape. The term of Circuit Court for this county was to be held about the 3rd Monday of May (1844) and to that term he instituted suit in assumpsit against me claiming $3,000 damages. My recollection is that he did not file his declaration in the suit so as to have a trial at that term or the next, his aim being, as I supposed, to hold the weapon of his malice over me as long as possible that he and his strikers might have as long time as possible to gloat over the ruin he was going to bring down upon my devoted head, and tantalize me as a cat does a captured mouse before giving it the mortal crush.

I continued right along with my business and waited. Our little store flourished and we increased its capital as we got money to put in, and had a very good trade. Many of our old Brownsville customers resided not far away and were glad to trade with me, as I

From Daniel H. Brush, *Growing Up with Southern Illinois*, Milo M. Quaife, ed. (Chicago, 1944), pp. 140-149, 164-165. Reprinted with the permission of R. R. Donnelley & Sons Company, The Lakeside Press. Footnotes in the original have been omitted.

had always done the fair thing by them. Mr. Hanson was also well liked. He was honest and people knew it, so they were not afraid of our firm.

Nothing of importance happened during the summer. In the fall there was a good deal of sickness. The unaccountable disease called Milk Sick was prevalent, brought on by using milk of cows that were allowed to run at large on the range in the Muddy River bottom. I believed that the complaint was only a malignant type of bilious fever and could not be brought on by drinking milk, so I let my cow go to the range and drank her milk when I felt like it, but when her sucking calf took the Trembles I quit using it. Not long afterwards the disease struck me, and for two or three months I was of but little account. My system seemed fully saturated with the poison, which finally worked its way out in risings like boils on various parts of my body and my hands especially became very sore and painful. I changed my notion about Milk Sick and thereafter kept my cows up in the season of its appearance.

. . . .

The remainder of this year (1845) transpired without any very important matters happening. We had a fair trade and in the late fall and winter took in country produce to the amount of a thousand or twelve hundred dollars which was shipped to Memphis by flatboat in the spring of 1846, Mr. Hanson going along and selling the stuff at a small loss, say about $35 on the lot. We could stand this pretty well, as we had thus turned goods into money and our profits on the goods recouped our loss and we were still ahead.

In the fall and winter of 1846 we had two flatboats built and purchased pork, wheat, corn, etc. to the amount of about $3,500 to load the boats to take down the River. It happened that in the spring of '47 there was a scarcity of such produce as we had purchased and prices advanced.

Speculators came to us from St. Louis and offered to buy our boats and all the stuff we had to load them with at a price that would yield a good profit and we concluded to sell and did so, clearing some five or six hundred dollars. Here the Logan-Jenkins spite again bared its cloven hoof in trying to poison the minds of the purchasers when they came to receive the produce, intimating that it might be well to watch out for their interests in the weighing etc., and so young John A. Logan, then a dapper boy of 18 or 20 years, was brought along to witness. I understood the move but did not care as I knew no wrong doing on our part was intended. The persons who purchased were French, and did not fully understand English. They soon discovered that we designed no wrong to them and we had no trouble. They got what they bought of us. We received of them the money for it, and they went on their way rejoicing and, I understood, made good sales.

Aside from business, sad times came upon Murphysboro people this winter (1847) in the shape of scarlet fever that broke out in most malignant form in midwinter and claimed victims from almost every family. In some households every child was taken. Myself and wife tried to shield our two children, Rowland and Lucretia, from the scourge by keeping them close at home and away from exposure. A girl of about 12 years that we had taken to raise at her father's request, notwithstanding our strict orders not to go to any house where the disease had made its appearance, called in at a neighbor's where there was a case, and the first we knew about it she was attacked and very bad off with the fever. We hired a girl whose father resided with his family a few miles in the country to help us take care of the sick one and in a very short time she was stricken down. Her sister then came to nurse and it was not long until she, too, was prostrated. Then our two little ones were attacked and so we had five cases of the pestilence in our small house at the same time.

The sickness attacked our children very differently. The boy was chilly and cold, and his throat and lungs soon became affected and he was hoarse as with violent cold, while Lucretia from the first was burning up with fever. I sent to Du Quoin for Doctor Wall who had a reputation as a successful physician. He came but misapprehended, as I think, the difference in the two cases. He required both to be kept cool and treated them as would probably have been entirely proper where the fever first developed; the treatment suited the little girl's case but was just the reverse with the boy as it increased the obstruction in his throat and lungs and induced croup which caused his death. He was not even confined to his bed and we did not consider him dangerously sick, but his hoarseness increased and the time soon came when his windpipe became so clogged with phlegm that he could not breathe, and at the last he rushed into my arms and looked up in my face in silent appeal as though he thought I could give him relief, and choked to death in my arms. No soul can depict my anguish at that time. I thought no greater could befall me but there was in store for me a sorrow much more poignant, when his mother died.

Our remaining child, Lucretia, was at death's door for months. We were up with her nights and taking rest by turns for months. Her throat was very much affected and swelled into a great lump on one side that had to be lanced to let the dead matter escape. We called in Doctor Sams, whose close attention and watchful care I think saved her life.

. . . .

The next day was Sunday. All nature seemed bright and cheerful and I anticipated the enjoyment of a pleasant Sabbath with my wife and children. About 10 A.M., however, a messenger appeared with word from brother James that he was ill and desired me to go to him, with a doctor. I was alarmed and at once started with a physician. When we reached the place, we found James up and around without pain, but having symptoms of the cholera in the shape of bowel discharges which were of that colorless watery type indicative of the dread disease. He had arrived at his home apparently all right, but in the night had occasion to be up often, and the increasing frequency of the discharges had signified to him the necessity of medical attention.

The doctor at once commenced treating him with a view to checking the dangerous symptoms, but with no success. The discharges continued to increase and it was but a little while until the patient was utterly prostrated and unable to rise from his bed. Cramps set in, commencing in the extremities of his limbs, thence gradually extending towards the vitals, accompanied by painful writhings fearful to behold. I was over him rubbing and bathing his distorted and cramped-up limbs with hot wetted cloths for hours without ceasing until his heart was attacked and the death struggle came for a moment and all was over with my dear brother. His sufferings after the cramping commenced were most intense, and he so signified as long as he could express his feelings. The disease ran its course in about 12 hours after the first symptoms appeared. His sudden death most powerfully impressed upon my mind the importance of preparing for the great change that would come to me as to all. I went home to Julia with the sad news and said to her that I had resolved to try to be ready and wanted her to join with me in intercessions to our God for His assistance and forgiveness, and we then and there commenced the family devotions that we ever after kept up by daily reading of the scriptures and prayer to the throne of the Most High.

The death of my brother was a great calamity to all his relatives. To his wife and family of six small children, the eldest but 12 years old, his loss was irreparable. He had commenced his married life in poverty, and with perseverent industry had just got fairly started in the way towards independence and prosperity. He was amiable in disposition and noble in character, entirely free from bad habits and honorable in his business dealings.

. . . .

In 1952, Harry Edward Pratt edited and published documents dealing with the Swedish immigrant colony at Bishop Hill (just north of Galesburg) and the murder of its founder, Eric Janson. A native of Cambridge, Illinois, Pratt received his doctorate from the University of Illinois in 1927. Before becoming the state historian at the Illinois State Historical Society in 1950, as well as editor of the Society's *Journal,* he taught at Wesleyan and Ball State universities. Pratt published extensively on Abraham Lincoln: some of his better known works are *Lincoln, 1809-1839* (1939), *Lincoln, 1840-46* (1941), and *Concerning Mr. Lincoln* (1944). For a full account of the Bishop Hill colony, see Olav Isaksson and Søren Hallgren, *Bishop Hill: A Utopia on the Prairie* (Stockholm, 1969).

The Murder of Eric Janson

HARRY E. PRATT

At Bishop Hill, in Henry County, a few miles west of Galva, Illinois, there flourished from 1846 to 1861 a communal colony composed of Swedish emigrants. It was dominated by Eric Janson, not only spiritually, but in almost every phase of living. Janson was to the "world a misguided fanatic; to his followers, a God-given prophet." The group engaged in agriculture, linen weaving, and the manufacture of wooden goods from pans to wagons. Cholera reduced their number in 1849, but in 1850 there were 550 residents.

The murder of Janson at the age of forty-two, in the spring of 1850, following ten weeks of turmoil, hurt the Colony's prestige. It is an involved story, but a contemporary account is given in six documents in the Governor Augustus C. French Papers in the Illinois State Library.

John Root, the murderer of Janson, came from a good family in Sweden. Well educated, with pleasing manners, he had served in the American Army in the Mexican War prior to taking up residence in Bishop Hill in 1848. He courted and married Janson's cousin, Charlotte Louise Janson. He is supposed to have signed an agreement that his wife would always remain a member of the Colony. This Root later denied, but he felt free to come and go and took no part in the group activities. After their child was born in the fall of 1849, Root tried to persuade his wife to leave. She refused, and then, on March 3, 1850, Root and a friend named Stanley forcibly seized and compelled her to go with them in a carriage.

From Harry E. Pratt, ed., "The Murder of Eric Janson, Leader of Bishop Hill Colony," *Journal of the Illinois State Historical Society,* XLV (1952), 55-69. Reprinted by permission of the Illinois State Historical Society. Footnotes in the original have been omitted.

This opened a series of kidnappings, rescues, warrants for arrest, three mob invasions of Bishop Hill, and the rally of neighbors to aid the colony and appeals to Governor French for troops. Janson and other leaders fled to St. Louis and did not return until Saturday, May 11. The Sunday following, Janson preached a farewell sermon, sensing death was near.

On Monday he went to Cambridge, Illinois, to defend several suits brought against the Colony in the Henry County Circuit Court. It was during the noon recess that Root appeared and fired two shots, one striking Janson above the heart and causing instant death. Root was captured and indicted that afternoon for murder before Judge William Kellogg. To prevent his release by the mob he was placed in the jail at Toulon, Illinois. His trial was postponed until the November term, when his "not guilty" plea was withdrawn.

His attorneys, for various reasons, got the trial postponed until September, 1852, when it was heard at Knoxville in the adjoining county of Knox. Three days were spent examining 219 people before a jury was selected. Root was found guilty of manslaughter and sentenced to serve two years in the Alton Penitentiary. He was pardoned a year later by Governor Joel A. Matteson.

I. State's Attorney Harman G. Reynolds to Governor French

Cambridge, Henry Co. Ill. April 23 1850

Private & Confidential
Dear Gov;

I have long hesitated as to my duty in relation to the unfortunate difficulties in our Co. I have at last however, concluded to presume a little upon our old acquaintance, and to state, shortly the true state of affairs, so far as I can learn—*as a private citizen.* I have read the article from the Mo. Republican, and the Peoria Dem. Press. They are gross perversions of the truth.

The Swedish Colony at Bishop Hill was planted in the Autumn of 1846, in the S.E. part of Henry Co., by one Eric Janson, who pretended to be inspired of God, something like Joe Smith, having a catechism explaining the Bible to suit his views.

His people treat him with extraordinary reverence, and receive his teachings with as much respect and regard, as the jews respect the laws of Moses. They believe in him implicitly.

At first, there was no marriage, but soon, this feature was abandoned, and marriage was encouraged. A short period before Marriage commenced among them, *John Root,* who is an educated Swede, and a gentleman in his manners and intercourse in Society,

Olaf Krans' painting of Bishop Hill, Illinois

and was mustered in luxury and indolence, came among these people, and sojourned.

He sought his present wife in marriage, and the bargain with Janson was consummated. Janson says, Roots wife was ever to remain. This, Root denies. Root was treated with respect, did as he pleased, went and came, lived, and enjoyed, with his wife, her society, little or much as it pleased him. Having received some money, Janson wished Root to place the same in the common fund, which Root refused to do. All the while, Root's wife labored as one of the Colony, until last summer, when the cholera carried off 130 out of about 600 in a few short weeks. In consequence of Root's refusal to deposit his money in the common fund, an estrangement ensued between him and the colony, until it grew into mistrust and mutual dislike. In the time of the cholera, Root wished his wife to go away with him to some safer place, which she refused to do, and a great variety of reasons are given by different ones for her refusal. The Swedes say, she did not want to live with Root; in the face of this Root lived with her when he pleased, at Bishop Hill. Some of the American's say that she wanted to live with him at Bishop

Hill—not elsewhere—others, that she was far advanced in pregnancy, could not speak English, and did not want to go for that reason—others again, that she was only restrained by the doctrine taught her by Janson, that if she or any of them left, they would be damned.

In the meantime, she gave birth to a child. Root waited a proper time and was more anxious for her removal than ever.

He tried to get people about Cambridge, and in other parts of the Co. and also in R. I. [Rock Island] Co. to assist him in bringing her away, which they utterly refused to do. He then begged them to go with him to Bishop Hill and stand about, saying, that if they were there, the Swedes would not interfer. Not any would go for a long time. At length, about the 2nd or 3rd of March Root wrought so powerfully upon the feelings of a young Mr. Stanley, that he went with him. From what I can gather from Root, from Stanley, and from Americans now and then in the employ of the Swedes, and with whom I am well acquainted, the facts are about these.

Root went to his wife, and wanted her to go away. She refused. He then said he would take the child, and then she consented to go: Got her clothes, fixed up her babe &c., went voluntarily down stairs, Stanley carrying the child. Root in presence of Swedes & Americans, helped his wife into the buggy, his wife took the child. Stanley got in behind, & they drove away. The alarm was given, and a large number of Swedes on horseback, followed after, overtook them, stopped their horse by force, and in the confusion, Root dropped his pistol, which a Swede seized, and they took his wife and child forcibly from the buggy & back to the Hill.

The following day, Root got a Capias* for Johnson [Janson] & others for Riot. Johnson feigned sickness and was not arrested. The Swedes got a continuance for counsel. Mrs. Root had been sub-peonaed as a witness & was in Cambridge when the continuance was granted. How much force was used in detaining her I am unable to say. She was detained against her will, and the following day, evidently against her will was conveyed in the waggon of one Wesley Hanna to Rock River in the North part of the Co. All this was in Co. Courttime—a great many were in Cambridge, and the excitement very great.

On Wednesday [March 4], the trial was to come on, or rather the examination. Root had gone away, and did not return in time, & the matter was dismissed. I am informed that a lawyer of some celebrity then told Janson to take her wherever they could find her. All went home, and the general belief was that the matter was at an end. Not so. Root took his wife to Chicago. The Swedes kept

*A court order demanding custody.

a look out, ascertained where she had gone, and dispatched some of their men to Chicago for her.

I will not detail what I learn had transpired there, only Root says, they had some sort of warrant for him and his wife, which they showed to the States Attorney, and which he denounced. They then tried to get a warrant for Root & wife, intending to fling Root in jail & get away with the wife. They were foiled in this. In the evening when Root was away, by means of a Swede living there, said to be brother to Eric [Janson], she was asked to the door, and taken away. On Roots return, he made what search he could but could not find her. He then got out a warrant for kidnapping, and came back to this Co. He also got a warrant here, to *search for the woman (search warrant for a person)*. The warrants were placed in hands of a constable, and he summoned a posse to take the kidnappers and find the woman. The posse consisted I am told of 56 embracing some of the very best men in Henry Co. They went, undoubtedly influenced by passion, and in no proper mood for such business, for in addition to what I have said, the Swedes had *Philip* Hanna, who had had nothing to do in the matter, arrested

Krans' painting of corn-planting near Bishop Hill

Courtesy of the Illinois State Historical Library

and taken to Wethersfield about 35 miles, on a charge of some criminal matter, which inflamed the public mind greatly.

No injury was done at Bishop Hill to property, to speak of. Some wild fellows, commenced tearing off clapboard, and pulling out brick, when they could not find Roots wife, but were compelled to desist by the American's themselves, and orders given to arrest the first one who should be found doing the like again. That hard language was used, and hostile demonstrations exhibited; that private apartments and sleeping rooms were unceremoniously invaded, I firmly believe. Nothing was to be found however of Janson, Bloombergson, or Mrs. Root. Janson & Mrs. R. had left for St. Louis, and the kidnappers for California. The people went away, saying that they must have Mrs. Root the next day. The Swedes offered no resistance, treated the Americans kindly—fed and lodged them.

The Americans returned the following day, but it was only a repetition of the scenes of the previous night. In the meantime Mrs. Janson had left. Some threats were used, as might be expected. Arms too, were at hand.

All this was done under pretence of the warrants. While these two gatherings were had, I (the State's Attorney) was at Peoria. Learning what was going on, I hastened home. Apparently, every thing was at peace. The Sheriff had done all he could to induce the inhabitants to forbear in the matter. Soon, however it was reported that Roots child was dead, and the excitement became more intense than ever. The people were ready for another rising, when I (the State's Attorney) interposed, and told the people that if they interfered, they were in danger of the District Court. Root, finding no prospect of raising a crowd about Cambridge, went to the north. He came back saying that the people would be on hand on Wednesday, the Sheriff remained at Cambridge to prevent any further interruption all day Wednesday, and part of Thursday. All came to the conclusion that the danger was over, & the Sh'ff went away. He had not been gone over an hour before about three waggon loads came hooting from the north part of the Co., some quite intoxicated. At the advice of all present, I (the District Attorney) refrained from addressing [them] all saying "its no use talking to a drunken crowd." A suitable alarm however was given, and a large number of Americans from Walnut & Red Oak Groves, met to defend the Swedes. A magistrate, Esqr Piatt, interposed his authority at every point, and no injury was done: Yet, great threats were made, and hosti[li]ty plainly manifested. Root however, had the warrants, and was not there. So this crowd had no excuse. This crowd then became exasperated with Root, returned to Cambridge, and but for the interposition of the people, I do not believe that Root would now be in the land of the living. As to the burning of the Hay stacks at Bishop Hill, the story is false. The Hay stacks were burned by some Californians, and the destruction of the only house at Lilly Hill from the fire, was prevented by this identical Root.

The people are so irritated with Root that further danger to the Swedes is not probable. The people are tired of it. They have been mislead. They greatly regret it. The people of this Co. are a law abiding people, a peaceable people. They have been excited by extraordinary representations of abuse—of the instructions from Janson &c.

Now Root has resorted to legal means to recover his wife, notwithstanding. Great abuse, great wrong, great violation of law, has been done. But before your Excellency decides upon a district Court, allow me to request you to send an agent to investigate the true state of matters here.

I must say, that if the people insist upon prosecutions, Henry is not the place for the trial. It would be a mockery of all public justice.

I have consulted with no one concerning what I have written, I would be glad if you would send Maj. W. B. Warren, or some gentleman experienced in Hancock matters to look into it.

The Swedes are first in wrong. The Americans are also wrong. I fear that political animosities—that religious prejudice has had too much to do with it.

The people at Bishop Hill appear to be the happiest people in the Country. They seem contented, are industrious, moral, and but little can be alleged against them, except their faithlessness in regard to their contracts.

Excuse this long letter—I have done what I thought my duty. Should you desire a statement from me as States Attorney, I will give it, but do not desire this to be seen by any but yourself.

Very Respectfully, & Fraternally,
Yours &c H. G. Reynolds.

II. Britton A. Hill to Governor French

St Louis April 8th 1850.

To His Excellency, Augustus C. French,
Governor of the State of Illinois;

Sir;

I have been applied to, by Eric Johnson [Janson] & wife & others, in regard to the Swedish Colony, located in Henry County in your State, which is now threatened with extermination, by a band of lawless men, of about seventy in number, collected together from Cambridge and Rock river in that County, and led on by John Root, Daniel Stanley, Jarvis Pierce, Capt Hanna and others. Root was formerly a member of the Colony of Swedes, and during his residence with them, married Charlotte Louise Johnson, a member of the Colony, and in consequence of domestic difficulties and ill treatment she left her husband and fled from Chicago to some of her friends near that place; and finally came to her relations in the Colony for protection against the violence of her husband, on the 21st day of March last past.

About the 26th of same month, Root came to the Colony with a mob to force his wife to go with him, but she had previously left for a place of safety. Root being irritated by this desertion of his wife, determined to avenge himself upon the innocent inhabitants of the Colony, and the relations of his wife, who were members of it. Incited by the enraged husband the mob paraded through the streets of the little village with guns, threatening to burn up the houses & kill the inhabitants; and after alarming the people very much by their threats, and after searching the whole place during the night, they left, and on the night of the 27th March again returned, & began to break the boards on the church & some of the houses; fired off guns; and ordered the inhabitants to leave their houses, so they could burn them down. The mob then drove all the men of the Colony, into the basement of the church, and the women and children into the Hospital. After keeping them in suspense & finding that these poor people whose faith is non resistance, obeyed their unlawful commands without a murmur, the mob suffered them to go again to their home and did not do any further violence that night.

On the following day, the mob, burned the hay stacks of the colony and set fire to the buildings at Little Hill about two miles west of Cambridge. The pastor of the Church, his wife, and other members of the Colony, fled from the fury of the mob, and are now in the City of St. Louis. No member of the Colony has had any concern with the quarrel between Root & his wife. She left her husband of her own accord, and fled to her relations her natural protectors, and for this, in which the Colony has no interest or part, the mob threatens fire, destruction & death to these poor people.

Root to accomplish these nefarious objects & designs, circulates the most foul slanders and excites the mob to violence thereby, pretending that these people have robbed him of his wife & child, & that the practices & designs of the Colonists are against law & the usages of christians. All impartial persons in the County, acquainted with these people, know them to be simple, industrious, innocent & unoffending persons. They are Christians, and worship God according to the Bible, which is their sole guide. According to the command of our Saviour, they sat at a common table, and all work for the common benefit; but each family has its separate organization, & they live according to the law of God & their profession. The law of marriage is the same as the laws of Illinois sanction. In no particular do they differ from other evangelical christians, than as above stated. They have suffered much from the cholera during the last season, and there are now about seventy widows with their children left dependent upon the Colony for support; and there are no resources but the property of the Colony to keep them from want.

The colonists own about 4000 acres of land, with a church, a large four story brick dwelling house, two other brick houses, five frame buildings & other small buildings for store rooms; a windmill, a large flax machine, two saw mills, a grist mill, & a steam flouring mill. A large part of the land is improved & fenced. The property of the colony, exclusive of their personal effects, amounts to $50,000 and upwards. The population of the colony is about 100 men, 250 women & girls and 200 children; and they are divided into farmers, artisans & mechanics.

These poor unoffending men, women & children, are now trembling under the hourly expectation of being driven forth from their homes, at this inclement season, by fire & sword. Though innocent of any crime and entirely unconnected with the quarrel between Root & his wife, they are in danger of being sacrificed to the fury of a ruthless mob. Meek and unresisting, they oppose no obstacle to the violence of their persecutors. Trusting in that God, "who tempers the wind of the shorn lamb" they do not oppose, they appeal to the laws of your state for protection. They are strangers in our land, from a far country, the land of Sweden; they have crossed the seas, to find in our free and glorious republic an asylum, secure from the heel of the oppressor & the grasp of the tyrant, and now from their little settlement, their new home, their wives, widows and helpless babies, implore and invoke, the protection of the State against lawless violence.

By late advices from the Colony, it is reported, that the mob have appointed a day, for the destruction of their little village, unless the wife of Root is before then surrendered to him. These people cannot coerce the wife of Root to such a course; if they had the power they would not exercise it, for in it they have no concern. It is believed that the authority of the State can alone, save the colony from destruction, and the lives of the relations of

Root's wife. They have appealed to the laws in the County of Henry, but no officer will serve process in the case. They are satisfied that the local authorities will not protect them.

The terrible example of the Mormon war & massacre, and the consequences thereof; the deplorable inefficiency of all local authority and the termination of that bloody era in the history of your state, induce the present petitioners to make early application to the Executive. This letter is sent to you in advance & Eric Johnson [Janson] will follow it, if able to do so; & accompanying this I send you a letter from Wm. W. Drummond Attorney of Stark Co. Illinois, & affidavits of part of the colonists, to the truth of the facts stated in this letter.

May you be able to save these unfortuante colonists, from harm, & your state from the further reproach of innocent blood, by exercising that authority which the law & constitution have placed in your hands, for the execution of the laws & the suppression of insurrection—

I have the honor to be your obedient servant
Britton A. Hill
Atty at Law
17 Locust St
St Louis

One of the clearest signs of the passing of the Illinois frontier was the arrival of the railroad. George M. McConnel recalls some of the events associated with the construction of the Northern Cross Railroad between Quincy and Springfield in the 1840s. McConnel, who was born in Jacksonville in 1833, received a law degree from Harvard University and after 1875 served as the literary and drama critic for the *Chicago Times*. For historical works on Illinois railroads, see R. C. Overton's three books on the Burlington line; the most recent is *Burlington Route: A History of the Burlington Line* (New York, 1965). Two other standard works are Carlton J. Corliss, *Main Line of Mid-America: The Story of the Illinois Central* (New York, 1951) and Robert Casey and W. A. S. Douglas, *Pioneer Railroad: The Story of the Chicago and North Western Railroad* (New York, 1948).

The Coming of the First Railroads

GEORGE M. McCONNEL

The Illinois people were too weak financially to do more than talk until in February, 1837, the state as such took up the work on its own credit and struck out a great system of "internal improvements," including the building of eight distinct lines of railway; *first*, the Central from Cairo to Galena; *second*, a branch of same from Hillsboro eastward to the Indiana state line; *third*, the Southern Cross road from Alton to Mt. Carmel; *fourth*, the Northern Cross road from Quincy, via Jacksonville, Springfield and Decatur, to the Indiana state line nearly due west from Indianapolis; *fifth*, from Peoria to Warsaw; *sixth*, from Alton eastward to intersect the Central, though there seems now some doubt whether this was not included in the Mt. Carmel-Alton project; *seventh*, from Belleville to intersect the Southern Cross, and *eighth*, from Bloomington to Mackinaw with branches to Peoria and to Pekin, all of which it was estimated would cost nearly ten million dollars.

While the bill was pending, Senator Vance of Vermilion county, one of the strong opponents of the whole scheme down to that time, suddenly declared, for some unknown reason, that if the friends of the bill would insert a provision that the Northern Cross road should be built first of all, he would support the bill and this was accordingly done, though the result showed that the bill would have passed without his vote.

It seems absurd, now, that a road from Quincy eastward through Springfield should be called the Northern Cross, but the fact that it

From George M. McConnel, "Recollections of the Northern Cross Railroad," *Transactions of the Illinois State Historical Society*, XIII (1908), 147-152.

was so named is clear proof of where the vast preponderance of the population of the State then lay. Except for the little lead mining city of Galena, the trading post at Peoria and a few other isolated communities, the great mass of the State's people then dwelt south of the Springfield line of latitude.

. . . .

Only a few weeks after construction began in 1837, the great financial panic of that year broke out and thence forth the work was urged against an increasing sea of difficulties that might have appalled the managers had they better known the real proportions of their task. So great were they that though the western half of the fifty-five miles, or nearly half was in active operation early in 1839, the road was not completed to Springfield till in May, 1842.

. . . .

Mr. Ridgely of Springfield . . . in 1847 . . . bought from the State at public auction the road and all its belongings. This, it is remembered, was rebuilt in the Springfield shops, after the re-organization effected by Mr. Ridgely, under the careful direction of Mr. Tilton, who for some years managed the rehabilitated road, was named the "Phoenix," a queer looking machine even for fifty and more years ago, and was used for doing a variety of light work through several years.

The road was built by laying parallel lines of mud sills, eight or ten inches square, under where the rails would come, save where the earth bottom was judged firm enough to lay cross ties much as is now done, only much further apart than now. On these ties were laid "stringers" of oak probably 4 X 6, or 4 X 8 inches, notched and pinned together and on these were spiked flat strap iron rails, some 2 1/2 inches wide, five-eighths of an inch thick and probably twelve or fifteen feet long, with ends mitred, or slanted, so as to take the weight of a wheel on each rail before it had quite left the other. The frequent result may be easily imagined. These ends gradually curled up as the wheels rolled over them, till the points, rising higher than the wheel center, became what were called "snake heads," were under-run by the wheels and shot up through the car and sometimes through an unfortunate passenger or employé.

The only passenger coaches the road possessed were about of the size and "build" of the big omnibuses of the past generation. The seats ran along each side, like those of the omnibus, and the coaches were equally destitute of any and every other appliance for the comfort or convenience of the traveler, other than to sit down and "hang on"—if he could. The speed of the trains was very low, as speed is now measured, but it was, relatively to that to which that generation was accustomed, nearly as high as we now habitually know, the roadway was very uneven, there were no straps to hang to and the lurching about of passengers unfortunate enough to be obliged to stand, their stumbling over and trampling upon the feet of the seated travelers, into whose surprised embraces they not infrequently stumbled and sprawled, were often vastly amusing to onlookers howsoever exasperating to the participants. It was often equally disagreeable when passengers were few. There were no divisions of any kind in the seats. Along each wall of the coach ran a smooth stretch of bench like seat and a sudden lurch of the coach would often slide a sitter half the length of the coach and land him, or her with a gruesome bump in the middle of the floor.

These were specimen inconveniences for travelers, while the want of some of the simplest of the railway devices of the past twenty years brought serious hardships and hazards to the employés. Cars were coupled only with the long link and pin, operated by hand and resulting in any train of a number of cars suddenly stretching or shrinking in length with sudden changes of speed as much as a score or more of feet with sudden jars and hazards unknown on modern trains. There was no means then known for warming the water in the tank of the locomotive tender and the only known means of conveying it from the tank to the boiler was by ordinary leathern hose swinging freely enough between the two to assure immunity from breaking in any one of these sudden elongations of the train. Often a stop of two or three minutes at any station exposed to the bitter cold blasts of winter would suffice to freeze the water in these hoses, tying up the train for from a few minutes to several hours, destitute of any means of informing anybody of the cause and probable duration of the delay. A few minutes of delay in pushing through a snow-drift far from any station would bring the same frozen hose, far from even the useless but sympathetic knowledge of the denizens of a bit of prairie station.

Then it became necessary for the train crew to take wood from the locomotive tender—the art of burning coal in a locomotive furnace had not then been discovered—and carefully built a fire on the ground between the rails and under the hose where it passed in festoons from tank to boiler, watching it like a hawk lest it scorch the leather, in which case the hose would crack and burst and the locomotive be left hopelessly "dead," till drawn away by some force other than its own.

What this task must be for two or three men crouched in the narrow space under a locomotive cab, with a maniac-like northwest wind howling like a legion of devils across the open prairie, driving clouds of stinging snow before it, may be partly guessed by those who have seen a prairie blizzard but can never be fairly appreciated save by him who has taken part in the torturing task.

The facilities for supplying locomotives with fuel and water were very meagre, and when the train stopped at any "wooding" station, the whole train crew and not infrequently some of the passengers, joined in throwing the sawed wood into the great box of the tender, sometimes even having to add to the labors of the sawyers to fill the needed quantity. In many cases some slight accident has caused a stop at some point remote from the scanty water stations, and lines of disgusted passengers trudged back and forth for hours between the impotent train and the nearest creek or farm well, often a distance of miles, each with one or two pails of some kind, carrying water to put into the tank.

These are but a few of the embarrassments of railroading in those days. There were scores of others, for the signal code, the air brake, the automatic coupler, the toilet devices of today, the sleeping car, the dining car, steam heated cars, all lights save candles alone, the use of the telegraph in operating trains, these and many another commonplace of today, were as yet undreamed of. I speak only of such as I saw something of in my boyhood.

The observer of today, if he stops to think, will feel a new respect for the general sagacity of the men who projected the eight lines of road before spoken of. Little of the vast area covered was much beyond the wilderness stage, most of it not at all beyond. Yet the majority of the lines they laid down are now literally or substantially parts of more or less important railway routes. The main line of the Wabash railway of today, pushed southwestward from the head of Lake Erie, intersects the line of the old Northern Cross about at Decatur, and follows it almost foot by foot westward to the Mississippi.

. . . .

One incident I recall witnesses the human quality of that day not a whit different from that of our day. As surveyed by Engineer Bucklin under the official supervision of Commissioner McConnel, the railway line passed along the northern verge of the village of Jacksonville, precisely where the line of the Wabash now passes. But certain of Commissioner McConnel's townsmen insisted that this was because McConnel "owned property on that side of town," and they were highly indignant that he was thus benefiting himself. "The whole town," they said, "should be benefited by locating the road right through the middle of town, along State street and through the public square!"

Why! bless you," said McConnel, though he may not have used the word "bless," but its next door neighbor on the theory that "extremes meet,"—"the engineers did not know I owned any property when they located the line. You can have it on State street if you wish and see how you like it."

And so, to the disgust of the engineers two long transverse curves were interjected into an otherwise straight road, turning it into West State street over the ground where the high school now stands, and sending along the chief street and through the central square of the town, the locomotives belching their smoke in the aristocratic front windows of Col. John J. Hardin as the road left State street on the eastern verge of town and went back again to the surveyed line.

The indignant citizens who thought they should share in a "graft" that existed only in their imaginations, were glad enough to get the track back again on the survey ten years later after the sale to Ridgely, but none of them ever made public acknowledgement that the Commissioner and the engineers were in the right from the first.

Once more let me remark that the fact that along these fifty-five miles of road the line of today follows foot by foot the survey of seventy years ago, is no small testimony to the sagacity, the foresight, the sincerity, the intelligence of the men who established these lines when there was yet no historic past in railway building by which they could guide their footsteps. They broke a way for civilization in the Mississippi valley, and a way whose fashion was yet wholly new to mankind.

3: Mid-Century Expansion

Arthur Cole, in *The Era of the Civil War, 1848-1870* (Springfield, 1919), points out that the year 1848 was a pivotal one in Illinois history. By this time the frontier had been mastered, constitutional difficulties overcome, and the groundwork laid for a decade of record growth and prosperity. Cole, a professor of history at the University of Illinois during the teens and at Ohio State University during the twenties, contributed a number of papers on Illinois to *Transactions of the Illinois State Historical Society*, including "Lincoln and the American Tradition of Civil Liberties" and "Lincoln and the Presidential Election of 1864." During the fifties, Illinois encountered the first stage of urbanization, an experience which fundamentally altered life in the Prairie State. But with progress came problems. Most pressing to many Illinoisans, as Cole points out, was the rapid increase of the foreign-born population. In an article on the Know-Nothing movement in Illinois, the editor of this documentary explores the dynamics of the nativist response to the "foreign problem," especially as it affected state and national politics. For other accounts of the Illinois Know-Nothings, see M. Evangeline Thomas, *Nativism in the Old Northwest* (Washington, D.C., 1936), chapters twelve and thirteen; Don E. Fehrenbacher, *Prelude to Greatness: Lincoln in the 1850s* (Stanford, 1962), pp. 7, 32-33, 46-47, 86-87; Thomas M. Keefe, "Chicago's Flirtation with Political Nativism, 1854-1856," *Records of the American Catholic Historical Society of Philadelphia*, LXXXII (September 1971), 131-157. General studies of the movement include: Eric Foner, *Free Soil, Free Labor, Free Man: The Ideology of the Republican Party before the Civil War* (New York, 1970); Ray A. Billington, *The Protestant Crusade, 1800-1860* (New York, 1938); Carleton Beals, *The Brass-Knuckle Crusade: The Know-Nothing Conspiracy, 1820-1860* (New York, 1960); George M. Stephenson, "Nativism in the Forties and Fifties, with Special Reference to the Mississippi Valley," *The Mississippi Valley Historical Review*, IX (December 1922), 183-202.

The Passing of the Frontier

ARTHUR COLE

The year 1848 marks the beginning of a new epoch in Illinois history. Not only had the polity of the commonwealth found it necessary to lay aside its swaddling clothes for a new constitution, but its citizens began to move forward in strides that rendered obsolete existing institutions and prevailing methods in almost every phase of the life of the times. Agriculture was revolutionized in many of its aspects; urban life discarded more and more of the traces of the frontier; the prairies were filled up by a progressive population which flowed in from every corner of the new and the old world; industry developed into new and untried fields; and the state came to take a front rank among Mississippi valley commonwealths. The way was prepared for the leading rôle Illinois was to play in bearing the burdens of the union in the storm and stress of civil war.

The outstanding feature of life in Illinois during the fifties was the passing of the frontier. Every aspect of its social and economic make-up declared that the spirit of western pioneering could not perpetuate its dominance over the growing commonwealth. Every stroke of a hammer, every rattle of a farm machine, every puff of a locomotive, was a blow at the peace and calm of the untamed prairie wilderness, still the haunt of the rabbit, the deer, and even the wolves—a taunt to the slow and inefficient man power of the primitive first settlers.

The upbuilding of towns and cities was one of the strongest indications of the rapid development of the state. Illinois of 1850 boasted only ten incorporated cities: Chicago, Alton, Springfield, Beardstown, Pekin, Quincy, Peoria, Bloomington, Galena, and Rock Island. Inasmuch, however, as several of these had been insignificant hamlets in 1840, this represented a remarkable development toward a more highly civilized commonwealth. There were in addition, moreover, towns of from three to five thousand inhabitants in places to which ten years before not so much as a trail had led. It was noted that the growth of towns and villages seemed to run

From Arthur Cole, *The Era of the Civil War, 1848-1870* (Springfield, 1919), pp. 1-3, 5-7, 16, 19-26. Footnotes in the original have been omitted.

parallel with the growth of grain; cities grew up only at points of special vantage for the penetration of interior districts by incoming settlers and for the ready exchange of farm products for the finished output of the factory and workshop. For this reason the river towns of the forties had swelled into thriving cities, their life supplied by the sonorous breathing of steam engines; and a business formerly confined to the barter of hazelnuts, butter, and eggs, for buttons, beads, cap ribbons, powder, and shot, was replaced by a business of thousands of dollars in merchandise and produce. For this reason, too, the network of railroads that came to traverse the states developed the municipalities in the fifties; while the smaller communities were receiving new accretions by the hundreds, Chicago increased from a city of 29,963 in 1850, to 80,028 in 1855, and 109,260 in 1860.

Rapid accumulation of population prevented the municipal improvements that might well have been expected of places of such size, for in most senses the cities and towns were mere overgrown villages. Housing facilities could not keep pace with such rapid growth; dwellings were small and crude, often mere shacks. Bloomington erected over 250 new dwellings in 1850, and a scarcity was still noted, while newcomers to Springfield, after looking in vain for some place of residence, passed on in hopes of finding a more favorable location. Home-owning was fairly general among the older townspeople; but rents for the newcomers were uniformly high, sometimes exorbitant. There was a steady shortage of dwellings in Alton, and houses were "worth from fifteen to twenty per cent. per annum on their cost." In Chicago houses that cost $500 sometimes rented for $300 and $400 a year; "a moderate little tenement which might be got in the suburbs of London for £25 per annum here fetches £200," reported a visiting Britisher.

Alongside these conditions, however, were others which showed how hard it was for Illinois to outgrow entirely the frontier atmosphere that had shortly before prevailed in most parts of the state. The backwoods pioneer was not wholly out of his element in the cities, still less in the towns and villages. Even the editor of the *Charleston Courier* protested at the "enormous rent" he had to pay for his newspaper plant, $60 a year. At the same time the sturdy shoemaker at Morris had high hopes of establishing his economic prosperity on a capital of $50; he proposed to build a "small house 12 by 12 middling lumber nails, doors, windows, $12.00 put up by a few neighbors gratis. $25.00 for stock in my line of business which is shoemaking and the Ballance as a reserve and i am certain of doing well." Both men applied to the governor of the state for the necessary loans, the one as a political backer, the other as a

A view of Chicago from the prairie, 1840

stranger whose only security was "the word of a man of honor," and who submitted as a text Raleigh's lines, "True nobleness is not confined to palaces alone." It is to be hoped that Governor French was able to justify their confidence—the sublime confidence of the pioneer in the spirit of democratic coöperation.

No town or city was sufficiently urban to develop a drainage system. In bad weather the streets approached the condition of a quagmire with dangerous sink holes where the boatman's phrase "no bottom" furnished the only description. An absence of civic pride made them the dumping ground of the community rubbish so that the gutters were filled with manure, discarded clothing, and all kinds of trash, threatening the public health with their noxious effluvia.

. . . .

Chicago, the "garden city," became in this period a cosmopolitan metropolis, the commercial emporium of the Lake Michigan region and the adjacent states. The foreign born population came to outnumber the native born, with a considerable representation for every national group. After the completion of the Illinois and Michigan canal the current of trade which formerly flowed down the Mississippi was turned eastward, making Chicago the great

Courtesy of the Illinois State Historical Library

market place of the west to the disadvantage of St. Louis which had
previously dominated the situation. Excellent and extensive railroad
connections next brought additional advantages; in 1854 seventy-
four trains a day tapped the upper Mississippi and the whole
northwest. By 1851 the total value of the trade on the lake port
reached nearly $30,000,000; in 1855 it had a grain trade of
20,487,953 bushels, nearly twice that of its rival on the Mississippi.
It had already become the greatest primary wheat depot in the
world; in spite of a chronic complaint of a shortage of capital, by
1860 over five million dollars of capital were invested in Chicago.

This precocious western city presented many incongruities. In
1850 it had several impressive public edifices, "large warehouses
and stores, five or six stories high, splendid hotels, five public
schools and dwellings, frequently magnificent churches;" ten years
later it had taken on even more metropolitan atmosphere. Yet at
the same time these massive stone and brick stores, warehouses, and
factories, even "palatial" hotels, were surrounded by wooden huts
and shanties. Rough stumps of pine trees were set along the roads in
all directions to carry telegraphic wires. On the occasion of the visit
of the Prince of Wales in 1860, the *London Times* correspondent
reported that Chicago was an "extraordinary *mélange* of the Broad-
way of New York and little shanties of Parisian buildings mixed up

Courtesy of the Illinois State Historical Library

John Deere and his helpers making plows

in some way with backwoods life." The streets, though filthy, were generally broad and pleasant; and a commendable zeal for planting rows of shade trees furnished the beginnings of city beautification. An extensive park system was planned and given authorization by the state legislature. Regular omnibus service was started on the principal thoroughfares in 1850, while the State street horse railroad was opened in April, 1859. The community supported seven daily papers in 1853, besides weeklies and monthlies. With the westward march of the American people, Chicago came to have a central location; equipped with fifty-seven hotels in 1855, eight of which were "first class," it had come to be a point of attraction as a convention city.

Springfield, the state capital, a city of 4,533 in 1850 and of 9,320 in 1860, was a place of few attractions. It had little civic beauty, was famous for the wretched condition of its streets, and for a long time lacked a single good hotel. Citizens talked of a waterworks system during the entire decade without accomplishing anything; nor did it acquire any other public utilities. It was amazingly slow in starting a system of public schools. Yet it had all the optimism of the day; lots on the public square sold as high as $100 a foot and farming property on the outskirts was worth up to $100 an acre; its citizens always vigorously opposed the numerous proposals from rival cities to move the state capital to a more suitable point.

Alton, an important port on the Mississippi, struck out aggressively for a railroad connection with Chicago and for a cross-state line to Terre Haute; these brought so important a westbound traffic to the city that, with the rush of settlement to Kansas, a direct steamship line to that territory was established which, as the easiest route, gave the city many of the economic advantages that St. Louis had previously secured from this movement. Peoria was a beautiful young city in 1860 with an important commerce sustained by a tributary agricultural region of unsurpassed fertility and first-rate facilities for manufacturing. In the decade it had passed Galena, to become, with a population of 14,045, the second largest city in the state.

Cairo was in this period Illinois' great city of prophecy, the speculation of a company of eastern capitalists. Situated at "the most important confluence of rivers in the world" and at the center of the American republic, at the southern terminus of the Illinois Central, it was expected—as the *entrepôt* between the northern and southern markets—to dominate commercially the Ohio, Wabash, Tennessee, and Cumberland valleys as well as the great northwest, becoming, as a great inland emporium, the largest city in the world.

In 1850, however, it was an embryo city of 242 inhabitants, living largely in wharf boats and small temporary shanties.

. . . .

Crowded cities of the old world poured forth a mighty stream of immigrants, whom Illinois received with enthusiastic welcome. With almost every national element already represented in the population of the state, Illinois offered the bewildered immigrant a hospitable asylum among friendly fellow-countrymen. The hardy workmen found places on the vast system of public works just being under-taken; to the more prosperous newcomers were offered the fertile farms of the state.

Of the European nations, Germany and Ireland made the largest contributions to Illinois; in 1860 there were in the state 130,804 Germans and 87,573 Irish. Illinois drew so large a quota of the immigrants from all countries that even before 1850 it could boast of 111,860 foreign born settlers, or one-eighth of the total popula-tion of the state; by 1860 their number had nearly tripled, reaching a total of 324,643. Chicago, rapidly becoming an important im-migration depot, retained so large a number of the new arrivals that the foreign born population of the city actually outnumbered the natives.

For a considerable period Illinoisans seem to have been unaware of the size of this foreign element. In January, 1854, however, the ice in the Mississippi held up fourteen steamers loaded with two thousand German and Irish immigrants, who, landed near Cairo and suffering greatly from cold, want of food, fever, and cholera, drew attention to the fact of the heavy foreign immigration. It became evident that the German and Irish emigrant societies of St. Louis who aided in the relief work had no effective Illinois counterpart, although a few local German societies had their agents on the ground. It became widely published, also, that of the emigrants landing at New York in 1856 seven per cent went to Illinois, but they brought with them over fourteen per cent of the "cash means" listed with the immigration authorities. Inducements to foreign immigrants to come to Illinois were therefore urged; a proper immigration system at Chicago was especially favored.

. . . .

During this decade Illinois acquired two Portuguese settlements, one in north Springfield and one in the vicinity of Jacksonville. In each case they were Protestant Portuguese exiles from the island of Madeira; the first company of 200 arrived November 1, 1849, followed by groups of from 60 to 150, until each settlement

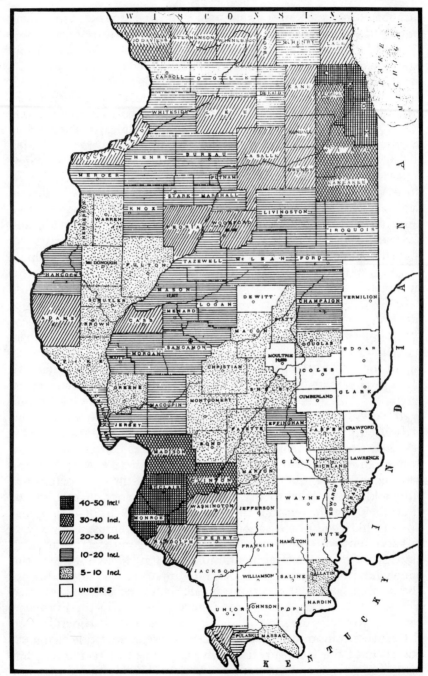

Courtesy of the Illinois State Historical Library

The foreign population of Illinois in 1850

numbered 500 persons. These exiles proved to be thrifty and industrious workers and rapidly attained material prosperity. They promptly built homes for themselves and the Springfield group established a Portuguese school and church where they zealously guarded the cultural atmosphere of their native land.

So considerable an increase in the Scandinavian population was made during the fifties that by 1860 it numbered well over 10,000. The Norwegians located largely in and around Chicago. They began to arrive in numbers about 1848; a year later there were nearly 600 in Chicago and by 1853, a Norwegian paper, the *Banner of Freedom*, was started in that city. Toward the end of the decade the Norwegian population of Chicago was variously estimated at from two to twelve thousand, with three Norwegian churches in the city. Chicago acted as a great distributing station from which Norwegians were supplied to other regions of the state; Norse groups gathered at "Old Sangamon Town" and in the "Kincaid neighborhood" north of Athens. Most of them, however, hired out with the farmers.

. . . .

The great works of internal improvement of the forties had brought vast hordes of brawny Irish to the Illinois prairies, many of whom took their place in the permanent population of the state. A Chicago Hibernian Benevolent Emigrant Society was organized in January, 1848, to encourage and assist immigrants seeking locations in the west. The railroad construction work of the fifties now offered employment to those still on the ground and attracted a new immigration, mainly of those unfortunates driven from home by the potato famine. The Irish remained to a large extent a restless floating population, little attracted by agricultural opportunities, but looking primarily to the cities for the essence of real life; in 1860 they constituted four times as large an element of the population of Chicago as of the agricultural regions of Illinois.

There seemed to be two strains, sometimes combined in the same individuals, in the Irish population of the state. There were on the one hand the brilliant idealists who supported the cause of civil liberty and liberal institutions in all its forms and expressions, whether in the Irish struggle for independence or in the European contests for self-government. Their local and state Hibernian societies were important agencies for the expression of this high ideal as well as of the feeling of brotherhood among the Irish. Irish relief work was carried on, and men like Senator Shields held themselves in readiness to join in the redemption of their native land when the hour to strike should come.

But to the people of Illinois the Irishman more often appeared in another guise. To them he was pictured as the noisy, quarrelsome seeker after excitement, who found it in the company of John Barleycorn, in bloody street brawls, and even in the lower depths of crime. When an overwhelming majority of the visitors at police court were repeatedly reported to be Irishmen, it was not surprising that the public should make such adverse deductions. The common practice of contemporary journalists was reflected in the point raised by the *Chicago Tribune*, December 23, 1853: "Why do our police reports always average two representatives from 'Erin, the soft, green isle of the ocean,' to one from almost any other inhabitable land of the earth? . . . Why are the instigators and ringleaders of our riots and tumults, in nine cases out of ten, Irishmen?" There followed the report of a riot at La Salle and of the murder of a contractor by a set of Irishmen. The *Tribune*, aroused to the point of approving action under lynch law, declared: "Had the whole thirty-two prisoners that were taken been marched out and shot on the spot, as the citizens did the Driskells in Ogle County, some years ago, the public judgment would have sanctioned it at once."

A more careful analysis, however, revealed a situation that scarcely warranted such a superficial judgment. The railroad contractors were often shrewd schemers and hard men who sought to impose upon the ignorant Irish laborers and to direct matters to their own advantage. Palpably unfair treatment was almost certain to arouse the temper of the hot-headed Irishman. As it was, however, thousands quietly submitted to conditions upon the public works that brought death or ill health, "from exposure to miasmi, bad accommodation in camps and shanties, and from improper diet;" when sickness fell upon them they were discharged and turned loose upon the world. It is to be remembered, moreover, that the Irishmen who drew the fire of public criticism were largely members of the sturdy band of humble toilers, brutalized by the religious and political oppression and economic exploitation of their native Ireland and, in this land of opportunity which they had so eagerly sought, deprived of contact with the finer forces.

The German "forty-eighters," the unsuccessful revolutionists of 1848, fled to America in a steady stream and were led to Illinois by Friedrich Hecker, the organizer of the revolt in Baden. Conditions continued favorable to a heavy emigration of refugees from the political and economic oppressions of the fatherland. The German population of Illinois in 1860 was 130,804, with Chicago, Belleville, Galena, Quincy, Alton, Peoria, and Peru as the chosen places of settlement. This influx was directed to Illinois by the guidebooks of

John Mason Peck and similar works. Charles L. Fleischman, United States consul at Stuttgart, prepared in 1850 to write an emigrant's guidebook exclusively on Illinois, having previously written two general works.

Early in 1854 a number of prominent Chicago business men enlisted their support in a movement in favor of a law to create the office of commissioner of emigration, whose principal duty it should be to travel through Germany for the purpose of directing the stream of German emigration to Illinois. The *Illinois Staats-Zeitung*, however, opposed the move as a sharp business transaction and a political maneuver in the interest of ambitious local politicians. Nothing developed along this line; instead, taking their cue from the Irish, Chicago Germans organized a society for the protection of German immigrants arriving at that city and employed an agent to devote his time to the care of the new arrivals. Similar societies were organized, as the need for them was felt, at other points of German settlement and carried on an important relief work.

In this period a new center of German culture was developing at Chicago. There the Teutonic immigrants created a set of social institutions in which the familiar atmosphere of the fatherland was transplanted. German Lutheran churches and parochial schools under Lutheran preachers—the only schoolmasters—had appeared at an early date to perpetuate their fundamental social traditions. Now the refinements which they had sorely missed in their new western home were enthusiastically added: a German theater which made brilliant the dramatic atmosphere of Chicago; an orchestra which built up a musical reputation for the city, and a Männerchor, in which the lusty "liedersingers" vied with each other in the attempt to produce a spirited ensemble. The German brass band, the German militia companies of black jäger rifles, of Washington rifles, of Washington grenadiers, and of Washington light cavalry were features of many a gay procession. A German Odd Fellow lodge fostered the fraternal spirit among these settlers in true American style. Meantime other German settlements actuated by the same cultural impulse were acquiring the same institutions and stimulating the spiritual development away from frontier conditions.

There was much of an atmosphere of revolutionary democracy in these German circles. The forty-eighters were full of the failure of their cause. Many were downhearted, but others looked upon their residence in the United States as a training for future revolutionary attempts. In 1852 they invited Dr. Gottfried Kinkel, the German revolutionist, to include different Illinois groups in his tour of the country to collect funds for the German revolutionary committee which they hoped would soon strike another blow. This erstwhile professor of history and literature at Bonn was welcomed at Chicago and Belleville with elaborate orations, and generous contributions were made to his fund.

The hopelessness of the revolutionary cause, however, caused the German population in general to settle down into more conservative channels. The Turnverein was introduced into Illinois in 1851 with a company at Peoria and Chicago; Belleville and Springfield soon had their own German gymnastic companies. The Northwestern Turnerbund held its annual meeting in 1858 at Belleville, and in the following year the United States *Turner* organization met in convention as the guests of the Chicago society. The social democratic atmosphere of this movement, however, had not been transplanted to America; and the political significance of the movement was very slight. The meeting at Belleville was addressed by Friedrich Hecker of that city, one of the originators of the *Turner* movement in America; his brilliant attack upon Douglas and his plea for the republican party showed that American issues had replaced the problems of the fatherland in the minds of leading revolutionary exiles. In 1850, however, the centennial of Schiller's birth was commemorated in festivals at Chicago and Belleville which did much toward arousing a feeling for German nationality on a democratic basis.

Rich as was the cultural atmosphere of their communities and content as they were with the surroundings they were able to create, these Germans could not confine their influence within these narrow barriers. Politically courted by both parties, their leaders took a prominent part in democratic politics and later transferred their allegiance to the new republican movement. Gustave Koerner continued a prominent figure in the politics of Illinois; with him were associated men like Caspar Butz, a prominent Chicago politician; George Schneider, editor of the *Illinois Staats-Zeitung*, and one of the founders of the republican party of Illinois; Friedrich Hecker, a republican elector on the Fremont ticket in 1856; and George Bunsen, an early advocate of a public school system, and an important influence in the educational development of the state. The German voters held the balance of power between the whig and democratic parties before 1856 and between the democratic and republican parties after that date. The democrats rewarded them by giving Koerner the lieutenant governorship in 1852, and the republicans in 1860 honored in the same way Francis Hoffman, a Chicago banker and a former whig. The Lutheran and Catholic clergy exercised a strong political influence upon their congregations; being conservatives like the rest of their profession, they were slower to see that they were acting "*wickedly*, and against God's Holy will, by their supporting the Democratic party." Those in the outlying towns of Washington and Clinton counties were a unit for Buchanan in 1856, but in 1860 their ranks were broken as the result of an aggressive campaign by republican agents.

The German press of Illinois, firmly grounded in this decade with a daily in every important center, showed better than anything else that the Germans had turned their backs upon Europe and taken up the political issues of the state and nation. These papers were naturally democratic organs until the slavery issue led them into the new republican party. The *Illinois Staats-Zeitung* was established at Chicago in 1848 and, under the editorial direction of George Schneider and his associates, wielded an important influence. It became a daily in 1851. Other experiments to establish German papers in Chicago inevitably failed after a short struggle. This was true in other Illinois German centers where a single paper was successfully established, and other attempts to enter the field fell stillborn.

As thus these different racial elements began to make potent their distinctive contributions to the evolution of the prairie state, it became increasingly evident that the simple society of the frontier state was giving way to the complexity of a mature commonwealth.

Against the 'drunken Dutch and low Irish': Nativism and Know-Nothings in Illinois

ROBERT P. SUTTON

Over sixty years ago, the first—and last—examination of nativism in Illinois appeared in the journal of that state's historical society. According to this interpretation, Know-Nothingism in the Prairie State was from beginning to end a political phenomenon rather than an expression of xenophobia, and it was largely untouched by the bigotry which characterized the movement elsewhere. There was nothing in any of the evidence which that author examined that bore "any resemblance to the issue which gave rise to the party in the East." Public opinion "was shaped by the moral and political

issue of slavery and not by any opposition to foreigners or to the
political influence of the Roman church."[1]

This view of Illinois Know-Nothingism raises a number of un-
answered questions. Most importantly, was the "eastern issue"
really that peripheral? If so, why was Illinois unique? Then there
remains the curious but largely unexamined relationship between
Stephen A. Douglas and the American party in Illinois. And what
made the citizens of the counties that voted Know-Nothing
majorities in the elections of 1854 and 1856 more responsive than
others to the Know-Nothing campaign?

Whatever revisions are made in our understanding of the Know-
Nothing movement in Illinois, a few points will remain unaltered. It
was clearly short-lived, encompassing the years 1853 to 1858. There
is also agreement about conditions in the state during the heyday of
the American party. By any standard, Illinois was in a phase of
astonishing growth. In the decade of the 1850s its population more
than doubled, from 851,740 to 1,711,951—a growth rate three
times faster than the national pattern. A high percentage of the new
citizens were foreign-born, who "nearly trebled their numbers . . . [rising] from 13 percent to 19 percent" of the total
population; they settled in the northern half of the state in two
pockets along the Mississippi and Wabash rivers.[2] This foreign-born
population, moreover, expanded in political significance as well as
in number. The Irish Catholics, coming mainly as laborers, provided
a loyal addition to the ranks of the Democratic party. The others—
Germans, English, and Scandinavians—resented the proslavery bias
of the "Democracy," and their votes were curried by politicians
opposed to Stephen Douglas. "Courted and exploited, amenable to
mass influence and posing the most serious threat to the purity of
elections," as one historian has observed, "they were a force to be
reckoned with at every turn."[3]

Such conditions resulted in strained relations between some
native voters and the new immigrants, and by the middle of the
decade newspapers began to call attention to the "foreign problem." The *American Era*, published at Grayville, and the *Canton
Register* condemned the special treatment being offered to
foreigners in order to get their vote. The *Alton Daily Courier*
published an account of the "bloody riot" in St. Louis in the
summer of 1854 in which "about fifty Irish barooms . . . were
destroyed with axes . . . and the office of the *Anzieger* was attacked

[1] John P. Senning, "The Know Nothing Movement in Illinois," *Journal of the Illinois State Historical Society*, VII (April, 1914), 25-26.
[2] Don E. Fehrenbacher, *Prelude to Greatness, Lincoln in the 1850's* (Stanford, 1962), p. 6.
[3] Ibid.

with stones and other missels" (Aug. 9, 1854). In Chicago, an anti-foreign-born, anti-Catholic campaign was begun by Henry Fowler of the *Tribune* and William W. Danenhower of the *Chicago Literary Budget*, both of whom sounded the alarm concerning the increase of Irish Catholics, whose numbers burgeoned from 30,000 in 1850 to 110,000 in 1860.

In this expanding and heterogeneous society the Illinois Know-Nothing movement took shape. By 1854, Know-Nothings had organized lodges in Joliet, Ottawa, Grayville, Canton, Vermont, Quincy, Alton, and Chicago. Their earliest known political activity was in April 1853, when the Quincy lodge ran unsuccessful candidates in the municipal election. The following year the Alton chapter claimed at least 300 members who gathered in clandestine meetings "in the culvert under Piaza street" to discuss the city elections (*Daily Courier*, Aug. 17, 1854). In Chicago, a lodge was formed by Danenhower, the Philadelphia-born publisher who claimed association with the national order going back to 1845. Danenhower, who was supported for a time by the *Tribune*, put together a "middle coalition around the anti-Catholic and anti-foreign themes . . . avoiding the slavery issue at all costs" (Chicago *Times*, Mar. 3, 1855).

By the summer months of 1854, newspapers began to warn of a new force at work in the coming election. In July the *Illinois State Journal* described it as "a movement among the people—a spontaneous one—which Whigs cannot control—if they desired." This "new, secret political organization," it predicted, could become "a formidable party, sufficient to control our general elections" (July 22, 1854). In August, the Democratic *Illinois State Register* mentioned Know-Nothingism but lamented that because of their secrecy "no one knows anything of them or what they design" (Aug. 16, 1854). By late October, the Joliet *Signal: Courier* admonished: "Democrats, Beware of Secret Societies!" (Oct. 29, 1854).

Stephen Douglas, fully aware of the threat to his political future posed by the anti-Nebraska response in Illinois, saw in Know-Nothingism "an opportunity to win back that which had been lost by the Clayton amendment—the foreign vote."[4] In a speech at Philadelphia in August he attacked the proscriptive stand of the order, hoping to drive "the Germans and all other foreigners and Catholics" to his side (Alton *Telegraph*, Aug. 4, 1854). Another Douglas tactic was to link the Know-Nothings with radical anti-slavery groups and thereby pull moderate voters, Democrats and Whigs alike, to the popular sovereignty Democracy. In a letter to

---

[4] John S. Wright, "The Background and Formation of the Republican Party in Illinois, 1846-1860" (unpublished doctoral dissertation, University of Chicago, 1946), p. 159.

James W. Sheahan, who had recently been appointed editor of the Chicago *Times,* he emphasized the need to blur any existing distinction between the American party and the abolitionists. If this could be done, he wrote, the party "will gain more votes than we lose on Nebraska and No Nothingism [*sic*]." "Charge into them every day boldly and disputedly," he advised.[5] In October, in a Bloomington speech, he alerted his listeners to the fact that the Know-Nothing party was a real challenge to Illinois Democrats and, because of its secrecy, a difficult enemy to combat. Nevertheless, he said, loyal Democrats were at that very moment infiltrating the order and soon the truth about the movement would be known.

In the November election, Know-Nothing candidates won in the third and fourth congressional districts, lost by one vote in the seventh, and combined in an anti-Douglas coalition to control the General Assembly.[6] The Joliet *Signal: Courier* described the election as a "perfect political tornado . . . never before have the democracy of Illinois been so completely vanquished." The Know-Nothings were voters who "regard Catholicism as far more aggressive and far more dangerous than slavery" and who feel "threatened by the growing rivalry of foreigners in all departments of labor" (Nov. 14 and 18, 1854). From Alton, the correspondent of the Chicago *Times* attributed the Democratic defeat there to "a secret party founded for the specific purpose of striking [a] blow at civil and religious liberty in the persons of foreigners and Catholics" (Feb. 21, 1855). Stephen Douglas confided his impression of the election to his old friend Charles H. Lanphier: "The Nebraska fight is over, and Know Nothingism has taken its place as the chief issue in the future."[7]

Scarcely did Douglas have time to assess his position in the wake of the Democratic defeat when the Know-Nothings recorded a second victory. In March 1855, in a contest billed as a fight "between Religion, Law, and Order on one side and Romanism, Priestley Intolerance, Rum and their concomitants on the other," the American party came to power in Chicago (Chicago *Tribune*, Mar. 6, 1855). There, Danenhower and lawyer Henry S. Jennings, evoking the themes of nativism and temperance against the "drunken Dutch and low Irish," elected Dr. Levi Boone (grandnephew of the legendary Daniel) mayor. In addition, the American ticket "emerged victorious except in three predominantly Democratic wards—the Seventh, Eighth, and Ninth," and won "other

[5] Stephen A. Douglas to James W. Sheahan, September 14, 1854, in *The Letters of Stephen A. Douglas*, ed. Robert W. Johannsen (Urbana, 1961), p. 330.
[6] For official returns, see *Illinois State Register*, Nov. 17, 1854.
[7] Stephen A. Douglas to Charles H. Lanphier, Dec. 18, 1854, in Johanssen, p. 331.

administrative posts plus seven councilmanic seats" (Chicago *Times*, May 10, 1855).

Triumph in Chicago, however, marked the apex of the Know-Nothing movement in Illinois. By the spring of 1855 the party began to come apart at the seams. One cause of the trouble was the effort by Illinois Whigs to control the order and use it to revive their own dilapidated opposition to the Democrats. This meant that the Whigs, unless they were prepared to become nativists themselves— and most were not—had to push the American party away from its antiforeign, anti-Catholic moorings and toward an issue they themselves embraced, opposition to the spread of slavery. The effort to graft a Whig antislavery platform on a movement based on other issues not only failed to revive the Whig party but destroyed whatever chance Know-Nothingism might have had to become a major force in Illinois politics.

First signs of the fatal division between nativists and the anti-slavery Know-Nothings appeared in Chicago within two months after the municipal elections. At a meeting of the state council held May 1-3, 1855, the so-called Jonathans, supported by former Whigs Joseph Gillespie, Dr. William Jayne, and Lincoln's mentor, Judge Stephen T. Logan, adopted an antislavery resolution—ostensibly to get the Protestant German vote (Chicago *Times*, May 10, 1855). Opposing any discussion of the slavery issue one way or the other were Danenhower and Jennings and their followers, called "Sams," supported by "old Hunker Whigs, Old Hunker Democrats, and old fogies" (*Times*, May 5, 1855).

In July of that year another state council of 124 delegates convened at Springfield. Although Danenhower was chosen the presiding officer, the "Jonathans" from northern and central counties predominated and, by a vote of 74 to 35, adopted a plank affirming the authority of Congress to deal with slavery in the territories. They also diluted the "Sam" position on proscription by asking for the restriction only of alien paupers and felons. The single point of agreement between the two factions was a pledge of continued resistance to "the corrupting influences and aggressive policy of the Roman Church." As a last order of business, the council affirmed that it would "cheerfully cooperate with any party as a national party, whose object it will be to carry into effect the above statements."[8]

Abraham Lincoln, a close observer of the Know-Nothing movement, felt that by August 1855 the worst of the threat had passed, but conceded to Owen Lovejoy that "know-nothingism has not yet

[8] Keefe, "Chicago's Flirtation with Political Nativism," p. 147; 156, n. 71.

entirely tumbled to pieces."[9] Douglas was more optimistic. Writing to Lanphier from Chicago in July, he stated that the growing chaos in the Know-Nothing opposition meant that "the prospects [for the Democracy] were never brighter in this part of the state." "Under these circumstances," he predicted, "I do not see how we can fail to elect the Dem. nominee for President next year."[10] Douglas' sanguine estimate turned out to be correct. The 1856 elections did place Buchanan in the White House and ended the Know-Nothing movement in Illinois.

*   *   *   *   *

The Chicago municipal election, scheduled for March 1856, shaped up to be a test case of whether the American party could hold together through the upcoming national campaign. In the ensuing municipal campaign Danenhower organized a ticket around former mayor Francis Sherman and mounted a "simon pure" nativist attack that threatened "to hold the noses of the Dutch and Irish to the grindstone" and boasted of "3,000 Americans . . . ready to grind them into the dust." Douglas' Democratic convention nominated Thomas H. Dyer and went for the city's Catholic vote. Dyer and the Democracy responded to Danenhower and Sherman by posing as the sole protectors of the "whole immense naturalized vote." Only Dyer, the Democrats cried, could "save them harmless from the bloody Know Nothings."

On March 4 both Democrats and Know-Nothings anticipated victory in an election that by all accounts was tumultuous. In the Seventh Ward, on the north side, "men were imported . . . to vote" for the Democrats from "the bawdy houses, the gambling-halls, and the grog shops. . . . They filled the Dyer carriages, they carried Dyer flags, they strained their throats in hurrahs for Dyer" and guzzled "whiskey for Dyer's honor" (Chicago *Tribune*, Mar. 5, 1856). In other wards, Democrats reportedly received support from a motley collection of "proslavery Know Nothings, drunken, priest-ridden Celts, blacklegs, pimps, hackmen, and loafers" (*Tribune*, May 13, 1856). The Sherman men, on the other hand, were charged with illegally opening the banks in order to get money to bribe votes for the Know-Nothing candidates (Chicago *Times*, Mar. 5, 1856).

When all the returns were in, Dyer had defeated Sherman by a narrow vote of 4709 to 4123, with the Democrat carrying five of the city's nine wards (*Times*, Mar. 13, 1856).

The Chicago success was to many Democrats a harbinger of the

[9] Abraham Lincoln to Owen Lovejoy, Aug. 11, 1855, in *The Collected Works of Abraham Lincoln*, ed. Roy P. Basler, IX (New Brunswick, N.J., 1953), p. 316.
[10] Douglas to Charles Lanphier, July 7, 1855, in Johanssen, p. 339.

upcoming general election. One downstate Douglas man, upon hearing the results, predicted that "nothing can check the reaction that has taken place in favor of the Democracy" now that it had carried "that d____d nigger hole Chicago by 800 votes—the place where but a little over a year ago Douglas could not be heard."[11]

The Know-Nothing National Council, which was meeting in Philadelphia at the same time the Chicago campaign was taking place, nominated Millard Fillmore and adopted a mildly worded plank against the repeal of the Missouri Compromise. This had an important effect on the Illinois Know-Nothing movement. The Greenville *American Courier,* expressing the reaction of many members of the order, condemned the stand on slavery, maintaining that "the conventions of the 18th and 22 of February had so far departed from the original landmarks of Americanism as to have un-Americanized themselves and thereby absolved every American from all obligation to sustain the nomination as an American nomination" (July 31, 1856). The *Tribune* predicted that because of the divisions over slavery the leaders of Illinois Know-Nothingism, "who now keep together the struggling squads . . . will throw up their hands and declare the game ended." "It will be a sad disappointment," it announced, "to those who have pinned their faith to this modern political Mephistophilies to see it die so soon . . ." (Feb. 16, 1856).

Despite the deepening schism within the order, Danenhower, upon returning from the national meeting in Philadelphia, called a state council in Springfield. There he hoped to refocus on the issues of immigration restriction and the Catholic threat. But it was apparent from the start of the council that a reconciliation was futile: some northern counties with Know-Nothing lodges refused to send delegates.

After some discussion about the advisability of even running candidates for state offices, the 100 delegates drew up a ticket. The platform approved by the council at last reflected the conservative views of Danenhower and the "Sams." Essentially nativistic, it reversed the antislavery position taken the year before and concentrated instead on proscription, anti-Catholicism, and the threat to national union posed by the "sectional" Democratic and Republican parties (*Illinois State Journal,* May 10, 1856).

The Springfield proceedings convinced the *Tribune* that the same conspiracy it detected in the Chicago election was functioning in the state campaign. The Know-Nothing ticket and platform, it

[11] William Snyder to John F. Snyder, May 24, 1856, Snyder Papers, Illinois State Historical Society.

charged, was a "scheme concocted between the Danenhower clique and the Douglasites to put a Know Nothing State ticket for the purpose of securing the State for the Black Democracy" (May 8, 1856). It denounced the American party as a "tool for Douglas," and charged that even though some of its candidates were men "who oppose its pro-Slavery attitude" this was only a clever ploy to fool the voters (May 12, 1856). "If a full-blooded, pro-Slavery proscriptive Fillmore ticket had been nominated," it said, "there would have been none at the polls to support it." Danenhower's "grand object" was to "secure success to Douglas, Richardson, and Slavery" (May 18, 1856).

In the face of an increasingly divided Know-Nothing opposition, both Democrats and Republicans pushed hard for victory in November. Republican newspapers reported widespread desertion of Know-Nothings to their party in the northern half of the state. Some editors described growing Republican strength in downstate counties. Democrats, encouraged by their Chicago victory, mounted an active campaign designed to keep opposition votes divided between the Republicans and the Know-Nothings. By midsummer local Democrats were holding "mass meetings" in central and western counties. And in a September speech in Chicago, Douglas opened a personal campaign that took him first to Springfield and then to appearances at sites from Galena to Carbondale.

Meanwhile, the Know-Nothing campaign fell apart. The difficulties of putting together a state ticket were augmented by the lackluster support of Know-Nothing politicians. Prominent leaders of the order openly embraced another party. Others, like Joseph Gillespie, posed as loyal to the American party but privately moved away from the order.

William Danenhower, returning to the state in late July after a two-month visit with party leaders in various Eastern cities, predicted success in "the central and southern part of the state" but admitted defeat in advance in the northern half because of the antislavery "fanaticism" there (Chicago *Weekly Native Citizen*, Sept. 6, 1856). Beginning his itinerary with a speech in Hancock County on September 1, he crisscrossed the state between the Mississippi and Wabash rivers for thirty separate appearances, ending with a rally at Cairo on the ninth of October.

Even as Danenhower was stumping the hustings for Know-Nothingism, the *Tribune* continued its bizarre charge of a conspiracy. Labeling him as an "emissary of Buchanan, nothing more, nothing less," the paper described the "fusion" which "was hatched in this city and is being spread over the state" (Aug. 4 and 20, 1856). In places such as Kankakee, Bloomington, and Chicago, "we

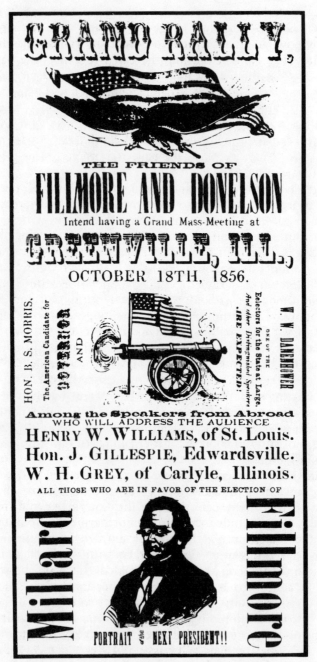

Advertisement for a Know-Nothing party rally,
Greenville *American Courier*, October 16, 1856

see Douglas and Danenhower . . . working together against Fremont
and Free Kansas," while "Judge Morris and Col. Richardson are
cheek by jowl in their efforts to defeat the gallant Bissell" (Sept.
17, 1856). The cement holding the cabal together, the paper said,
was the proslavery bias of the "Sams" and the Democracy. Specifically, the *Tribune* alleged that Danenhower was using Morris as
"a bridge to carry such old Whigs over to Richardson as he can" and
to serve "as a sponge to absorb from Bissell those who are not yet
willing to vote for the Border Ruffian candidate." In the presidential contest, "Fillmore plays the part of a bridge to Buchanan and a
sponge from Fremont."

Despite Danenhower's efforts to pull together a Know-Nothing
campaign, signs of apathy and futility were everywhere. By September, the *Native Citizen* anticipated an even race at best between
Fillmore and Buchanan in the southern region, noting the likelihood that the German vote there would go to Fremont (Chicago
Weekly Native Citizen, Sept. 6, 1856). By October some reports
were a little more optimistic. Politics around Mascoutah, said the
American Courier, "indicate . . . a strong vote" for the American
party (Sept. 25, 1856). The most encouraging news of all was an
account of a Know-Nothing rally in Springfield in October that was
described as "the largest meeting ever congregated in Illinois."
"Thousands turned out," the correspondent wrote, to hear speeches
by "Merrs. Bucknor S. Morris, W. W. Danenhower, of Chicago,
Joseph Gillespie of Madison County," and other Know-Nothing
leaders (*Carthage Republican*, Oct. 16, 1856). Most indications,
however, showed that the American party was "disgraced," as
Danenhower phrased it, in the northern half of the state.

In Know-Nothing speeches, letters, newspaper reports, and
broadsides, the focus of the campaign had been on two points: the
evils of foreigners and Catholics, and the dangers of the slavery
question to the union. Shortly after the American party announced
its ticket, for example, the Greenville *American Courier* had reprinted on its front page a vicious nativist attack warning that
America's freedoms were threatened by "shiploads of immigrants"
sent over by "foreign powers" to "buy lands, gain wealth, make
homes" in order "to assist the secretive, dastardly, cowled monk to
gain permanent power in America." These foreigners, estimated to
be over 2,700,000 in number, "cherish feelings of animosity against
our religion . . . erect walled convents . . . to consumate their foul
plots . . . and satiate their evil passion" (May 22, 1856). The editor
of the paper exhorted "the American Party of Southern Illinois," in
the face of these dangers, to "wake from their lethargy and arouse
to activity the time has come . . . let us work!" (Aug. 21, 1856). In

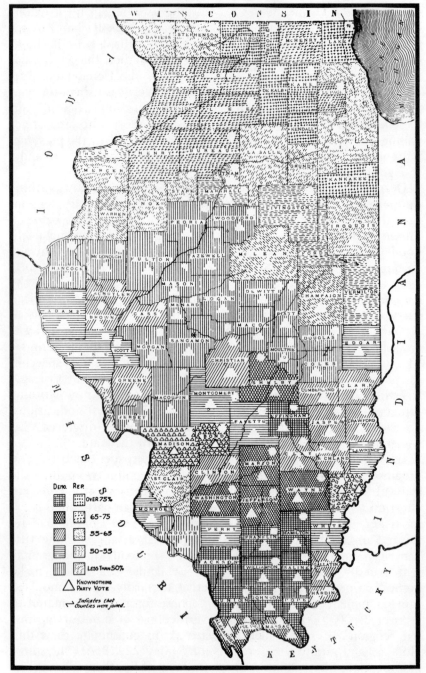

Courtesy of the Illinois State Historical Library

Party voting in the Illinois popular presidential election, 1856

September the *Native Citizen* blamed all "our present difficulties" on the "foreign element in our elections who blindly vote for the radical parties." Foreigners, it went on, "are easily made the tools and instruments of demagogues who flatter their rich German accent and blarney their 'swate' Irish tongue, nauseating to all sensible men" (Chicago *Weekly Native Citizen*, Sept. 6, 1856). The *Grayville Herald* wrote that American-born Catholics were equally suspect since they were "under the *temporal* as well as *spiritual* dominion of the Pope of Rome." In order to keep the nation free, it said, all Catholics and foreigners should be opposed at the polls. "Let Americans rule Americans!" it enjoined (Sept. 6, 1856). The paper charged that Democrats "hug the veriest spawn of European pauperism and felony . . . to get a vote in the ballot. . . ." Vote the American ticket, the editor commanded, and reject the impudent Democratic appeal "to save the government in the hands of the Foreign-Rule party and foreigners by placing their leaders and flatterers in power." "It is a fact," it stated, "that those who now call themselves Democrats take pleasure in defending the Holy Father; and a few of the leaders would have no objection to kiss his big toe the hottest day in August" (Aug. 21, 1856).

Democrats and Republicans alike were assailed as "sectional" parties willing to divide the union over slavery. The Know-Nothing press charged that a vote for the "black Republican" party was a vote for abolitionism, and that a Democratic victory would find the "white laboring man reduced to starvation in trying to compete with slave labor" (*Grayville Herald*, Sept. 6, 1856). The way out of the dilemma was for voters to support the national party of Fillmore and the Know-Nothings. Local American party candidates promised to "quell the agitation" of the slavery issue if elected (Greenville *American Courier*, Oct. 9, 1856). Time and again they stressed Fillmore's experience, reputation, and honesty. The *Carthage Republican* had called him a "truly *national* man uncontaminated by that fanaticism and sectionalism so prevalent at the north . . ." (July 1, 1856). The *Grayville Herald* expressed a widely heard Know-Nothing pledge when it said that "Millard Fillmore will be a president not of the North or South alone, but of this whole glorious confederacy" (Nov. 1, 1856). Buckner Morris, after charging that Buchanan's election would set off the "violent feelings of hatred and blind prejudice of the people of the North" and that the man voting for Fremont "will be guilty of moral treason to his country," went on to praise the unblemished record of Fillmore. "His election," Morris asserted, "will restore peace and confidence to the people . . ." (*Illinois State Register*, Aug. 16, 1856).

The returns in November bore out the worst of the Know-

Nothing fears. In the presidential race, of a total of 238,975 votes cast, Fillmore received only 37,451. Morris made a still poorer showing, with only 19,941 votes of a total of 237,956.

In evaluating the significance of the outcome of the election, the Chicago *Times* speculated that the figures showed "that all the Know-Nothings of the state, except 37,451, voted for Fremont," and that Bissell also "got the Know Nothing vote" (Nov. 27, 1856). Only five counties gave the Know-Nothings a majority in the presidential fight, and of these only Piatt County gave them a majority in the gubernatorial race.[12]

*   *   *   *   *

Why did the voters of Wabash, Edwards, Madison, Bond, and Piatt counties respond more favorably than other voters to the Know-Nothing campaign? Perhaps no definitive answer can be found to this question; but something can be said about the people who lived in these three Know-Nothing pockets in the 1850s. This in turn could suggest some factors that may have influenced their voting behavior. Local and county histories, while helpful as starting points of investigation, are of uneven quality and tend to concentrate on events after the Civil War. However, there is a reliable but largely neglected source of information about local social history which can be employed: the national and state census manuscripts.

A profile analysis of the Know-Nothing counties based on census data reveals one important characteristic: the voters of these five counties were not typical of the voting population of Illinois as a whole. According to the noted Lincoln scholar Don E. Fehrenbacher, a representative sampling of Illinois citizens in the 1850s would have shown that 40% were born in the state, 12% came from the Old Northwest, 12% from the Middle Atlantic states, 4% from New England, and the remaining 32% from the South and from foreign countries.[13] By contrast, the voting population of Madison and Bond counties contained only 12.6% Illinois natives; in Edwards and Wabash counties this figure was 17.9%; and in Piatt County this element constituted only 1.6% of the adult males. Voters born in the Old Northwest in Madison and Bond counties numbered only 3.9%, and in Edwards and Wabash counties 5% of the total. But in Piatt County, this group was atypical in the opposite extreme: 41.3% of the adult males numbered in the 1850 census were born in

<hr />

[12] Fillmore did receive support in twelve other counties, even though support fell short of a majority. These were: Jersey, Perry, Union, Fayette, Montgomery, Sangamon, Menard, Mason, Moultrie, Richland, Lawrence, and White. Morris came close to winning in five counties besides Piatt: Madison, Bond, Fayette, Alexander, and Edwards.

[13] Fehrenbacher, *Prelude to Greatness*, pp. 5-6.

the Old Northwest, and in 1860 this group made up 38.7% of the voting population. Those born in the Middle Atlantic states numbered 6.1% of the voters living in Madison and Bond counties, 9.8% in Edwards and Wabash counties, and 16.3% in Piatt County. New England voters made up only 3% of the voters in Madison and Bond counties, 3% in Edwards and Wabash counties, and 1.8% of the adult males in Piatt County.[14]

The census data also reveal some interesting characteristics of the foreign-born population of the five counties. In the two western counties the foreign-born adult males made up 25% of the total population, with a concentration of 39.4% of the Madison County voters. Most foreign-born voters were German: 45%, or 956, of the adult males were born in that country. In terms of occupation, the foreign-born adults in these counties made up an equal share of those listed in agriculture (58.5% foreign adults to 59.4% American adults), but they showed significant variances in the skilled crafts and laborers. Foreign voters outnumbered American craftsmen 14.7% to 12.6%, and in the labor market they outnumbered Americans more than two to one—34.4% to 15.6%.[15] Symptomatic of the xenophobia of Bond County citizens were the editorials of the Greenville *Advocate*, which regularly printed the most virulent antiforeigner attacks found anywhere outside of Chicago.

In the Wabash River pocket, foreign-born adult males made up 17.9% of those listed in the 1850 census. Edwards County, like Madison County on the other side of the state, had a disproportionately high concentration of the foreign-born, 39.6%; half of these voters were born in England and Wales, two-fifths in Germany and Holland, and the rest in Ireland and Scotland. Like the Greenville *Advocate*, the columns of the Grayville *Herald* printed a steady diet of antiforeign material. Know-Nothingism may well have appealed to voters in these counties because it was this part of the state, beginning with the Birkbeck colony of English farmers in Edwards County in the 1820s and the establishment of the New Harmony community shortly afterward across the Wabash River in Indiana, which had seen a continual increase in the numbers of foreign-born voters.

The occupational profile of the alien adults there was similar to that of Madison and Bond counties. Their percentage of farmers was close to that of the native Americans—63.5% to 72.8% of native farmers. However, in the skilled crafts the percentage of the foreign element exceeded that of the American two to one—21.9% to

[14] Population schedules of the seventh and eighth censuses of the United States: The National Archives and Record Service, General Services Administration, Washington, D.C.
[15] Population schedules, Madison and Bond counties.

11.2%. And the foreign-born voters listed as laborers outnumbered American laborers by a ratio of three to two.[16] On this point the Grayville *Herald* wrote: ". . . here we have more foreign laborers than we need" (Sept. 29, 1855).

In Piatt County, the foreign-born voters, while not numerous in absolute numbers, did increase at a fourfold rate, becoming 13.1% of the adult males by 1860. The immigrants were mostly Irish workers, and they made up 50% of the 1860 adult work force in Willow Branch Township, 35.4% in Sangamon Township, 36.3% in Cerro Gordo Township, and 70% in Bement Township. Germans settled in the town of Monticello, which in 1860 listed eight of its 30 skilled craftsmen and businessmen as German-born; one, a butcher, was Irish.[17]

Know-Nothingism in Piatt County also appealed to a number of voters whom the *Monticello Times* dubbed "old fogies." These were the Piatt County arch-conservatives, who bitterly resented the signs of change that were appearing in the county during the 1850s: the arrival of the railroads and their hard-drinking Irish work crews, demands for increased taxes for public improvements, the start of a newspaper supporting the railroads, the Irish in general, and Stephen Douglas. The editor of the *Monticello Times* (Feb. 12, 1856) had this to say about his neighbors:

> We confidently expect, ere long, to see a railroad running through our place. This *will be*, sooner or later. When this period arrives farewell to *old fogyism*. The first shrill note of which proclaims the advent of the 'iron horse' will find the superannuated relics of an almost extinct generation taking up their lonely march to some benighted corner of the earth, where they will be troubled 'nevermore' with school teaching, lecturing, printing presses, telegraphs, railroads, or any other internal improvements. And it may be set down as an unalterable fact, that the same old Fogy spirit will . . . oppose every improvement which the people of the county undertake. Try and keep awake . . . O! Ye sleepy inhabitants of Piat County.

Whatever the social profile of Madison, Bond, Edwards, Wabash, and Piatt counties, in 1856 the American-born voters in these counties gave a majority vote to the Know-Nothing party. Extant returns by township in Bond County and by ward in Alton, for example, clearly indicate that the Know-Nothing vote came from the American-born voters. Township returns show that in the Know-Nothing pocket along the Mississippi Fillmore lost only Alton and Highland, both of which supported Fremont by heavy

[16] Population schedules, Wabash and Edwards counties.
[17] Population schedules, Piatt County.

margins (Alton *Campaign Courier,* Nov. 20, 1856). In Edwards County, the Know-Nothings lost only Philipstown and Carmi to the Democrats. Wabash County voters split their votes between Fillmore and the Republican candidates for state offices, although American party nominees for state representative and other local offices won comfortably in the townships of Mt. Carmel and Friendsville in the eastern part of the county (Grayville *Herald,* Nov. 8, 1856). In Piatt County, the vote was close throughout, with victory often determined by a few votes. Piatt County Know-Nothings, in contrast to voters in Wabash County, voted almost a straight party ticket (*Monticello Times*, Nov. 6, 1856).

*   *   *   *   *

Illinois Know-Nothingism never recovered from the 1856 elections. In Chicago, the one-time center of the movement, the end came with dramatic suddenness. "The day after the election," one scholar has written, "the *Native Citizen* discontinued publication, thereby extinguishing the last flickering light of political nativism in Chicago."[18] The five counties that voted for Fillmore in 1856 did cast ballots for Bell in 1860, but by then most Know-Nothings had switched to the Republican party. "Bond, Edwards, Madison, and Piatt counties supported Lincoln in 1860; he ran a close second in Wabash."[19]

Thus Know-Nothing voters in Illinois, as in other states, were absorbed by the Republicans. Even Danenhower turned up a Republican during the Civil War and was recommended by Lincoln for a patronage job in Washington.[20] After 1856, Lincoln himself solicited the support of Know-Nothings, stressing in the process the similar views of the two parties on foreigners and Catholics. It was not accidental, as one writer has maintained, that "there was no word of anti-nativism in the Republican platform of 1860." [21] Moreover, in that year "Know Nothing support was . . . a major reason of Lincoln's nomination" and "the Know Nothings were clearly responsible for the election of Lincoln to the presidency." [22]

---

[18] Keefe, "Political Nativism," p. 152.
[19] Charles G. Hamilton, *Lincoln and the Know-Nothing Movement* (Washington, D.C., 1954), pp. 13-14.
[20] Abraham Lincoln to Salmon P. Chase, April 11, 1861, in Basler, IV, p. 327.
[21] Hamilton, p. 12.
[22] Hamilton, p. 20.

The original narratives concentrate on the reaction of the average citizen and traveler to the changing social setting. Charles B. Johnson recalls scenes of everyday life in Pocahontas, a village near Greenville in Bond County. This selection was published in the *Transactions of the Illinois State Historical Society* of 1912 from a paper read by the sixty-nine-year-old physician. After receiving his medical degree from the Ohio Medical College in Cincinnati, Johnson established a practice in Champaign. In addition to his medical practice, he was the author of *Illinois in the Fifties, or A Decade of Development, 1851-1860* (1918) and *Musket and Medicine, or Army Life in the Sixties* (1917).

Daily Life in Pocahontas

CHARLES B. JOHNSON

At the period of which I write there were none but subscription schools. With the thought of teaching in a given locality a teacher would visit the various families and get their pledges for as many "scholars" as possible. A "scholar" in this sense was the attendance of one pupil for the full time the school was taught. About 1855 what was called the "free school law" went in force and under its provisions teachers were paid from a public fund set aside for this purpose and since that date no Illinois pupil has been kept from the public schools because his parents or guardian would be required to pay tuition.

When the second half of the nineteenth century was very young the good people of Pocahontas and vicinity saw the need of better educational advantages for their children and with this thought uppermost in their minds erected a most respectable building that was called "The Pocahontas Academy," a name which it retained for many years. However very soon after the "free school law" went into effect the academy was taken over by the local school district and used for regular school purposes. To the satisfaction of those who were instrumental in putting up this building it turned out that from the time it was erected till its fiftieth anniversary was celebrated some of the higher branches were at all times taught.

From Charles B. Johnson, "Everyday Life in Illinois Near the Middle of the Nineteenth Century," *Transactions of the Illinois State Historical Society*, XVII (1912), 49-52.

Consequently, "The Pocahontas Academy" at least fulfilled some of the objects for which it was originally intended.

. . . .

In my school days very much more was made of arithmetic, grammar and spelling than is done today. We used the old blue-backed, Webster's Spelling Book with its temple of fame near the title page and the picture of the boy stealing apples from the enraged gentleman well along towards the end of the book. We also used McGuffy's series of readers. Not the so-called McGuffy of today, but the genuine true, McGuffy as it was published fifty years ago. I have heard more than one person of good literary taste of my generation say that it was to the fine selections in these old McGuffy readers that they owed their love for good literature. I have often wondered who McGuffy was and not long since my curiosity was to a degree gratified when I ran across an article that gave a few particulars concerning his life. He lived in Cincinnati, Ohio, was a teacher and gave much time and thought to his readers. It may be a weakness, but nevertheless I confess to no little sentiment in my remembrance of McGuffy and his series of readers.

Perhaps the fact that literature of all kinds was very scarce fifty odd years ago was one reason why McGuffy's readers were so much appreciated. In many families no newspaper of any kind was taken, and up to the breaking out of the Civil war I think but one daily paper was taken in the village of Pocahontas. At long intervals I would see a copy of Harpers' New Monthly Magazine, and about the time its publication began a little more than fifty years ago, I saw the Atlantic which looked precisely as it does today. You will notice that I said I occasionally saw the Atlantic and Harper, but when it came to reading them that was a privilege accorded to the fortunate few in my young days.

In the village of Pocahontas the women had an organization known as "The Ladies' Sewing Society," the objects of which were industrial and social. This organization accumulated a fund that about 1857 was used to purchase books for a modest but well selected village library. In this small collection I recall the works of Irving, Bancroft, Macauley, Prescott, Addison, J. S. C. Abbott, etc.

A little later our school was supplied with a library that I remember contained Irving's life of Washington, Ford's History of Illinois and more of the same kind.

Beginning with about 1850 perhaps half the people had abandoned their log cabins for frame houses, many of which were one-room structures with a shed or lean-to at the back of each. The more ambitious built two-story houses of six or eight rooms. When very young I recollect a new frame house on the prairie which on account of its coat of clean white paint and green window blinds attracted much attention.

About the time frame houses began to be common, heating and cook stoves came into use. My people got their first cook stove in the spring of 1849. Tallow candles were used for lighting purposes, as also were grease lamps. I have seen a room lighted by igniting a piece of cotton cloth that had been twisted and laid in a saucer of melted lard with of course the burning end protruding out of the fluid and over the vessel's edge.

One evening in, I think, 1859 I attended a social gathering at the village doctor's when we were all surprised and delighted at a very brilliant light from a small lamp in one of the rooms. Upon inquiry we learned that the lamp contained a new burning fluid called "rock oil," or kerosene.

In my childhood matches were by no means common and not unfrequently I was sent to the neighbors to "borrow some fire," that is to get a shovel full of coals to start up a fire.

In my boyhood all the boys attended school during the winter months and worked on farms in summer time. In those days the hours were very long and sometimes to the village lad work on the farm seemed hard and monotonous. But it toughened his muscles and brought him in contact with nature and he learned much of plant and animal life. During the decade between 1850 and 1860 many labor saving devices were introduced on the farms. Among these may be noted, in much the same form that we have them today, the mower, reaper, threshing machine, grain drill, corn planter and hay rake.

In this age of plutocracy with a millionaire in almost every neighborhood it is hard to realize that fifty odd years ago a man in Bond County worth ten thousand dollars was counted rich. However, most people were frugal and careful of their expenditures. I remember in my childhood that one family was rated extravagant because in their sitting room they burned two lighted candles at once.

In my boyhood I attended the Pocahontas school and here in addition to the usual English branches got a little taste of Algebra, Chemistry, Latin, Natural Philosophy, etc. These last whetted my appetite for more knowledge and better educational opportunities and I began to look about me. Thirty miles to the southwest was McKendree College, at Lebanon; forty miles northwest was Shurtleff College at Alton; and sixty miles north was Illinois College at Jacksonville. Save at Ann Arbor, Mich., State Universities, such as we know them today were unknown. I had heard of Michigan University in a way that interested me greatly and finally I mustered up courage to write to the president of that institution for a catalog. But it would surprise the reader to learn how many sheets of paper and envelopes I spoiled before I was even measurably satisfied with my efforts at letter writing where so dignified a character as a college president was involved.

Well, in due time the catalog came and it was about the size of an old-fashioned almanac. In my mind I often compare the few-paged pamphlet received from the University of Michigan fifty years ago with the plump, bulky catalogs today issued by that and the numerous state educational institutions all about us. This comparison in catalogs is one means of noting the educational progress made in this country since the time of the Civil war.

During the winter of 1860-61 when one after another of the southern states seceded, we all wondered where it would end. Then in the spring of 1861 when Fort Sumpter was fired on we wondered all the more when and where would be the final outcome. Following the fall of Fort Sumpter came President Lincoln's first call for troops. Of these Bond County furnished its full quota. During the winter of 1861-62 I taught school in a neighborhood remote from news centers. One day in February we heard cannon firing that from the peculiar condition of the atmosphere reached us all the way from St. Louis, forty-five miles away. In a day or two we learned that it was a salute in honor of a great Union victory and that Fort Donelson and fourteen thousand Confederate soldiers had been captured. Of the man who brought the news I asked the name of the Union commander. In reply he said his name was Grant. "Grant," I said, "who's Grant?" "Don't know," he answered, "never heard of him before."

In the same remote Bond County community where I taught school during the winter of 1861-62 I engaged in farming during the spring and early summer of 1862. On rainy days and during noon hours I gave such attention as I could to Latin, Geometry and some other branches. My dreams and anticipations were all in the direction of going to college and improving my education. Meanwhile the Civil war had entered upon its second year and from time to time news from the front reached our quiet neighborhood. Finally late in July came the startling news that McClellan had been repulsed and was retreating from before Richmond. Upon the heels of this came President Lincoln's call for 300,000 volunteers. A call that a little later was increased to 600,000. I now realized that my time had come and that for me the hour had struck. With a number of boy friends on August 7, 1862, at Greenville, Bond County I enlisted in Co. F., 130th Illinois Infantry and saw service continuously at the front till the war ended three years later.

I am convinced that the present generation is without a proper appreciation of what the Civil war cost this county in young manhood fifty years ago.

In conclusion and by way of illustration permit me to give a relatively infinitesimal item of this cost that came under my observation. At a farm house in Bond County in the spring of 1861 were six stalwart young men ranging in age from seventeen to twenty-three years, and of these I was one. In the ensuing eighteen months all of these young men had become soldiers and were in the enemy's country.

At the end of the war and after four years service one of them came home shattered in health. After three years service and with the end of the war a second came home shattered in health. At the end of the war, likewise shattered in health, I returned home after three years in the enemy's country. A fourth was killed at the battle of Belmont in November 1861. A fifth was killed at the siege of Jackson, Miss., in July, 1863, and finally the sixth member of the party of boys and young men at the Bond County farm house in the spring of 1861 was killed at the battle of Atlanta in 1864.

Pennsylvanian W. W. Davis visited Illinois in 1851 by rail and stage. He traveled from Alton to Springfield and from there to the Illinois River, where he boarded the steamboat to Peru, finally crossing west to the Rock River by rail. Davis became a resident of Sterling, Illinois, and was active in county and state historical societies during the first decade of this century, serving as a member of the Board of Directors of the state historical society.

Downstate, 1851

W. W. DAVIS

It was a great undertaking for that day. It meant a round trip of 3,000 miles by rail, canal, stage and steamboat. There were no railroads across the continent, and traveling was tedious. Iowa and

From W. W. Davis, "A Trip from Pennsylvania to Illinois in 1851," *Transactions of the Illinois State Historical Society*, IX (1907), 198-204.

Illinois were on the frontiers, and Ohio was the focus for most emigration. People generally moved by wagon, and the journey from eastern Pennsylvania occupied a month. They took a solemn farewell of their friends as they never expected to see them again.

. . . .

From St Louis, 20 miles up the Mississippi to Alton. Here we had to take stage across the country. Our introduction to the Sucker stage. No luxurious Concord coach with upholstered backs, but a rough spring wagon with a canvas cover and soft boards for seats. What roads! A series of swamps.

We traveled all night, but the continued jolting prevented sleep. Happy dreams of Pullman cars would have lightened our slumbers. We reached Jacksonville about dinner time; 79 miles from Alton in 23 hours. Jacksonville was already the seat of asylums, the blind, deaf and dumb and insane, and also of Illinois college. Here we struck the railroad from Naples on the Illinois river to Springfield, and boarded the first train for that city. This was our destination, and for two weeks we enjoyed the society of our relatives and early friends of my father, who had moved from Pennsylvania.

Dr. William S. Wallace opened a drug store on the east side of the square, married a sister of Mrs. Lincoln, was long a popular physician, and was appointed paymaster during the Civil war. J. Roland Diller was in the postoffice. Obed Lewis carried on the carriage business, married a daughter of Major Iles, and was elected mayor. Reuben F. Ruth opened a harness store on the south side of the square, and was in later years president of the Marine bank. Roland W. Diller and his brother, Isaac R., joined the colony afterwards. Roland and his friend Corneau continued the old Wallace drug store, which for years was the popular rendezvous in the city for men of all politics. Around the rusty stove gathered Lincoln, Douglas, Judge Logan, Baker, and the worthies of that day whose names have since become so familiar.

. . . .

During our stay in Springfield, Mrs. Wallace gave a tea party in our honor, inviting her sister, Mrs. Lincoln, Mr. Lincoln and a few others. A table full, a lively company, but of the sayings and doings of the occasion, there is no record. Often since have I wished for the memory of Macaulay and the pen of Boswell to chronicle the table talk of that assembly. The Lincoln of 1851 was not the Lincoln of 1861, whose fame gave every utterance widespread importance. In Congress from 1847-1849, but with no reputation outside the State. No doubt, he told some of the jokes that

Courtesy of the Illinois State Historical Library

A farmer riding Danford's mowing machine, 1854 (a newspaper advertisement)

afterwards went the rounds of the papers, and made him the popular storyteller of his time. . . .

Springfield at that day gave little promise of its present beauty and prosperity. All business centered on the public square and the old State house was the most commanding object. Here Lincoln sat as a member of the legislature, and was one of the "Long Nine" who led in the removal of the capital from Vandalia. . . . On the north side of the square was a succession of little houses, called by the citizens "Chicken Row." The town had about 4,000 people.

Turning our faces homeward we went by rail from Springfield to Naples, on the Illinois river, 70 miles, and at Naples boarded the steamer Connecticut for the voyage up stream. Heavy rains made the river look like a vast lake, bottom lands covered to the distant hills. We arrived at Peru the next day, a sail of about 200 miles, the limit of navigation on the Illinois. Here, again, the Sucker stage was a change in our method of locomotion, and we were soon floundering through the sloughs of the rolling prairies. It was in early summer and flowers and grass were waving in all their luxurance.

. . . .

From Peru to Dixon, an all-day stage ride of 60 miles, a distance now traversed by the Illinois Central trains in two hours. At Dixon, on Rock river, we hired a special team to take us to Sterling, 12 miles west, also on the river. Here we were again among friends from Pennsylvania. Hugh Wallace and brothers, Geo. Woodburn and Ezekiel Kilgour, from Cumberland county. They came in 1837. Hugh Wallace was perhaps the most prominent citizen. He graduated at Washington college, read law with General Porter in Lancaster, was a member of the Illinois legislature 1846-1852, and was appointed by Pierce, register of the land office at Dixon. At his hospitable frame cottage, known as "the fort," he and his noble wife, née Mary Galt, entertained Senator Douglas, U. F. Linder, Judge Leffingwell and other noted men of that time. The western part of Sterling is built on his old farm.

. . . .

Sterling stood high and dry on its limestone hills along the river, with a population of 200, in houses scattered over the prairie, east and west of the court house. It was a "green county town," as William Penn wrote of Philadelphia in its infant days.

Our visit at Sterling ended, we left Dixon on our last stage ride, for Aurora, 70 miles, and reached there at noon the next day, having stayed all night on the way. The railroad from Aurora to Chicago was the only one in Illinois in 1851, except that from

Naples to Springfield. Chicago had only 30,000 inhabitants, but was beginning to boom. Buildings low; no skyscrapers, many of frame. Our hotel was the old Tremont. The streets were covered with plank. Omnibuses were the only means of transit. No union depots, as no through lines of railroads radiated from the city. The purchase of some good corner lots then on State street would have associated our name with Marshall Field's.

From Chicago, a varied and delightful course homeward.

. . . .

The Scots scientist William Ferguson, who also passed through the central and southern counties by wagon and rail, describes that part of the state during the mid-1850s. His journey begins on the Illinois Central Railroad out of Chicago. His account was part of a general travelogue entitled *America by River and Rail*, published in London in 1856. An interesting aspect of the story of that line is told by Paul W. Gates in *The Illinois Central Railroad and Its Colonization Work* (Cambridge, 1934).

Illinois by Rail, 1855

WILLIAM FERGUSON

Monday, June 4.—We left Chicago this morning at a quarter past eight, by train on the Chicago branch of the Illinois Central railway, and reached Urbana, one hundred and twenty-eight miles, about four o'clock. . . .

On leaving the shore of the lake, the railway enters flat prairie land, with some young wood. Some eight or nine miles out, it crosses the line of the Michigan Southern and Northern Indiana railway. Beyond this, it lies for many a mile in open prairie. It is only when approaching the bank of some stream that wood is found.

. . . .

From William Ferguson, *America by River and Rail; or, Notes by the Way on the New World and Its People* (London, 1856), pp. 370-388. Footnotes in the original have been omitted.

Until this railway was made, this part of the State was quite inaccessible; and still tracks, miles in extent, are without a house. Stations are put down every ten miles or so; and already little villages are clustering around them, and the lands are being rapidly settled. The early settlements are all on the banks of streams. Reaching the Iroquois river, we find on its banks, a mile and three-quarters from the station, the old French settlement of Bourbonnais. It contained, by the census of 1850, 1719 people; and it presents features of improvement, in new buildings, &c. At the station, a new town called Kankakee, is springing up. Eighteen months ago, there were at this place one log-hut on an eminence, and one shanty or small house of boards at the station; now, there is a flourishing little town of 1500 to 2000 people. The situation is very favourable for a town, there being a flat meadow bottom along the Iroquois river, and a rising ground beyond, well timbered. It is on the ridge of this rising ground that the town (which is to be the county-town of Kankakee county) is springing up, and a court-house is in the course of erection now.

. . . .

The thirteenth station is Urbana—128½ miles from Chicago. Here we stopped—there remaining 122 miles to be finished before this branch joins the main line at Centralia. There is a patch of wood close to Urbana, of 15,000 acres, and an old and new town; the latter at the railway station, and about two miles from the former. In 1853, the old town contained about 400 inhabitants, and the new town did not exist. It is calculated that the old town now contains 1200 or 1500 inhabitants, and the new town about 800— so rapidly does the building up of towns go on in these new countries.

We observed another interesting instance of the mirage. We were passing over a long reach of level railway, where, without any cutting or embankment, the track was simply laid on the prairie; nevertheless, it assumed the appearance of having disappeared through a deep cutting outlined against the sky, while an engine, following us at some distance, looked as if suspended in the air, some little way above the road.

We reached about four. There is a hotel close to the station, where we got a tolerable tea (our kind cicerone, Mr. Johnson, had brought a basket of sandwiches, and we dined on them in the train), and then we got into a waggon with a pair of horses, and drove through the old town of Urbana, and out upon the great prairie. I do not fancy there exists in the old world such a sight as we beheld. From an eminence, as far as the eye could comprehend the scene, it traversed the richest undulating fields of grass, almost unbroken by fence, plough, or house. We walked some distance up to the knees in the luxuriant herbage. It is said that this is the character of the country nearly all the distance from this to the junction with the main line, 122 miles; except that as you get further south there are more streams, and consequently more timber. The agricultural resources of this country are incredible. We made a detour from this edge of the grand prairie, by cultivated fields, till we reached the timber; and skirting it, returned to Urbana.

Tuesday, June 5.—Mine host would have devoted two of us to one bed—the household one, if I mistake not, for there was women's gear about; but at last a bed was "raised" for me in the hall above. It was a good bed, though rather public; for, being at the head of the stair, it had to be passed and repassed by those who slept on that floor. However, I slept very comfortably, till knocked up at half-past five this morning. This is a superior specimen of an Illinois country inn:—a frame-house, with a good deal of accommodation of that rough sort; and good enough food, badly cooked. Withal—what is rarer—a most civil landlord.

We got breakfast, and by half-past six were again seated in the waggon, with a day's provisions, to cross the prairie, sixty miles, to Decatur. There is a shorter route, but we took the one we did to see a herd of fine cattle, belonging to Mr. Frank Harris. They were out on an extensive prairie, and we discovered them by means of a glass. We went as straight as we could, through the prairie, some mile or two, to where they were—losing sight of them most of the while, from the rolling of the ground. At last we got near them, and the sight was indeed worth going a long way to see.

. . . .

As we were walking about among them, one of our party called out, "There's a snake"; and sure enough there lay a rattle-snake, three or four feet long, coiled up, and with elevated head, hissing and shaking his rattling tail. Our herd-boy friend soon made an end of him, planting one heel upon him, he stamped him to death with the other. The rattle, which was carried off in triumph, had eight rings, betokening a serpent of ten years. The boy said, he had killed probably fifty of them. They sometimes bite the cattle, when whisky and tobacco is applied, and this allays the inflammation. It is affirmed, there is no authenticated instance of any one in Illinois having ever died from the bite of these prairie rattle-snakes.

. . . .

The rest of our route was nearly all the way through the timber which skirts the Sangamon river. About half-way, we stopped in the woods to dine and rest the horses. Drawn up beneath the shade of a spreading live-oak, a napkin was spread out on the front seat of the waggon; and from a miscellaneous collection of sandwiches, cheese, crackers, hard-boiled eggs, and pickled cucumbers (salt was not forgotten), we made an *al fresco* mid-day meal, pretty near the heart of Illinois.

Water is rather scarce on some parts of these prairies. At one cottage, where was a well, the people refused to permit us to take any; but about four in the afternoon, we came to a farm-house, where the people not only permitted us to have water, but helped to draw it. While our horses were drinking, we had some interesting conversation with the farmer and his brother. He owns a farm of 1960 acres. A single field in front of his house contained in one unbroken expanse forty acres of wheat, and seven hundred acres of Indian-corn. He keeps fifteen teams or pairs of horses. We saw eleven of them engaged at one time hoeing the corn. He can make a profit by selling Indian corn at fifteen cents, or sevenpence half-penny per bushel. He has made, he says, as much money as he wants; and wishes to sell his farm as it stands, with its improvements, at fifteen dollars or three pounds per acre, all round. It is five miles from the Great Western railway of Illinois, and about mid-way between the Chicago branch and the main line of the Illinois Central railway—about sixteen miles from each.

. . . .

We got into Decatur about half-past eight, by which time it was just dark enough to be out on the prairie; four miles of which we had to cross before entering the town. The whole ride to-day, both in its prairie, and forest, and river features, has been one of very great interest. Such a body of rich land is inconceivable. It must be seen to be appreciated; and even then, its extent and value are beyond what can be duly recognized.

. . . .

Wednesday, June 6.—Breakfasting at the early hour of half-past six, we had more than an hour to wait at the station. We left at nine; but the morning being very wet, we could not to-day, any more than last night, see much of Decatur. It is a large place, and is increasing rapidly. In 1850, its name does not occur in the census report. In 1853, it had about six hundred inhabitants; and the present year, it is estimated to have three thousand. There are several hotels in the town, and one building at the railway-station. A farm was pointed out to us, a little way from the station, which had been offered last autumn, with all its improvements, for $45, or £9 per acre; and the one between it and the town was stated to be likely to fetch $90, or £18 per acre; while land in the town itself would be worth $150, or £30 per acre.

. . . .

Ere we are many hours out of Decatur, the climate becomes perceptibly warmer. The flowers are further out, and different. The prairie-rose is in bloom, also several pink and scarlet flowers, and a showy chrysanthemum, and various others common in our gardens.

Vandalia, 142½ miles from Cairo, is the old capital of the State, and contains about a thousand people. It is a very prettily-situated little town. The country around is finely varied and well-timbered, that is, the trees are large and well-grown. The neighbourhood is fairly settled, and being fast cleared. Fine woods and fields of wheat, together with the general fencing and cultivation, give somewhat the appearance of English scenery. The town itself is not increasing. A little south of the town, the Kaskaskia river is crossed; and there is near it a good deal of broken ground and low-lying bottoms, subject to be overflowed. They were so this morning. The railway is carried through them on trestle-work, which will be ultimately converted into embankments, when experience has taught how much water-way it will be needful to leave.

A little to the north of Duquoin is the first place where it has been attempted to work coal on the line of the road in the south of the State. The train was stopped to allow us to examine the coal-pits. There has been one shaft sunk perpendicularly 74 feet,—in reaching which depth it has passed through a bed of limestone, 4 feet thick, then shales, and lastly, the coal-bed, which is 6 feet 8 inches thick. The limestone is very compact, crystalline, and not fossiliferous, as far as I could judge on a hasty glance. They are now sinking an incline to reach the coal on a slope. They have got down 150 feet, but have not reached the coal yet. As I stood at its mouth looking down, a blast exploded at the bottom, and made me start. A small quantity of coal has as yet been taken out, as the mine is only in course of being opened. It is supposed they have got to about the centre of the basin, for the coal rises on each side from this shaft. It crops out about half a mile to the east, and again on the banks of the Bigmuddy river to the west. It is stated that the coal can be sold at the pit-mouth at $1, or 4s. per ton. . . .

We now enter the hilly country of the south, and there is no more prairie. Some sixty miles north from Cairo we crossed Bigmuddy river, which well deserves its characteristic name. It looks small, but it is deep. Coal is found along its banks, and is floated to the Mississippi in barges to supply St. Louis, and other towns. In making the railway, the rails were brought by water to this point. Six miles beyond, we reach Carbondale, through a timber country, with clearings here and there. Dead trunks of trees, standing up among the wheat, remind one of Pennsylvania and Ohio. There is fine wheat-land all around. We saw some fields already beginning to change colour. The road is now ascending, at the rate of about thirty-six feet in a mile. Carbondale is a station for some towns near, the country back from the line of railway being well settled. Tobacco is grown in this neighbourhood, and forwarded from Carbondale. As we passed, we saw five hogsheads on the platform, waiting to be taken away.

. . . .

As we neared the town of Cairo, we had the swamp forest, with its multitudes of fire-flies, on the west; and on the east, the broad Ohio placidly reflecting the failing light; beyond, the wood-covered hills of Kentucky; and here and there, on the bosom of the river, the star-like light of some boat.

Presently, we emerged form the thicket, and its place was taken by an open space, flickered here and there by the light from an open window. The train stands still. We are on the high bank of the levee. Down on the one side, the shining waters of the Ohio; down on the other, the shining lights of the few scattered wooden houses which constitute Cairo. It has begun to rain. We descend twenty steps, cross on a gangway of planks some fifty yards of an incipient lake (!), and reach a new hotel—the Taylor-house.

The Taylor-house is large and roomy, but it is new; and many of the rooms are but partially furnished, others not at all. Some of us get rooms supplied with beds on a bedstead; others are not so fortunate, for their beds are spread on the floor. A few months ago, we would have fared worse. Travers, who drove us to-day, has often slept at Cairo, stretched, for warmth and shelter, on a board below his engine.

There were lots of people just arrived from New Orleans, all looking wretched in the rain. We are in a different climate altogether from Chicago. I have on the clothes to which the cold winds of the lakes had driven me, and now they are thoroughly wet with perspiration. The air is hot, close, and oppressive. I escape to my room. A solitary chair does duty for itself, wash-stand and toilet-table. I have placed my lamp upon it, and sit on the bed-side, to read for a little. I open the Olney Hymns, and read—

"Strange and mysterious is my life!"

when a vivid flash of lightning lights up my room, the court, and beyond. Flash succeeds flash, with roll of distant thunder. The rain comes down in torrents, splash, splash, in the already circum-ambient waters; and thinking I have got into somewhat of a bog, I prepare to put myself to bed in the future "city" of Cairo.

Thursday, June 7

. . . .

Cairo is the southern terminus of the railway, situated on the confluence of the Ohio and Mississippi. From this point southward, the river is always navigable, and nearly always free from ice. It is about 180 miles below St. Louis, and 509 miles below Cincinnati. To each of these cities, and, consequently, to all places beyond them, the navigation is liable to frequent stoppage,—in summer, from want of depth of water; and in winter, from ice. This point is, therefore, likely to become a great shipping-place for produce going south, and for merchandise, &c., coming from New Orleans; while the saving to passengers going to Cincinnati and St. Louis is such, that they are already preferring to land at Cairo and go by railway, although, in the present state of connecting lines, this route is a long one.

. . . .

It is computed there are from 1000 to 1200 people in Cairo, two-thirds of whom have come here within a year from this time. There are about sixty houses, including the hotel, which is quite full of people. The city is laid out in lots of twenty-five feet front, and one hundred and twenty-five feet in depth. Three of these, on the front level, had been sold at $1500 each, to make a beginning. The price for good lots range as high as $2500. On the back streets they may be had for $350, and upwards.

The high prices for which the trustees are holding out, has helped to delay the rapid development of Cairo; but within a month or two they have adopted a different policy, and several "substantial build-ings are now erecting; and in the autumn, others, already contracted for, will fairly start the place."

The levee round the town is the work of the Illinois Central railway. It has been completed sufficiently to protect the town, and for a mile is finished for the accommodation of business. The rail-way buildings are only partly erected, and but temporary; but both levee and buildings will be finished as fast as the business of the road and the growth of Cairo demand. For this service, the railway receives from the trustees ample land for depôt purposes on both rivers; and when all the arrangements are perfected, the railway will surround the town, leaving it, on the north side, at a point about equi-distant from each river.

Chicago during the 1850s is the subject of William J. Onahan's recollections, published in the *Transactions of the Illinois State Historical Society* of 1916. Largely anecdotal, it touches only slightly on the issue of immigration, which at the time so deeply influenced the Chicago political climate and divided its electorate.

Sixty Years in Chicago

WILLIAM J. ONAHAN

My recollections go back to 1854—when I first set foot in Chicago.

It was before the days of horse cars, no electric conveyances had then been invented—The Killomobile—was undreamt of. We made our limited trips within the city on foot or by omnibus—these latter made the journey on the south side from the Courthouse to State and Twelfth Streets—over a planked roadway—on the west side to Halsted Street and later to the "Bulls Head"—now Ashland Avenue and on the north side to Chicago Avenue. Pedestrian exercise within the city was in those days a precarious and often a perilous experience owing to the inequality of the sidewalks—scarcely any hundred feet being on the same level. It was up and down—up and down—all the time nor did the street offer an inviting alternative since few if any were paved.

There were no "sky scrapers" in those days—the buildings seldom rose higher than three stories and the third story was usually difficult to rent—there being no elevators to ease the burden of climbing. The population of Chicago when I came was I should say

From William J. Onahan, "Sixty Years in Chicago," *Transactions of the Illinois State Historical Society*, XXII (1916), 79-88.

Courtesy of the Illinois State Historical Library

Chicago in 1853

principally from New England and Old Ireland. The German population had begun to arrive, but there were few or no Poles or
Italians—and none at all of the various slavic peoples who now form
so numerous a part of Chicago's population.

The New England or strictly American citizens mostly engaged in
commercial pursuits—these controlled the business interests of the
city. My countrymen were engaged in the more laborious and less
profitable employments—and of course had already begun to be
quite an influence and factor in local politics—almost all being
Democrats and naturally ardent and devoted followers of Senator
Douglas. Since I am speaking of the Irish element in Chicago allow
me to quote and adopt as my own judgment this testimony to their
influence and character, which I find opportunely at hand. It is
from the pen of James O'Shaughnessy, President of the Irish Fellowship Club.

"The Irish in Chicago's History, by James O'Shaughnessy, former
President Irish Fellowship Club. Irish influence in Chicago from the
beginning of its continuing history has been large. The first Fort
Dearborn was built by an Irish-born soldier of the revolution. The
first man to till a farm and the first white family to which a child
was born, as well as the first to teach a school where now Chicago
stands, were all Irish. The two heroes of the Fort Dearborn massacre were Irish. The beginning of Chicago proper was made possible
by the influence in France of an Irishman who found the money for
the Illinois and Michigan Canal. The first man of prominence,
influence and ability to proclaim Chicago a future great city was an
Irishman. The first great builder of churches, hospitals and institutions of learning that attracted the first large influx of Irish home-
builders was an Irish bishop. Since its corporate existence the
percentage of Irish in its population has been very large—and so
potent as to exert a marked influence on the commercial spirit, civil
pride and social life of the community. . . ."

This brings to mind an Irishman who was a well known character
in my early days—Doctor William B. Egan. Although by profession a
physician he was more given to real estate—than to pills and
potions. Once when prescribing for an old lady she asked him
"How often am I to take this, Doctor"? The Doctor who at the
moment was thinking of his real estate deals absently replied—"Oh—
a quarter down. The balance canal time, one, two and three years"
—the terms for land deals then much in vogue. I heard another story
of Dr. Egan worth telling. The Doctor I should say was a man of
fine education, a classical scholar and an attractive public speaker.
He had been nominated by the Whig party for the office of
Lieutenant Governor—unlike most of his countrymen in Chicago—

he was a Whig—of course, he was not elected—but to the story: At the opening of the Illinois and Michigan Canal a grand celebration was planned to be held at the Chicago end, or beginning—at Bridgeport at the time and for long afterwards settled by Irish people—many of whom had been engaged in work on the canal.

For this celebration Dr. Egan was selected as the orator of the occasion. The time was midsummer, and naturally a crowd was expected. The Doctor had taken thought as to the conditions and being largely interested in Bridgeport lots he conceived a plan for unloading a few.

The night before the celebration he sent out a barrel of Bourbon whiskey—which then was very cheap, and had it dumped into a well that had been opened to provide the thirsty and perspiring crowd with liquid solace.

The heat of the day and the crowds quickly drew the people to the well—and there sure enough it was flowing with tempting toddy! This was a revelation and a temptation—and it is said every Irishman in the crowd—hurried to the Doctor's agent who, providently had a real estate shanty nearby in order to secure a lot in the near vicinity of the wonderful well! . . .

It may be of interest here to note that the Irish settlements along the line of the Illinois and Michigan Canal from Joliet to LaSalle—were due in part at least to the hampered condition of the State finances. When the State was unable to pay the canal contractors the alternative of land scrip or land warrants was resorted to. These gave the holders the right to take upland within the limits of the grant given by the U.S. Government in aid of the canal. So it was that Irishmen in large numbers, who as contractors or laborers, were engaged in the work, failing to get cash, took the land scrip and so settled on the land contiguous to the canal, thus making the Irish settlements once well known from Joliet to LaSalle.

. . . .

Senator Douglas had become the idol of the Illinois Democracy. I heard him speaking from the balcony of the Tremont House in one of his most famous speeches, which resulted in the nomination of Lincoln for the Presidency—though Douglas won in the issue then in question, the U. S. Senatorship for Illinois.

I would not be an impartial witness—even now of the merits of the discussion in the famous debates. I was then a young Douglas enthusiast, and had little or no esteem for his rival. I marched in the funeral procession of Senator Douglas from Bryan Hall where he had been carried from the Tremont House (where he died) to the site of the present Douglas monument, where his remains were laid. Bishop Duggan, the Catholic bishop of Chicago, delivered the oration at the grave, the Senator having been received into the church in his last days.

. . . .

Gustaf Unonius was born in Finland but raised in Sweden, where he was educated at Uppsala University. He then studied law part-time as a government clerk in the city. In 1841 he moved to America with his bride and settled in Wisconsin. In 1857 he visited Chicago, and the following year returned to Sweden, where he remained until his death. This selection depicting the fast-changing physical appearance of the city is from Unonius' memoirs, *A Pioneer in Northwest America, 1841-1858*, published first in Sweden in 1861 and translated into English in 1950 by Jonas Oscar Backlund for the Swedish Pioneer Historical Society.

Chicago, 1857

GUSTAF UNONIUS

I remained two weeks in Chicago, the Garden City, as it was called, but at that time anything but a garden. Though most of the houses had a pavilion-like appearance there was nothing beyond that appearance to give them the character of inviting garden pavilions. The surroundings also harmonized with the general character of the city—with few exceptions resembling a trash can more than anything else; the entire area on which that "wonder of the western world" was to grow up might best be likened to a vast mud puddle. The principal site of the city is low and swampy, almost at the same level as Lake Michigan, and most of the buildings were at that time erected close to the lakeshore or on the miry, alluvial soil which time and again was flooded by the river flowing right through

From Gustaf Unonius, *A Pioneer in Northwest America, 1841-1858: The Memoirs of Gustaf Unonius*, trans. Jonas Oscar Backlund, ed. Nils William Olsson (Minneapolis, 1950, 1960), II, 174-188. Copyright by the Swedish Pioneer Historical Society. Reprinted by permission. Footnotes in the original have been omitted.

the city. Certain other parts consisted of waste expanses of sand without a blade of grass, and from them a floury dust was carried in blinding clouds over the clayey streets, sifting into the houses, making them as dusty inside as the outdoors was muddy and unpleasant. During the rainy season, and sometimes far into the summer, the streets were almost impassable for driving as well as for walking. To be sure they were supplied with board sidewalks, but crossing from one side of the street to the other entailed decided difficulties. I recall how during my first year in Chicago I saw again and again, elegantly dressed women standing on streetcorners waiting for some dray on which they might ride across the street. But even for vehicles, the streets were sometimes impassable. Horses and wagons sometimes sank down in the clayey mud and had to be pulled out with great labor and difficulty.

This will give the reader an idea of what Chicago was like at that time [1845], when it was estimated that its population was something like 20,000. Twelve years have passed, and what a change in its appearance as well as in its population, which is now 120,000! The formerly low, swampy streets have been raised several feet and paved with planks or stone. The river has been dredged and widened; its shores have been supported with piles, evened off, raised well above the water level, and are now occupied by loading piers or used as foundations for gigantic warehouses or factories. The older buildings, most of which had been erected in such a hurry that they would soon have tumbled down anyway, have either been burnt to ashes in the fires that frequently broke out (and which greatly assisted in the improvement of the city) or have been torn down to make way for new buildings of brick, stone, iron, and even marble, on far better foundations. It is now a city in which private and public buildings have been erected that compare favorably both in size and style with the most spendid structures in the capitals of Europe. In a single summer, in 1855, 2,700 new houses were built, many of which would be a source of pride to any city. The following year an even greater number were erected, which, inclusive of churches, railroad stations, and other public buildings, were said to have entailed expenditures of more than four million dollars. Some of the older wooden buildings which had been built in what is now the better part of the city have been moved on sled-like runners to outlying districts where new streets are constantly being laid out; eventually they will be moved even farther away to make room for modern and more beautiful buildings.

Some of the houses thus moved from one place to another are not so small as one might imagine. I have seen even three-story buildings travel down the street. The contrivance by which this is done is really quite simple. A capstan is used, seldom drawn by more than one horse, around which a chain is wrapped and fastened to the rollers placed underneath the building after the foundation has been removed. The capstan is moved from place to place according to the length of the chain, and while the chain is rolled up on it the house is pulled forward; a few men are kept busy moving the planks and rollers under the runners, and the house is pulled evenly and steadily to its new site. When they are to make a turn the capstan is moved to the side, the chains are fastened to the corner of the building, which is carefully turned and faced in a new direction. This kind of work has become almost a new trade in the growing cities, and housemovers are seldom idle or in want of a good income.

Until one has become accustomed to this kind of transportation, it seems rather strange. Often the entire width of the street is blocked by a house that is out for a walk and extends from one side of the street to the other, but neither drivers nor pedestrians complain because they are compelled to make a small detour. Anyway, it does not take long before the street is clear again. Moving the house does not necessarily mean that those living in it must move out. I have seen houses on the move while the families living in them continued with their daily tasks, keeping fire in the stove, eating their meals as usual, and at night quietly going to bed to wake up the next morning on some other street. Once a house passed my window while a tavern business housed in it went on as usual. Even churches have been transported in this fashion, but as far as I know, never with services going on.

. . . .

Thus Chicago has undergone a complete transformation. Located on an almost completely level prairie upon which it extends itself farther year by year, lying as it does on the shore of a boundless inland sea, having extensive parks, magnificent buildings and attractive villas surrounded by beautiful flower parterres, orchards, and terraces, it now really deserves the name it has adopted, the Garden City. It is now displaying, perhaps in a greater degree than any other city in the Union, one of the most indisputable proofs of the industrial advance and the virile power which, while it is evidenced in the smaller communities, has lifted, and will continue to lift, the great, robust nation to a position as one of the most powerful dominions in the world. Did we not know it to be an indisputable fact, one might well believe that the description of Chicago, its discouraging beginning, the changes that have taken place in the course of a few years, its incredible growth—ten thousand added to its population in a single year—and the position it occupied today in the business life of America, had been culled from an Arabian Nights tale.

There are persons still living in the city from the time when the first log cabin was erected by the side of the red man's wigwam. When I moved to the city its oldest native-born inhabitant was a rosy-cheeked girl of seventeen. But the oldest inhabitant, reckoned from the time the first white families settled here, is John H. Kinzie, Esq., still in the best years of his manhood, one of the principal and highly honored citizens of Chicago. When the government in 1804 built a small fort at the mouth of the Chicago River, with a garrison of fifty men as a frontier guard against the Indians, Mr. Kinzie's father settled opposite the fort, on the other side of the river, and there built the first dwellinghouse. He also established a trading post among the wild tribes that were roaming the land which they had recently ceded to the United States but which, with the exception of these Indians, was almost completely uninhabited. The son, who at that time was only a few months old, is now occupying a sturdy house on the spot where the original cottage was. As a young man he secured appointment to an office in the service of the government, but after a few years he returned to his hometown, which was then hardly any more advanced than when he left it. There he settled with his talented young wife who has, since then, published a well-written and entertaining story of the early settlements and of the bloody scenes which they were later to witness during the war with England. The Indians, who gained possession of the fort, cruelly and treacherously murdered the greater part of the garrison and the women and children of the settlers, and carried several of them into captivity, among them a young girl belonging to Mr. Kinzie's own family. Again and again, in that cultured and respectable family, who from our first arrival in Chicago showed us much friendship and kindness, I have listened to their description of the childhood of that remarkable city which they had seen grow up. Kinzie was at first the owner of most of the ground on which Chicago is now built. Had he been able to foresee its future importance, and had he realized that in a few years every foot of the sandhills where he had played as a child would be sold at a price for which he could have purchased an entire section, he would probably not have practically given away tracts that, had he retained them, would have made him one of the richest men in America. He told me, for instance, that he had once traded off for the colt of an Indian pony a few muddy acres which would now be worth over $100,000, not counting the buildings erected on them, though he himself, as well as others, thought at the time that he had made a good trade.

In 1816 the fort which had been destroyed by the Indians was rebuilt and remained standing till only a couple of years ago, as a venerable relic of the childhood of the city. In buildings within that memorable stockade, now without defenses or defenders, a temporary refuge was provided by public benevolence for many Swedish immigrants who, on their way to distant regions in the West, have arrived in Chicago sick and homeless. The modern improvement craze finally committed the sacrilege of razing the monument from a past time and in its place a railroad terminal was erected from which might locomotives now roll out of the city on their iron rails, linking Chicago with the Gulf of Mexico and the Atlantic Ocean.

In 1829 the place had five dwellinghouses in addition to the fort and a few outlying log houses. In 1831 the population was increased by a few dozen families. The merchant fleet of the city consisted of four small vessels which unloaded in Chicago everything that was required for the northeastern part of Illinois and the northwestern part of Indiana. As yet the place had no postoffice, but an Indian was sent every other week to bring letters and papers from a small village in Michigan. In 1833 a few more families settled in Chicago and from that year we may date its existence as something more than a pioneer settlement. However, it was not incorporated as a city until four years later when it had acquired a population of 4,170.

The growth of the city during the last sixteen years seems almost miraculous—even for America. In 1848 a canal was completed, a hundred miles long, by which Chicago secured direct communication with the Mississippi River, and consequently also with the Mississippi valley, all the way down to New Orleans, and all the way up to the land around the source of the giant river with its three thousand miles of navigable water. Through this canal the state of Illinois, which in fertility is surpassed by no other state in the Union, became commercially the most important state in the West, and the city of Chicago became the center of trade in products of America and other countries. The canal became the first powerful force leading to the present greatness and is still the artery through which rejuvenating strength flows into the constantly growing city.

However, the web of railroads which Chicago has spun around itself during the last ten years is the thing that more than anything else has contributed to its wealth and progress. In 1851 the first locomotive was to be seen rolling along on a track that extended only a few miles outside the city. Now Chicago is the terminus of more than a dozen trunk lines from which almost twice as many branch lines extend in every direction. Thereby the city has communication with the rich copper districts and other mining regions around Lake Superior, with Canada, with all the Atlantic states, with the rich grain-producing lands beyond the Mississippi, and with the cotton states around the Gulf of Mexico. While a few years ago it took eight to ten days to travel from New York to Chicago, the traveler may now make his choice among three different railroads and cover that distance in thirty to thirty-six hours. More than one hundred twenty trains, some of them consisting of up to forty fully loaded freight cars, arrive and depart each day from the railroad stations in various parts of the city. Some of these stations are still uncomfortable and primitive, showing how people in the West try to get along as best they can with what they have. On the other hand, many compare very well in size, architecture, furnishings, and beauty with the best in other countries. It should be mentioned that all these railroads, altogether measuring five thousand miles in length, which radiate from Chicago as a central point in that immense iron web, the threads of which now cross each other everywhere in the extensive Mississippi valley, are private undertakings. Neither the state nor the city has spent a single dollar on these projects or voted any public funds to realize them. They are ventures entirely undertaken and brought to completion with wonderful energy and foresight by private companies which, operating under a charter issued by the state, independently attend to all the affairs associated therewith; the public has not ventured a penny on these railroads. In that respect Chicago differs from many other American communities which have grown up overnight and engage in extensive undertakings in which unscrupulous demagogues discover some way of fattening their purses at the expense of the general public only to bring eventual loss and dishonor to the community whose confidence they have succeeded in gaining.

But not only canals and numerous railroads have made Chicago one of the most important business centers of the Union, without a doubt the most important in the interior of the country. Its favorable location contributes fully as much if not more. Located at the extreme south end of Lake Michigan, the point of departure for all of the great watercourses, it is, one might say, the source of the extensive navigation maintained on those immense lakes and through the great navigable rivers connected with them. Thus it has direct communication by water with Canada and the Atlantic and even with transatlantic ports. Chicago is connected by the canal with the almost inexhaustible coalfields in southern Illinois and has easy access through the St. Mary's Canal to the mining regions around Lake Superior. These conditions will be important in promoting the future growth and prosperity of the city. It has already become the center for great iron-manufacturing mills which are now employing thousands of workmen and which will in the future certainly be still more developed. . . .

At present grain may be regarded as the city's principal business commodity and export goods. It is possible to form some conception of the scope of the business carried on in that line when we learn that in 1855 a single firm shipped 500,000 bushels to Buffalo. This is natural, for the city is the most easily available and most important trading center for the 130 million bushels of corn and 120 million bushels of wheat which in addition to other grains are produced annually by the fertile state of Illinois alone. This is according to a report of 1855, following which time, since more land has been put under cultivation, the yield must have increased by millions of bushels.

. . . .

In addition to what has already been mentioned, Chicago has a great number of establishments, all of which testify to the speedy and constant development in all kinds of industries and business undertakings. Great locomotive works, car shops, foundries, and all kinds of machine shops employing thousands of workmen receive orders from almost every state for manufactures that a few years ago could be secured only from the eastern states. Among factories, McCormick's establishment for the manufacture of agricultural machinery deserves mention. Among other things, it annually produces several thousand harvesting machines—Mr. McCormick's invention which is now being used almost everywhere in Europe.

Add to this the fact that Chicago has more than fifty churches, some of them really excellent structures in Gothic style, twenty-five newspaper presses, about a dozen banks, and a countless number of stores and hotels, which in the matter of elegance, comfort, equipment, and stock cannot only be compared with, but also surpass, most establishments of that kind in the European capitals. All of these things will give the reader an idea of how the city has grown from practically nothing during the last twenty years, and he will therefore realize that it is not an exaggeration to predict that within another score of years, when it is likely that the electric spark, crossing the Rocky Mountains, will bring messages from one ocean's shore to the other, and the locomotives which roll across the land from San Francisco and New York will meet in Chicago—that this city will become the central metropolis of the great North American continent, an emporium for the products of Asia, Europe, and America. Not only commercially may we predict for this city a great future of vast importance to the world, but also in other respects. Culture and education have, like Columbus, found land in the West, and the Mississippi valley and its metropolis are a star in the banner of the United States that like the "changeless star of the North" knows no setting.

The exploding issue in Illinois and the nation during the 1850s was the slavery question: would the South's "peculiar institution" spread up the Mississippi Valley and perhaps ultimately extend to the West, thus gaining sufficient Southern political support in Congress to make slavery legal in the free states? This was the central question put by Lincoln in an address delivered at the end of the Republican State Convention in Springfield on June 17, 1858. In the parts of the "House Divided" speech reprinted in this section, it is interesting to see how skillfully Lincoln develops the slave-power conspiracy to suggest that the conspirators are none other than the leaders of the Democratic party and the Chief Justice of the United States Supreme Court, i.e., Stephen Douglas, Franklin Pierce, Roger Taney, and James Buchanan. Douglas tried in vain to refute these charges in a series of debates with Lincoln during the senatorial campaign of 1858. In the last selection in this volume, a correspondent for the New York *Evening Post* comments on one of those debates, held on August 21 in Ottawa, and his inclination toward Lincoln is explicit. Among the voluminous material available on Lincoln, some of the excellent recent works are Don E. Fehrenbacher's *Prelude to Greatness: Lincoln in the 1850s* (Stanford, 1962) and Robert W. Johannsen's *The Lincoln-Douglas Debates in 1858* (Oxford, 1965) and *Stephen A. Douglas* (Oxford, 1973).

Lincoln's House Divided Speech

Springfield, Illinois, June 17, 1858

Mr. President and Gentlemen of the Convention:

If we could first know where we are, and whither we are tending, we could better judge what to do, and how to do it. We are now far into the fifth year since a policy was initiated with the avowed object and confident promise of putting an end to slavery agitation. Under the operation of that policy, that agitation has not only not ceased, but has constantly augmented. In my opinion, it will not cease until a crisis shall have been reached and passed. "A house divided against itself cannot stand." I believe this government cannot endure permanently half slave and half free. I do not expect

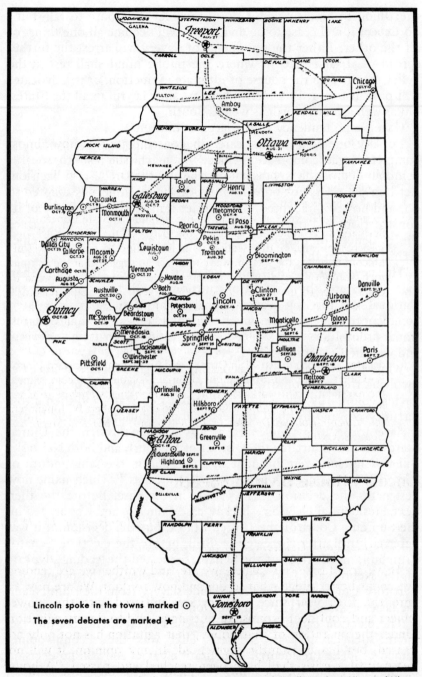

Lincoln's speaking dates in the 1858 senatorial campaign

the Union to be dissolved; I do not expect the house to fall; but I
do expect it will cease to be divided. It will become all one thing, or
all the other. Either the opponents of slavery will arrest the further
spread of it, and place it where the public mind shall rest in the
belief that it is in the course of ultimate extinction, or its advocates
will push it forward till it shall become alike lawful in all the States,
old as well as new, North as well as South.

Have we no tendency to the latter condition?

Let any one who doubts, carefully contemplate that now almost
complete legal combination—piece of machinery, so to speak—
compounded of the Nebraska doctrine and the Dred Scott decision.
Let him consider, not only what work the machinery is adapted to
do, and how well adapted, but also let him study the history of its
construction, and trace, if he can, or rather fail, if he can, to trace
the evidences of design, and concert of action, among its chief
architects, from the beginning.

The new year of 1854 found slavery excluded from more than
half the States by State Constitutions, and from most of the
National territory by Congressional prohibition. Four days later,
commenced the struggle which ended in repealing that Congressional prohibition. This opened all the National territory to slavery,
and was the first point gained. . . .

While the Nebraska Bill was passing through Congress, a *law case*,
involving the question of a negro's freedom, by reason of his owner
having voluntarily taken him first into a free State, and then into a
territory covered by the Congressional prohibition, and held him as
a slave for a long time in each, was passing through the United
States Circuit Court for the District of Missouri; and both Nebraska
Bill and lawsuit were brought to a decision in the same month of
May, 1854. The negro's name was "Dred Scott," which name now
designates the decision finally made in the case. Before the then
next Presidential election, the law case came to, and was argued in,
the Supreme Court of the United States; but the decision of it was
deferred until after the election. Still, before the election, Senator
Trumbull, on the floor of the Senate, requested the leading advocate
of the Nebraska Bill to state *his opinion* whether the people of a
Territory can constitutionally exclude slavery from their limits; and
the latter answers: "That is a question for the Supreme Court."

The election came. Mr. Buchanan was elected, and the indorsement, such as it was, secured. That was the second point
gained. . . . The Presidential inauguration came, and still no decision
of the court; but the incoming President, in his inaugural address,
fervently exhorted the people to abide by the forthcoming decision,
whatever it might be. Then, in a few days, came the decision.

The reputed author of the Nebraska Bill finds an early occasion to make a speech at this capital indorsing the Dred Scott decision, and vehemently denouncing all opposition to it. The new President, too, seizes the early occasion of the Silliman letter to indorse and strongly construe that decision, and to express his astonishment that any different view had ever been entertained!

At length a squabble springs up between the President and the author of the Nebraska Bill, on the mere question of *fact*, whether the Lecompton Constitution was or was not in any just sense made by the people of Kansas; and in that quarrel the latter declares that all he wants is a fair vote for the people, and that he cares not whether slavery be voted *down* or voted *up*. I do not understand his declaration, that he cares not whether slavery be voted down or voted up, to be intended by him other than as an apt definition of the policy he would impress upon the public mind. . . . That principle is the only shred left of his original Nebraska doctrine. Under the Dred Scott decision "squatter sovereignty" squatted out of existence, tumbled down like temporary scaffolding; like the mould at the foundry, served through one blast, and fell back into loose sand; helped to carry an election, and then was kicked to the winds. His late joint struggle with the Republicans, against the Lecompton Constitution, involves nothing of the original Nebraska doctrine. That struggle was made on a point—the right of a people to make their own constitution—upon which he and the Republicans have never differed.

The several points of the Dred Scott decision, in connection with Senator Douglas's "care not" policy, constitute the piece of machinery, in its present state of advancement. This was the third point gained. The working points of the machinery are:

Firstly, That no negro slave, imported as such from Africa, and no descendant of such slave, can ever be a citizen of any State, in the sense of that term as used in the Constitution of the United States. This point is made in order to deprive the negro, in every possible event, of the benefit of that provision of the United States Constitution which declares that "The citizens of each State shall be entitled to all privileges and immunities of citizens in the several States."

Secondly, That, "subject to the Constitution of the United States," neither Congress nor a Territorial Legislature can exclude slavery from any United States Territory. This point is made in order that individual men may fill up the Territories with slaves, without danger of losing them as property, and thus to enhance the chances of permanency to the institution through all the future.

Thirdly, That whether the holding a negro in actual slavery in a

Courtesy of the Illinois State Historical Library

George I. Parrish's painting of the Lincoln-Douglas debate at Alton, October 15, 1858

free State makes him free, as against the holder, the United States courts will not decide, but will leave to be decided by the courts of any slave State the negro may be forced into by the master. This point is made, not to be pressed immediately; but, if acquiesced in for a while, and apparently indorsed by the people at an election, then to sustain the logical conclusion that what Dred Scott's master might lawfully do with Dred Scott, in the free State of Illinois, every other master may lawfully do with any other one, or one thousand slaves, in Illinois, or in any other free State.

Auxiliary to all this, and working hand in hand with it, the Nebraska doctrine, or what is left of it, is to educate and mould public opinion, at least Northern public opinion, not to care whether slavery is voted down or voted up. This shows exactly where we now are; and partially, also, whither we are tending. . . .

Why was the amendment, expressly declaring the right of the people, voted down? Plainly enough now,—the adoption of it would have spoiled the niche for the Dred Scott decision. Why was the court decision held up? Why even a Senator's individual opinion withheld, till after the Presidential election? Plainly enough now,—the speaking out then would have damaged the "perfectly free" argument upon which the election was to be carried. Why the outgoing President's felicitation on the indorsement? Why the delay of a reargument? Why the incoming President's advance exhortation in favor of the decision? These things look like the cautious patting and petting of a spirited horse preparatory to mounting him, when it is dreaded that he may give the rider a fall. And why the hasty after-indorsement of the decision by the President and others?

We cannot absolutely know that all these exact adaptations are the result of preconcert. But when we see a lot of framed timbers, different portions of which we know have been gotten out at different times and places and by different workmen,—Stephen, Franklin, Roger, and James, for instance,—and when we see these timbers joined together, and see they exactly make the frame of a house or a mill, all the tenons and mortises exactly fitting, and all the lengths and proportions of the different pieces exactly adapted to their respective places, and not a piece too many or too few, —not omitting even scaffolding,—or, if a single piece be lacking, we see the place in the frame exactly fitted and prepared yet to bring such piece in,—in such a case, we find it impossible not to believe that Stephen and Franklin and Roger and James all understood one another from the beginning, and all worked upon a common plan or draft drawn up before the first blow was struck. . . .

Lincoln and Douglas at Ottawa

Chicago, August 23, 1858

Saturday, the 21st, was the day of the first discussion between Lincoln and Douglas. It was held at Ottawa, a city of about 900 inhabitants, on the line of the Chicago and Rock Island Railroad on the Illinois canal, and at the junction of the Fox and Illinois rivers. I arrived late the night before at Ottawa, and was accommodated to a sofa at the hotel. The city was already even full. Saturday was pleasant, but warm day, and Ottawa was deluged in dust. By wagon, by rail, by canal, the people poured in, till Ottawa was one mass of active life. Men, women, and children, old and young, the dwellers on the broad prairies, had turned their backs upon the plough, and had come to listen to these champions of the two parties. Military companies were out; martial music sounded, and salutes of artillery thundered in the air. Eager marshals in partisan sashes rode furiously about the streets. Peddlers were crying their wares at the corners, and varied groups of politicians were canvassing and quarreling everywhere. And still they came, the crowd swelling constantly in its proportions and growing more eager and more hungry, perhaps more thirsty, though every precaution was taken against this latter evil. About noon the rival processions were formed, and paraded the streets amid the cheers of the people. Mr. Lincoln was met at the depot by an immense crowd, who escorted him to the residence of the Mayor, with banners flying and mottoes waving their unfaltering attachment to him and to his cause. The Douglas turnout, though plentifully interspersed with the Hibernian element, was less noisy, and thus matters were arranged for the after-dinner demonstration in the Court House square, where the stand was erected, and where, under the blazing sun unprotected by shade trees, and unprovided with seats, the audience was expected to congregate and listen to the champions.

Two men presenting wider contrasts could hardly be found as the representatives of the two great parties. Everybody knows Douglas, a heavy, thick-set, burly man, with large round head, heavy hair, dark complexion, and fierce bull-dog bark. Strong in his own real power, and skilled by a thousand conflicts in all the strategy of a hand-to-hand or a general fight. Of towering ambition, restless in his determined desire for notoriety; proud, defiant, arrogant, audacious, unscrupulous, "Little Dug," ascended the platform and looked out impudently and fearlessly on the immense throng which surged and struggled before him. A native of Vermont, reared on a soil where no slave ever stood, trained to hard manual labor and schooled in early hardships, he came to Illinois a teacher, and from one post to another had risen to his present eminence. Forgetful of the ancestral hatred of slavery to which he had been heir, he had come to be a holder of slaves and to owe much of his fame to his continued subservience to southern influence.

The other—Lincoln—is a native of Kentucky, and of poor white heritage, and from his cradle has felt the blighting influence of the dark and cruel shadow which rendered labor dishonorable, and kept the poor in poverty, while it advanced the rich in their possessions. Reared in poverty and the humblest aspirations, he left his native state, crossed the line into Illinois, and began his career of honorable toil. He was first a laborer, splitting rails for a living—deficient in education, and applying himself even to the rudiments of knowledge—he, too, felt the expanding power of his American manhood, and began to achieve the greatness to which he has succeeded. With great difficulty struggling through the tedious formularies of legal lore, he was admitted to the bar, and rapidly made his way to the front ranks of his profession. Honored by the people with office, he is still the same honest and reliable man. He volunteers in the Black Hawk war, and does the state good service in its sorest need. In every relation of life, socially and to the State, Mr. Lincoln has been always the pure and honest man. In physique he is the opposite to Douglas. Built on the Kentucky type, he is very tall, slender and angular, awkward even, in gait and attire. His face is sharp, large-featured and unprepossessing. His eyes are deep set, under heavy brows; his forehead is high and retreating and his hair is dark and heavy. In repose, I must confess that "Long Abe's" appearance is *not* comely. But stir him up, and the fire of his genius plays on every feature. His eye glows and sparkles, every lineament now so ill formed, grows brilliant and expressive, and you have before you a man of rare power and of strong magnetic influence. He takes the people every time, and there is no getting away from his sturdy good sense, his unaffected sincerity, and the unceasing play of his good humor, which accompanies his close logic and smoothes the way to conviction. Listening to him on Saturday, calmly and unprejudiced, I was convinced that he has no superior as a stump speaker. He is clear, concise and logical; his language is eloquent and at perfect command. He is altogether a more fluent speaker than Douglas and in all the arts of debate fully his equal. The Republicans of Illinois have chosen a champion worthy of their heartiest support, and fully equipped for the conflict. . . .   Yours, &c.,

Bayou

Index of Parallel Readings

Note: This collateral index is provided to assist teachers and students of Illinois history who are using Robert P. Howard's *Illinois: A History of the Prairie State* (Grand Rapids: Eerdmans, 1972) as a standard textbook. The lefthand column lists the chapter titles of Howard's history up to the Civil War period; the righthand column lists the pages in this documentary history which cover the historical material corresponding to each of those chapters.

Index